Praise for *Experiences of Test Automation*

"What you hold in your hands is a treasure trove of hard-w
and what doesn't in test automation. It can save you untold ...
away from paths that lead nowhere and guiding you towards those that lead to suc...

—Linda Hayes

"From tools to methodology, Dorothy Graham and Mark Fewster weave a compelling set of stories that provide a learning experience in automation. This comprehensive tome is the first of its kind to take the reader deep into the world of automated testing, as depicted by case studies that show the realities of what happened across a multitude of projects spanning a wide variety of industries and technology environments. By identifying similarities and repeated themes, the authors help the reader focus on the essential learning lessons and pitfalls to avoid. Read this book cover to cover for inspiration and a realization of what it takes to ultimately succeed in test automation."

—Andrew L. Pollner, President & CEO of ALP International Corporation

"Many years after their best-seller *Software Test Automation*, Mark Fewster and Dorothy Graham have done it again. Agile methodologies have given test automation a dominant presence in today's testing practices. This is an excellent, highly practical book with many well-documented case studies from a wide range of perspectives. Highly recommended to all those involved, or thinking about getting involved, in test automation."

—Erik van Veenendaal, Founder of Improve Quality Services and vice-chair of TMMi Foundation

"This book is like having a testing conference in your hand, with a wealth of case studies and insights. Except that this book is much cheaper than a conference, and you don't have to travel for it. What impressed me in particular was that it is all tied together in a concise 'chapter zero' that efficiently addresses the various aspects I can think of for automation success. And that is something you will not get in a conference."

—Hans Buwalda

"An exciting, well-written, and wide-ranging collection of case studies with valuable real-world experiences, tips, lessons learned, and points to remember from real automation projects. This is a very useful book for anyone who needs the evidence to show managers and colleagues what works—and what does not work—on the automation journey."

—Isabel Evans, FBCS CITP, Quality Manager, Dolphin Computer Access

"*Experiences of Test Automation* first describes the essence of effective automated testing. It proceeds to provide many lifetimes worth of experience in this field, from a wide variety of situations. It will help you use automated testing for the right reasons, in a way that suits your organization and project, while avoiding the various pitfalls. It is of great value to anyone involved in testing—management, testers, and automators alike."

—Martin Gijsen, Independent Test Automation Architect

"This offering by Fewster and Graham is a highly significant bridge between test automation theory and reality. Test automation framework design and implementation is an inexact science begging for a reusable set of standards that can only be derived from a growing body of precedence; this book helps to establish such precedence. Much like predecessor court cases are cited to support subsequent legal decisions in a judicial system, the diverse case studies in this book may be used for making contemporary decisions regarding engagement in, support of, and educating others on software test automation framework design and implementation."

—Dion Johnson, Software Test Consultant and Principle Adviser to the Automated Testing Institute (ATI)

"Even with my long-established 'test automation won't work' stance, this book did make me pause and ponder. It opened my mind and gave me a few 'oh, I hadn't thought of that' moments. I would recommend this book as an initial reference for any organization wanting to introduce test automation."

—Audrey Leng

"This book is a stunning achievement. I believe that it is one of the best books ever written in test automation. Dot and Mark's approach presenting 28 case studies is a totally new concept including eye-catching tips, good points, and lessons learned. The case studies are coming from life experiences, successes and failures, including several aspects of automation, different environments, and a mixture of solutions. Books are 'the' source of wisdom, and what a good idea for using storytelling to increase our learning through triggering our memories. This book is a must for everyone who is thinking of or involved in test automation at all levels. It is truly unique in its kind."

—Mieke Gevers

EXPERIENCES OF TEST AUTOMATION

EXPERIENCES OF TEST AUTOMATION

CASE STUDIES OF SOFTWARE TEST AUTOMATION

Dorothy Graham
Mark Fewster

✦✦ Addison-Wesley

Upper Saddle River, NJ • Boston • Indianapolis • San Francisco
New York • Toronto • Montreal • London • Munich • Paris • Madrid
Capetown • Sydney • Tokyo • Singapore • Mexico City

Many of the designations used by manufacturers and sellers to distinguish their products are claimed as trademarks. Where those designations appear in this book, and the publisher was aware of a trademark claim, the designations have been printed with initial capital letters or in all capitals.

The authors and publisher have taken care in the preparation of this book, but make no expressed or implied warranty of any kind and assume no responsibility for errors or omissions. No liability is assumed for incidental or consequential damages in connection with or arising out of the use of the information or programs contained herein.

The publisher offers excellent discounts on this book when ordered in quantity for bulk purchases or special sales, which may include electronic versions and/or custom covers and content particular to your business, training goals, marketing focus, and branding interests. For more information, please contact:

U.S. Corporate and Government Sales
(800) 382-3419
corpsales@pearsontechgroup.com

For sales outside the United States, please contact:

International Sales
international@pearson.com

Visit us on the Web: informit.com/aw

Library of Congress Cataloging-in-Publication Data

Graham, Dorothy, 1944-
  Experiences of test automation : case studies of software test automation / Dorothy Graham, Mark Fewster.
    p.   cm.
  Includes bibliographical references and index.
  ISBN 978-0-321-75406-6 (pbk. : alk. paper)
  1. Computer software—Testing—Automation—Case studies. I. Fewster, Mark, 1959- II. Title.
  QA76.76.T48G73 2011
  005.3028'7—dc23

                                                                              2011040994

ISBN-13: 978-0-321-75406-6
ISBN-10:   0-321-75406-9
Text printed in the United States on recycled paper at RR Donnelley in Crawfordsville, Indiana.
Second printing, August 2012

*To my husband, Roger, for your love and support,
your good ideas, and for making the tea!
And to Sarah and James, our wonderful children.
—Dot Graham*

*To my wife, Barbara, for the good times we've shared.
And to my terrific son, Rhys, for the good times you bring.
—Mark Fewster*

CONTENTS

FOREWORD

Automated testing—it's the Holy Grail, the Fountain of Youth, and the Philosopher's Stone all rolled into one. For decades, testers have looked to automated testing for relief from the drudgery of manual testing—constructing test cases and test data, setting system preconditions, executing tests, comparing actual with expected results, and reporting possible defects. Automated testing promises to simplify all these operations and more.

Unfortunately, successful, effective, and cost-effective automated testing is difficult to achieve. Automated testing projects are often initiated only later to stumble, lose their way, and be thrown onto the ever-growing pile of failed projects.

Automation fails for many reasons—unachievable expectations is perhaps the most common, followed by inadequate allocation of resources (time, people, and money). Other factors include tools that are poorly matched to needs, the sheer impatience for success that hinders quality work, and a lack of understanding that automated testing is a different kind of software development, one that requires the same professional approach as all other development efforts.

Dorothy and Mark's previous book, *Software Test Automation: Effective Use of Test Execution Tools*, published in 1999, set the standard for books on this topic. The first part detailed practices found in most successful automation efforts—scripting techniques, automated comparison, testware architecture, and useful metrics. The second part described the experiences of a number of organizations as they implemented test automation efforts. Now, with an additional 10 years of industry knowledge behind them, Dorothy and Mark provide another set of organizational and personal experiences to guide our automation work. It brings us up to date, describing both the classical and most modern approaches to test automation. Each chapter tells a story of a unique automation effort—including both successes and failures—to give us guidance.

Certain themes reoccur in *Experiences in Test Automation*: reasonable and achievable objectives; management support; metrics, including return on investment; required skills; planning; setting expectations; building relationships; tools; training; and politics—all necessary to make test automation successful. However, these same themes are equally applicable at both the project and personal levels. One great benefit of this book comes from stepping outside the test automation realm and considering these themes in the larger context.

I first met Dorothy and Mark at the 1998 EuroStar conference in Munich. I was impressed with both their knowledge of and passion for helping others do great automated testing. I congratulate them for their outstanding accomplishment and commend this book to you.

—Lee Copeland
December 2011

PREFACE

Test automation tools have been around for about 30 years, yet many automation attempts fail, or at least are only partially successful. Why is this?

We wanted to understand if the principles of effective automation, as published in our previous book, *Software Test Automation*, are still relevant and what other principles now apply, so we began gathering information about real-world test automation implementations. This led us to a rather pleasant discovery: Over the past 10 years, many people have had good success with software test automation, many of them using our book. Of course, we are not the only ones to have described or discovered good automation practices, yet successful and lasting automation still seems to be an elusive achievement today. We hope the stories in this book will help many more people to succeed in their test automation efforts.

This book brings together contemporary automation stories. The technology of test automation has progressed significantly since our last book on automation was published in 1999. We wanted to find out what approaches have been successful, what types of applications are now being tested using test automation, and how test automation has changed in recent years. Different people have solved automation problems in different ways—we wanted to know what can be learned from their experiences and where and how test automation is being applied in new ways.

The case studies in this book show some approaches that were successful and some that were not. This book gives you the knowledge to help avoid the pitfalls and learn from the successes achieved in real life. We designed this book to help you get the most out of the real-life experiences of other professionals.

The case studies in this book cover mainly the automation of test execution, but other types of automation are mentioned in some chapters. We focus primarily on system-level automation (including user acceptance testing), although some chapters also cover unit or integration testing. Test automation is described for many types of applications, many environments and platforms; the chapters cover commercial, open source, and inhouse tools in traditional and agile development projects. We are surprised by the number of different tools being used—around 90 commercial and open source tools are listed in the Appendix (which includes any tools used by the chapter authors, not just testing tools).

The experiences described in this book are all true, even though in some cases the author or company name is not revealed. We encouraged the case study authors to describe what happened rather than offer general advice, so this book is very real!

In collecting this book's stories, we were struck by the pervasiveness of test automation into every industry and application. We were also impressed with the dedication and persistence of those who have developed test automation within their companies. Unfortunately, we were also struck by the difficulties that many of them encountered, which sometimes resulted in failure. We are sure the experiences described in this book can help you to be more successful with your test automation.

Case Studies Plus (Our Added Value)

This book is more than a collection of essays; we worked closely with the authors of the chapters to produce a book with information that we felt would be most useful to you. Our review process was thorough; we asked questions and suggested changes in several rounds of reviewing (special thanks are due to the chapter authors for their patience and additional information). Our "old versions" folder contains over 500 documents, so each chapter has been carefully crafted.

We help you get the most from this book by offering Good Points, Lessons, and Tips. Each chapter includes our own comments to highlight points we think should stand out at a glance. Watch for these helpful notes:

- **Good Points,** which are well worth noting (even if they are not necessarily new).

> **Good Point**
>
> Management support is critical, but expectations must be realistic.

- **Lessons,** often learned the hard way—things it would have been better not to do.

> **Lesson**
>
> Automation development requires the same discipline as software development.

- **Tips** on ways to solve particular problems in a way that seemed new or novel to us.

> **Tip**
>
> Use a "translation table" for things that may change, so the automation can use a standard constant term.

We picture these interjections as our way of looking over your shoulder as you read through the chapter and saying, "Pay attention here," "Look at this," and "This could be particularly useful."

How to Read This Book

Each case study is a standalone account, so the chapters can be read in any order. The arrangement of the chapters is designed to give you a variety of experiences if you do read the book from front to back.

To decide which chapter you would like to read first or read next, look at Table P.1, a "chapter selector" that summarizes characteristics of the various chapters. The table enables you to see at a glance which chapters cover a particular application, tool, development methodology, and so on, and helps you to quickly find the chapters most directly relevant to you. After Table P.1 are one-paragraph summaries of each case study chapter.

Following this Preface, the section titled "Reflections on the Case Studies" presents our overall perspective and summary of the management and technical issues discussed in the chapters along with our view and comments on those issues (and our diagram of testware architecture). In this section of the book, we distill the most important points of advice to those currently involved in, or about to embark on, their own automation. This is the "executive summary" of the book.

Chapters 1 to 28 are the case study chapters, each written by an author or authors describing their experience in their specific context: what they did, what worked well, what didn't, and what they learned. Some of the chapters include very specific information such as file structures and automation code; other chapters are more general. One chapter (10) is an update from a case study presented in *Software Test Automation*; the rest are new.

Chapter 29, "Test Automation Anecdotes," is a mini-book in its own right—a collection of short experience stories from over a dozen different people, ranging from half a page to several pages, all with useful and interesting points to make.

Finally, the Appendix, "Tools," covers the commercial and open source tools referred to in the chapters.

Table P.1 Case Study Characteristics

Chapter	Author	Application Domain	Location	Lifecycle	Number on the Project
1	Lisa Crispin	Financial, web	USA	Agile	9–12
2	Henri van de Scheur	Database	Norway		30–3
3	Ken Johnston, Felix Deschamps	Enterprise server	USA	Traditional with agile elements	>500
4	Bo Roop	Testing tool	USA	Waterfall	12–15
5	John Kent	Mainframe to web-based	UK	Traditional	40
6	Ane Clausen	2 projects: pensions and insurance	Denmark	None and agile	3–5
7	Elfriede Dustin	Government: Department of Defense	USA	Agile	100s
8	Alan Page	Device drivers	USA	Traditional	Hundreds
9	Stefan Mohacsi, Armin Beer	European Space Agency services	Austria, Italy, Germany	Traditional	>100
10	Simon Mills	Financial: insurance	UK	Chaotic and variable	Dozens
11	Jason Weden	Networking equipment	USA	Traditional (waterfall)	25

Time Span	Tool Type(s)	Pilot Study?	ROI Measured?	Successful?	Still Breathing?
1 yr, report after 6 yr	Open source	No	No	Yes	Yes
5–6 yr	Inhouse	No	No, but 2,400 times improved efficiency	Yes	Yes
~3 yr	Commercial, Inhouse	No	No	Yes	Yes
1 yr, 2 mo	Commercial	No	No	No	No
23 yr	Commercial	Yes	No	Yes	Yes
6 mo 1 yr	Commercial	No Yes	No Yes	No Yes	No Yes
4½ yr	Commercial, Open source, Inhouse	Yes	Yes	Yes	Yes
9 yr	Commercial, Inhouse	No	No	Yes	Yes
6+ yr	Commercial, Open source, Inhouse	No	Yes, projected payback after 4 cycles	Yes	Yes
15 yr	Commercial	No, but began small scale	No, but now running 5 million tests per month	Yes	Yes; client base still growing
3 yr	Inhouse	No	No	Ultimately, yes	Yes

Continues

Table P.1   Case Study Characteristics (Continued)

Chapter	Author	Application Domain	Location	Lifecycle	Number on the Project
12	Damon Yerg (pseudonym)	Government services	Australia	V model	Hundreds
13	Bryan Bakker	Medical devices	Netherlands	V model	50
14	Antti Jääskeläinen, Tommi Takala, Mika Katara	Smartphone applications in Android	Finland		2
15	Christoph Mecke, Melanie Reinwarth, Armin Gienger	ERP Systems (SAP), 2 projects: health care and banking	Germany, India	Traditional	10
16	Björn Boisschot	SAP applications in the energy sector	Belgium	Traditional	12
17	Michael Williamson	Web-based, distributed	USA	Agile	15
18	Lars Wahlberg	Financial marketplace systems	Sweden	Incremental to agile	20 (typical)
19	Jonathan Kohl	Various, web to embedded	Canada	Agile and traditional	A few –60

Time Span	Tool Type(s)	Pilot Study?	ROI Measured?	Successful?	Still Breathing?
11 yr	Inhouse	Yes	No, but comparable manual effort calculated	Yes (peaks and troughs)	Yes; thriving and forging ahead
1.5 yr	Commercial, Open source, Inhouse	Started small	Yes	Yes	Yes
6–8 mo	Commercial, Open source	Entire project is a pilot study	No	Yes	Yes
4 yr 2 yr	Commercial, Inhouse	No	No	Yes	Yes
6 mo	Commercial	Yes	No	Yes	Yes
6 mo	Commercial, Open source	Yes	No	No	No
~10 yr	Open source	Yes	Yes, projected payback for tests run daily, weekly, or monthly	Yes	Yes
Various	Commercial, Open source, Inhouse	Yes, in some cases	No	Yes	Yes; some still in use

Continues

Table P.1 Case Study Characteristics (Continued)

Chapter	Author	Application Domain	Location	Lifecycle	Number on the Project
20	Albert Farré Benet, Christian Ekiza Lujua, Helena Soldevila Grau, Manel Moreno Jáimez, Fernando Monferrer Pérez, Celestina Bianco	4 projects, all medical software	Spain, USA, Italy	Spiral, prototyping, waterfall	2–17
21	Seretta Gamba	Insurance	Germany	Iterative	27
22	Wim Demey	Customized software packages	Belgium	Traditional V model	
23	Ursula Friede	Insurance	Germany	Traditional (V model)	30
24	John Fodeh	Medical applications and devices	Denmark	Traditional (V model), incremental	30
25	Mike Baxter, Nick Flynn, Christopher Wills, Michael Smith	Air traffic control	UK	Traditional	15–20
26	Ross Timmerman, Joseph Stewart	Embedded: automotive systems	USA	Phased waterfall	8

Time Span	Tool Type(s)	Pilot Study?	ROI Measured?	Successful?	Still Breathing?
5 yr 2 yr Few months 1 yr	Commerical Inhouse Commercial Commercial	No	No	Yes Partly No Yes	Yes Yes No Planned
12 mo	Commercial, Inhouse	Yes	No	Yes	Yes
4 mo	Commercial, Open source	Yes	No	Yes	Yes
~6 mo	Commercial	No	No, but quantified savings of €120,000 per release	Yes	Yes
6 yr	Commercial, Inhouse	Yes	No	Yes	Yes
Cycles lasting 3–12 mo	Commercial, Open source, Inhouse	Yes	No	Yes	Yes
5 yr	Inhouse with commercial hardware	No	No	Yes	Yes

Continues

Table P.1   Case Study Characteristics (Continued)

Chapter	Author	Application Domain	Location	Lifecycle	Number on the Project
27	Ed Allen, Brian Newman	Web-based, mobile, desktop, social channels (voice, chat, email)	USA	Traditional	28
28	Harry Robinson, Ann Gustafson Robinson	Problem reporting for telephone systems	USA	Waterfall	30 overall 4 on project

Chapter Summaries

Chapter 1, An Agile Team's Test Automation Journey: The First Year

Lisa Crispin describes, in her very engaging style, what happened when an agile team decided to automate their testing. Given Lisa's expertise in agile, you will not be surprised to see that this team really was agile in practice. One of the interesting things about this project is that everyone on the team (which was fairly small) was involved in the automation. Not only did they excel in agile development, they also developed the automation in an agile way—and they succeeded. Agile development was not the only component of this team's success; other factors were equally important, including building a solid relationship with management through excellent communication and building the automation to help support creative manual testing. Another key factor was the team's decision to build in process improvement along the way, including scheduling automation refactoring sprints twice a year. You are sure to agree that what Lisa and her team accomplished in their first year is remarkable. The project was done for a United States company in the finance sector.

Time Span	Tool Type(s)	Pilot Study?	ROI Measured?	Successful?	Still Breathing?
1 yr	Commercial, Inhouse	No	No, but benefits measured	Yes	Yes
1.5 yr	Inhouse	No	No	Yes	No

Chapter 2, The Ultimate Database Automation

Henri van de Scheur tells a story that spans half a dozen years, relating what happened when he and his colleagues developed a tool for testing databases in multiple environments. They set good objectives for their automation and a good architecture for the tool. They automated so many tests that they developed a lifecycle for automated tests that included periodic weeding. Tests were run nightly, weekly, or with special scheduling. Despite great success, a number of problems were encountered, and Henri describes them honestly. The development of this database testing tool (now open source) was done in Norway by a small team, over several years, and it achieved a very impressive return on investment.

Chapter 3, Moving to the Cloud: The Evolution of TiP, Continuous Regression Testing in Production

Ken Johnston and Felix Deschamps from Microsoft describe how they moved from product-based to service-based automated testing by implementing the automation in the cloud. Testing of Microsoft Exchange servers was already extensively automated, and much of the existing automation was reusable. Testing in production seems a foreign concept to most testers, but this chapter explains why it was necessary and beneficial to move to continuous monitoring and contains useful tips for anyone considering a similar move. This experience takes place in the United States, over three years, and unsurprisingly, Microsoft tools were used.

Chapter 4, The Automator Becomes the Automated

Bo Roop takes us on a guided tour of attempting to automate the testing of a test automation tool. One of the first questions to ask a tool vendor is "Do you test the tool using the tool?" But the answer isn't as straightforward as you might think! With his lively writing style, Bo gives an honest description of the difficulties and challenges he encountered, particularly in the verification of test results. It is a good idea to find out what others have tried, and Bo shows the advantages of doing so. His sensible approach to automation is to start by automating the easier components before tackling the more complex. Unfortunately, this story does not have a happy ending. It illustrates how presumably well-intentioned management actions can sabotage an automation effort. For reasons that become obvious when you read this chapter, the tool vendor is not identified: a fictitious company and tool name are used instead. This experience takes place in the United States with one automator (the author) and covers just over one year.

Chapter 5, Autobiography of an Automator: From Mainframe to Framework Automation

John Kent tells us how and when test automation started and offers surprising information about the origins of capture/replay technology. Understanding how automation worked on mainframes shows how some of the prevailing problems with test automation have developed; approaches that worked well in that environment did not work well with GUIs and the need to synchronize the test scripts with the software under test. The principles John discovered and put into practice, such as good error handling and reporting and the importance of testing the automation itself, are still relevant and applicable today. John's explanation of the economic benefits of wrappers and levels of abstraction are compelling. He ends with some recent problem/solution examples of how web elements can trip up the automation. This United Kingdom–based project involved mainly commercial tools.

Chapter 6, Project 1: Failure!, Project 2: Success!

Ane Clausen tells of two experiences with test automation, the first one unsuccessful and the second one a solid success, largely due to what she learned from her first experience. Lessons are not always so well learned—which is a lesson in itself for everyone! Ane's first story is told honestly and highlights the serious impact of insufficient management support and the importance of choosing the right area to automate. In her second story, Ane designed a three-month pilot study with clear objectives and a good plan for achieving them. Many useful lessons are described in this chapter, such as good communication (including using the walls), limited scope of the early automation efforts, good use of standards in the automation, a good structure (looking for common elements), and keeping things simple. The continuing automation was then built on the established foundation. Ane's experience was with pension and insurance applications in Denmark, using commercial tools.

Chapter 7, Automating the Testing of Complex Government Systems

Elfriede Dustin, well known in the test automation world, shares her experience of developing an automation framework for real-time, mission-critical systems for the U.S. Department of Defense. Because of the particular type of software that was being tested, there were specific requirements for a tool solution, and Elfriede and her colleagues needed to spend some time searching for and experimenting with different tools. Their clear statement of requirements kept them on track for a successful outcome, and their eventual solution used a mixture of commercial, open source, and inhouse tools. They met with some unexpected resistance to what was technically a very good system. This story covers hundreds of testers and tens of automators, testing millions of lines of code, over a period of four and a half years.

Chapter 8, Device Simulation Framework

Alan Page from Microsoft tells a story of discovery: how to automate hardware device testing. We all take for granted that our USB devices will work with our computers, but the number of different devices that need to be tested is very large and growing, and it was difficult to automate such actions as unplugging a device. However, a simulation framework was developed that has enabled much of this testing to be automated in a way that has found widespread use inside and outside of Microsoft. The chapter includes numerous examples showing both the problems encountered and the solutions implemented. This story is from the United States and was an inhouse development now used by hundreds of testers.

Chapter 9, Model-Based Test-Case Generation in ESA Projects

Stefan Mohacsi and Armin Beer describe their experience in using model-based testing (MBT) for the European Space Agency (ESA). Their team developed a test automation framework that took significant effort to set up but eventually was able to generate automated tests very quickly when the application changed. This chapter includes an excellent return-on-investment calculation applicable to other automation efforts (not just MBT). The team estimated break-even at four iterations/releases. The need for levels of abstraction in the testware architecture is well described. The application being tested was ESA's Multi-Mission User Information Services. The multinational team met the challenges of automation in a large, complex system with strict quality requirements (including maintainability and traceability) in a waterfall development—yes, it can work! If you are thinking of using MBT, you will find much useful advice in this chapter. A mixture of inhouse, commercial, and open source tools were used by the team.

Chapter 10, Ten Years On and Still Going

Simon Mills updates his case study from our previous book, *Software Test Automation* (Addison-Wesley, 1999). Still automating 10 years on is a significant achievement! The original story is included in full and contains excellent lessons and ideas. The success and continued growth of this automation is a testament to the sound foundation on which it was built more than a decade ago. The case study describes many lessons learned the hard way and some amusing observations on Simon and his team's first automation attempts. Their automation architecture separated their tests from the specific tools they were using—a wise move as was proved later. They devised a reliable way to document their tests that has stood the test of time. This story takes place in the United Kingdom, uses commercial tools, and covers about 15 years.

Chapter 11, A Rising Phoenix from the Ashes

Jason Weden tells a story of initial failure leading to later success. The failure of the first attempt at automation was not due to technical issues—the approach was sound. However, it was a grassroots effort and was too dependent on its originator. When he left, the automation fell into disuse. But the phoenix did rise from the ashes, thanks to Jason and others who had the wisdom to build on what had gone before, making many improvements to ensure that it was more widely used by business users as well as technical people. Their "test selector" for choosing which tests to execute gave the test engineers flexibility, and they ensured their legitimacy by keeping stakeholders informed about bugs found by automated tests. The small team that implemented automated testing for home networking equipment is based in the United States.

Chapter 12, Automating the Wheels of Bureaucracy

Damon Yerg (a pseudonym) tells of experiences in automating large systems for a government agency, over more than 10 years, with hundreds of developers and testers and more than a dozen automators. After some uncertain starts, external pressure brought the right support to move the automation in the right way. The tests to be automated covered diverse applications from web-based to mainframes, all with environmental factors. This story brings home the need for automation standards when many people are using the automation. Damon and his colleagues organized the regression library into core and targeted tests to enable them to be selective about which tests to run, and they related the automated tests to risk factors. The basic design of the automation supported business expert testers and offered technical support as needed. One of the most powerful things they did to ensure continuing management support was to develop a spreadsheet describing the benefits in a way that communicated effectively to stakeholders. This is a very successful large-scale automation project from Australia.

Chapter 13, Automated Reliability Testing Using Hardware Interfaces

Bryan Bakker tells of automating testing for medical devices, an area with stringent quality requirements and difficulties in accessing the software embedded in devices such as X-ray machines. Bakker and his team's starting point was simple tests that assessed reliability; functional testing came later. The automation was developed in increments of increasing functionality. The chapter contains many interesting observations about management's changing views toward the automation (e.g., management was surprised when the testers found a lot of new bugs, even though "finding bugs" is what management expected of them). The team developed a good abstraction layer, interfacing through the hardware, and were even able to detect hardware issues such as the machines overheating. The results in the test logs were analyzed with inhouse tools. The reliability testing paid for itself with the first bug it prevented from being released—and, in all, 10 bugs were discovered. Subsequent functional testing was smoother, resulting in cutting the number of test cycles from 15 to 5. This story is from the Netherlands, and the project had excellent success using commercial and inhouse tools with just two people as the test automators.

Chapter 14, Model-Based GUI Testing of Android Applications

Antti Jääskeläinen, Tommi Takala, and Mika Katara tell how they used model-based testing (MBT) in a substantial pilot study, testing smartphone applications—specifically Messaging, Contacts, and Calendar—on the Android platform. They used domain-specific tools rather than generic testing tools and a mix of commercial, open source, and inhouse tools, including two MBT tools. Testing in a huge state space was quite a challenge, but they give clear examples of the types of tests they were automating and good explanations of the algorithms used. They include many helpful ideas for making testing easier, such as using correct syntax for keywords and converting testware to more usable formats. This story covers a pilot project in Finland.

Chapter 15, Test Automation of SAP Business Processes

Christoph Mecke, Melanie Reinwarth, and Armin Gienger tell how automation is used in testing major application areas of SAP, specifically banking and health care. Because SAP applications are deployed in many client sites and have a long life, the test automation is on a large scale, with over 3 million automation lines of code and 2,400 users of the automation. The testware architecture of the tool they developed is modular. The standards and guidelines put in place ensure the automation can be used in many areas and in many countries, and the tool can be used by SAP customers as well. The automated tests must be ready to go as soon as new software is delivered to enable the testing to help speed delivery rather than slow it down. Some of the problems they encountered concerned testing parallel versions and multiple releases, consistency of test data environments, setting of customized parameters, and country-specific legal issues. One particularly good idea the authors relate is to have a tool do static analysis on the test automation scripts. They also warn about ending up with "zombie scripts": dead automation code in a script. This story takes place in Germany and India over several years.

Chapter 16, Test Automation of a SAP Implementation

Björn Boisschot tells how he developed a generic framework based on his observations while setting up automation for various clients. He explains how he used the framework and extended it in the automation of the testing for two SAP applications in the energy sector. The groundwork for the project is well laid, with a proof-of-concept forming the basis of the go/no-go decision. Björn gives good examples of communicating with managers, explains why capture/playback does not work, and emphasizes the importance of setting realistic expectations. The framework, now a commercial product, used good automation and software development principles to construct a modular structure that successfully scaled up. The layers of abstraction are well implemented, separating the automated tests from the tool and giving users access to tests without having to program. He ends by showing how multilingual tests were implemented through a translation table and some of the challenges of that project. This case study takes place in Belgium and is the origin of a commercial framework.

Chapter 17, Choosing the Wrong Tool

Michael Williamson tells the story of trying to use a tool (which he inherited) that he later realized was not suitable for what he was trying to test. He was trying to automate the testing of major functionality in web development tools at Google, where he was new to testing and test automation. Some assumptions that seemed obvious at first turned out to be not as they seemed. His approach to taking over the use of an existing tool seemed sensible, yet he encountered a lot of problems (which are illustrated), particularly in automated comparison. Michael found it was difficult to abandon something you have put a lot of effort into already, yet in the end, this was the best approach (and he was surprised when he discovered what had really been hindering his efforts). This story is of one person in the United States attempting to use a commercial tool.

Chapter 18, Automated Tests for Marketplace Systems: Ten Years and Three Frameworks

Lars Wahlberg gives an insight into his 10 years of test automation for marketplace systems, including the development of three automation frameworks. One of the key messages in this chapter is the importance of having the right abstraction level between the technical aspects of the automated tests and the testers. Lars describes how they addressed this issue in each of the different frameworks and some of the problems that occurred if the abstraction layer was too thick or too thin. As Lars and his team moved into agile development, they found the process worked best when they had people who could be both tester and test automator, but the role of the test automation architect was critical for smooth implementation of automation. The chapter illustrates the progression of a test from manual to automated and the automated checking of preconditions. Lars also includes an illuminating assessment of return on investment for automation based on how often tests are run, the costs of automating, and the number of tests that are automated. This work was done in Sweden using open source tools.

Chapter 19, There's More to Automation than Regression Testing: Thinking Outside the Box

Jonathan Kohl takes us through a set of short stories, each illustrating a variation on the theme of automating things other than what people usually think of, that is, thinking outside the box. The stories together demonstrate the value of applying ingenuity and creativity to solve problems by automating simple tasks, or processes other than test execution. Full-scale automation is not necessarily a practical option in some cases, but small and simple tool solutions can provide significant benefits and savings. Jonathan shows that even devising "disposable" automation scripts can be very useful. These experiences from Canada cover small to large applications, from web-based to embedded systems, using commercial, open source, and inhouse tools.

Chapter 20, Software for Medical Devices and Our Need for Good Software Test Automation

Even if you are not working with medical devices, this chapter, written by Albert Farré Benet, Christian Ekiza Lujua, Helena Soldevila Grau, Manel Moreno Jáimez, Fernando Monferrer Pérez, and Celestina Bianco, has many interesting lessons for anyone in automation. For the safety-related applications they test, a strict, formal test process is used with a risk-based approach to the implementation of the automation. Their story shows how success can be mixed even across different projects in the same organization; attempts to resurrect previous automated tests that had fallen into disuse resulted in different outcomes in different projects. In some cases, unrealistic imposed objectives ("total automation") virtually guaranteed failure. However, they did progress, devising a good list of what they wanted to use automation for and what they wanted to avoid automating. The problems encountered included some that are unique to regulated industries (where test tools need to be formally validated before their results can be used in the qualification testing of the software), problems with hardware interaction, and problems with custom controls (overcome by an abstraction layer). Their honest description of problems, solutions, and lessons learned in the four projects described is as useful as it is interesting. These stories from Spain involve commercial and inhouse-developed tools and cover projects lasting a few months to five years.

Chapter 21, Automation through the Back Door (by Supporting Manual Testing)

Seretta Gamba tells of the difficulties she and her team experienced in trying to progress automation, even though it had a good technical foundation. She shows how they addressed the real needs of the testers and provided support where testers needed it most, which was in manual testing. The really interesting twist is how they were able at the same time to harvest things that would progress the automation—win-win situations. Their approach is described in detail, showing how they implemented levels of abstraction, separating tests from application detail such as the GUI, and they include an example of a user interface (UI) to the tests. They developed what they call command-driven testing, which is based on a form of keyword-driven testing and worked well for them. This case study takes place in the insurance industry in Germany.

Chapter 22, Test Automation as an Approach to Adding Value to Portability Testing

Wim Demey describes how he developed an inhouse tool to work with commercial and open source tools to enable parallel testing of different configurations. Testing the installation of packages that are developed with a common core but customized for different customers is important because failures in installation may have serious impacts not just on the system but on market perception as well. But testing the ports of the different packages on a large variety of configurations (operating systems, browsers, databases) can be a time-consuming and resource-hungry process, so it is a good candidate for automation. Wim used virtualization to run portability tests on many configurations at once through a custom-built tool that launches the portability tests in the virtual environments. The chapter offers many good lessons, including the importance of automating the activities surrounding test execution, for those considering a similar task. This story comes from Belgium and involves financial client software.

Chapter 23, Automated Testing in an Insurance Company: Feeling Our Way

Ursula Friede describes the experience of "feeling their way" to better automation. She and her team did not plan the steps they ended up taking, but it would have been a good plan if they had. They began by just experimenting with a tool but soon realized its limitations, so they decided to focus on the most pressing problems by changing their automation. In each of four phases, they successfully addressed an existing problem but then encountered new problems. They calculated an impressive saving per release after they had implemented their improvements. Ursula was based in Germany at the time and was automating tests in the insurance sector.

Chapter 24, Adventures with Test Monkeys

John Fodeh tells of his experiences with automated random test execution, also known as "monkey testing," for medical devices used for diagnosis and in therapeutic procedures. John describes the limitations of automated regression testing and why few bugs are found that way. Using test monkeys enabled him to find many bugs in the devices that otherwise would not have been found before release. Inputs are selected from a list at random, and all crashes are investigated. Test monkeys can be implemented with commercial execution tools or inhouse tools. This approach borders on model-based testing and also is close to exploratory test automation. John's team was able to calculate the reliability of the devices over time, which helped in the release decision. Many other interesting metrics are described in this chapter as well. An honest assessment of the limitations of the technique makes this a well-balanced description of an interesting use of tool support in testing. This story takes place in Denmark.

Chapter 25, System-of-Systems Test Automation at NATS

Mike Baxter, Nick Flynn, Christopher Wills, and Michael Smith describe the automation of testing for NATS (formerly called National Air Traffic Services Ltd.). Among its other responsibilities, NATS provides air traffic control services for the airspace over the eastern North Atlantic Ocean. Testing a safety-critical system where lives are at stake requires a careful approach, and the requirements included special technical factors, human factors, and commercial considerations. The tool used was able to test the software without affecting it, and it was also useful in some unexpected ways, such as in training. The authors provide a helpful checklist for deciding which tests to automate and describe lessons learned, both general and technical. This case study is from the United Kingdom and involves commercial, open source, and inhouse tools.

Chapter 26, Automating Automotive Electronics Testing

Ross Timmerman and Joseph Stewart tell about the inhouse testing tools they developed over the years to test automotive electronics systems at Johnson Controls. In 2000, no commercial tools were available for this niche area, so the Johnson Controls team chose to develop their own tools, which was done initially by the test team and later by an offshore team. Both benefits and problems arise from writing your own tools, but the team dramatically increased the number of tests they were able to run. They also discovered ways to automate things they initially thought had to be done manually. In their second initiative, they built on the success of the earlier tools but provided more functionality, using off-the-shelf hardware modules with their own software to get the best results. This case study covers five years and is based in the United States.

Chapter 27, BHAGs, Change, and Test Transformation

Ed Allen and Brian Newman tell of their experience in automating the testing for a customer relationship management system. The problems they encountered ranged from technical issues, such as environments, testware architecture/framework, and "script creep," to people issues, including management support, working with developers, and when to ignore a consultant. After several false starts, they were challenged by some "Big Hairy Audacious Goals" (BHAGs) and were given support to meet them. They achieved good benefits in the end and provide some intriguing metrics about the number of defects found by different ways of testing (automated, manual scripted, exploratory testing, and bug fixes). This story is based in the United States with a team of 28, including 25 from quality assurance and 3 from development.

Chapter 28, Exploratory Test Automation: An Example Ahead of Its Time

Harry Robinson and Ann Gustafson Robinson describe Harry's experiences in doing what seems on the surface like an oxymoron. How can testing be both exploratory and automated? There are a number of requirements to make it possible, but when it can be done, it provides a way to explore test input spaces that are far too large to be tested in any other way. This chapter takes us step by step through Harry's journey of implementing what has now become known as model-based testing. The effort was far more successful than anyone thought possible at the time, which had an unexpected side effect on Harry's career! Although this story takes place rather a long time ago, the techniques described are now "coming into their own" because better tool support makes them applicable to more systems in a wider context. (Note: Although this chapter has two authors, it is told from Harry's viewpoint for easier reading.) This story comes from the United States.

Contributors and Acknowledgments

Submissions for inclusion in this book came from people we knew, people we met at conferences, and those who responded to the appeal for authors on our websites and in our newsletters. We began work on the book in autumn 2009, and from December 2009 until December 2011, the two of us put in over 850 hours on this book; this does not include the effort from all of the chapter and anecdote authors.

Thanks to all of the chapter authors for their tremendous efforts, more often than not on their own time, to produce their respective chapters and liaise with us through the production of this book. Thanks to the authors who contributed to Chapter 29: Michael Albrecht, Mike Bartley, Tessa Benzie, Jon Hagar, Julian Harty, Douglas Hoffman, Jeffrey S. Miller, Molly Mahai, Randy Rice, Kai Sann, Adrian Smith, Michael Snyman, George Wilkinson, and Jonathon Lee Wright.

Thanks to a number of other people who helped with this book, including Claudia Badell, Alex Blair, Hans Buwalda, Isabel Evans, Beth Galt, Mieke Gevers, Martin Gijsen, Daniel Gouveia, Linda Hayes, Dion Johnson, Audrey Leng, Kev Milne, Andrew Pollner, David Trent, and Erik Van Veenendaal. Thanks to authors for co-reviewing other chapters.

Thanks to the Pearson publishing team for their help, encouragement, and all the work they have done to make this book a reality: Christopher Guzikowski, Raina Chrobak, Sheri Cain, Olivia Basegio, and freelancer Carol Lallier.

—Dorothy Graham
Macclesfield, United Kingdom
www.dorothygraham.co.uk

—Mark Fewster
Llandeilo, United Kingdom
www.grove.co.uk

December 2011

REFLECTIONS ON THE CASE STUDIES

Dorothy Graham
Mark Fewster

Successful test automation needs both ingenuity and perseverance. Your experience may have similarities to some of those described in this book, but everyone's story is unique. The journey to success is not straightforward, but success can and has been achieved in a great variety of application areas, environments, and development life-cycles, as shown by the case studies in this book.

In this reflection, we draw together the themes and threads that have emerged from this book's case studies and anecdotes. This chapter can be read as an initial high-level summary of the most important lessons learned from current experience. You might also want to read this chapter (again) after you have read through the case study chapters.

What main factors contribute to success in test automation? What common factors most often lead to the failure of an automation effort?

There are no simple universal answers to these questions, but some common elements exist. We believe that two of the most important elements are management issues and the testware architecture:

- Management support for automation, such as setting realistic objectives and providing sufficient and appropriate resources to achieve a planned return on investment (ROI).
- A good technical architecture for the automated testware, having the right levels of abstraction to give flexibility and adaptability while minimizing costs not just of testware maintenance but of all aspects of automation.

In addition to the common elements, a number of other aspects, some surprising, may help you achieve better success in your own automation efforts. This is our hope and purpose in producing this book!

In most of the following subsections, we highlight the chapter numbers where a specific topic is discussed. The topics may be discussed in other chapters, too—the ones listed are where we note the discussion on the topic especially.

We discuss management issues first in Section A, but managers also need to be aware of the technical issues we describe in Section B.

A Management Issues

It is clear from many of the case studies that management support can make or break an automation effort. For example, chapters 4, 6, 11, 17, and 20 all recount situations where inadequate management support for the automation led to failure.

A.1 Objectives for Automation

Having good objectives for an automation effort is critical to achieving them! This seems obvious, but it is surprising how many times an automation effort is begun without any clearly defined objectives or with only the vaguest of platitudes ("faster testing," "do better," "save time"). The more specific your objectives are, the more likely they are to be well evaluated (to see if they are realistic and achievable) and achieved.

It is important to distinguish objectives for automation from objectives for testing. Automation is a way of running tests, whether those tests are good or poor. A good objective for testing would be "find lots of bugs." This is not necessarily a good objective for automation: If you are automating your existing regression tests, which are normally run to give confidence that a recent change has not broken the system, these tests rarely find new bugs. This does not mean that the automation was not successful, just that it had the wrong objective. But if a high-level manager perceives that automation has not met its objective (even if it was misguided), then funding may be withdrawn.

There are some cases in which automation is effective at finding bugs, as discussed in Section B 9. Good objectives for automation are discussed in chapters 1, 2, 3, 6, 7, 10, 11, 12, 14, 20, 21, 25, 27, and 29.

A.2   Management Support

Successful automation rarely grows within an organization without being nurtured and guided. It is fine for individuals to begin experimenting on their own, but if you want automation to scale up and provide the significant benefits it has the potential to deliver, then it needs to have adequate management support. A "bottom-up" approach is not a sustainable long-term road to good automation.

Management support is vital to success; we see this in many, if not most, of the case studies in this book. This support takes many forms: funding for tools, funding and release of time for a pilot project and testware architecture development, as well as taking an interest in what the automation is doing and monitoring costs and benefits. (See Section A.3 on ROI.)

It is also vitally important that managers are educated and informed about what the automation is capable of providing and the effort and timescales needed to achieve those results. Those involved with building and maintaining the automation regime need to communicate clearly and often and in terms their managers understand.

In some cases, high-level managers are not adequately informed or educated about what good automation entails. This could be because they have not investigated it well enough themselves, but another factor may be that the people doing the automation have not communicated the issues as well as they could have done.

The importance of good communication with management is highlighted in chapters 1, 4, 6, 13, 20, and 29, and education is covered in chapters 16, 19, and 29. Management support is highlighted as a key factor in the case studies in chapters 1, 2, 6, 11, 18, 21, and 29.

A.3   Return on Investment and Metrics

A popular misconception is that the only investment needed for successful automation is to acquire a tool (so if you get an open source tool, you do not need to spend anything). If your investment in the automation is zero, then your return on that investment could be negative. Putting it succinctly: If you put nothing in, you'll get trouble out!

Investment is needed to research and experiment with ideas; to design and develop (or select) a good testware architecture; to learn and understand the success and failure factors; to find a solution tailored to your unique situation; and to communicate the plan, progress, and ways of using the automation.

ROI is often estimated at the beginning of an automation project. This is a sensible thing to do: Are you likely to get back more money in benefits and savings than it will cost to develop the automation? This justification for test execution automation is normally done by comparing the time taken to run tests manually with the time to run those same tests automatically. Although this is a useful way to justify automation, just executing tests is not the whole story. The time to implement an automated test, the maintenance of the automated tests, the time taken to analyze failed tests, and other tasks may take significantly longer with automation than with manual testing. These other tasks can be a significant additional cost and should also be taken into account. Be aware that if you use a tool-vendor ROI calculator, these other costs may not be included in their ROI calculations.

Other factors to consider include greater coverage (the amount of the system that has been tested), shorter time to market, and increased confidence, but these benefits may not be realistic in the early days of automation implementation. They may only become reality once test automation has become established. They are also harder to quantify, so could be considered just as additional benefits.

Once an automation effort is established, it is also important to see whether you have achieved what you thought you could achieve, so a similar comparison (taking all factors into account) is good to do at regular intervals, and it is vitally important to communicate this information to the level of management that is responsible for funding its continued life.

Many people confuse benefits with ROI. Benefits are just that, the benefits, whereas ROI effectively compares the benefits with the costs.

Remember that the metrics you decide to collect may be misinterpreted and may not communicate what you had hoped for. Beware also of metrics that are no longer useful in a new context; a career-changing effect of this is described in Chapter 28.

ROI and quantified benefits are discussed in chapters 1, 2, 9, 12, 13, 18, 23, 26, and 29. Chapter 9 has a good example of an ROI calculation using model-based testing to justify their investment.

A.4 Automation in Agile Development

As agile development becomes more pervasive, automation becomes more important. Continuous integration *is* test automation; regression tests are run every day, if not more often. The automation also needs to be responsive to change, just as agile development is, so the testware architecture is more critical. (See Section B.1.) Test automation is successful in traditional as well as agile development, but agile development cannot succeed without test automation.

Agile techniques such as test-driven development (TDD) should ensure the automation of unit tests, but system-level testing is also needed for systems developed using agile methods. Chapter 1 focuses on automation in agile development; automation in agile projects is also covered in chapters 6, 7, 17, 18, 19, and 21.

A.5   Skills

The skill set of a tester is not the same as the skill set needed for a test automator, a role that bridges between the tester and the tool. (See Section B.1.)

The test automator role may include a distinction between a high-level designer of the automation (the test architect) and the implementer of the automated testware, or the term *test automator* may apply to both roles. The test automation architect is the person who designs the overall structure of the automation or selects and adapts the framework used to achieve a good testware architecture. The test automator is responsible for designing, writing, and maintaining the automation software, the scripts, the data, the expected results, and additional tools and utilities. The test automator implements the levels of abstraction (discussed in Section B.1), making it possible for testers to use the automation without technical programming knowledge. The test automator also supports the testers by helping them with technical problems, determining cost/benefit ratios, implementing support for new test requirements, and so on. The test automator *must* have good programming skills.

There is a trend to have testers become multiskilled, meaning that they are also developers. If a tester is also a good programmer, then that person could be both a tester and a test automator—we are talking about different roles, not necessarily different individuals.

However, many testers are not technical and do not want to become programmers. As Hans Buwalda says, forcing a nontechnical tester to become a programmer may cause you to lose a good tester and gain a poor programmer. Nontechnical testers should have access to test automation, too! If they are excluded from automation, the full extent of their skills may not be realized, nor will the full potential of test automation.

The roles of the tester and test automator are discussed in chapters 10, 12, 18, 19, 20, 23, and 29.

A.6   Planning, Scope, and Expectations

An automation effort is more likely to succeed when it is well planned. Plans should include time for experimentation without allowing a project to drift. A time-boxed pilot project with a few clear objectives and adequate resources, for example, can help you see more clearly how to achieve your long-term goals for automation.

Don't expect your automation projects to be problem free; nothing ever is! Build in contingency for problem solving. Remember that even the best plan is only a guide—be prepared to revise the plan in the light of reality.

Set realistic expectations for what can be done within a timescale, and define the scope of the project. Don't focus on too low a level, or you will not achieve the potential benefits that could be achieved within your organization. Focus on achieving some useful results early on rather than seeking to build too extensive a library of reusable scripts at the expense of useful automated tests. Once the automation is up and running, continue to seek improvements and set new goals for automators to achieve aimed at reducing costs and increasing benefits.

See chapters 1, 5, 6, 11, 16, 20, 25, and 29 for discussion of these issues and chapters 1, 3, 23, and 27 for discussion of continuous improvement within an automation effort.

A.7   Relationship with Developers

One factor that was present in the successful automation experiences was a good relationship between the testers, test automators, and developers. A poor relationship can make the automation much more difficult than it needs to be even if it still gives some benefit in the end. If the software is not designed with automation in mind, it can be much harder to automate tests. For example, if the software uses nonstandard controls, it may be difficult for the automated tests to interact with them. The testers or automators might say to the developers, "Please use only standard controls—that will make things much easier for us." But the developers, who are probably rather pushed for time, may respond, "Why should we do something for you when there is no benefit for us?" This is not the developer being contentious; this is a perfectly reasonable response (though some testers would argue this point).

A better approach is to ask the developers how the automation could help them and to seek a cooperative relationship with them. For example, if you can run tests in the test environment within 15 minutes of a new function being coded, you will give the developer useful information (bugs found or tests that have passed) within a timeframe that is of the greatest use to them.

Developer relationship issues are discussed in chapters 1, 2, 6, 9, 17, 20, 27, and 29.

A.8   Triggers for Change and Getting Started

What is it that causes an organization to decide that test automation is the way to go? Sometimes, a serious problem or near disaster due to insufficient testing can be the catalyst for change; sometimes, an outside view can show a better way; sometimes, management decides that test automation is needed for the company's survival. Real change often doesn't happen unless people have felt the pain first.

The most important advice for people starting out in test automation is to start small. A pilot project is a good idea, testing out different approaches on a small scale to see what works best before attempting to spread the automation to more people.

These issues are discussed in chapters 1, 9, 10, 12, 17, 23, 26, 27, and 29.

A.9 Tools and Training

A question often asked is, *Which tool is best?* This is like asking which car is best. One person's best car might include space for four children and two dogs; another person may prefer speed and performance; another, economy. There is no such thing as the perfect tool, but there are many tools that would be adequate for a given situation.

Actually, it is possible to have the wrong tool, as shown in Chapter 17, and it is important that the tool you choose is appropriate for the job. The same tool that was wrong for Chapter 17 was used successfully in chapters 7 and 25.

But the tool is not the most important aspect of test automation. Yes, you usually do need to have a tool to execute tests, but the other aspects of good automation far outweigh the differences between individual tools in most cases. Having a great tool does not guarantee success in test automation—the whole test automation regime, of which the tool is only one small part, must be planned, tailored, and maintained.

Failing with one tool does not mean you will succeed with another; some organizations have tried several tools and failed in the same way with each one. Unfortunately, the tool and/or the people are often blamed for the failure, when in fact the automation project was not adequately planned and managed.

The best use of tools is to support people! The testers and people who will be using the tool should have a say in how that tool is to be used, and the infrastructure should be put in place around it to support them.

Training is important for whatever tool you have. Those who will use the tool directly need to have in-depth training of some kind early on, whether through vendor courses or online tutorials. If you bring in an outside consultant or vendor to provide training, space the sessions far enough apart that trainees can absorb and experiment with what they learned before the next session. Later, provide training in how your automation works to those who will be using it—this is internal rather than external training. Good training can prevent a lot of wasted time.

Tool issues and training are discussed in chapters 1, 6, 11, 12, 13, 18, 19, 21, 23, 25, 26, and 29.

A.10 Political Factors

Some factors arise that are completely outside the control of the testers, test automators, and even managers or stakeholders; for example, a successful automation effort may be cancelled along with the rest of a major project.

Many testers and automators struggle with what seem to be completely arbitrary decisions made by their managers. Several of the anecdotes in Chapter 29 give examples of this, as does Chapter 4, where the automation was killed by a manager's actions (though it was probably manslaughter, not murder). Chapter 28 illustrates what can happen when improvements are so drastic that managers don't believe the results.

Political factors are part of life; decisions are not always made as rationally as we would like.

B Technical Issues

The most important technical issue in our view is the testware architecture and levels of abstraction. *Testware* is all of the artifacts created for testing, including the scripts, data, documentation, files, environment information, and so on, that is needed for testing. The testware architecture is the way in which these artifacts are organized and how they relate to each other—for example, high-level scripts that use low-level scripts to interact with the software under test.

B.1 Abstraction, Abstraction, Abstraction: The Testware Architecture

When a test execution tool is first acquired, the testers are often expected to be the ones to start using the tool. What happens when the testers are not developers? Now they suddenly need to become programmers, learning the scripting language of the tool. If they don't have a programming background, they won't know how to build solid (automation) code, so what they produce may be very costly to maintain when any changes occur to the software being tested that result in changes needed to the automation code. High maintenance cost is what normally puts a test execution tool back on the shelf!

There are (at least) two major abstraction levels (or layers) needed for successful test execution automation: separate the tool and tool-specific detail from the structured testware, and separate the tests (i.e., what the testers work with) from the structured testware. These are described in more detail in sections B.1.1 and B.1.2.

The test automator is responsible for implementing these levels of abstraction; if they are not implemented well, the automation will be expensive to maintain and difficult to use. Figure 0.1 shows our view of a good testware architecture, including the test automator's role in achieving these levels of abstraction.

B.1.1   *Separate the Test Execution Tool from the Testware*

A good testware architecture is what gives test automation its real power. The test automation architect is responsible for designing the architecture of the testware: scripts, data files, utilities, and so on, that are needed for automated testing. Other test automators must then comply with and contribute to the architecture. Good programming practices are needed here: well-structured, modular code conforming to sensible standards that encourage simplicity and reuse. When some aspects of the software change, the testware may need to be updated, but a good architecture will keep these updates to a minimum.

The architecture may be implemented by a framework that may be part of or separate from the test execution tool, or it may be implemented by a separate test control program or test interpreter.

People sometimes refer to *wrappers* around user interface objects, such as buttons and edit boxes. Wrappers are a good starting point and are necessary (but

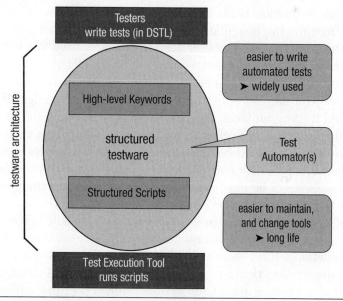

FIGURE 0.1   Levels of abstraction

not sufficient) for good automation. Having an *object map* for the names of GUI objects is another example of what may be needed to achieve an appropriate level of abstraction.

Another important aspect is that the higher levels of testware should not be directly related to any particular tool or tool language. Of course, at the tool interface, the scripts must be in the language of the chosen tool, but that is the bottom level only; structured scripts should be written in a tool-independent way. You may think that your current tool is ideal, so why bother? But tools change over time, applications change in unanticipated ways, your systems may move to other environments or platforms, and the tool that seemed ideal 3 years ago is no longer such a good fit. If your testware is tightly bound to that tool, you may end up throwing much of your testware away. If you have achieved this level of abstraction, you will be able to keep much of your structured testware and will only need to change the lowest-level, tool-specific scripts.

This abstraction level is what gives your automation a long life. With the right level of abstraction, your automation can outlive changes to your application as well as changes to the tool you are currently using. All of the case studies that were successful have implemented this level of abstraction to some extent.

B.1.2 Separate the Tests from the Testware

The top level of abstraction is the separation of the basic idea of the test (what is being tested) from the implementation of that test (how this automated test will be built). The testers describe the test they want to run by writing that test in a way that is meaningful to them, using high-level (and domain-specific) keywords.

This level of abstraction is most critical for testers who do not have programming skills. Their expertise may be in business or application knowledge. If the tests are being developed by programmers, they are likely to understand the technical implementation of the tests, so this level of abstraction may be less important for them; the high-level keywords that would be most appropriate to developers would be considered too technical for business users. However, don't underestimate the importance of having the automation be easy to use for whoever will be writing or maintaining tests, whether they are programmers or not.

The job of the tester is to test (see also Section A.5 on skills). The testers should not have to think about implementation details when they are concentrating on how best to test something. They should be able to write tests using a language that is meaningful to them rather than a programming language that is meaningful to a tool. Their thoughts about testing are related to their domain (i.e., the application they are testing), so their tests should be related to that domain.

For example, a tester with business knowledge in insurance would be thinking about insurance policy claims and renewals. A tester whose knowledge is in mobile devices would be thinking about testing network connections, conference calls, and so on. The high-level keywords would be very different at this level for people in different industry sectors even though some of the low-level keywords may be the same. This is why we like the term *domain-specific test language*, which Martin Gijsen has written about (www.deanalist.nl).

If testers without any programming experience can both write and run automated tests, then the automation will be of great use to the business domain and is much more likely to be widely used, further increasing the ROI.

Case studies that talk specifically about this level of abstraction include chapters 2, 11, 12, 14, 15, 20, 21, 27, and 29.

B.2   Automation Standards

Left to their own devices, most people will construct the automation and testware in a way that makes sense to them, but each way will be different. If you want to have automation used by a lot of people, then it is essential that standards for the automation are defined and adhered to. Standard naming conventions; standard places to store testware items; standard ways of constructing tests; standard ways of documenting tests; standard names for objects, scripts and data files; a standard header for each script—the number of things that need to be agreed on and used in a common way is more than you might expect. In addition, the more people who will use the automation, the more important and beneficial a standard approach becomes.

Definition of these automation standards is best started in a pilot project, where alternatives can be tried out and a consensus reached. Then the agreed standards must be communicated to anyone who will be using the automation, whether they are defining automated tests using a domain-specific test language or developing reusable scripts. It is also possible (and recommended) to build some of the standards into the tool support for testing, making it possible to automate more of the testing "housework" and thereby reducing human errors.

These standards should not be set in stone, however. As the automation matures, it is a good idea to ensure that the standards can be changed and updated in line with new (improved) approaches. It is also important to allow exceptions to the standards when justified. As automation is scaled up, it becomes even more important to have the standards centralized and communicated to all. Standards are discussed in chapters 6, 9, 12, 15, 16, 21, and 29.

B.3 Reusability, Documentation, and Flexibility

Although it can sometimes be useful to have "disposable scripts" (Chapter 19), in much of test automation, individual scripts have a long life and need to be reusable and reused in many ways. If a script is used many times, then it is well worth the effort of ensuring it is as well built as it can be, by including good error handling, for example, and also by making sure that it has been tested and reviewed. Look for modules that could be reused rather than building them from scratch.

In order for the test automators to be able to find and use a reusable module, it must be well documented. Information about the testware item should be easily accessible and in a standard format. For example, at the head of each script, document the purpose of the script, how to use it (data it expects, data it returns) together with any preconditions and postconditions. Additional information such as what happens under possible error conditions may also be helpful. This information should be easily searchable. In fact, the collection of all such information can form the documentation for the testware, and it is usually straightforward to automate the assembly of this information into a separate document or central place for searching.

Flexibility is important in running tests. For example, if a script is processing data from a spreadsheet, and not all items are required, a more flexible script will allow a field to be skipped if it does not have a value, making it easier for testers to specify a rich variety of tests.

It is also useful to tag each test with an indication of the category of the test, such as smoke test, bug fix test, or a test of function X. This "test selector" can be used to quickly select different subsets of tests to be run at a given time.

These topics are discussed in chapters 3, 5, 11, 14, 21, and 29.

B.4 Test Results and Reporting

Assessing the result of a test is the essence of what testing is about: If you don't care what the answer is, it's not a test! Checking the results of an automated test may not be straightforward and is particularly difficult when done at the level of bitmaps of screen images (which are best avoided if possible).

The tool doesn't tell you if a test passed or failed; it can only tell you if a result matched or didn't match a result that you asked it to compare its result to. If your expected result is wrong, the tool will happily pass all your tests when they are doing the wrong thing!

Sometimes, automated tests can fool you into thinking they are checking things when they are not—a test that passes is not usually investigated but may harbor serious problems, as chapters 15, 19 and 29 illustrate. (Chapter 15 calls these "zombie tests.")

Reporting of test results should be done in a way that is meaningful to the people receiving the reports; additional work may be needed to filter and interpret the raw results, but the better communication that results is worth the effort. This is discussed in chapters 3, 5, 13, and 20.

Sometimes, the automated tests can usefully check limited aspects of a test outcome rather than complete results by using a partial oracle. For example, exploratory test automation (chapters 28 and 29), monkey testing (Chapter 24), and reliability testing (Chapter 13) may be checking that the system is still running rather than that every calculation is correct. When large numbers of tests can be automatically generated, simply checking system survival may be worthwhile.

See chapters 3, 5, 10, 13, 14, 17, 19, 20, and 29 for more on test results and reporting.

B.5   Testing the Tests: Reviews, Static Analysis, Testing the Testware

Automation code, including scripts, is software and, like all software, can have bugs and therefore must be tested. Reviews, even inspection, of automation testware can help find problems and bugs in the testware itself and can help to ensure that the automated tests are fit for purpose. They can also help to spread knowledge among the team about the details of the testware. You don't need to review everything—choosing a representative sample of test scenarios to review with stakeholders is an effective way to see if you are on the right track.

Another technique from software development, described in Chapter 15, is static analysis of test scripts. Static analysis tools can find bugs in code (including automation code) that can be difficult to spot in a review and may not always be found in testing. Although it doesn't find all bugs, it is very quick and cheap to find the bugs it is capable of finding.

These topics are discussed in chapters 1, 5, 7, 10, 15, 17, 21, and 29.

B.6   What Tests to Automate

Chapters 2 and 12 demonstrate that there is no point in automating tests that do not provide value—first, make sure the tests are worth having, and then automate only those tests that are worth using repeatedly.

Which tests should be the first to be automated? Tests that are boring for people to perform, that are mundane and repetitious, or that are very complex all make good candidates for the top of your list depending on the problem you most need to solve. Above all, automate tests that will provide value to testing.

Chapter 25 gives an example of a checklist for deciding whether or not a test should be automated. It is important to know what not to automate as well as what should be automated. Being overly ambitious can harm your automation efforts because you may not achieve some of the "quick wins" that will demonstrate the value of automation more effectively.

This topic is discussed in chapters 2, 8, 19, 20, 22, 25, and 29.

B.7 Test Automation Is More than Execution

Most people think of test execution tools as just that—tools to execute tests. However, good automation is far more than having tool support for only that one activity. Many of the case studies show the benefits, often surprisingly significant, of thinking much more creatively about which testing activities can be supported by tools—and not just by the traditional commercial tools but by inhouse utilities, scripts, macros, and so forth. In addition to Chapter 19, which focuses on this topic, useful tips and ideas that have worked are included in chapters 3, 4, 5, 14, 21, 22, 24, 25, and 29.

One area of automation that is often overlooked is that it can actually help to support manual testing. Chapter 21 tells an interesting story of improving the automation at the same time as supporting manual testing, and this topic is also covered in chapters 1, 8, 12, and 19.

Another area is the automation of preprocessing and postprocessing tasks. If these tasks are not automated, then test automation becomes embedded in a manual process—this rather defeats the object of automation! See chapters 2, 10, 11, 18, and 22 for more on this topic.

B.8 Failure Analysis

Analyzing the cause when a test fails can take significant time, more so for automated tests than for manual tests. For example, when you are testing manually, you know exactly what went on before you noticed a bug, so you have the context of that bug in your head at that time. When an automated test fails, you may only know its identity and have no idea what that test was doing, the point it had reached, or what else had been happening. This context needs to be reconstructed before you can write a bug report, which takes time. With this in mind, automated tests should be designed to log additional information that may be helpful to the person who has to investigate the test failure. Failure analysis is discussed in chapters 20, 23, 27, and 29.

B.9   Automation Finding Bugs?

We mention in Section A.1 that finding bugs is a good objective for *testing*, but not really a good objective for automated regression tests. However, in some instances, automation does enable new bugs to be found. If the automation allows tests to be run that otherwise would not have been run (because running them manually is time consuming or impractical), then they have increased the coverage of the software being tested and can find bugs in the software that otherwise may have been missed.

Model-based testing (see chapters 9, 14, 24, 28, and 29) can reveal bugs through the development of the models as well as when the model-based tests are executed.

When automation can run long sequences of tests that would not be possible or practical manually, such as in monkey testing, reliability testing, or exploratory automated testing, then bugs can be found that would not be found with manual testing.

If you want to keep track of which bugs were found by the automation as opposed to other ways of testing, Chapter 11 advises identifying those bugs in some way in your bug-tracking system. Chapter 27 has some interesting statistics about the number of bugs found by automated tests (<10%) compared with manual scripted tests and exploratory testing.

B.10   Tools and Technical Aspects

In Section A.9, we talked about tools from a management perspective; you must consider their technical points as well. If you develop your own tools, you may be able to make them do exactly what you want; ideally, you would then have the best tool for your needs. However, developing a tool takes effort (usually more than you expect), so a compromise is often needed between the functions desired and the resources available.

One thing to explore is the use of a number of tools to accomplish a goal that no single tool could do on its own. Don't hesitate to adapt the tools to maximize their usefulness.

Tools that are specific to the domain you are testing can assume knowledge of that domain, making them easier and less error prone to use.

If you are considering what language to use for the testware, choose one that is already familiar to and popular with developers. This is much more likely to result in available help for problems in the testware.

The environment of the test needs careful attention; you want your tests to fail because they have found real problems, not because something in the environment has been forgotten. The setup of many environmental factors can be automated, making them less prone to human error.

Synchronization of tests with software can be a problem, particularly where the software under test is not confined to the use of standard GUI controls. While many tools offer excellent support for synchronization, this issue may not be solved in all instances. Furthermore, it may not be possible to adequately resolve all synchronization issues. This may mean a small reduction in the scope of which tests can be automated, at least for a while (new technical solutions may emerge later on).

See chapters 7, 8, 14, 17, 18, 19, 24, 26, 27, and 29 for discussion of these points.

C   Conclusion

Test automation is moving beyond a luxury and becoming a necessity for systems; as applications and systems grow ever larger and more complex, manual testing simply cannot keep up. As technology changes, testing must adapt—and quickly.

The experiences of test automation described in this book contain a snapshot of test automation at the start of the second decade of the twenty-first century. These stories incorporate both pain and pride, both failure and success, both brilliant ideas and unbelievable decisions. Listen to the stories and heed what the chapter authors have learned, and your own experience of test automation is more likely to be successful.

An Agile Team's Test Automation Journey: The First Year

Lisa Crispin

Look at "How to Read This Book" (page xxxiii) and "Reflections on the Case Studies" (page 1) for an overview of all chapters.

Lisa Crispin describes, in her very engaging style, what happened when an agile team decided to automate their testing. Given Lisa's expertise in agile, you will not be surprised to see that this team really was agile in practice. One of the interesting things about this project is that everyone on the team (which was fairly small) was involved in the automation. Not only did they excel in agile development, they also developed the automation in an agile way—and they succeeded. Agile development was not the only component of this team's success; other factors were equally important, including building a solid relationship with management through excellent communication and building the automation to help support creative manual testing. Another key factor was the team's decision to build in process improvement along the way, including scheduling automation refactoring sprints twice a year. You are sure to agree that what Lisa and her team accomplished in their first year is remarkable. The project was done for a United States company in the finance sector. See Table 1.1.

Table 1.1   Case Study Characteristics

Characteristics	This Case Study
Application domain	Financial services, web-based J2EE application
Application size	226,000 LOC: 95,000 legacy covered mainly by GUI smoke tests; 131,000 new architecture covered by 4,364 JUnit tests (in 2004, we had 128,000 legacy, 20,000 new with 473 JUnits)
Location	United States
Lifecycle	Agile, both legacy system maintenance and new development
Number on the project	9–12 (4–5 programmers, 1–2 testers, 1 database administrator, 1–2 system administrators, 1 ScrumMaster, 1 manager)
Number of testers	1–2
Number of automators	All involved in automation
Time span	Case study covers mainly the first year or so but tells where we are after 6 years
Dates	2003 to 2011
Tool type(s)	Open source
Pilot study undertaken	No
ROI measured	No hard measures, though we did track defect numbers and velocity (story points per sprint)
Successful?	Yes
Still breathing?	Yes

1.1   Background for the Case Study

Let's face it: Test automation is hard when you haven't done it before. This is a story about how a team went from no automated tests and a poorly designed legacy system to automating all of their regression testing in a little more than 1 year. In the ensuing years, I've talked to dozens of other teams who faced similar obstacles and found similar solutions. Come along with me on my team's journey. See if our barriers sound like yours, and consider experimenting with similar approaches.

1.1.1 The Problem

Here's where we start: We need to deliver new functionality to production every 2 weeks, but our code is buggy and we have no automated tests. We have plenty of showstopper bugs in production, though! How do we break out of this?

1.1.2 Our Goals

We're committed to creating the highest quality code that we possibly can, but where do we start? As a self-organizing Scrum team, we are comforted that we're all in this together. It's 2003, and some of us have good test automation experiences on other teams—there has to be a way. A safety net of automated regression tests would let us work faster. If we knew right away that a particular code change introduced undesired behavior, we could stabilize our code base. Continuous integration with adequate test coverage would enable us to have a stable build each and every day. Right now, it's hard to get a stable build by the end of the iteration, so this sounds good!

It doesn't sound easy, though. Let's look at what helped us create a successful strategy to implement an automated regression test suite.

1.2 Whole Team Commitment

We're a team of programmers, a tester, a database administrator, a system administrator, and a ScrumMaster. Our company's business experts are ready to help anytime. Our whole team pitches in to execute our manual regression test scripts before every release. Because we release every 2 weeks, this means that we take 1 or 2 days out of every 2-week iteration to manually test. We don't have enough time for the important exploratory testing that might help us find serious problems before our end users do.

> **Good Point**
>
> Everyone on the agile team does the manual testing, so all of them appreciate the benefits of automation.

We all care about quality, and we're all committed to ensuring all testing activities are planned and executed each iteration. This is a good start!

1.3 Setting Up the Automation Strategy

We need to confidently release new features without breaking existing functionality. We have to know quickly whether a new code change caused a regression failure. The manual regression testing only gave us feedback at the end of each 2-week iteration, and we didn't have time for as much regression testing as we wanted.

Some of us have worked on other agile teams that practiced test-driven development (TDD). We noticed that TDD helps produce well-designed, robust code.

Our existing regression tests are done manually, by the whole team, using scripts written on our team Wiki. That effort is about 20 percent of the whole team's time for each 2-week period. These tests provide the bare minimum of coverage, only for the most critical parts of the application. Defects reported in production show us that regression failures still slip by us. We spend at least 20 percent of our time each iteration fixing production bugs, limiting the amount of new functionality we can deliver.

Automating regression tests with more appropriate coverage would require a big investment of time, money, and brainpower. We would need hardware and software to set up a build process, environments where we could run the tests, and frameworks and drivers to automate them. However, since we figure that this automation will give us back 40 percent of our time, which we could devote to more valuable activities such as new development, the benefits far outweigh the cost.

Continuing with manual regression testing would certainly lead to failure. We need a sensible strategy for automation.

Because we're all doing the manual regression testing, everyone feels the pain of not having automation. We're motivated to come up with some way to tackle this problem. First, we need . . .

1.3.1 A Testable Architecture

TDD is the way to go, but automating unit tests seems daunting with our current code in which business logic, database access, and the UI are jumbled together. It's hard to isolate any one component for testing.

It seems smart to come up with a new architecture that isolates the various layers of the software for testing. We'll develop all new features with this new architecture.

It doesn't make sense to automate if automating costs more than the benefits it provides. We study the test automation pyramid shown in Figure 1.1. (This pyramid was proposed by Mike Cohn, who was our manager at the time). Unit-level tests generally have the best return on investment (ROI). The programmers can write them in minutes, they run in seconds, and they're easy to update as needed. We want unit-level tests as the strong base of our automated regression tests.

Our business logic is pretty complex. Our new architecture separates this logic from the database and UI layers, so we can test it by setting up data in memory and operating on it with production code. This is the middle layer of our pyramid—fewer tests than the bottom layer but still significant.

We still need to test the UI, but tests automated via the UI are inherently more fragile, expensive to maintain, and slower to run. Eventually we want to minimize the percentage of UI tests so they'll be the small tip of our pyramid. Like many teams, though, we have to start with GUI smoke tests just to get some protection around our code. Our pyramid is going to start out upside-down, but that's okay—we'll flip it over eventually. (It would ultimately take us about 4 years to get the triangle shape we were shooting for!)

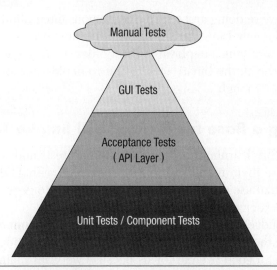

FIGURE 1.1   Test automation pyramid

> **Tip**
>
> The best way to get where you want to go may not be the most direct route.

We now understand what we need to do, so we start in on the tasks that will give us the biggest bang for the buck.

1.3.2 Setting Up the Build Process

We have only four programmers, but they're constantly checking changes into our source code control system. We want to make sure they don't step on each other's toes or break any existing functionality. Also, I (the tester) have sometimes had to wait several days for a build of the code that I can deploy in the test environment. An automated build process would ensure that a deployable version of the latest code is available within a few minutes of each check-in.

Our management assures us that quality is our number one goal, and they're willing to let us budget some time to set up a good infrastructure.

> **Good Point**
>
> Good management support allows time to develop the automation infrastructure.

We stop what we're doing and set up a continuous integration (CI) process using CruiseControl and a new Linux box. We don't have any tests to run yet, so it simply compiles the code and builds deployable binary files. I can see what check-ins went into each build and pick the binary files I want to deploy into production. This is a big help! But it's not enough.

1.3.3 Getting a Base for Testing: GUI Smoke Tests

The programmers are learning how to automate unit tests and write code test-first, but it's going to take them months to really get traction with TDD. With our legacy code, smoke tests that use the GUI would be a quick way to get some automated test coverage. But what tool would be best?

We have the budget to buy a vendor tool, but the programmers on the team are Java programmers; they don't want to have to use another scripting language for tests. Capture/replay isn't a good avenue for us because we want maintainable, solid test scripts. We settle on Canoo WebTest, an open source framework that lets us specify tests in XML files and run them with Ant. It integrates easily with our build process.

> **Good Point**
>
> Expensive commercial tools are not necessarily the best option.

I ask the business experts to prioritize the critical areas of the system that need to be protected with smoke tests. We budget time each sprint for me to automate test scripts with WebTest. We go for "quick wins" first, automating tests of the basic functionality for each user role in the system.

At first, our CI build runs a few unit tests and some GUI smoke tests that cover the high points of the system. As we get more tests at both levels, we move the GUI tests into a separate build that runs only at night, because otherwise our feedback is too slow.

At the same time, the unit tests and GUI smoke tests for each new user story we do are completely automated within the iteration. The new functionality will be covered by automated unit and GUI tests. Once the programmers are competent at TDD, we'll get started on that middle layer of our pyramid.

1.3.4   Driving Development at the Unit Level

Only one of our programmers has ever done TDD. Everyone buys into the idea. We bring in the best consultant we could find, as recommended by others, to help us learn how, and we spend lots of brown-bag lunchtime sessions experimenting with TDD. Here's the bad news: It's hard to learn! Our team needs time to master it.

Our management understands this learning curve: Our directive is to write code we'd be proud to take home to our moms to put on the fridge. Our company, a startup in business for only 3 years, almost went out of business because of problems with the web application and inability to deliver new functionality in a timely manner. Our business partners were ready to give up on us, but since we implemented Scrum, they are starting to see small steps toward stability and responsiveness. Our executives are committed to making the investment needed for long-term success.

> **Lesson**
>
> A near disaster sometimes can be the impetus for great improvements.

We know that these unit-level tests will have the best ROI. And we understand that TDD is really about code design, not testing. Thinking about what the code should do helps the programmer get the right code written. The tests run fast, and fast feedback is critical.

The best thing about unit-level tests is that they give us fast feedback. After some research of good practices, we decide to keep our build under 10 minutes. This requires occasional refactoring of the unit tests. Early on, our unit tests accessed the database. The programmers on our team learned how to fake, stub, and mock this out as appropriate to keep the tests fast while still providing proper test coverage.

1.4   Applying Acceptance Test-Driven Development (ATDD) to Test behind the GUI Using FitNesse

It's now 8 months into our automation journey, and the programmers have built a useful library of automated unit tests. We have smoke tests for all the critical areas of the application, and maybe 100 JUnit tests done, which cover a tiny percentage of the code. But we have nothing in the middle. TDD has now become a habit. It's time to fill in the middle part of our test automation pyramid.

1.4.1   In-Memory Tests

Our financial services product has a lot of complex algorithms that can be tested by providing inputs in memory. The tests are too high level to do with unit tests, but we don't want to have to do them through the GUI either, because that would be slow and expensive. We find it's easy and quick to write FitNesse fixtures to automate this type of test. We start using FitNesse tests to drive development of new user stories at the customer test level. These tests use fixtures to build test inputs in memory and send the inputs to the application code, which operates on it just as it would do in production. The fixtures then bring back the actual outputs from the code and check them against the expected results that are specified in FitNesse tables.

Testers and customers write the FitNesse test cases, and the programmers automate them with fixtures. This means we have to talk! Improved communication is one of the biggest benefits of automating tests with this type of tool. We testers sit with our product owner and other stakeholders to work through examples of desired and undesired behaviors for each user story. We turn these stories into FitNesse test case tables and review them with the customers to ensure our tests, when passing, will prove that their requirements are met. We also review the tests with the developers to make sure we are all clear on the requirements and to confirm that the test design is compatible with the code design. The developers write the fixtures to automate the tests. This process is repeated in many small iterations for each user story until development and testing are complete.

1.4.2   Tests Using the Database

Our application is data intensive, and we want to automate some tests that are more end to end. We can also test our legacy code with FitNesse tests by setting up test data in the database and operating on it with the legacy code.

   This type of test is more expensive to write and maintain. As FitNesse newbies, we make some mistakes. We couldn't figure out how to modularize components of our tests, which is done with the !include widget of FitNesse. We violated the "Don't Repeat Yourself" maxim of code design in a big way. For example, we had tables to set up the same employee on dozens of different test pages. If a new column was added to the employee table, we had to add it to dozens of tests. By the time we learned how to do this properly, we had a big mess that was hard to fix.

> **Lesson**
> Tool training early on can save a lot of wasted time later.

   We automated every test case we could think of, including the low-probability, low-impact edge cases, and kept all of them in our automated regression suite. It wasn't too long until our suite took a lot of time and machine power to run, and it got expensive to maintain. We learned to think carefully about which tests were really needed to provide adequate test coverage and to keep only those in our regression suite.

> **Tip**
> Lean regression suites help keep maintenance costs low while still providing value.

   Just as we do with production application code, we now continually revisit and refactor our FitNesse tests to ensure we have the coverage we need without slowing the feedback cycle too much or spending a lot of time maintaining the tests.

> **Good Point**
>
> Regularly review automated tests to ensure they are fit for purpose.

1.4.3 Benefits of FitNesse Tests

Our FitNesse tests provide faster feedback than the GUI test suite, though it's much slower than the JUnit tests. The FitNesse suite takes 60 to 90 minutes to run, whereas the JUnit tests run in under 8 minutes. We integrate our FitNesse tests into our build process and run them in the same build as the GUI test scripts. At first, we run this "full build" only at night, but this doesn't provide timely feedback, and if the tests fail, we won't know until the next night whether the problem is fixed. We invest in more hardware so we can have this full build of all the tests above the unit level run "continuously." Like the build that runs our unit-level tests, this is set up to run whenever a check-in is committed to the source code control. It takes about 90 minutes to run, so it's usually testing several new check-ins at once.

1.5 Use an Incremental Approach

Like so many teams, we find ourselves at the end of our 2-week iteration with unfinished testing tasks. Sometimes stories don't get finished. For example, we start on a story that has a five-page wizard in the UI, and only four pages get done.

One of the programmers proposes that we identify a "steel thread" for complex stories—a thin slice of functionality that cuts through the functionality from one end to the other. We write tests for that, write code, automate the tests, and then move on to the next thread. That way, our test automation, even at the GUI level, keeps up with development. The first automated test might be simplistic, but we can add on to it incrementally.

> **Tip**
>
> Steel threads are a way to make sure the automation gets finished within the sprint.

This works great, so for every complex feature we plan, we first diagram our threads on a whiteboard and make sure to finish one thread—automated tests and all—before moving on to the next. Soon, we don't have to carry over test automation tasks from one iteration to the next.

1.6   The Right Metrics

How do we know we're making progress? How do we measure success? We need some metrics. Our build process counts tests, so it's easy to keep track of the number of tests at each level: JUnits, FitNesse assertions and test pages, Canoo WebTest assertions.

The raw numbers don't mean as much to us as the trend. We want to see those numbers go up every iteration. So do our business managers. Every iteration, we send them a calendar with days colored green if all the regression tests passed at least once that day, red if the builds weren't all green. The business people actually pay attention. If they see two red days in a row, they ask us why. They also get a report every iteration with the number of JUnit, FitNesse, and Canoo WebTest tests. When test numbers go down, they notice and ask questions.

> **Good Point**
>
> Make your benefits visible to managers. You need to continually "sell" the benefits of automation.

Making test results visible is a form of publicity. We increase awareness of automated regression tests across the whole company. They see the number of tests go up, they see more functionality getting delivered. When we ask for time to refactor our tests or improve our build process, our customers understand why.

We need fast feedback, so the time each build takes is a critical metric. If the continuous build that runs JUnit tests takes longer than 10 minutes, check-ins start to back up, and it gets harder to identify which test caused the failure. When the JUnit build takes longer than 10 minutes, we stop and identify what's slowing it down. We refactor tests, add hardware, upgrade operating systems, configure the tests to run in parallel, whatever it takes to keep the feedback loop fast. The same goes for the builds that run higher-level tests. If our FitNesse tests take longer than a couple of hours to run, the feedback will be too slow. We have to strike a balance between test coverage and speed. Fortunately, innovations such as virtual machines have made it inexpensive to run many test suites concurrently, shortening the feedback cycle.

Tip

Never stand still with your automation: Refactor when needed, get new hardware, reorganize tests. Keep the goal in mind (fast feedback here) and change the automation to achieve it.

1.7 Celebrate Successes

One hundred JUnit tests isn't a lot, but each test represents many assertions, and it's a milestone worth celebrating. When we get to 1,000 JUnit tests, we feel that deserves a companywide party. Pizza is brought in for the whole company. We celebrate 2,000 JUnit tests with an after-work party that includes drinks and hors d'oeuvres. Some people have asked us if these celebrations might encourage the wrong thing: padding the numbers with unnecessary tests. However, since each small test is written right before the little piece of code that makes it pass, we don't have any extraneous unit tests. If any code that has tests is removed, the tests are removed as well.

As we near 3,000 JUnits, the ScrumMaster asks me to compose an explanation of what a robust suite of regression tests at the unit level means to our business. I provide a high-level description of test-driven development, how it helps us produce robust, maintainable code and provides us with a safety net of regression test coverage at the unit level. I try to make clear that the JUnits have a purpose—to help design the code. We don't just write unit tests willy-nilly. The ScrumMaster sends this report to everyone in the company and books a party at a local restaurant. Not only do we get a nice reward for our accomplishment but all the business stakeholders appreciate what it means.

1.8 Incorporate Engineering Sprints

Because we've taken time to explain our process and practices to the business managers, they understand the concept of technical debt. Whenever we have to cut corners to meet a business deadline, our code becomes harder to work with. If we don't have time to upgrade our tools to the latest versions, or we don't have time to try out the latest software that would help us work better, our velocity will go down. It's similar to falling behind in paying off credit-card debt—the interest rate will go up and we'll get further and further in debt. We won't be able to deliver the amount of software at the rate our customers expect if we're burdened by technical debt.

We get one iteration every 6 months where we don't have to deliver new business value. We call this our "engineering sprint." We can spend the time upgrading to the latest Java version, doing big code refactorings, trying out a new performance test tool, refactoring our FitNesse tests to eliminate duplication. In one of our engineering sprints, we switched our source code control from CVS to Subversion. In another, we switched our build process from CruiseControl to Hudson, which gave us more flexibility to shorten our feedback loop. Our business people can see the payoff of these investments when we are able to deliver more and better functionality in less time.

1.9   Team Success

Our team went from no automated tests to automating all of our regression tests within 1 year. Our test automation pyramid was still not quite the shape that we wanted, but we had good test frameworks and drivers to implement tests at each level (see Figure 1.2). We didn't get complacent, though. We continue to find ways to automate regression testing at all levels more efficiently and effectively. Once we had

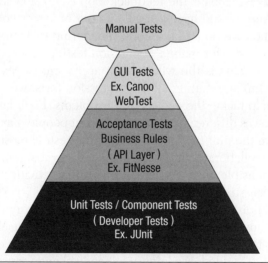

FIGURE 1.2   Test automation pyramid showing tools used

functional test automation under control, we moved on to automating performance testing. We don't run out of challenges to tackle!

Best of all, we have time to do enough exploratory testing for each story or feature set so that we rarely have nasty problems surface in production. We even have test automation that helps with our exploratory testing. We invested in creating highly flexible scripts using Ruby, the Watir (Web Application Testing in Ruby) test driver, and the test/unit framework. These accept runtime parameters and allow us to set up complex test data and scenarios in seconds or minutes rather than spending time in tedious manual test setup. The scripts put us right onto the screen where we want to test so that we can spend time exploring the software more deeply.

Good Point

Use automation to help support creative manual testing.

Our goal was to automate all of our regression tests, but this goal comes with some caveats. To get a reasonable ROI, automated tests have to be carefully designed for maintainability over the long term. This is why it helps to have programmers with good design skills help design automated tests at all levels. We continually refactor our tests to keep maintenance costs low. Also, teams must be judicious in choosing which tests to keep in their automated regression suites. You need "just enough" coverage. Too many tests means the feedback loop is too slow and the maintenance costs get too high. And we still have a small amount of legacy code not covered with automated tests. When we do a major code refactoring that might affect the legacy code, we have to plan time for manual regression testing.

The key to our success is the whole-team approach. Because everyone on our team was committed to automating all the regression tests, we had a lot of skill sets and viewpoints to help tackle the automation problems. Each layer of our test automation pyramid involves different tools, and different people may focus on each layer. The developers write the unit tests as they code, the testers most often automate the GUI tests, and both collaborate on the middle layer in FitNesse. However, everyone on the team is responsible for completing all testing activities for each user story before we can call that story done.

Our test automation gives us a quick feedback loop. Every day, we know within a couple of hours if any existing functionality has been broken. We plan time during engineering sprints to make changes we need to keep the feedback loop quick as more and more tests are added. We know what code change caused the problem, and we can fix it right away. We can meet our company's goal for the best-quality product while delivering new business value frequently.

1.10   Continuous Improvement

2011 was the eighth year of our test automation journey. There are always new challenges. As of this writing, our GUI test suite had grown to the point where it takes more than 2 hours to run. That's too long, so we split it into two suites and run them in parallel on different slave machines. This took some work, because some tests had dependencies on others, a bad practice and a compromise we made in the past that we have to pay for now. We have over 5,400 (and counting) JUnits, and our refactored FitNesse suites finish within 30 minutes.

We know our test coverage at the unit level, but not at the functional or GUI levels. We're currently experimenting with a tool that will measure how much of the code is covered by our FitNesse tests.

We know a lot more about automated test design than we did 8 years ago, and our tests need major refactoring. We try to improve the tests anytime we add a test or make a change, but we use engineering sprints to do the big refactorings. We watch what's going on with open source tools and try out new ones that we think might cut our test maintenance costs or provide faster feedback.

We've already done this with our GUI tests. A few years ago, we were finding that Canoo WebTest didn't support JavaScript well enough, and we started writing all regression tests for new functionality using Watir. A year or so later, Canoo WebTest was upgraded to handle JavaScript and Ajax better than Watir did at the time, and Watir was harder to integrate with our build process, so we switched back to WebTest, keeping our existing Watir regression scripts.

We're also looking into using Slim rather than Fit for our FitNesse tests. Again, we may not convert all our FitNesse tests to Slim right away, but we've found it's not a big problem to maintain multiple tools.

Through the years, our staffing levels have stayed fairly constant. A few programmers and one tester have come and gone, but the core of the team has remained. I think that is because good people like to work where they are able to do their best work, and on our team, we are allowed to do that—for instance, to do things like automate regression tests. We've had some interesting transitions. One tester decided he wanted to be a programmer, so he took some Java courses; the other programmers paired with him, and he came up to speed quickly. He has retained his interest in testing, especially performance testing. Another programmer never was able to adopt TDD, despite lots of pairing and coaching, and was eventually let go because his code wasn't up to par. We never filled the empty headcount, and our velocity actually went up. Every team needs the right people, and those people need to be allowed the time to learn, experiment, and improve.

1.11   Conclusion

What about *your* team? What's the biggest thing holding up your test automation efforts? Docs your team lack a particular skill set? Do you just need time to develop and implement your strategy? Are you waiting for the right hardware or software?

Think of something you can do today to make progress on automating tests and shortening your feedback loop. Be patient and take baby steps. Experiment, evaluate your results, and keep making small improvements. Before you know it, you'll be enjoying the benefits of automated tests.

CHAPTER 2

THE ULTIMATE DATABASE AUTOMATION

Henri van de Scheur

Henri van de Scheur tells a story that spans half a dozen years, relating what happened when he and his colleagues developed a tool for testing databases in multiple environments. They set good objectives for their automation and a good architecture for the tool. They automated so many tests that they developed a lifecycle for automated tests that included periodic weeding. Tests were run nightly, weekly, or with special scheduling. Despite great success, a number of problems were encountered, and Henri describes them honestly. The development of this database testing tool (now open source) was done in Norway by a small team, over several years, and it achieved a very impressive return on investment. See Table 2.1.

2.1 Background for the Case Study

This case study describes my experience in a fast-growing startup company: When I started, there were approximately 50 employees, and after just 5 or 6 months, it grew to more than 100. Because of this rapid growth, a large number of developers and testers were lacking fundamental knowledge of the product. Transfer of knowledge was perhaps neglected too much. As a consequence, both product and testing had poor quality.

Table 2.1   Case Study Characteristics

Classification	This Case Study
Application domain	Databases
Application size	
Location	Trondheim, Norway
Lifecycle	
Number on the project	30 to start with, 3 in the end
Number of testers	20 to start with, 5–6 in the end
Number of automators	5–6 to start with, 2 in the end
Time span	5–6 years
Dates	
Tool type(s)	Inhouse
Pilot study undertaken	No
ROI measured	No, but 2,400 times improvement
Successful?	Yes
Still breathing?	Yes

The office had 50 to 60 developers and 20 dedicated testers, residing in the same building but on separate floors. Testers reporting problems in the product tended to be ignored because of known poor quality of testing and a lack of knowledge and understanding of the product. By improving communication between the two groups—developers and testers—both product and tests benefited and quality in general improved. Improved communication was a prerequisite to even start thinking of automation at all.

Good Point

Don't try to automate poor tests; improve the tests first.

A typical release test with about 30 to 40 tests would take approximately 3 to 4 weeks for 15 to 20 testers to run on only one platform. Because a release typically had more cycles of bug-fixing and testing (typically four to six cycles), it took far too long before a new version of the product could be released. The need for automating this process was great: Cycles had to be shorter and use less human resources, and the tests had to be run on more platforms.

An inhouse tool was developed in Java with these requirements as a start. More and more requirements were added along the way, and newer versions of this tool were developed with increasing functionality. Tests were also developed in Java. Although automation started with a GUI focus, the command-line interface became increasingly important, enabling the team to more easily automate through scheduled batch-jobs.

Although some test suites were available at that time for testing databases, we were not aware of any tool for the automation of database testing. In addition, our database had some specific functionally that did not exist in the market at that time, and it required extraordinary functionality from a test tool. An inhouse tool already existed, but it was far too limited for our needs. At the same time, we suddenly had some resources available for starting such a project, so the scene was set for our tool development.

2.2 Software under Test

The software under test was special because it consisted only of databases. Some test suites are available for testing databases, such as suites for testing compatibility for a number of database APIs and query languages, including the Java Development Kit (JDK), JDBC, Open Database Connectivity (ODBC), and SQL. But the tools are not widely available, and/or they are too tailored for the database on which they are used, so both tests and test tools described in this case study were developed inhouse.

We defined a platform as a combination of an operating system, its brand, and a JDK version; we later included another axis: whether the platform was 32 or 64 bits. Examples include the following:

- Solaris 10 SPARC, JDK 6, 32 bits
- Solaris 10 x64, JDK 6, 64 bits
- Solaris 10 x64, JDK 6, 32 bits
- Solaris 10 x86, JDK 6, 32 bits
- Solaris 10 x86, JDK 5, 32 bits
- Windows Vista 64, JDK 6, 64 bits

2.3   Objectives for Test Automation

The book *Software Test Automation* (Addison-Wesley, 1999) contains a helpful table in Chapter 8 that lists different objectives for test automation. From this table, I assembled, in priority order, the objectives we had when we started:

- Increase confidence in software quality
- Earlier time to market
- Reduce cost of testing
- Consistent repeatable testing
- Run tests unattended
- Find regression bugs
- Run tests more often

After the first-phase implementation, the following objectives were added:

- Better quality software
- Test more software
- Measure performance
- Find more bugs
- Test on different operating systems

Good Point

Don't start with too many objectives; focus on a few initially and add to them later.

In addition, we created new objectives in new iterations of further automation:

1. Gather statistics for creating metrics (to answer the following questions):
   a. On which operating system did we find most bugs?
   b. Would we miss some bugs by cutting testing on an operating system?
   c. Which bugs were specific for which operating system?
   d. Which tests discovered most failures?
   e. Which tests never discovered failures?
   f. Which failures were uncovered by release tests and *not* by nightly testing? This helps analyze why such failures were discovered late in our release process.
2. Use the hardware not in use for anything else.

3. Use the hardware almost 24/7.
4. Shorten the time between when bugs are introduced and when they are discovered (initially from weeks to days, then to overnight, and finally to directly after checking in code).
5. Use our own databases to collect statistics to have our own data in a real production environment and possibly encounter failures otherwise not discovered (use your own medicine).
6. Enable test scenarios not possible to run manually.
7. Enable scenario lasting for several days.
8. Enable scenario with many users.
9. Reuse preprocessing tasks and automate these.
10. Reuse postprocessing tasks and automate these.
11. Automatically generate reports about results of tests.
12. Automate up to 100 percent of testing.

2.4 Developing Our Inhouse Test Tool

The most basic functionality was developed in 6 to 9 months with three to four developers. It was written in Java. After this first version, one person was made responsible for maintenance and for further development, which was gradually decreasing.

Figure 2.1 shows an overview of the Java Engine for Testing (JET) architecture. Each of the bigger squares is a computer that runs some software.

The runner computer is where you start to execute a set of tests. It uses JETBatch to start the test runs and to collect the results from them. The client machines run JAG (JET Agent), which JETBatch communicates with. It uses JAG to start JET to run a single test. The JETs read an XML document that tells them what to execute in a test and talks to the JAGs on the server machines to start the software you want to test. The complete set of machines comprises a test rig. By using different machines for different tasks, we avoided resource consumption of the framework itself influencing the tests being executed.

Because we had spent time and effort in designing our automation, we achieved almost all of our objectives. (Only performance testing was done with a separate tool that also was written inhouse. This is outside the scope of this case study.) Almost all tests were run through our tool automatically. There were only a couple of tests for which we concluded that the effort of automating was not worth the result. In the end, we had a tool with enormous capabilities and flexibility in a number of different areas.

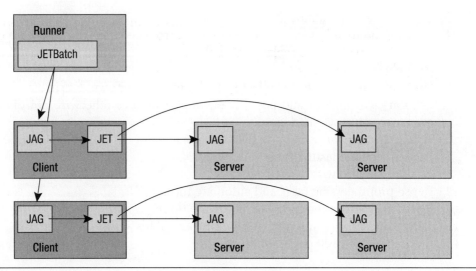

FIGURE 2.1   The architecture of the tool (from http://kenai.com/projects/jet)

2.4.1 Configuration

Configuration of tests: Our tests were defined in a database and could be selected through groups, individually, and in sequences of choice. The tool did an initialization before each test, avoiding a test influencing its successive test. The tool also cleaned up after each test. The tool collected and archived testware.

> **Tip**
>
> Implement preprocessing and postprocessing as part of the kickoff of a set of tests.

Configuration of the application under test: The version of the product could be selected, including debug versions and versions locally from developers' "sandboxes."

Configuration of platforms for servers and clients: We made it easy to define platforms and groups of platforms to run on. Tests were divided over the test rigs available within one platform group (for instance, Windows Vista, 64 bits,

JDK 6). We could set up a separate configuration for servers, with one or two platforms. We could also set up a separate configuration for clients, normally with one platform. For both clients and servers, different operating systems could be selected.

A typical test required four machines: one test machine, one client machine, and two servers with a database to be tested.

2.4.2 Resource Optimization

By adding more machines to a pool of test rigs, we could run tests in parallel. In addition, tests were queued: After a test was finished on a test rig, the next test in the queue was started.

2.4.3 Reporting

The tool created websites for its reports, and all results were also archived in detail in a database, enabling us to create detailed metrics, such as the following:

1. What bugs on which platforms and frequency (helping in prioritizing bugs)
2. General statistics per platform
3. Detection rate of bugs for tests
4. Redundancy for tests

After a test was finished, a summary email with the result was sent, and an XML-file was generated, containing all the information necessary to use for import to other databases or report generators.

The tool also made it easy to include information from an open source test-coverage tool (EMMA), again giving more insight into the quality of our testing—at least on the surface.

2.4.4 Failure Analysis

Automatic failure recognition was implemented with 60 to 80 percent of the failing tests correctly analyzed. This was done by defining patterns or signatures describing the failure, in most cases directly with the error message it generated in combination with the test name and test statement generating this failure. One bug could have more than one signature. More (manual) analysis was required for new failures or known failures with new symptoms, requiring new signatures.

In one of the first release tests performed with this new tool, it was a requirement that at least 75 percent of the tests would be run without any failures, independent of the cause, either product or test. In the end, this requirement was increased to 96 percent.

2.5 Our Results

After about 3 years of development and use, a release test with almost 200 tests on 6 to 10 platforms could be run by one person in 3 to 4 days. This would be the equivalent (in the way things were done before the automation) of 20 people (20:1 improvement) running 40 tests (5:1 improvement) on one platform (6:1 or more improvement) in 16 days (4:1 improvement). So our test automation process helped us improve our efficiency with a factor of at least *2,400!*

> **Good Point**
>
> Express your success in a way that communicates best with the people whom you want to know about it (here, 2,400 times efficiency improvement).

All other testers could now concentrate on test development and further tool development, and they had much less boring work compared to the repetitive tasks required in the beginning. The quality of both our product and our tests improved dramatically. Developers and testers had well-deserved mutual respect, and they challenged each other, making their work much more attractive.

Maintenance required less than 10 percent of one tester, a low number achieved partly because one of the requirements for further development of our product was backward compatibility. It was a rare occasion that the tests and/or the test tool itself had to be changed because of new functionality. On the other hand, new functionality often required new tests, in some cases replacing older tests.

2.6 Managing Our Automated Tests

Our test processes were improved continuously, and we devised a documented lifecycle for our tests, as shown in Figure 2.2.

After tests were developed, a review was performed, and after approval, a test was allowed to be included in the candidate batch (a set of tests "on probation" to

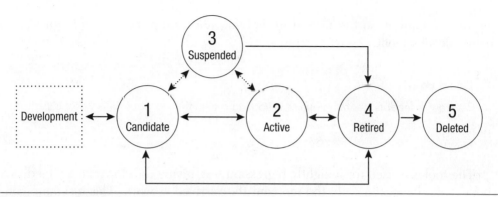

FIGURE 2.2   Lifecycle for tests

be included in the full automation suite). If a candidate test failed more than 4 days in a row, the test was withdrawn and went back to development. After showing no failures due to the test itself for a week, a test achieved active status and was ready to be included in the nightly and/or weekly test suites.

If the product functionality changed but the test had not been updated, the test could be suspended. Depending on the suspension cause, a test could become active again or would become a candidate again (after the cause of the failure was fixed).

Periodically, the contents of the different test suites were evaluated. Metrics were used to measure the value of running the specific tests. As an outcome of this process, a test could be moved from one test suite to another (to be run more or less frequently) or in some cases retired. If there was a certainty a specific test would never again be needed, the team could decide to delete it.

Lots of metrics were produced, sharpening both our priorities and our focus—to the great satisfaction of management. No doubt, their trust in the approval process of the product had increased greatly compared to earlier.

2.7 Test Suites and Types

Eventually, the tool was also used for approving developers' check-ins: Before they were allowed to check in new or changed code, they had to run a minimum acceptance test suite (MATS) on their code on three different platforms. These platforms were chosen, through experience, to be able to uncover specific and/or unique failures. This step helped to decrease the number of regressions and failures before the changes were introduced in the source code. The execution time of such tests was kept to a minimum so the tests were helpful, not a time-consuming hindrance to further development.

Good Point

Give quick feedback, and keep overheads to a minimum to provide the best support to developers.

The tool was used for a nightly regression test, giving developers daily feedback about their changes in code the moment they arrived at work. This test suite consisted mostly of shorter regression tests, run on a limited selection of platforms: typically three to five different platforms with a total execution time of approximately 12 hours.

A weekly test was done with a test suite running for 4 to 5 days, normally on three different platforms.

These regression tests had high priority and gained full support from management. Failures here had to be fixed as quickly as possible.

Besides these regression tests, other tests were run in candidate batches. These tests, typically tests for new and/or changed functionality for new releases, had a lower priority and were more closely monitored by the responsible developers and test developers. Candidate batches could also consist of nightly and weekly batches.

Project teams could define their own test suites to run on a schedule that best served their purposes.

In parallel with these tests run with our inhouse test tool, performance tests were run and compared against a baseline. These tests had their own framework, due to its very specific requirements for both tests and outcome. These tests were normally run on just one platform.

A release test normally contained all of the tests described, but they were run on up to 22 different platforms. This is shown in Figure 2.3.

In addition, the release test included other nonfunctional tests run with our test tool, such as the following:

- *Long-term testing:* Running for at least 10 days under different scenarios
- *Scalability:* Adding more hardware to divide load, typically run with 24 servers and 12 client machines

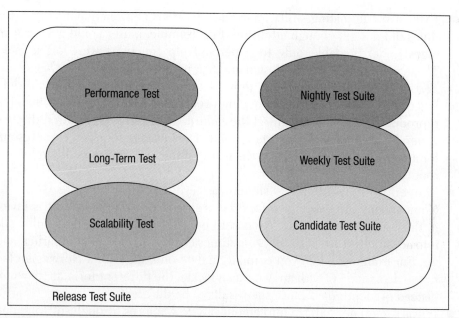

FIGURE 2.3   The contents of a release test

2.8   Today's Situation

The tool has been used for different database products and has now become an open source tool: See http://kenai.com/projects/jet.

2.9   Pitfalls Encountered and Lessons Learned (the Hard Way)

During these 3 to 4 years, we also encountered numerous pitfalls:

- Testing became very mature, sometimes causing us to forget the simple things. For example, complex SQL queries were tested, but a simple creation of a user without a user group was forgotten. Such a statement was not allowed and could cause big trouble due to unknown privileges set by user groups.

- Extensive automating shifts focus, and parts of nonfunctional testing sometimes did not get enough attention. For example, a user could get error messages understandable only to experts. Help functions were often lacking. These were both software design and test issues.
- Tests with randomly generated input data sometimes revealed serious defects but could not help in the debugging process because of the test's inability to reproduce the data that caused the failure. Those tests were often discussed, generally from an economic standpoint: They usually required extra resources for analysis, often failed to find the cause of the bug, and too seldom led to the root cause of a defect.
- The effort in automating should be evaluated for its effects on ROI! Comparisons can easily give false failures unless additional effort is invested in the comparison process. We had to be careful in comparing results, taking into account the use of locale, sometimes converting before comparing, and so on. For example, when you compare a date on a PC with a Norwegian locale to the date on a PC with an American locale, the different formats (day/month instead of month/day) cause the results to be different.
- It was sometimes hard to implement physical failures through software and to have these failures occur at exactly the same time on more than one computer. Simulating through software such situations as a power outage or a network outage can be different from the real event.
- Problems with false positives occurred because tests could report OK results even if they had encountered one or more failures. Tests that have been used over a long period without reporting failures are especially likely to overlooked for accuracy checking. But over time, these tests can accumulate errors and therefore should be checked occasionally for correctness in reporting.
- If minor bugs with lower priority were not fixed right away, they could mask major bugs, which were then harder to analyze because of the time elapsed since the bug was introduced.
- Waiting times had to be inserted and tailored to ensure previous mandatory processes had finished before testing continued. Replacing hardware with newer hardware often meant having to resynchronize this process.

Good Point

Anticipate things that may change, and make them easy to change when necessary (e.g., by keeping a central list of synchronization times).

- In some parts of the test suites, templates with expected results were used to compare the results. Such templates required a lot of maintenance. We therefore tried to change these template-based tests to assertion-based tests.
- Introducing new platforms sometimes caused trouble and required many resources to resolve. Operating systems needed to be monitored in increasing detail.
- For the Windows-based families, automatic updates had to be switched off, and updates had to be queued and were planned in advance in a timeframe where testing could be paused.
- We had to be aware of *everything* happening in the network in which the tests were running. For example, we were getting some unexplained failures once a month in the middle of the night. It turned out to be a nightly scheduled job on a machine from an ex-employee: The machine was not switched off and was still actively spamming the local network with queries.

Tip

Some things may seem obvious looking back but can trip you up if you don't anticipate them.

I think it is also advisable to do exploratory testing regularly. You would be surprised what you can find, and you can sometimes reuse the experience in new automated tests.

2.10 How We Applied Advice from the *Test Automation Book*

In developing our automation, we applied many useful points that we found in *Software Test Automation*:

- We had a long list of requirements for the tool before we started; we discussed and reviewed the list, and it proved to be a solid basis for our successful result. We involved key people in the project, each representing different needs: managers, IT operations people, release engineers, test managers, developers, and testers.

- The automation was only done for test preparation, execution, comparison, cleanup, archiving, reporting, and metrics. Processes before execution, such as test design, were not automated.
- We had strong support from management to implement this automation, and they had *realistic* expectations.

Good Point

Management support is critical, but expectations must be realistic.

- Without having brilliant experts in different areas, we would never have succeeded. Solutions and implementations were complex and presented a big challenge.
- We were lucky to not have to test any GUI for most of our products, which made automating much less cumbersome.
- The database with a GUI to test was considered for usability tests. Just specifying this type of test gave us many major improvements, leading to the usability test being postponed. To this day, it still has not been done, but we benefited from thinking about it!
- A big part of development was focused on the GUI part of the test tool. Later, this part was hardly used, because everything was automated through the command-line interface. Our earlier focus on the GUI occurred perhaps because we still had the mind-set of testing products manually.

Tip

Having a good user interface to the tool may be most helpful at the beginning of the automation project.

- Because of this automation, testers developed different skills and became more specialized in their areas of interest. Some focused more on test development, others more on executing and reporting.
- Always having further improvements in mind helped us take big steps forward. Group discussions of problems and how to solve them by automation ultimately lead to solutions.

- Letting all testers attend the International Software Testing Qualifications Board (ISTQB) course for Foundation certification improved communication. The same terminology was used *and* understood.
- An unplanned reduction in the workforce accelerated the process of automating: The need to use fewer resources had become even greater.
- Introducing small steps to the rest of the organization was also well received. Those small steps were easier to test before they were put into production.

Good Point

Look for quick wins; take small steps.

- The testing done through this automation became a core process for the business. Whenever failures occurred, they were flagged and reported to the whole department. This could have had a negative impact for development because developers became extra careful when changing code. The extra care was good for quality, but there is always a balance between quality and effort. Good enough quality was not defined and might result in too much effort in development, but this is just my hypothesis with no facts and/or metrics to support it. But having developers too concerned with quality is quite unusual in the software industry!

2.11 Conclusion

The quality of both our database product and our tests was very poor, and both were improved dramatically before automating of testing started.

A process was started to develop a tool for automating testing. A team was set up with a perfect mix of gatekeepers, experts, and stakeholders defining the requirements. Development was done with the highest expertise available, and automating of testing was gradually implemented, and each participant in this process played an important role: the tool champion and change agent, management, tool custodians, and the whole implementation team.

Early on, we achieved our first objectives for developing the tool, and then more objectives were met over time. Our efficiency was improved by a factor of at least 2,400, and we found ourselves with the perfect tool for our organization. The little maintenance it required to implement small fixes and/or enhancements also contributed to our success story. All of our hardware resources were utilized optimally: Most of the machines were being used 24/7 with just some short breaks.

For us, this was the ultimate automation.

2.12 Acknowledgments

I want to thank Yngve Svendsen and Jørgen Austvik for their helpful feedback and positive comments as I wrote this case study. In addition, I thank all the people involved in making this project such a big success, especially William Franklin, who continually supported our automation efforts and challenged us to do more. Thank you, also, to the two authors of this book for giving me the opportunity to publish this story.

CHAPTER 3

MOVING TO THE CLOUD: THE EVOLUTION OF TiP, CONTINUOUS REGRESSION TESTING IN PRODUCTION

Ken Johnston
Felix Deschamps

Ken Johnston and Felix Deschamps from Microsoft describe how they moved from product-based to service-based automated testing by implementing the automation in the cloud. Testing of Microsoft Exchange servers was already extensively automated, and much of the existing automation was reusable. Testing in production seems a foreign concept to most testers, but this chapter explains why it was necessary and beneficial to move to continuous monitoring and contains useful tips for anyone considering a similar move. This experience takes place in the United States, over 3 years, and unsurprisingly, Microsoft tools were used. See Table 3.1.

Table 3.1   Case Study Characteristics

Characteristics	This Case Study
Application domain	Exchange Server 2010—business-class email server
Application size	Very large
Location	Redmond, Washington, United States
Lifecycle	Traditional multiyear release cycle migrating to a 6-month ship cycle with agile elements
Number on the project	>500
Number of testers	>150
Number of automators	>150
Time span	About 3 years
Dates	2007–2009
Tool type(s)	Microsoft Visual Studio Team System; rest of tools were inhouse developed
Pilot study undertaken	No
ROI measured	No; product strategy change forced us to adapt, so ROI was never done
Successful?	Yes
Still breathing?	Yes

3.1 Background for the Case Study

Would you bet a billion-dollar business on the cloud?

Exchange 2007 was an exciting release for our team. At the time we shipped, we had successfully rearchitected our product to run natively on the .Net platform, made the transition to support server administration by "roles," made 64 bit our target platform, and adopted Windows PowerShell as our server management automation toolset. We were ready for the next challenge!

At that time, Ray Ozzie, Microsoft's new chief architect, was beginning to build a roadmap for the future of Microsoft and the cloud. It was clear to us that the cloud was going to be big and that Exchange was looking at one of those great opportunities that rarely come around in any business. We could help our customers lower their costs and improve their quality of service, and we could dramatically grow the Exchange business, all at the same time.

This decision to embrace the cloud led to even more questions. How do we build a set of features that would entice IT professionals to upgrade to our Wave 14 release (released as Microsoft Exchange Server 2010) while also targeting a service? How do we rearchitect the product to achieve the economies of scale needed to run a fully geodistributed service? Where do we even begin now that we have to deal not only with building the software but also with a data center?

We went into full prototype and discovery mode. We learned a lot of new web service concepts to help us scale the service up and out with redundancy:

- We needed to architect for multitenancy so that a single instance of the service could serve multiple client organizations (tenants).
- We needed to scale units (sometimes called pods) as logically grouped subsets of machines fulfilling a function and being useful when planning procurement units.
- Our service must be geodistributed to support business continuance planning (BCP) and to reduce latency by geographic markets.

We learned how the services worked as a business and how we had to manage our CAPEX (capital expenditures, such as purchasing new servers) and our OPEX (operational expenditures, such as support staff required to run the service) and manage our total COGS (cost of goods sold). The team learned that servers didn't just magically appear in the data center; rather, we had to plan our procurement a year in advance as well as plan for space, power, and network within our data center. For those individuals who have worked on services for some time, this sounds rather basic, but we wanted the entire organization to embrace services and really understand what it meant for us to bet our business on our cloud strategy.

Out of this learning process, we settled on a set of tenets to drive our Wave 14 release:

- Reuse and extend our existing infrastructure.
- Exchange will remain one codebase.
- We are one team and will not have a separate service engineering team or service operations team.

3.2 Moving Our Testing into the Cloud

For the test team, we quite simply had to figure out how to simultaneously test a server and a service. How do we pull our existing rich cache of test automation into the services space? The answer we settled on was to aggressively embrace testing in production (TiP), which at the time was seen as something you just didn't do. Our starting point was our existing tools and assets, which are shown in Table 3.2.

Because Exchange is one of the most complex products in the world, we had already built a very impressive engineering pipeline for developing and testing our product. Our test lab consists of roughly 5,000 machines that we use for running daily and pre-check-in test passes. We do something in the vicinity of *80,000 automated exchange deployments a week* on those machines, in various complex topologies that simulate our test scenarios (multiple AD [Active Directory] sites, different failover configurations, multiple role configurations, etc). At the end of 2007, we had written around *70,000 automated test cases for validating our product,* which we run each and every day and a subset of which are required to be run before anybody checks in any code. We used Microsoft Visual Studio as the development environment for our test automation. Automation is usually written in C#, but we also use JavaScript and C++.

Table 3.2   Existing Tools and Assets of Exchange Testing

Assets and Processes	Purpose
Topobuilder	Automated tool for building highly varied and complex server topologies
5000 machines in test labs	70,000 automated test cases run multiple times a day on these machines
Milestone-based development with long integration phase	Validate a broad array of scenarios after code completion and during a large test and stabilization phase
Dog food	Eat your own dog food; it's good for you and makes the product better for our customers (explained next)
Complex branch management	Multiple product units with independent source control branches eventually integrating into a single branch and release

As with most Microsoft product teams, we eat our own dog food. There have been many articles and blogs on the concept of dog-fooding a product. For this release, it meant that the entire Exchange team had their mailboxes hosted on either the corporate dog food environment or the cloud-based dog food environment. Adding to the complexity, we had to make the two dog food environments work together seamlessly even while upgrading them to the latest build every 2 weeks.

This level of automation allowed us to have a single main code branch with consistent file versioning across multiple product units. This was accomplished while maintaining the number of compile failures (build breaks) and regressions at a minimum. Having our own mailboxes in dog food allowed us to very quickly find functional issues that our testing may have missed and gave us confidence in the very features we were building. It was important for us to continue getting this level of confidence as we moved into the services world. The new tools and models we adopted are shown in Table 3.3.

Each of our new tools and processes drew on our experiences in shipping Exchange Server. The new twist for us was figuring out how to integrate with other services and how to execute traditional test activities in a production data center.

Table 3.3   New Tools and Models

New Innovations	Description
OneBoxes	One server/OS instance of major service components to allow for parallel independent testing. For Exchange, this meant running the Exchange store, SMTP, POP3, and web frontend all within a single OS. We also implemented OneBox for major platform components such as Windows Live ID.
Service dog food	Portion of Exchange team must be on the service dog food while the rest are on the corporate server dog food.
TiP service	Leveraging existing 70,000+ automated test cases that normally run in the test lab to test against and validate production.
TiP OneBox	Running our OneBox environments in the production data center as early as possible in the development process.

3.2.1   What We Wanted to Get Out of Our TiP Test Strategy

Our goals for our TiP strategy were to:

- Proactively find issues in production
- Actively test against service dog food
- Validate new production rollouts
- Confirm that a configuration change or upgrade didn't break anything
- Partner signoff tests with our dependent services, like Windows Live ID
- Leverage and help improve the existing SCOM (System Center Operations Manager) monitoring solution
- Detect latency
- Have engineering teams use these tests to understand production experience

With goals in place, we needed to develop our guiding principles for testing and particularly for TiP while ensuring they were in alignment with the overall project goals for Exchange. We settled on a core set of principles that focused on efficiency and reuse. The efficiency concept was around finding the right set of bugs as quickly as possible in the least complex environment. The OneBox was a major asset here. Additionally, we chose to host many of our OneBox test environments within the data center. That decision yielded many additional bugs caused by data center networks and security settings. Reuse for us became vital, because it meant extending existing assets and processes into the data center and production, yielding better early test results.

3.2.2   Guiding Principles

We used the following principles to guide our development:

- No separate teams means test teams of existing features get involved.
- Same codebase in production meant that we would try to reuse our entire product and test assets (the test automation, test harness, test tools, and processes), but now in production.
- Functional validation done in labs means we want to go further in production and act as a customer to validate the customer experience. Some TiP approaches use testability features to get deeper into the stack in the live site, but for our initial implementation, we chose to stick with an end-user blackbox test approach.

- Scenarios expressed as breadth, not depth, scenarios (cover as much surface area as possible on the scenario while making it as fast as possible).

Good Point

Know your objectives, and set the guiding principles for automation to best achieve them.

3.3   How We Implemented TiP

Our first step was to have the test managers buy into the guiding principles and then work closely with senior members of their teams to review these principles against all the main functional areas. This allowed us to ensure we had no gaps and that we could leverage the deep technical knowledge of testers in the various areas. This virtual team defined over 40 scenarios that represented the breadth of functionality deemed the most critical.

Good Point

Avoid reinventing the wheel; reuse existing automationware wherever possible.

Next was deciding how we would translate those scenarios into a concrete implementation that we could target at our production system. As mentioned, one of our tenets was reusing as much as possible of what we had, so we focused on defining and developing the desired tests as quickly as possible. For our initial implementation, we decided we would leverage our existing test execution framework to run the tests so that we could reuse our existing reporting tools, machine management, and so on. This also allowed us to take advantage of our existing test automation libraries.

What we ended up with as our first implementation is detailed in Figure 3.1. Every hour, our execution engine automatically deployed a new machine and installed the appropriate client libraries, tools, and tests. It also installed a "cloud definition" file that described the target environment in a generic way. The tests themselves do not know anything about the target, and we can, through the use of this abstraction, point to a data center, a scale unit, or an individual machine (which we actually do in our pre-check-in workflow now).

Tip

Another level of abstraction: Separate the tests from the machine and environment they run on.

Figure 3.1 shows our first version of the TiP system topology, which has the following characteristics:

1. Deploy an *automation host* that executes tests against a specific data center.
2. Send results to the Focus test execution (FTE) server, which processes results (Focus is the name of our tool).
3. Results are saved to a common database.
4. TiP diagnostic service periodically wakes up and aggregates the results across runs.
5. Aggregate results are streamed back to the database.
6. Product bugs are automatically opened for issues.

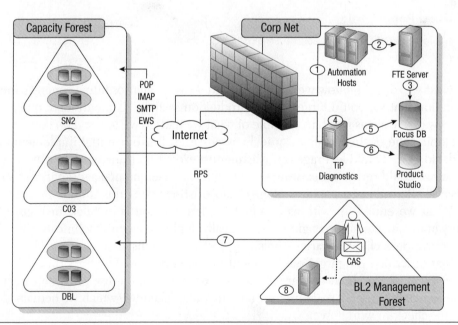

FIGURE 3.1   Exchange TiP, version 1 system topology

7. Diagnostic service sends a request to our management forest, which contains the logic for paging and alerting.
8. Request is sent to the SCOM root management system (RMS) for processing. SCOM alerts are fired, and on-call folks respond to issues found.

Initially, we used the tests to validate new deployments of the service before provisioning (signing up and creating mailboxes for) new users. We realized early on, though, that unlike the traditional software-only world where all we were responsible for was ensuring the quality of the software, we were now running a service that is always in flux. Not only are configuration changes always happening (Domain Name System [DNS], patches, new tenants, etc.), the sheer volume of updates means that over time we may run into an update or minor configuration change that we hadn't anticipated or tested for. In our experience, even a change to production that is considered safe can break the service. This is why we decided it was important to run not just once during deployment but in a continuous fashion.

TiP was able to function a bit like a production service monitor; however, the set of tests we ran were much deeper and more robust end-to-end scenarios than traditional lightweight service monitoring. As such, TiP tests became our canary in the coal mine, providing us with early alerts to potential customer-facing issues. We did use other agent-based monitoring solutions built on top of Microsoft System Center; however, these agents focused at the single-machine level. Our TiP tests ran as end users and alerted us when their experience was degraded.

> **Good Point**
>
> Don't use just one approach to automation; use any that are useful. They will complement each other and give greater value than only one.

As part of our overall strategy, we ended up using third-party services like Gomez and Keynote. While very important in our overall strategy, this type of monitoring focuses mainly on service availability of some narrow scenarios (such as login). While our breadth of TiP scenarios is not as large as the rest of our testing (only 40 high-level, end-to-end scenarios versus the more than 70,000 tests we run daily in our lab), they are certainly more in depth than we normally got from those services.

By using our own infrastructure, for example, we were able to easily add validation for ActiveSync protocols for mobile phones. This would be very difficult to reproduce in a traditional black-box monitoring environment because of the complexity of the protocol. Another point is that of agility. We can make changes and respond quickly to changes in the data center, in terms of both the production environment and the tests themselves. So, as it is with our single-machine-focused SCOM monitoring infrastructure, these TiP tests are meant to complement, not replace, external black-box testing.

3.4 Sample of Monthly Service Review Scorecards

Every month, we have an executive review of the overall quality of service (QoS) and the progress we have made on targeted improvements from the previous month. This review strikes a continuous cadence for overall service improvements and helps us to drive improvements into the TiP suite. The monthly review was initiated by our executive, and he participates every month, driving the question-and-answer (Q&A) sessions. It is his one chance each month to go deep into live site quality and drive improvements. Executive sponsorship is critical for any program like this, and we had it from the very beginning. An example of the scorecard is shown in Figure 3.2.

3.4.1 Reading Our Scorecard

One of the first questions that is typically proffered after someone sees the TiP scorecard is, *How do you read it?* Good question.

One important point is that the scorecard shown in the example is one of several slides in a PowerPoint deck that is reviewed monthly. The data is pulled into a rather large Excel spreadsheet, and then sections are pulled out of Excel into each slide for review by the larger team and executive management.

Figure 3.3 provides an area breakdown of the scorecard. Area 1 provides a reference to the rows in the Excel spreadsheet. Due to space limitations in PowerPoint slides, only the last 3 months of data are presented; the Excel spreadsheet contains many more months of data. During the review, everyone has a copy of the spreadsheet and quite often follows along with the presentation by reviewing the spreadsheet on their own laptop.

Area 2 is the title of the drill-down area. In the example provided the area was Incidents and Escalations.

Area 3 is pulled from the Excel spreadsheet report. It provides the metric name and the last 3 months of data. In the sample provided in Figure 3.3, data is presented for incident volume by month by service component. Every time a component of the overall Exchange cloud service has a failure that requires human intervention to resolve, it is considered an incident. With 3 months of data, we can identify positive and negative trends even if we are meeting the monthly goals.

Scorecard Rows 66-141	Incidents and Escalations				

Customer Impacting Escalations - 0 for month	Metric	Dec	Nov	Oct	
Provisioning Escalations (21)	Biz Hours Response Time in minutes	2.9	10.6	3.6	◐
• TIP tests failing	Off Hours Response Time in minutes	5.7	9	8.2	◐
• Response from SyndC	Biz Hours Escalations	34	52	30	◐
• Logging from SyndC	Off Hours Escalations	18	19	14	◐
• Majority false alarms	**Total Escalations**	**52**	**71**	**44**	●
	OWA	1	8	12	◐
OWA Escalations (1)	POP, IMAP, ActiveSync	17	48	1	◐
• Leaks (app pool)	Prov, Gal, Recipients, OAB	21	49	16	◐
• Operational burden	HA	3	51	3	◐
	Store	3	34	9	◐
Data Center Escalation (35)	Ops	9	19	10	◐
• Significant false alarms as new servers added to production	Data Center	35	17	10	●
	MOMT	1	3	2	◐◐
•Operational burden	Transport	1	1	0	◐
Long-term response to leaks - automation for the next regression?	**Service Impacting Incidents**	**0**	**3**	**0**	◐
	Missed by Monitoring	3	4	4	◐
.34 deployment Q&A	External Status Communication	-	-	-	

FIGURE 3.2   Incidents and escalations from the escalation scorecard

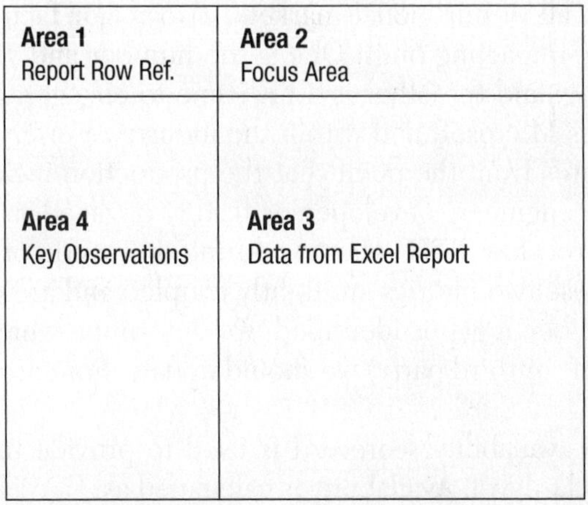

Area 1 Report Row Ref.	Area 2 Focus Area
Area 4 Key Observations	Area 3 Data from Excel Report

FIGURE 3.3   Incidents and escalations from the incident scorecard areas

Area 4 is the most important section of the scorecard. Before the monthly review, there is a prereview with the engineers responsible for improving their areas of the service. In the case of incidents and escalations, members of the test, development, and operations teams are typically involved in the prereview. The members analyze the data and look for outliers and negative trend lines. The areas of risk and concern are marked with green and red dots. In Figure 3.2, the solid black dots represent what would be flagged as red, or an area of concern in our PowerPoint slide. Sometimes, the team members may know why a metric is trending poorly, but often they can only develop a hypothesis. The vTeam (virtual team) members are then expected to follow up on finding out the root cause of the negative trending metrics and the outliers. The results of these investigations are the bullets seen in area 4 of the scorecard. Quite often, if the root cause of a negative trend is known, the recommended remediation may also be summarized in area 4.

Good Point

Tailor your reporting to give you the information you need to know.

3.4.2 What We Did with the Incident and Escalation Report

With the incident and escalation scorecard, we analyze all incidents raised from all sources. These sources include the server-level monitors of SCOM, the service-level monitors of TiP, and a limited set of monitors running with a third party ensuring we have connectivity to all of our global markets. Two major factors affect our ability to mitigate customer-impacting bugs: One is the number and severity of real issues missed by monitoring, and the other is TTE (time to engage). There are many formulas for TTE across Microsoft and within the industry. For Exchange, TTE meant the number of minutes from the point that the production incident began until we had the appropriate engineer (developer or tester) engaged in fixing the problem. The typical cause for a slow TTE, whether during or outside of business hours, is a missing monitor. These two metrics are tightly coupled and are ones we watch carefully every month. When a gap is identified, we determine which of the monitoring solutions (SCOM, TiP, or third party) we should update. Sometimes we add monitors to all three.

The TiP feature availability scorecard is used to provide indications of service availability at a granular level. Availability is calculated as:

$$\%\text{availability} = \frac{(\text{total minutes per month} - \text{minutes of downtime})}{\text{total minutes per month}}$$

By running TiP for each feature, we can detect when a small non-customer-impacting service outage, such as an ActiveSync outage, occurs. These short outages of some subservices may not directly impact the customer, but they do represent regressions and risk to the service. Intermittent failures or hung queues, as in provisioning, often show up on this scorecard but not on the one focused on escalations (see Figure 3.4).

Good Point

It is important to regularly use the information produced by the automation to monitor how things are going, look for further improvements, and keep the benefits of automation in the foreground.

Scorecard Rows 142 - 177	Customer Experience				
	TIP Feature Availability				
Provisioning and ECP availability issue cause by partner load last month is fixed for current month.	**Tip Feature availability**	**Dec**	**Nov**	**Oct**	**Sep**	**Aug**
	Provisioning	99.93%	94.01%	100.00%	100.00%	100.00%
	RBAC	99.93%	98.81%	100.00%	100.00%	99.93%
IMAP log file issue from last month resolved and IMAP back to 100% availability.	Outlook	100.00%	98.81%	100.00%	100.00%	99.95%
	ECP	100.00%	97.18%	100.00%	100.00%	99.97%
	Mailflow	100.00%	94.01%	100.00%	100.00%	99.50%
New: Powershell scripts experiencing intermittent failure	ActiveSync	100.00%	99.73%	100.00%	100.00%	99.63%
	UM	100.00%	99.68%	100.00%	100.00%	99.68%
Improvements	Calendaring	100.00%	100.00%	100.00%	100.00%	100.00%
• Content Delivery Network and DOMT tests added to address recent Incidents	Web Services	100.00%	100.00%	100.00%	100.00%	100.00%
	OWA	100.00%	100.00%	100.00%	100.00%	100.00%
	POP	100.00%	100.00%	100.00%	100.00%	100.00%
	IMAP	100.00%	89.87%	100.00%	100.00%	100.00%
	Remote Powershell	99.93%	100.00%	100.00%	100.00%	100.00%

FIGURE 3.4 The TiP feature availability scorecard

3.5 Exchange TiP v2—Migrating TiP to the Windows Azure Cloud

Although our version 1 service was clearly adding value to the organization and was one of our main tools for measuring and improving the live service, we had bold plans to address issues with the current service and to make it an even more valuable asset. The top three version 1 issues we wanted to address were the following:

- Move executions outside of the corporate network to address Redmond proxy issues.
- Increase frequency of test execution to 5 minutes or less.
- Expand coverage to all DAGs (Database Availability Groups) and mailbox databases.

Several options were considered in determining how we would resolve these issues (shown in Table 3.4).

Although we wanted to preserve the ease of use of our existing test execution harness, it became apparent that none of the potential environments available to us would be able to support it. That, coupled with the fact that all reporting, failure investigations, and workflows associated with our harness were not easily targeted at aggregated results, led us to the conclusion that we would have to replace the execution harness for our tests. We ultimately decided to move our TiP infrastructure to run in Windows Azure because of the benefits of the platform. The best part was that because of the way we had architected the tests, we did not have to make changes to them (in fact, we were able to simply move the tests to the new harness without having to recompile).

Table 3.4 Decision Matrix for Potential Execution Environments for TiP Framework

Requirements	Direct Internet TAP	Edge Network	Azure
Outside corporate	Green	Green	Green
Capacity	Yellow	Green	Green
Cost	Red	Yellow	Green
Manageability	Red	Red	Green
Execution harness	Red	Red	Red

TiP Windows Azure Architecture

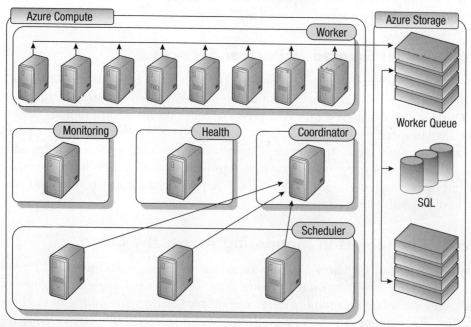

FIGURE 3.5   Exchange TiP v2 system topology

By moving our TiP framework from the test lab and into production, we were adopting the TiP concept of moving your test infrastructure from the lab and into the data center. In this case, we moved into the cloud and built a more scalable and flexible TiP service.

The framework in Figure 3.5 illustrates how we now execute our production tests. By using Windows Azure, we have the necessary capacity not only to cover all of our existing scale units but also to contemplate whole new scenarios not previously possible (e.g., simulating hundreds, if not thousands, of users concurrently in a slice of production prior to moving customers). This framework will of course continue to evolve over time to meet our expanding needs.

3.6   What We Learned

Our TiP tests have allowed us to find issues introduced during data center rollouts and sometimes in production before customers became aware of them. They have also, over time, allowed us to spot interesting trends in latency, performance, and overall feature behavior.

3.6.1   Issues Related to Partner Services

One of the important components where TiP tests have become vital is in finding issues related to the partner services that we take dependencies on and build on top of. Our service, like almost all cloud services, relies on many different services that specialize in specific areas. For example, we depend on Windows Live ID to provide the authentication layer. Another dependency we have is on the live domains service to provide for namespace management and provisioning. Our tests have been instrumental in finding issues with some of these dependencies that we would otherwise not have been able to catch.

3.6.2   Challenges in Monitoring Across the Cloud

A unique aspect of Exchange as a service is that our target customers are IT professionals. As such, they are used to being very cautious with upgrading to new services, and many large customers have custom solutions written on top of Exchange. Additionally, some of our customers are running in a hybrid mode with some users still running within their corporate Exchange Servers and some running in our cloud. Typical monitoring solutions are not well designed for significant longer-term variations in versions across a single cloud. Our TiP tests flow through the system with versions and configuration variations in a way that makes it much easier for us to measure and ensure quality across a heterogeneous cloud. These challenges are atypical for many cloud services, such as Bing, Facebook, and Twitter, that leverage their more homogeneous and loosely coupled service architectures to achieve a continuous deployment model.

Still, our service is layered and has dependencies that follow more rapid release cycles than the Exchange team. The network itself is a layer for us that is continually being updated with new firmware versions and Access Control List (ACL) changes. The black-box approach provided by monitoring services like Gomez or Keynote will alert our operations center of catastrophic changes in those layers but not of intermittent or edge cases. TiP allows us to go deeper and catch these dependency issues before they become catastrophic. In some cases, we even catch the issue during an upgrade of a partner service, and we can alert them to roll back the change.

3.6.3   Sample Issues Found in Production by TiP Tests

Here is a sampling of some of the issues found in production with our TiP tests:

- One of the Dublin provisioning queues hangs, but monitoring doesn't detect it.
- Provisioning latencies detected.
- Hotmail outages detected by TiP; Exchange team can stand down and wait for Hotmail Fix.
- Live ID outages impacting Exchange Cloud customers; escalate to Live ID operations.
- TellMe, a voice-over-IP gateway system that transfers calls between our system and phone switches (landlines handled by Quest/Verizon and mobile phones by T-Mobile), needed to be monitored for outages in end-user connection scenarios; TiP is the only method that can find problems with the phone numbers used in our integration pilot tests.
- TiP tests used to identify root cause of intermittent failures over time (% of failures found not in a single incident but over time).

3.6.4   Aggregating to Deal with "Noise" in the Results

We learned a lot about test execution against a live service. One of the first things we learned was that this sort of automated run can be quite noisy. As an example, because we were running from behind the corporate firewall, we were forced to route our requests through the Redmond proxies. These proxies are not intended to be used in this fashion, so this led to occasional dropped requests, failed host lookups, and other strange network failures. This quickly led to a second realization, which was that when you are running automation against a production system, what becomes important is not the individual passing or failing results but the aggregation of those results over time. Aggregating allows you to determine whether an issue is a persistent breaking issue or is simply a one-time network fluke, thus reducing the noise level enough to make a more accurate call on the health of the service. It also lets you spot trends over time, something that is not possible by simply looking at a single snapshot in time (e.g., latency degradation over time, failures in load balancing logic).

> **Tip**
> Monitoring the details is important, but so is keeping an eye on overall trends.

This last point regarding noise reduction becomes very important when you note that our tests ran only once an hour. This frequency was dictated by built-in assumptions in our test execution framework both about how a test pass should be configured (i.e., assuming each test run execution must occur in a newly deployed machine) and about how the tests themselves execute (i.e., assuming that tests must execute serially). We learned that those assumptions were flawed for many different reasons.

Another reason to run them just once an hour was the concern about consuming too much production capacity. What we have found over time is that a service must have extra capacity to support live site monitoring, peaks and valleys in utilization, denial-of-service attacks, and growth. If running a set of automated functional tests at an increased frequency of, say, every 5 minutes across each production cluster pushes the service over the edge, then we were running the service too hot anyway and needed to add capacity. For many IT organizations, the cost of procuring and housing dedicated hardware has made the approach of having some excess capacity unthinkable. However, with the move to cloud computing and the ability to have dynamic growth in computer or storage resources, it is becoming more affordable to build a service with some reasonable extra capacity that can be used for testing in production.

3.6.5 Pitfalls

One lesson we learned was that our test automation was more complete than our basic outside-in monitoring and, because of the quality of these tests, teams soon wanted to use the TiP system as an enhanced monitoring solution. The problem was that a timely reaction is simply not possible at a 1-hour frequency because it takes too long to collect enough samples to make an accurate call on whether or not an issue is real. The alternative is to implement some retry logic in the test, which can potentially further slow down your pass and can also give you a false positive as a result of transient issues (e.g., failure to send a message due to throttling policies).

The next lesson we learned was that when dealing with a scaled-out production system, not having a similarly scaled-out validation strategy for the test automation can lead to a false sense of security. In our initial implementation, we created a single set of mailbox accounts for each one of our scale units. The problem is, our scale units have a further level of granularity because they are composed of multiple servers, availability groups, and other resources not originally accounted for. In practice, that meant we could cover only a single availability group or mailbox database per site. This led to situations where an incident would not be caught by the infrastructure because the portion of a scale unit affected was not one of the ones we were covering.

In addition to being the canary for regressions, TiP tests like our system should be treated as an element of a more robust continuous improvement program (CIP). As with most CIPs, senior management involvement and sponsorship is a key element of success. Proper alignment will ensure the engineering teams are supported to continue to improve the production service and fill in the gaps for TiP and the other elements (per-server and outside-in) of a full monitoring solution.

3.7   Conclusion

Testing in production is necessary in the fast-paced world of online services. Test automation from the test lab can and should be extended into production. Because no service is ever an island unto itself, continuous execution of test cases that run through and validate key end-to-end scenarios will provide augmentation to simple per-server (SCOM for us) or outside-in (Gomez or Keynote) availability monitoring. Continuous regression tests do function like monitoring to alert the service team to service outages, and the approach is particularly helpful in the early identification of non-customer-impacting intermittent bugs.

Although this case study focuses on Exchange, the trend toward using test automation, especially rich automated scenarios, is growing rapidly across Microsoft service teams. The trend of running these solutions within the production cloud is also gaining traction. We expect the movement toward test automation as enhanced production monitoring to continue across Microsoft.

> **Tip**
>
> Testing in the cloud may be part of your future; learn from the experiences of this chapter's authors!

3.8   Acknowledgments

The authors want to acknowledge Keith Stobie and Andy Tischaefer as peer reviewers and Karen Johnston for copy editing.

CHAPTER 4

THE AUTOMATOR BECOMES THE AUTOMATED

Bo Roop

Bo Roop takes us on a guided tour of attempting to automate the testing of a test automation tool. One of the first questions to ask a tool vendor is "Do you test the tool using the tool?" But the answer isn't as straightforward as you might think! With his lively writing style, Bo gives an honest description of the difficulties and challenges he encountered, particularly in the verification of test results. It is a good idea to find out what others have tried, and Bo shows the advantages of doing so. His sensible approach to automation is to start by automating the easier components before tackling the more complex. Unfortunately, this story does not have a happy ending. It illustrates how presumably well-intentioned management actions can sabotage an automation effort. For reasons that become obvious when you read this chapter, the tool vendor is not identified: a fictitious company and tool name are used instead. This experience takes place in the United States with one automator (the author) and covers just over 1 year. See Table 4.1.

4.1 Background for the Case Study: My First Job

I was a fresh, young college graduate back in the mid- to late 1990s, and the only thing I knew when I graduated was that I wanted to do anything besides development work. I graduated college with an associate's degree in General Business and

Table 4.1   Case Study Characteristics

Classification	This Case Study
Application domain	Software test execution automation tool
Application size	Unknown
Location	United States
Lifecycle	Waterfall
Number on the project	12–15
Number of testers	2–4
Number of automators	1
Time span	1 year, 2 months
Dates	1999–2000
Tool type(s)	Commercial
Pilot study undertaken	No
ROI measured	No
Successful?	No
Still breathing?	Probably not

a bachelor's degree in Computer Information Systems and was ready to take on the world—if I could only find something to do with my degrees. I went to all the job fairs and interviewed with darn-near everyone. And I must have been pretty good at it, because I landed eight job offers, and after much internal debate, chose to work for one of the largest software houses headquartered in my home state. We'll call them Roboto Industries.

My career began smoothly enough; I went through Roboto's Introductory Professional Program, an extended training class that all new college graduates were required to pass through, and landed a position on one of the company's tech support teams. I was supporting this fancy automated testing package that we'll call The Automator. I was told that it did some sort of capture and replay and could verify windows and controls on the screen. I learned of a few more things it was capable of—the features were listed in the marketing pamphlets I was handed as an introduction to the product. I quickly learned that the tool did many more things, both documented and undocumented.

4.1.1   My First Role: Technical Support

By talking to our customers on the phone, I learned that some of them were real whizzes with this tool, and they pushed the darned thing to the radical edge of sanity where no one inhouse ever dreamed of using it, let alone developing features for it. I learned more from talking to these customers than I had ever learned before (and possibly after) about automation. I had to study relentlessly just to keep up with their technical support questions. This caused me to become one of the few power users in the group for this tool, and it offered me an opportunity that was rare on the technical support team: access to the pre-beta builds. Little did I know that I was becoming a tester! I took those builds and put them through their paces before any of the customers saw the software, and I was testing in parallel with the "official" quality assurance (QA) team.

I managed to last about 2 years on the phones on The Automator's technical support team. Voluntary turnover was high for those positions, and I was no exception. I was getting antsy for something new, something a bit more challenging, and something that would get me away from those irate customers. So began my official transition over to the QA team.

4.1.2   Joining the QA Team

It was a logical transition for me because I'd been using the product for about 2 years and had been unofficially testing the product prior to each release over the previous 6 months. I really thought I was a great fit for the team. I needed little to no training on the software and could be an effective tester within minutes of my arrival. And I fit right in; we were all used to testing the new software releases manually. Looking back now, this seems really odd to me; I mean, we were making an automated testing solution for sale on the open market for other companies to use for their software automation efforts, but we weren't using the tool ourselves. Did we think our own dog food was rotten?

Anyway, I remember it making perfect sense to me at the time. Everyone from my testing team manager to the product's development team members told me it wasn't possible to automate the testing of the tool itself. Manual testing was the best way to validate that the new features were implemented correctly while none of the existing features were being changed. What little did we know?

4.2   My Great Idea . . .

Now remember that this was back in the day when Windows 95 was the norm and only a handful of progressive companies had moved over to Windows NT 4.0. So although we had a newer 32-bit version of our software for the 32-bit operating systems, we also had to maintain the original 16-bit version of the application.

Wait a second! There was a 16-bit version of the product still hanging around? Yup!

"Gotcha," I said with an evil-looking grin sneaking across my lips. It was one of those great moments when a technological hurdle gets knocked over and forcefully shoved out of the way never to be worried about again. Triumph, I thought . . . if only momentarily.

I figured I could simply load up both versions of The Automator's packages, 16 and 32 bit, on a single Windows 95 system and then cross-automate the packages with each other. Both of them would install, launch, and remain useful to me . . . and to my automated testing. And luckily, they knew nothing about each other; they didn't share any files and didn't collide with each other if installed on the same computer. So I could begin my automation quest. I used the older 16-bit version of the product to capture/replay/verify the newer 32-bit version of the application. Life was good. I had a bit of perma-grin as I showed this off to a few select people within the organization.

4.2.1   But Would It Be Short-Lived?

I earned a few attaboys for my efforts but was quickly reminded that the 16-bit version of the software was going to be phased out soon and that any scripts created with it were only going to be able to run on the Windows 9x platform. By this time, Windows 98 was available and gaining momentum, but I only had a short time before the true 32-bit platforms would take over. So my testing manager wanted me to try to find a solution that would run on Windows NT. I was off on another quest.

I took my 16-/32-bit automation dog-and-pony show on the road, well, around the office, anyway. One day I got to sit down with one of the original developers of the 16-bit product, and I showed him my automation efforts. He quickly informed me about how he had tried something like this a few years back when the 16-bit product was the new kid on the block. He was a junior developer back then and was working part time as a tech support guy on the team while developing code. He used the predecessor to the 16-bit product to try to drive it. My excitement was dashed a little bit, but not too much, because he admitted he had never had as much success with his testing back then. The 16-bit's predecessor didn't have nearly as many features/capabilities. And this was exactly what I was finding with the automation involving the 16-bit product. There were new features that I would love to be using that were only available in the 32-bit version.

> **Good Point**
>
> Telling other people what you are doing can help you find ways to do it better yourself, make you aware of potential roadblocks, and help you garner support for your efforts.

My quest continued, but now I had a sympathetic ear and a bit of history to drive me. I also had a coworker who was excited to see this working—someone I could bounce ideas off of and ask for help. This meeting with the original developer also gained me a meeting with a second senior developer. I was asking around about why The Automator was able to learn all of these other software packages, but it never learned itself? It's like it was invisible even though I knew how the tool worked (by listening in on the Windows keyboard buffer, the mouse buffer, and the Windows event buffer and then replaying by sending those commands back through those buffers); I simply didn't understand how it was invisible to itself. But I was soon to find out that it had been created that way.

Of course! No real user of the software would want the tool to learn any actions against it, such as minimizing the window to the Windows taskbar while it was in learning mode. They just wanted to move it out of the way so they could drive their application under test. But I was different.

My poking and prodding also led to a rediscovery by that second seasoned developer: There was a hidden setting that would change the way the software could be used. This setting would allow the mouse and keyboard actions against The Automator's windows, dialogs, and controls to be learned. By switching this setting, I could capture and successfully replay scripts that would drive and verify the automated tool's own window. It took the developer a few minutes to find it, but by golly . . . it was in there. It was wisely tucked away from the general public and wisely-er left available for my exploitation (I mean use).

> **Good Point**
>
> Don't be afraid to ask questions if you don't understand something; the answers can reveal useful and sometimes unexpected information.

4.3 A Breakthrough

I was finally able to successfully capture and replay a script that maximized and restored The Automator's main window! That was the greatest thing I'd seen to date at this company. I was so excited! I know, I'm easily amused, but I could finally start my real automated testing efforts.

I feel the need to slow down and backtrack a little bit here. I was heading down this new automation path, but I also needed to remember many of the lessons I had learned along the way.

- Capture/replay is only the beginning (validation points are needed, conditional responses must be programmed into the script, and response timing issues can break script replay if not properly planned for).
- Learning anything by mouse coordinates on the screen is bad (controls move or get rearranged in the UI frequently).
- Starting from a known state is imperative to getting your scripts to replay reliably and correctly. (You need to be on the same screen that the script is expecting, or else it won't know what to do.)
- Some titles of windows or dialogs can change (e.g., the title of Notepad changes depending on which document is currently opened in it), so you need to wildcard out those differences in the scripts, or remove them.
- The names of controls sometimes change according to how the application was written. (For example, Windows calculator used to change the underlying button names based on whether you were running in Standard or Scientific mode. The buttons were created from a dynamic array and simply incremented a counter attached to the end of the control name. So btn_2 wouldn't always be the CE button when your scripts were replaying.)

Lessons

Capture/replay is not a long-term solution. Recording screen coordinates rarely works. Automation demands consistency.

Using my technical support experience as background, I had an idea of what to test and what to expect while running the automation. I even knew where to begin my testing, with the easy and/or boring stuff that was simple to automate and gave me a pretty good feel about the software's overall fitness for use by our external customers. Where could I get the biggest bang for my buck?

4.3.1   Getting into the Job

Well, I was already able to validate the default syntax that appears within every new script that the tool created. And every new installation of The Automator testing tool came with a sample database, which contained the tables that would soon house the scripts and checkpoints and the instructions on how The Automator recognizes windows and controls. All of those things were easy to validate. I just made a copy of the sample database and then performed a few DDE commands (Dynamic Data Exchange is a way for Windows applications to share data) against that database while connecting to my testing database, the one with my scripts. It seemed easy enough.

But where did I need to head with my newfound knowledge and ability to script the product itself?

Again, I chose to start with some of the easy stuff to automate that would provide me almost instant feedback and increase my comfort level with automating the tool with itself. The Main Window's menu structure was a logical choice for automation. Any changes there could be easily overlooked or missed by manual testing, and the tool could capture greater levels of detail with regard to these menus. It would see any changes in more than just the text. The tool would find any changes in the accelerator keys, the hotkeys, the positions or locations of the menus, and the same for the submenus—all at once! I got a lot of quick feedback by checking those menus for changes. And any changes that were found in these dialogs during the replaying of the scripts pointed to either a regression issue or a new implementation of functional code that would potentially change the way the application works. We didn't always receive up-to-date specifications, so a lot of our testing efforts came from discovery. I was already getting valid feedback from my automation.

> **Good Point**
>
> Consider using the capabilities of the tool to do more in-depth testing than would be done manually.

The next areas I focused in on during my testing were some of the most highly used areas in the software, the capture and replay of scripts and checkpoints. The scripts are the coding syntax files that the software uses to perform the automated testing, and the checkpoints are definitions the tool uses to verify that dialogs and controls are designed and implemented properly. For example, they can be used to validate text in a control or whether a control is enabled or disabled. But the only way to validate a checkpoint was to create another checkpoint. So I had to create a script that could do this. And while I was creating those scripts, I decided that I may as well validate that the scripts themselves were being generated accurately.

4.3.2 Validating Checkpoints

As background, whenever the user created a checkpoint in The Automator software, a popup dialog would appear onscreen asking for the pertinent information: a name for the checkpoint, the name of the control or dialog to verify (or you could use the identify tool and drag/drop a crosshair over the target to select it), any/all of the data points you wanted to verify, and so on. Some default values would appear and some controls on the popup dialogs would be disabled until certain conditions were met.

I started by opening each of those popup dialogs and validating the existence and state of the controls housed within. I created a new form checkpoint against each of the individual checkpoint dialogs. The form checkpoint was used to validate the default properties for each of the controls within the dialog that open with each new checkpoint being created. But remember that I was also capturing and learning this as I went into a new script, so I had to go back and modify the learned steps of creating the checkpoints and change them to run the checkpoints at the appropriate moment. The checkpoint syntax was wrong as I was creating it because The Automator was creating the syntax to open the dialog and then create a checkpoint against it. But what I really needed was syntax that would open the dialog and then run the new checkpoint against it.

That was a pretty easy concept for me to grasp. I only wanted to replay opening the checkpoint dialogs, perform the running checkpoint, and then close them. But the tool was learning that I opened the checkpoint popup dialog, created a new checkpoint, and then closed that popup dialog. If I didn't remove the previous checkpoint creation portions of the script prior to running it, the tool would stumble as it tried to create another new checkpoint and then tried to save it with an existing name (remember that tools only do as they're told, so it would reuse the same name that was learned during recording). Also, the original checkpoint would never run because the syntax to perform that checkpoint was never learned into the script. I had to manually interject that logic into the script.

See where I'm going? Hopefully you do, because I was quickly getting lost.

The next hurdle I encountered was trying to wrap my head around automating this automation! When I began validating that The Automator application was learning scripts correctly, I ran into a logic nightmare. Not with the software, but within my own head. I started trying to expand on the idea of having The Automator drive itself while learning itself and validating itself.

I started with a script that would drive to certain points within an application and then create some validation checks on that application under test (AUT). I chose to automate a simple application, one that was truly solid and would change very little over time—enter Notepad.exe. As an aside, I still love using Notepad for testing and for examples. We're all familiar with it, we all have a copy of it, we all know how it works, and we all know what it's capable of doing or not doing.

> **Tip**
>
> Try out your automation on something simple, such as Notepad.

Anyway, my new Automator database contained a script that would drive itself while learning a few actions against Notepad. I would open the Notepad text editor through the Windows Start menu and then type in a few words (the proverbial "Hello World" example). Then I would close the application and choose to not save my changes. Finally, The Automator's script would stop replaying and report back its findings. This automation was fairly easy. It made sense to me, and I could verify later that the scripting syntax learned by the tool had been created correctly. I would use the same DDE logic as described earlier: make a copy of the database and then go spelunking (also known as caving or potholing outside of the United States—I use the spelunking reference frequently when referring to software testing because we're essentially doing the same thing as cave explorers. We're often tasked with heading into the dark unknown with only a minimal tool set and just our skills, and a lot of safety lines, to rely on). Let's see what we can find.

4.3.3   Then Things Got Difficult

I found that not only could I compare the learned script to the expected results, but I could also replay the script and verify that this new script would drive the Notepad application as expected. After replay, I could verify the logging capabilities of the tool.

It was all becoming very circular and increasingly difficult to explain the testing concepts to some of my coworkers and managers. The internal testing team did not have a complete understanding of the need for and benefits of test automation. Manual testing and validation had always been used in the past and had been working (meaning no one was complaining).

They seemed to get it but didn't understand all the extra work that went into creating these scripts to automate the automation tool. I needed to do a lot of manual scriptwriting, and the database management became difficult as I tried to push the envelope even further. I had a copy of the default database that gets installed with the software, a second database that contained the automation scripts to run, and a third database that contained my expected results. Unfortunately, I wasn't used to using source control at that time, so I was saving away copies of my working databases on the network drives before becoming familiar with Visual SourceSafe. It seemed like everything came with a steep learning curve.

The real issues came into play when I went off and tried to validate whether The Automator's checkpoints were being learned and created properly. I would run my script to the point where I already had some text typed into Notepad. Then I would perform a text checkpoint to ensure that the proper string had been typed into Notepad while replaying the script; this would validate that the replay functions were working correctly. By creating a new form checkpoint at this point against The Automator's text checkpoint dialog, I could validate that all of the default values were being populated into the dialog's controls correctly and that The Automator was indeed learning against Notepad accurately. But remember that as I was replaying the script, the text checkpoint dialog would appear while capturing/learning against Notepad, and I had to open the form checkpoint dialog to validate against The Automator itself.

I learned that by using the built-in hotkeys to open the checkpoint dialogs, I could expand on my earlier validation logic on this new popup dialog. As I was creating a new form checkpoint against The Automator's popup dialog controls, the replaying text check verified the proper text value was typed into the edit control in Notepad. Running that new form checkpoint later would verify that the proper values appeared in the text checkpoint popup dialog.

Confused yet? I sure was.

4.3.4 The Beginning of the End

Not only was my head swirling with all of these circular references to checkpoints and scripts (both those being created and those running), but my databases kept growing as well and were requiring more and more time to keep them fresh.

Once the team started seeing the benefits of automation, they thought it was great. We were sending more consistent results back to the software developers faster than ever before, but the testing manager failed to understand why it was so difficult to automate the automation tool. She also forgot to budget time for maintaining those scripts, so making any changes to the existing scripts would cut into the time allocated to create new scripts. Sometimes educating your leaders is the most difficult hurdle you have to overcome.

Once my manager found out that the scripting was becoming functional, she passed the running of the scripts off to other testers in my group. She thought this would help free me up a bit to create more scripts and better tests.

I believe that if the offer were to be extended and I had the opportunity to do it all over again, I wouldn't change much. I think most of my decisions were good ones and that if we had had the resources to continue with our automated testing, the tool would have been even better than it was. Roboto Industries saw some of the successes in automating these tests as we got some quick, reliable, and valuable feedback from the scripts. And I could get a lot of testing done because new builds were being frequently sent over to the testing team. From my point of view, that's a success even if it's no longer being used.

CHAPTER 5

AUTOBIOGRAPHY OF AN AUTOMATOR: FROM MAINFRAME TO FRAMEWORK AUTOMATION

John Kent

John Kent tells us how and when test automation started and offers surprising information about the origins of capture/replay technology. Understanding how automation worked on mainframes shows how some of the prevailing problems with test automation have developed; approaches that worked well in that environment did not work well with GUIs and the need to synchronize the test scripts with the software under test. The principles John discovered and put into practice, such as good error handling and reporting and the importance of testing the automation itself, are still relevant and applicable today. John's explanation of the economic benefits of wrappers and levels of abstraction are compelling. He ends with some recent problem/solution examples of how web elements can trip up the automation. This United Kingdom–based project involved mainly commercial tools. See Table 5.1.

Table 5.1   Case Study Characteristics

Classification	This Case Study
Application domain	Mainframe to web-based
Application size	Various sizes
Location	United Kingdom
Lifecycle	Traditional
Number on the project	40
Number of testers	3 full-time testers, 40 end users (Maximo project)
Number of automators	2 automators (Maximo project)
Time span	23 years
Dates	1987–2010
Tool type(s)	Commercial
Pilot study undertaken	Yes
ROI measured	No
Successful?	Yes
Still breathing?	Yes

5.1   Background for the Case Study

5.1.1   Early Test Automation: My First Encounter with a Testing Tool

"Let's use the CA-VERIFY capture/playback tool to record what I do during the systems test," said Paul, the business analyst. "That way, we'll be able to see exactly what I input on each screen, and if we get strange results, we can check that I input the right thing." It was 1989 and I was a programmer at an insurance company working on a system called Paxus POLISY, which ran on an IBM mainframe. Paul and I were testing the screens we had developed for a new insurance product.

I had heard of VERIFY and became curious at this point. "Why don't people use VERIFY to actually replay tests?" I asked. "You could have a set of reusable tests that you could run against the system for lots of different projects."

"Because you record logging onto the system, and every time your password changes, the tests won't run," he replied.

"Oh," I said. It was the kind of "Oh" you say when you have a vague feeling that the answer you just heard is somehow not the complete picture, but you don't have time to delve further.

"We just use VERIFY to record our input," Paul said.

I didn't get to delve further, and actually play back tests until 1991 when I found myself in the independent testing group. I literally did find myself there. I'd been on holiday when the team was set up and, because no one wanted to join a "testing team, for goodness sake," it was decided to press-gang people into it. Like giving actions to the people who are not at a meeting, I was moved, in my absence, to testing. On the first day back, I knew something was up because my colleagues wouldn't talk to me except to say, "You need to talk to the team leader." Later, as I packed my things, programmers came up to me and said how sorry they were and how badly treated I had been to be condemned to spend all my time testing.

5.1.2 Overcoming Problems to Use the Tool to Replay Tests

In the test group, I had the luxury of time to be able to work out how to use VERIFY. Implementing it on an actual project would have been difficult and high risk.

I realized later that this was a good idea, to set aside time to trial a new tool in a non-project setting before using it "for real." This trial highlighted issues and gave me a good idea of how long it would take to get tests up and running and reliable. Trying to deliver automated tests in a project, with no prior knowledge of the tools, is likely to be too difficult and stressful to be successful.

I got around the password problem by getting some user IDs set up with no expiry. I grabbed some time on a spare test version of the system and started recording tests, called Streams in VERIFY parlance, and rerunning them. In hindsight, getting the tests to run using the VERIFY mainframe test tool was relatively easy compared to today's script-based automation tools (such as QuickTest Professional [QTP] and TestPartner) because the mainframe tools worked very differently from today's tools.

5.1.3 How Mainframe Dumb Terminal Systems Worked and Why Capture/Replay Was a Good Idea

In a mainframe system, the dumb terminal on which the user works communicates with the processor and thus invokes the software to be tested only when he or she presses Enter or a Function key. Between each press of the Enter key, data can be input into the screens, but nothing is sent to the processor until the Function key is pressed. The system sends a screen to the dumb terminal; the user inputs information into the screens, but the software under test does not run until the Function key is pressed. See Figure 5.1.

Thus, the mainframe text-based automated tools do not need to record low-level user actions; rather, they record terminal/processor conversations. The user can tab around the screen, enter data into fields, delete data, but the software under test does nothing until the user presses Enter. CA-VERIFY recorded these conversations.

The test streams are recordings of what is sent to the processor on pressing the Enter (or Function) key and what is sent back to be displayed on the user's screen by the software under test. A recording or Stream in VERIFY is a series of pairs of images of the screens: one sent to the processor from the dumb terminal and one sent back from the processor. Paul could record his keyboard actions and print out that recording, which showed all the screens in the test he had executed.

Lesson

Allow time to experiment and explore with tools before expecting real benefits to be achieved on a project.

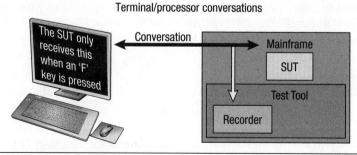

FIGURE 5.1   Automated green-screen testing

5.1.4 Attended Replay and Its Advantages

When VERIFY reran a test, it would compare each screen with the recording, and if there was a difference, it would stop the run. This meant that you could not leave the tests to run unattended, but VERIFY would let you correct the recording and continue. VERIFY would stop the test on a difference between the current run and the recording and allow you to accept the changes or even allow you to record some more screens that were inserted into the recording, so you could, for example, change an incorrect screen navigation sequence. A critical factor was that the only problems that could stop the run were differences in the comparison of the recording and the actual screens. There were no synchronization problems because the tool simply waited for screens to be sent from the processor to the dumb terminal and back.

There were a few problems getting the tests to rerun:

- *System and other dates that changed between runs.* VERIFY allowed you to mask areas of the screens to be excluded from the comparison of actual and recorded screen.
- *Screens that changed with new releases of the software under test (SUT).* VERIFY allowed you to edit fields in recordings for all instances of a particular screen. An additional and most excellent feature was that when it was rerunning a test and stopped because of a difference between actual and recorded screens, it let you record the new screen (or screens) and insert it into the recording for future use.
- *Screen navigations that changed in new releases of the SUT.* The editing features previously mentioned allowed you to change the screen sequences and insert new screens.

VERIFY (now CA-Verify) is a great tool—it truly is record/playback. So are the other green-screen test tools like Compuware's CICS-Playback (later called Hyperstation) and IBM's TPNS.

I believe the fact that, in the mainframe tools, record/playback was practical and contributed to the record/playback myth for the later, script-based test automation tools.

Good Point

Knowing how record/playback worked on mainframes shows where later misperceptions and unrealistic expectations came from.

5.2 A Mainframe Green-Screen Automation Project

5.2.1 Scaling Up

Once the tool had been proven to work, it was used on a very large project. I was lucky to be working with an excellent project manager, Fergus McLachlan, who really needed the test automation because the testing required for the project was so extensive that he simply could not get it done manually. The project was a major reengineering of a system and we were lucky the changes were mostly confined to the backend—with few changes to the screens.

It turned out to be one of the biggest automation projects I've ever been involved in. All of the inputs from five end users were recorded over 4 weeks. The recordings contained over 100,000 screens in total. The largest recording consisted of 7,000 screens (five users keying over 1 day), and it would run in 30 minutes. A database dump was taken just before the recordings. When the tests were to run, the database was restored to the beginning so that the automated tests always ran against the same database image. Also, the system date was reset to the original date on which the tests were recorded.

5.2.2 Using the Tool on the Tool Scripts

We developed a way of changing the screens en masse. VERIFY had a find/replace feature in its test stream editor. *Test Stream* was the CA-VERIFY name for the recording that could be viewed as a series of pairs of screens: one screen for what was sent to the processor and one for the screen that was sent back to the dumb terminal. We wondered if we could start a VERIFY recording, and then record going into the VERIFY editor and change a lot of recordings using the find/replace. We tried it and it worked like a dream. It meant that we could use VERIFY to replay recordings of it running itself and changing field values in all of the recordings. All we needed to do was change the find/replace values to change recordings en masse. We called it the Total Improbability Drive.

Once you have the luxury of knowing that the data input is the same as when the recordings were made, you can introduce another powerful technique and do database comparisons. An excellent inhouse tool called TEDSUP was used to compare the databases, and we noticed rounding errors in some field values in the reruns. This defect would not have been found and fixed without the automated tests.

5.2.3 Success

The project was a great success. The automated tests reduced rerunning the regression test to 3 weeks as opposed to 3 months without VERIFY. (The 3 months was an estimate because the project would never have gotten the go-ahead to run a 3-month regression test.) Defects were found that would not have been found any other way.

Fergus seemed to get the testing bug during that project and is now a test consultant and trainer.

Note: Having proven that the automation tool works, don't go and automate a large test project. We did it because we didn't know any better, and we were lucky to be working on a green-screen automation project. You, dear reader, know better because you have this book.

Software development is a bit like quantum mechanics. Behavior in small-scale projects can be very different from behavior of large scale projects. Trying to deliver large-scale automated tests in a project, with no prior project experience of the tools, is likely to be too stressful to be successful. Start small and work your way up.

5.2.4   Who Wants It Now?

Interestingly, after the project was finished and the automation was a huge success, we could find no one who would maintain the automation pack. An automation pack must be run against each release of the system to keep it up to date. This pack was ideal for regression testing, but no one in the organization was interested in owning it. It soon became out of date as system changes were released. A few years later during the Y2K project, a completely new automation pack was built at great expense. This was partly an internal "political issue"; an evaluation was never done to look at the relative merits of updating the pack versus rebuilding the automation from scratch.

> **Tip**
>
> When an organization embarks on large-scale test automation, it should be aware that it needs to provide the resources to maintain and nurture the test automation.

A test automation pack is not just for now and again—it's for life.

5.3   Difference between Mainframe and Script-Based Tools

5.3.1   Level of Interaction

Unlike with the green-screen automation project, with modern script-based automation tools, you wouldn't be able to record five users over 1 day and expect it to rerun. You can't rerun a recording of one user over 1 day, let alone five. Why not?

Because the recordings in mainframe test automation tools, as we have seen, are recordings of conversations between the dumb terminal and the processor; these tools are "true" record and playback. They did not have to deal with synchronization problems, only with differences between recorded and actual results. Because what these tools were doing was relatively simple without the difficulty of synchronization problems, it was fairly easy to make playback successful.

With the introduction of PCs and then GUIs, the user–software interaction became much more complex. With PCs, each user has his or her own processor rather than having to share one processor with many others, as in mainframes. This means that in PCs, the user–software interaction is much closer. In a GUI application, the software is invoked not just when the user presses Enter—a GUI system can respond to any key press or mouse click or even by just putting the mouse over a particular part of a window. GUI software is said to be *event-driven* because the application responds to a variety of low-level user actions, including mouse clicks, mouse movements, and key presses. Because of this closer user–software interaction, automated test tools could no longer simply play back the text on a screen; rather, they needed to be able to play back detailed users' *actions*. The way to do this is to have a list of actions that are performed on the SUT, called *scripts*, and thus the tools became *script-based*.

5.3.1.1 *Synchronization*

In script-based tools, each low-level user action must be synchronized with the UI of the SUT. With a GUI, the very act of inputting the data into an object may invoke events in the SUT that change the status of other objects in the window. It is no good playing an action into the SUT until the system is ready to accept it, and the previous action may have caused the system to do some work first. Furthermore, with modern time-sliced operating systems, the same action may take different amounts of time to complete because the processor may have other tasks to attend to at the same time. Script-based automated testing is like two people dancing together: the SUT's UI and the test automation. You can't have one dancer going at one speed and the other dancing at a faster rate. Unless the two are performing the actions together, it won't look good.

The synchronization problem is exacerbated by modern *n*-tier systems in which the client UI may have to wait for actions to be performed on a server. Although it is possible to use "wait functions" to synchronize the automation, the problems are what to wait for and how to choose the right synchronization point. This is especially important with very dynamic browser-based systems, where an object may be visible on the page but the page has not finished talking to the server. It is easy to choose the wrong wait point to apply the synchronization, and such an automation solution is not 100 percent reliable.

So, synchronization is key to understanding one of the major difficulties of script-based automated test tools.

5.3.1.2   *User Interface Objects*

Another difficulty is that the tools have to interact with many different objects in the windows. The tools need to know not only when to put data into or retrieve data from objects (the synchronization problem) but also which objects to use at any given time.

Windows or screens that form a UI for a computer software system are collections of UI objects. In Microsoft Windows, these objects are called *window controls*. In UNIX X-Windows, they are called *widgets*. Many different types or *classes* of window control are available. Standard classes of window controls include:

- textboxes
- combo boxes
- buttons
- option buttons
- checkboxes
- menus
- list boxes
- grids

There are many more types of controls that may be implemented in standard or nonstandard ways depending on the language in which the UI is written. Test tools largely cope well with standard controls, but nonstandard controls may require more programming or adjustment of various settings to make it possible for the tool to interact with them successfully.

5.4   Using the New Script-Based Tools

5.4.1   Trying to Use New Tools the Old Way

After the VERIFY automation project finished in 1992, I moved on to GUI automation. The insurance company was building its first client/server application, a customer management system running on a UNIX backend with a PowerBuilder frontend. We performed a tool evaluation and settled on MS-Test from Microsoft. MS-Test was later renamed Visual Test, and later still Rational acquired it. Again, I had the luxury of time to work out how to use the tools.

The script-based tools looked very different from the old green-screen tools. The most obvious difference was that these tools were programming environments. MS-Test contained a programming language based on BASIC, which had added testing functions. You could do all the usual things you wanted to do with a programming language: statements, conditionals, loops, functions, and subroutines. One telling question to ask is why you need a programming language if the tools are record/playback. MS-Test, being a product that Microsoft wasn't really interested in selling, did not play up the record/playback part of the tool and instead emphasized programming the tool to get it to run tests.

I tried recording scripts and replaying them. The replay was much less reliable than in the green-screen case. I soon realized that we were not going to be able to record testers and expect the tests to replay. This was in part due to the lack of synchronization and object interface issues just described.

There was another problem. PowerBuilder used very nonstandard controls called Data Windows, and MS-Test could not identify or talk directly to these controls. The task I had been given was to load extensive details of several hundred customers into the system at the beginning of systems test so that the manual testers had a lot of data to perform their tests with. This was lucky because MS-Test could not actually identify the PowerBuilder controls in the windows, so getting data out of them would have been difficult. For my task, I didn't have expected results. I just needed to get the data loaded into the windows correctly. I worked out that I could activate a control with a mouse click and then type the data into it. This worked for textboxes, list boxes, and combo boxes.

When you get a scripted test tool these days, you have the option of selecting add-ins for the types of objects in your UI. You may have a Java add-in, a .Net add-in, and so on. These add-ins enable the test tool to identify and interact with the controls on your UI. Nowadays, the first question I ask when faced with building automation for a new application is, "What is the UI built with?" The backend, middleware, Active Server Pages (ASP), Java Server Pages (JSP), and database don't matter. The test tool is used to simulate user actions, so it has to communicate with the UI. The test tool's ability to talk to whatever the UI is built with is important.

5.4.2 Programming the Tools

As a programmer, the recorded scripts looked wrong to me. They were long lists of actions with mouse click coordinates. Programs should have a structure and reuse functionality. The manual testers were keen to get their hands on these new wonder tools and record their tests. I knew that if they did that, there was no way we could maintain all the thousands of recorded scripts we would end up with.

I recorded some actions, put a loop around the script, and drove it from a data file in order to get repeatable actions with different data. Even this seemed to be not quite right. I had been lucky enough to attend a talk about green-screen automation given by Ian Weavers, a test expert. He said, "What we need to aim for is to have our screens defined only once for all tests." I realized this was what we needed to do: put the definitions of the window controls in one place and have programs that employed reuse. I set about developing a structure for the automation code.

> **Good Point**
>
> Structure the automated testware for reuse.

5.4.3   Building the Framework

Taking a programmer's view of what the structure of the test automation code should be and having listened to Ian Weavers, I decided two important things:

- There should be one function for each window, and this function and only this function would be called to perform all actions against its window. These I eventually called *window wrappers* because each was one function that dealt with everything to do with its window (i.e., it wrapped the window).
- There should be one function for each type or *class* of UI control, so one function would handle all actions on all buttons and another function would handle all actions on all textboxes, and so on. These functions I later called *control wrappers*. Nagle calls control wrappers *component functions*. (http://safsdev. sourceforge.net/FRAMESDataDrivenTestAutomationFrameworks.htm)

Looking back, window wrappers were what are now called GUI maps (or object repositories in QTP). They contained the object identifiers—mouse coordinates in this case—and also called the control wrappers for each of the objects on the windows. For example, a Login window is shown in Figure 5.2.

A pseudocode version of the Login window wrapper would look a bit like Listing 5.1.

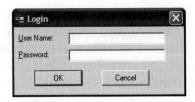

FIGURE 5.2   Login window

Listing 5.1   Login Window Wrapper

```
Function LoginWindow (Parameters...)
'User Name text-box:
If (the action is for this control) Then
Call Wrapper_Textbox(UserNData, UNx1, UNy1, UNx2, UNy2)
End if

'Password text-box:
If (the action is for this control) Then
Call Wrapper_Textbox (PWData, PWx1, PWy1, PWx2, PWy2)
End if

'OK Button:
If (the action is for this control) Then
Call Wrapper_Button(OKx1, OKy1, OKx2, OKy2)
End if

'Cancel Button:
If (the action is for this control) Then
Call Wrapper_Button(Cx1, Cy1, Cx2, Cy2)
End if

End Function
```

This function checks which control the action is for and then calls the control wrapper for that type of control. It passes the data and the identification properties for it. This case was unusual in that the identification for the controls were the X and Y coordinates. Usually, we try to avoid using XY coordinates at all costs (using a unique, position-independent identifier instead), but as said earlier, MS-Test could not recognize the PowerBuilder controls.

There would be one function or window wrapper for each window in the SUT. The test data looked a bit like Table 5.2.

A driver program read through the data sequentially and called the specified window wrapper for each line, passing it the data. The window wrapper then called the control wrapper appropriate to that type of control. The control wrapper performed the action on that UI control. This was the structure of the test automation code. All together, this code structure was what many people would now call a keyword-based framework, although it is actually a very low level of keyword implementation, very close to the UI. Keywords can be used at a high level (sometimes called a domain-specific test language) where they are more closely related to business or user tasks. However, even using this low level of wrapper-type keywords brings a level of abstraction and benefits to the automation.

There are a few things to note:

- The test data could be built by a tester with no knowledge of the test automation tool.
- Every window had a window function or wrapper, and every control was included so the tester building the data could build tests that could navigate to every window in the system and use any control.
- Notice that there is no "action" in this test data. Because these tests were only loading data into the system via the frontend, there was only one action for each control type. For buttons, the action was "click"; for textboxes, the single action was "set" the value.

Table 5.2   Test Data

Window Wrapper	Object	Data
Login	UserName	admin
Login	Password	apassword
Login	OK	
MainWindow	NewCustomerMenu	
CustomerWindow	FirstName	Smith
And so on . . .		

5.4.4 Other Features of the Framework

I thought the test automation should get itself out of trouble if necessary. If the SUT did not behave as expected, I wanted the automation to close the system down and get on with the next test. This is called recovery in automation circles. Although MS-Test could not see the PowerBuilder controls, it could identify the windows by their titles. I built some code to put into each window wrapper to record an error if the expected window was not displayed. The driver would then call the recovery routine that would close the application down and move to the next test.

Another important feature was to capture as much information as I could about what the automation and the SUT were doing during the automation run. It is no good having the automation perform a lot of actions if you can't see afterwards what happened during the test.

> **Good Point**
>
> Visibility of the results of automated tests is essential.

Recovery and logging were important in the *development* of the automation because they meant that:

- Tests could run unattended.
- Test runs could be analyzed later to see what actually happened.
- Most important, a large number of tests could be tested (yes, you have to test the test automation).

5.4.5 The Software Test Automation Paradox: Testing the Tests

In test automation, we face an inevitable paradox: We must *test the automated tests*. When we run an automated test against a new release of the SUT, we are testing two software systems: First, we are testing the SUT. Second, and there is no way around this, we are testing the test automation. The test automation is a software system that has a requirement to be able to test the latest release of the SUT, but this automation itself may be faulty and failures may occur. This paradox forces us to conclude that we must build automation code structures in such a way that they can be rigorously tested so that we can have a high degree of confidence that the automation software is reliable.

It is ironic that these tools are used by test teams who often do not recognize that the software produced using these tools needs to be tested. As testers, we know we must strive for the highest test coverage we can manage for any software product we have—including test automation software.

The paradox that we must test the test automation should not be underestimated. It is a fundamental problem that must be resolved for successful, large-scale test automation.

> **Good Point**
>
> Automated tests are also software and must be tested.

For the client server project, I had another piece of luck in that the systems windows had been prototyped, and their design agreed well in advance of the system being built. In prototyping, the windows are built with very little of the actual programming done. Just enough code is built to move from one screen to the next. This allows the physical design of the windows to evolve with approval from the end users. I was able to use this prototype to *test* the automation before the system was delivered into systems test. This was essential to the success of the automation project. I was extremely lucky that the behavior of the prototype and the delivered system were close enough for me to develop and test the automation on the prototype and then modify it when I had access to the development version of the system in time for systems test.

It is unusual to build test automation in time for the very first delivery of a system into systems test. Again, I didn't know any better at the time and I would not have been able to build the automation without the prototype.

5.5 Automating Tests for IBM Maximo

5.5.1 Moving on to 2010

In 2010, I was working as test manager at a large energy company. I was responsible for the testing of the Maximo system. Maximo is a web-based application that has a UI, importantly from an automation point of view, built in HTML. It is a work and asset management (WAM) system and is used to define all of the assets in the power stations such as turbines, pumps, and so on. It also manages the maintenance work performed on these assets using work orders that define the tasks to be carried out.

This is safety critical; if work is done in the wrong order or is not rigorously controlled, accidents can happen, causing serious injury or even death. Power stations can be very dangerous places.

Large amounts of data defining the assets and work orders were loaded into the system prior to going live, and it was this data we were primarily concerned with in our testing. We wished to automate some tests so we could check that the work orders loaded into the system would work correctly. We could only check a relatively small number of these manually and wanted to extend the test coverage to find any problems lurking within the large number of work orders.

We had little time to get the automation up and running because we were busy with manual testing, but we found a 1-week window in which to get it started. This would have been impossible in that time without a prebuilt framework and without the control wrappers already built for HTML objects. The control wrappers are key here because once they are built, they can be used for any system that has the same UI technology. Luckily, this was HTML in this case, and the control wrappers had been built and tested a long time ago.

5.5.2   The Liberation Framework

My current framework, now called Liberation (previously called ATAA), has been developed over the years since that first project, and it retains basically the same structure. It has been translated from Visual Test into AutoTester, WinRunner, QARun, Robot, and QTP. In this case, we used the QTP version of the framework.

It no longer has window wrappers, which are replaced with the object repository that comes with the tool (known as the GUI map in WinRunner). However, it does have the all-important control wrappers for each class of object in the UI. It is map-based in that the objects are defined in the object repository in QTP. No code is written at the application UI level—only the control wrappers are used. The UI objects are mapped for each page in the UI, and tests are created in Excel spreadsheets with instructions for the actions to be performed on the UI. Testers use an Excel add-in to help with creating tests. It reads the QTP (in this case) object repository to determine what objects are available in a page. The tests have the structure shown in Table 5.3.

The automation driver reads in each line of this data. It identifies which window or page the instruction is for and the logical name of the object within that page. The first two lines set the value of the UserID and Password textboxes. The next two lines click a button and a menu item.

The way the object is identified is defined in the UI object repository but the automation engine does not need that information, only the object repository name of

Table 5.3 Test Data for Map-Based Automation Is at the UI Object Level

Window/Page	Object	Action	Data
Login	UserID	Set	user1
Login	Password	Set	password
Login	OK	Click	
MainMenu	WorkOrders	Click	

the object. The automation engine reads the UI object map to find out what class the object is and then calls the control wrapper that deals with objects of that class and performs the required action upon the object, using the data if required. No automation code for a specific *instance* of an object is needed, only for *classes* of object.

The framework has other important features:

- Synchronization for each individual action
- Recovery
- Logging for fault diagnosis
- Test reuse: Tests can be specified at a higher level, which is abstracted from the UI

The control wrappers approach gives major benefits. It minimizes maintenance, and it gives high reliability because it provides a structure that can become highly tested over time. Maintenance with the framework only involves keeping the object map and the test data up to date with the changes to the system under test. No code has to be changed and retested.

High reliability can be achieved because all actions are performed by a small number of reusable functions (the control wrappers). With greater usage over time, bugs in these functions are found and fixed, so eventually high reliability is achieved. Because the code does not have to be changed during maintenance, it does not have to be regression tested and its reliability is not compromised. Thus, the framework overcomes the Test Automation Paradox.

Once you have the control wrappers built, not only can you create more tests without having to build automation code, you can define more windows, screens, and web pages in the object repository and not have to increase the number of code lines at all (unless a new *class* of UI object is introduced). All that is necessary is to define the new windows in the UI object map. In fact, you could use the same framework and control wrappers on many different systems with the same UI object classes without having to write virtually any more automation code.

> **Good Point**
>
> Once the reusable elements are there, new automated tests can be added very easily.

We were able to get the automated tests up and running very quickly. For Maximo, we had to tweak the code a bit, but this was in the order of 120 lines of code in total.

Because the framework had already been built before the project, it offered the following advantages:

- Virtually no automation code needed to be written.
- The control wrappers were highly tested and reliable before the start of the project.

5.5.3 Technical Challenges

Having gotten the automated tests up and running, we had to overcome a number of technical challenges, which are briefly described next.

5.5.3.1 Synchronization

Maximo has, for a web-based application, quite a lot of code at the UI level in the form of JavaScript events for each object. These events need to be triggered as if a user were using the keyboard and mouse, but the automation tools do not always do this precisely. For example, sometimes the Maximo system has not finished processing one object before the next object to be worked on is available. The automation can perform actions on the second object too soon. The solution was to ensure all objects were at the ready state before each and every action was performed.

5.5.3.2 UI Object Recognition Problem

One of the problems we had was with object recognition of some tables. HTML tables, which were identified and acted on by QTP most of the time, would cause an "Object not Found" error in certain circumstances. It turned out that another table with the same name was being created as a hidden table—when the tool found two the same, it didn't know what to do, so it raised an error. We needed to make sure that all tables had a unique identifier that was not likely to change.

5.5.3.3 *The Tool Works Differently from Human Users*

The tool was putting text into webedit boxes, but Maximo was behaving as if there were no text there. This would cause failures, for example, when the data was saved because Maximo would be unaware of text in mandatory fields.

The automated tools can put text into objects in an unnatural way so that the object's events are not fired. We needed to make sure that events were fired when needed by putting this into the control wrapper.

5.5.3.4 *Automation's Three Rs*

Run the tests as often and repeatedly as you can. Many of the problems we found only came to light as intermittent faults in the automation and would not all have been discovered without the repeated testing of the tests. Test automation needs to be reliable so that when it fails, it is because of incorrect system behavior, not a problem with automated tests. It is a good idea to put a set of tests in a loop and run them overnight.

Remember the three Rs of test automation: Run it and Run it and Run it.

5.5.4   Results of the Test Automation

Despite having only a week in the first instance, to get the automation up and running, over 20 tests were automated. These were mostly in the work order area of Maximo functionality. Using the test reuse features of the Liberation framework, these tests were run against several hundred work orders. Several defects were found, including one where a number of work orders had invalid general ledger (GL) codes in them. This was especially nasty for some work orders because the GL codes could only be changed when the work order was in a certain status, but Maximo would not let the status be changed because of the invalid GL code.

The automation was later used for quite a lot of checking of loaded data, and more recently, when a new power station's data was loaded, it was used to create and progress to completion over 500 work orders. This gave greater confidence because during systems test and user acceptance tests, only about 20 work orders were completed manually. About a third of the regression test pack was also automated.

5.5.5 Rolling Out Automation to the Rest of the Organization

The use of automation in the project was fairly ad hoc. There was no senior management buy-in prior to use. We simply implemented the framework so that we could extend our test coverage and do a better job. After the implementation of the system was over, there were discussions about rolling out the test automation to other projects and putting it on a more formal and supported footing.

The IT director had been pushing for test automation for some time, and having proven the concept to some extent, this seemed like the ideal time for the test team to take a closer look. The test team, however, seemed reluctant to even look at the automation we had for Maximo. I found this reluctance difficult to understand at first, but then I realized that they were very busy testing the systems they had and that there was no slack there for them to take on anything else. They did what a lot of test teams do, which is say, "I'm going to start building automated tests with QTP soon." Soon never comes because they already have a heavy workload. Very often, and it happened in this case, test managers give one of their testers an automated test tool to use "when they have a spare moment." I think they were right not to be jumping into test automation. If you are very busy, the last thing you want to do is get involved in something complex and technical that will not immediately lighten your workload. Test automation is a difficult thing to do. It must be—otherwise, everyone would be doing it. You cannot build a test automation framework in the odd spare moment.

Eventually, a sponsor was found who was willing to put up some money for a proof-of-concept. This is ideal. You might think that we had already proven the technology by building and running the tests, but this was done in isolation and without an eye on the return on investment. A proof-of-concept demonstrated all issues and provided the organization with a detailed view of the real costs and benefits. The Liberation framework is now being rolled out to two other systems.

5.6 Conclusion

It is more difficult to build automated tests for modern computer systems than for mainframe systems because there is a closer interaction between the user and the software. Synchronization has to be performed for every interaction with every object, whereas in the mainframe case, synchronization was simply not a problem.

Automators soon found out that building automated tests using record/playback with the new script-based test tools had severe limitations that made it impractical for large-scale test packs. More efficient approaches were incorporated into new automation frameworks. A key part of this was adopting a control wrapper approach that meant that automation code need be built only at the UI object class level rather than at the SUT UI level. This offers many advantages, but there are two important ones. The first is that the code does not need to be changed as the system changes, thus reducing maintenance and the need to retest changed code. The second is that the more it is used, the more reliable the automation code becomes because a control wrapper for a particular class of UI control will be used for each and every interaction with that class of control. For example, the function or control wrapper for HTML textboxes in Maximo has been run over a million times, and it is now very reliable.

Having a framework prior to the project offered the following advantages:

- Virtually no automation code needed to be written.
- The control wrappers were already highly tested and reliable before the start of the project.
- Without a prebuilt framework, we would not have had time to get the automation up and running.

5.7 Additional Reading

Buwalda, Hans. (1999). "Testing with Action Words." In Mark Fewster and Dorothy Graham, *Software Test Automation*, Chap. 22. Harlow, UK: Addison Wesley.

Dwyer, Graham, and Graham Freeburn. (1999). "Business Object Scenarios: A Fifth-Generation Approach to Automated Testing." In Fewster and Graham, *Software Test Automation*, Chap. 24.

Fewster, Mark, and Dorothy Graham. (1999). *Software Test Automation*, Harlow, UK: Addison Wesley.

Hayes, Linda G. (2004). *The Automated Testing Handbook*. Richardson, TX: Software Testing Institute.

Kaner, Cem. (1997). "Improving the Maintainability of Automated Test Suites." Paper presented at Quality Week 1997, San Francisco, California.

Kent, John. (1997/2000). "An Automated Testing Architecture." Paper presented to the British Computer Society SIGST, London, July 1997, and EuroSTAR 2000, Copenhagen, Denmark.

Kent, John. (1999). "Generation of Automated Test Programs Using System Models." Paper presented at Quality Week 1999, San Jose, California, and EuroSTAR 1999, Barcelona, Spain.

Kent, John. (1993/1994). "Overcoming the Problems of Automated GUI Testing." Presentations to British Computer Society SIGST, London, December 1993, and STAR 1994, Washington DC, May 1994.

Kent, John. (2007). "Test Automation: From Record/Playback to Frameworks." EuroSTAR 2007, Stockholm, Sweden. Also available at www.simplytesting.com.

Lalwani, Tarun. (2009). *QuickTest Professional Unplugged*. New Delhi, India: KnowledgeInbox.

Nagle, Carl J. (no date). "Test Automation Frameworks." Available at http://safsdev. sourceforge.net/FRAMESDataDrivenTestAutomationFrameworks.htm.

CHAPTER 6

PROJECT 1: FAILURE!, PROJECT 2: SUCCESS!

Ane Clausen

Ane Clausen tells of two experiences with test automation, the first one unsuccessful and the second one a solid success, largely due to what she learned from her first experience. Lessons are not always so well learned—which is a lesson in itself for everyone! Ane's first story is told honestly and highlights the serious impact of insufficient management support and the importance of choosing the right area to automate. In her second story, Ane designed a 3-month pilot study with clear objectives and a good plan for achieving them. Many useful lessons are described in this chapter, such as good communication (including using the walls), limited scope of the early automation efforts, good use of standards in the automation, a good structure (looking for common elements), and keeping things simple. The continuing automation was then built on the established foundation. Ane's experience was with pension and insurance applications in Denmark, using commercial tools. See Table 6.1.

6.1 Background for the Case Study

I have been working with automated tests in two companies. For both companies, the automated test was to be created on the application GUI used by an insurance agent (i.e., an end user). The tools used for both companies were Hewlett-Packard's HP Quality Center (QC), using business process testing (BPT) and Quick Test

Table 6.1   Case Study Characteristics

Characteristics	Project 1	Project 2
Application domain	Pension	Insurance
Application size	250,000 LOC	1,000,000 LOC
Location	Denmark	Denmark
Lifecycle	No method	Agile
Number on the project	5	3
Number of testers		
Number of automators		
Time span	6 months	1 year
Dates	2005	2007–2008
Tool type(s)	Commercial	Commercial
Pilot study	No	Yes
ROI measured	No	Yes
Success?	No	Yes
Still breathing?	No	Yes

Professional (QTP). In BPT, you design business components and incorporate them into business process tests. One business component tests a single business action that performs a specific task in a business process. An example is given in Section 6.3.4.3, "Application Knowledge." Often, business components are just called components, and a BPT has the same meaning as a test case.

The first project, started in 2005, failed, whereas the second project, started in 2007, was a success. I provide a more detailed description of the second project because the experiences from this project show how we achieved success with automated tests.

There was one major difference between the two projects: In the first project, the automated test was created on a developed project that was not yet put into production. This meant that we did not have the production system to build on but had to use a system that was under development and not yet specified. In the second project, the automated test was built on the production system and the automated test was executed on any new release that was extended to the production system.

6.2   Project 1: Failure!

We were a team of five persons working part time on the automated test project. Only one person had a little experience in working with the capture replay method in QTP and QC, and none of us knew how to work with business process components.

One of the team members described how to understand the business process components, but it was more like a guide for understanding how they worked than a description of best practice for our purposes. So we were all working differently with the business components in the project, which in the end meant that the business components could not be incorporated together in one BPT.

> **Lesson**
>
> It is important to have everyone working in a consistent way.

Furthermore, each team member was working on automated test in different areas of the application but did not cooperate to find the general components. One consequence of this was that a lot of common components were designed, and the overview and benefits of reusable components were lost.

Unfortunately, we were all part time on the automated project, which meant that we did not have enough time and "peace and quiet" around the project. We were all working on different projects, and it was seen as better to work on those projects than on the automated test project. It also meant that we did not join the automated test group at the same time during the working week, so we were not updated with common information. When we had time to work on the automated test project, we were often working on our own.

The automated test project was not embedded in the organization. It was only initiated in the test department. Because the project was not prioritized in the organization, the management team did not take serious notice of the project. Furthermore, other people in the organization did not know anything about the automated test project, which meant that they did not have any interest in using their time to help us with it.

> **Lesson**
>
> Starting automation "bottom-up" is difficult. Senior management support is needed for long-term success.

None of the five team members had an overview of the application that was going to be automated. It caused some serious problems:

- The system was under development, so we could not obtain any experience from doing an automated regression test on an existing system.
- A lot of changes were made to the system even though the specifications were approved, so we often could not complete an automated test because we had to do a lot of maintenance.
- The changes caused a lot of maintenance of business components, but because we did not have an overview of the business components, it was difficult to maintain.
- We just started on a pilot project without any clear goals and strategy. The pilot project ended up being used as the real project without spending any time on learning and reflection, so we did not really have a pilot project.
- The test cases were not built according to the application. The test cases were built with no standards or naming convention. The same component could be found many times but with different names. The test case structure was confusing and managed in an unstructured way. It was impossible to find the right business components and incorporate them into a business test case.

> **Lessons**
>
> Many lessons were learned the hard way on this project: the need for clear goals, a pilot project, building for ease of maintenance, and standards.

After about half a year, the project failed and was closed down. The group decided that we could not continue on this project. There was no progress at all, and the project members were frustrated. After talking to the project manager, all the group members returned to the projects they already were participating in. There was no follow-up at all. For this project, everything that could go wrong went wrong.

6.3 Project 2: Success!

The second automated test project was in a different company, also in the insurance industry. The automation project was started because the IT systems were becoming increasingly complex, and resources were insufficient to do an adequate regression test on the releases going into production. The only regression test that was executed was done by one person in a few hours. She had only time to do a small functional test and to perform a lookup in the application to validate the system. It was actually just a sanity test of the application. This little regression was too risky for the business, so a real regression test was needed.

We had four major reasons to do the automated test project instead of using a manual regression test:

1. We had many releases to production and also hot fixes, and the regression test was more and more time consuming. (A hot fix is program code that is put into the production system very quickly outside the normal release plan, often to fix defects in the production system.)
2. There were not enough resources to do a manual regression test.
3. We wanted to be sure that exactly the same tests were executed every time, and a manual operation is always associated with a high risk of mistakes. Often the manual tester could not describe exactly what and how she had tested.
4. We had calculated that we would break even on our investment in a reasonable time (see the next section).

6.3.1 Our Estimated Return on Investment

We calculated that in a year's time, we would break even on the cost for automated regression testing compared to manual regression testing. The cost figures for manual regression testing are based on there being no automated regression tests.

A project initiation document was used to describe the automation project. A lot of factors were described, such as how many end users were dependent on the system, how many customers we had, how many hot fixes we had, how many errors we found in projects and in production, what kind of test we did, and what the economy was for introducing automated test. This large document involved different stakeholders, such as the CIO for agents, for IT, and for customers, as well as team leaders and the maintenance group. The document was specific for this company and contained confidential information.

Among a lot of detailed description, there was also a spreadsheet showing a breakeven point at the end of 1 year. Table 6.2 shows our estimated fixed costs per test case. Table 6.3 shows the number of releases and test cases (just one in this example). Table 6.4 shows the accumulated costs, taking into account the investment in the automation in year zero. As shown in Figure 6.1, this was projected to give a return on investment (ROI) after just one year.

To find the cost, we estimated (in hours) the cost per test case for a manual and automated perspective. We did not look at the cost for the automation tool because we already had the tools and licenses inhouse. (The company had a good offer from Hewlett-Packard, so it bought QC and QTP at the same time, and there was no need to investigate other tools.) The company needed the cost for human resources to do the test automation so that the software quality could be ensured. This is shown in Table 6.2.

Good Point

Even with an existing tool, investment is still needed in the people using the tool in order to achieve good and lasting benefits.

Next, we looked at how many times a test case should be executed in the regression test. We had 10 releases per year, so one test case would be executed 10 times a year. This is shown in Table 6.3.

Table 6.2 Estimated Fixed Costs per Test Cases

	Fixed Costs	Startup Cost Hours Per Test Case
A	Describe the test case; whether for a manual or automated test, the description is the same	2
B	Execute one manual test	2
C	Design one automated test ready for execution	10
E	Execute one automated test (3 min)	0.05
F	Maintain one manual test (12 min)	0.2
G	Maintain one automated test (12 min)	0.2

Table 6.3 Number of Releases and Test Cases per Year

	Number of Releases	**year**
L	Number of releases per year	10
T	Number of test cases	1

We estimated the manual and automated tests with these equations:

$$\text{Cost per test case} = \text{Test cases} \times [\text{Describe test} + \text{Releases} \times (\text{Execute test} + \text{Maintain test})]$$

$$\text{Cost per manual test case} = T \times [A + L \times (B + F)]$$

$$\text{Cost per automated test case} = T \times [(A+C) + L \times (E + G)]$$

This gives us the information shown in Table 6.4.

Finally, the accumulated cost estimation from Table 6.4 is shown in the graph in Figure 6.1. The breakeven point is estimated to be 1 year.

6.3.2 The Start

We started with three persons who were 100 percent dedicated to the automation project. Consequently, we were working full time and were not interrupted by any other projects while working on our project. The management wanted to know if test automation would be viable, so they gave us 3 months to say "go" or "do not go." With this in mind, we decided to work on a pilot project to gain a common knowledge and do the practical test automation.

Table 6.4 Accumulated Cost per Year per Test Case

Year	0	1	2	3	4	5
Manual test cost	2	24	46	68	90	112
Automated test cost	12	14.5	17	19.5	22	24.5

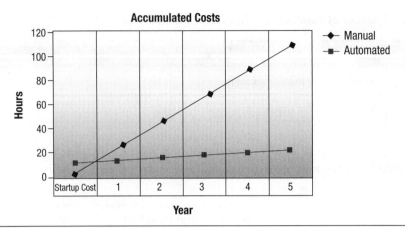

FIGURE 6.1   Accumulated cost for one year

The 3 months of the pilot project were divided into two time periods:

- The first month was a learning process to understand the task and the tools and to scope the pilot project. We achieved the common knowledge to handle the rest of the pilot project properly.
- The next 2 months were the practical implementation, automating a set of real tests for the application.

Good Point

A well-planned pilot project gives a sound foundation for automation.

6.3.3 Pilot Project Goals

We chose two easy products in the insurance application and decided to automate them end to end. This means from logon to logoff as seen from an insurance agent/ end user's perspective. The automated test went through the most important functionality in the application and through the GUI actions, such as dropdowns, popups, menus, and lists, providing us with a good overview. We also gained experience on how to work with automated tests and ensured that our goals could be achieved. We learned that we could run the entire automated test from the same starting point.

This meant that we could make an automated test covering as many areas as possible in the application, including new policies, different types of policies, claims, address changes, and so on. We also ensured in the test that all popups, menus, and lists were available and not missing. The manual tests tended to focus on limited areas, and often a menu or list was inadvertently omitted from the test. After release to production, we often found that a link or list was missing. The automated tests should prevent that in the future.

6.3.4   The First Month: Understanding the Task and the Tools

Lessons were learned and applied to the new project from the failure of the earlier automated project. With this in mind, we started the pilot project as follows.

We knew that the knowledge of automated tests and the tools we had to work with were very different for each team member. We decided to work on a pilot project to learn how to use the automated test with the tools QC with BPT and QTP. We began by sharing knowledge of the tools and by examining the possibilities and scope of the pilot period. By doing this pilot project, we made sure that we all had:

- Shared knowledge of tools and strategy.
- Tool knowledge so we could use the tool according to our task.
- Documentation so we could capture both standard practice and best practice.
- A general methodology and strategy so we could have a uniform solution.
- Application knowledge so we could scope the task.
- Management support so we could keep on working on our task in the best way.

6.3.4.1   *Common Understanding and Tool Knowledge*

To obtain the same level of knowledge for working with automated tests using QC and QTP, we decided to start the pilot project by taking lessons from a tool vendor consultant. We arranged a consultant from Hewlett-Packard (HP) to come to our office three times. We felt it was important to use the tool in a consistent way and according to best practices. After meeting with him for 2 days to learn to use the tools, we worked in close contact with each other to put the tools into practice. When we met the HP consultant the next time, we had both issues and more understanding. It was necessary for us to know all the general areas in the application so we could create reusable business components.

> **Tip**
>
> Kick-start a pilot project by training all involved, but space out the days; this gives you time to learn more thoroughly, experiment, and have better questions for the next visit.

6.3.4.2 Documentation

We wrote a quick guide to QC and QTP in the way that we wanted to use the tools. We also maintained a log of best practice and standards used in our project and recorded them whenever we had new and better experiences.

We had a common-issue log where we described all the problems and places where we got stuck. Sometimes we could solve the issues together. Other times we had to ask the consultant.

This structured way of working together ensured a uniform solution. Using an agile testing approach within the automation team (on iterative deliveries of business components) focused us on testing newly developed code until quality was achieved. Team members tested weekly deliveries of developed components. If errors were found in a component, they were reported back to the developer. By sitting side by side, it was easy to talk about a fix for the component. A week later, in the next release, the component should be ready for retesting. Often a component was approved after just one or two test cycles.

6.3.4.3 Application Knowledge

While learning the tool, we were also learning about the application. We experienced how the application was structured, the flow, the behavior, and how areas were grouped logically. By having the first overview of the application, we set up the scope for the pilot project.

6.3.4.4 General and Specific Areas in the Application GUI

We printed all the pages of the whole application and hung them on the wall. We had a lot of screenshots because we covered the whole application, including dropdowns, menus, lists, and popups, with scenarios from logon to logoff. This gave us a good overview of the entire application and the flows. For all the screenshots we investigated, we marked general areas used more than once with a red pen—we drew a red box around that area. If we could find a specific area used only one time, it was marked up as a blue box with a blue pen. The red areas represented either general or custom areas that could be reused. The blue areas represented areas that would be run only once but would achieve coverage.

Good Point

Make things visible at a glance (color is helpful to distinguish different categories).

We also considered what kind of data to validate and the timeframes for validation. We chose to validate the insurance premium, or the customer's payment for insurance, because it is highly sensitive data that must be right all the time. We validated that the premium was the same every time the test case was executed.

In this company, the premium is increased every year. Therefore, a year later we had to update the automated tests for all the test cases that had a premium calculated because the premium was validated.

It was easy for us to do because only one data field in one business component had to be updated. If there had been a lot of data fields in many business components to update, then it would have been time consuming.

Figure 6.2 shows an example screenshot from the application. This was one of the pages we hung on the wall. Every screenshot was analyzed for general and specific areas, and these areas were transferred to components.

6.3.5   The Strategy and Plan

In our case, the strategy of the pilot project was to use either ordinary capture/replay or BPT with keyword-driven automated components. BPT enabled us to create and modify the steps of the automated business components in a keyword-driven way. Using the BPT method, we could design business components and incorporate them into business process tests. A business process test has the same meaning as a test case, and business components are often just called components.

With our knowledge about the whole GUI, we chose how we wanted to use the BPT method. This method required that we knew all the general and specific areas in the GUI application so we could reuse components, so we created a structure and a plan according to the business components.

We planned how and when the business components should be delivered, so we all knew when we could run the entire test case composed of business components. The plan was created according to the importance of the general and specific areas using agile testing. We had weekly deliveries of components that were tested within few days, which resulted in quick testing progress.

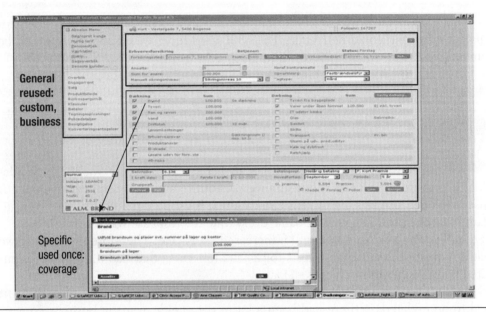

FIGURE 6.2   Example showing areas highlighted as specific or general

Also, the time schedule was created according to the importance of the insurance products so that the tests for the most important products were automated first.

Good Point

Remember to consider prioritization of tests when they are automated.

6.3.6   The Agile Testing Method

We wanted to have quick progress, so we chose to use agile testing. Agile testing focuses on testing iteratively against newly developed code or, as in our case, business components. It matches the method for using BPT because business components are independent, single-business actions that are incorporated into business process tests.

For example, when a customer wants to insure a farm with cows, the insurance agent follows these steps:

1. Logs onto the system.
2. Fills in details about the customer, such as address, age, and so on.
3. Enters information about the customer's business type (e.g., agricultural business).
4. Enters the type of coverage the customer wants (coverage for cows in this case).
5. Submits the policy. The system calculates and displays the premium.
6. Logs off the system.

A business process test simulates the use of the application made by the end user using components. From the previous scenario, the components could be composed in the BPT as follows:

Logon

Customer details

Business type

Farm cows coverage

Policy

Logoff

In this example, the business process test consists of six business components, and they run in sequence from top to bottom.

The first three and last two components are general because they contain information needed every time an insurance policy is created, whereas "Farm cows coverage" is specific because it is used only when a customer has a farm with cows to be insured. To be able to test this flow, we need to place business components into a business process test.

If we want to test the component "Farm cows coverage" in the flow from "Logon" to "Farm cows coverage," then the first three general components must be available. That is, when an automated test is done in a specific flow, it is dependent on delivery of general components according to the plan.

6.3.6.1 Management Support

We ensured that all the stakeholders knew about the automated test project. In that way, we were allowed to talk to all groups of people, such as the business team, the production team, the delivery team, and the development team. We reported status on the project frequently to maintain the managers' interest and support.

> **Good Point**
>
> Maintain stakeholder interest and support with frequent reports about the
> automation.

6.3.7   Result of the First Period

The result of the first time period was that we could set up a realistic scope for both the rest of the pilot project and the whole project. The whole test team had:

- Management support
- Clear goals
- The same knowledge level
- Understanding of the tool
- Real application knowledge on the GUI
- Strategy for the task handling
- Methodology to use, including a description for best practice
- A realistic plan
- A realistic time schedule

6.4   The Next Time Period: Testing for Real

One team member had to leave the project, but the two who were left were still 100 percent dedicated to the project. Our goal for this period was to obtain a real automated test of the application. To reach this goal, we needed to have a good and structured process for the automated test, documented according to the plan. Our plan contained agile testing with weekly deliveries of business components. The general business components were delivered first.

> **Good Point**
>
> Start simple!

The status of the business components showed us if the business component was:

- Ready
- Under development
- Had errors
- Being modified

This meant we always had a full overview of the progress for the business components and thereby the whole test.

Every component under development was tested by the responsible developer. When the developer found the component to be reliable, it was marked with status "ready," meaning that the component was ready for all the team members to use.

If a business component failed in a test case, it was marked with the status "error," and the responsible developer had to redesign the component or, in rare cases, create a new component if no changes could be done. The failed component should be fixed and "ready" to test by the next weekly release. Every release contained fixed and new components ready to test. In this way, we ensured quick progress.

6.4.1   What to Automate

We were dependent on having operational test automation within 2 months, so we decided to start with functionality that was:

- Simple, so we would not get stuck.
- Stable, so we would not have too many changes.
- Positive tests. Just to keep it simple, we could extend this later by doing negative tests on error messages.
- Easy to continue to work with, so we would not have to find a new way of doing the automated test.
- Described as best practice (see Section 6.4.3 for more detail).

We did some functional coding as well but only on a small scale because we did not want to be dependent on a code specialist (in the maintenance of the automated test).

6.4.2   Stakeholders' Involvement

First, the business team told us about the simplest functionality in the insurance products that could be automated. This gave us a good knowledge of an easy application. The business team also prioritized the insurance products according to the benefit it would give the business to have the products automated.

Second, we talked to the developers to hear how they had coded the GUI so that we were prepared to do the test automation. The developers were told that any changes in the GUI would also create changes to the automated test, so they agreed to use a coding standard.

The developers had a meeting, and we all saw a benefit in using coding standards. The developers were also doing maintenance, so they could see that this would make things easier for them. We told them about the automated test project so they could think of us as partners and not annoying people interrupting their work. Consequently, we had a close cooperation with the developers: They told us when there were changes in the GUI, and we did some automated test when they wanted us to do so. They were happy for us to execute the automated tests in the development environment to find errors early on in the development phase. The developers couldn't run the automated tests themselves because we didn't have enough licenses for QC and QTP.

> **Good Point**
>
> Cooperate with developers; help each other.

Third, we talked to the delivery manager to hear what was the most stable part in the GUI and what changes were planned in the next delivery. This helped us minimize the number of changes in the automated test and be prepared in time to do automated test in the releases to production.

6.4.3 Uniform Solution

Armed with this information, we could choose to automate a limited scope end to end with the overall philosophy of "keep it simple." This helped us:

- Ensure a simple and uniform solution and thereby avoid having a complicated and unintelligible solution.
- Have a solution that was not too difficult in order to avoid getting stuck. When we had a problem, it was written in an issue log. The group could often find the answers themselves.
- Keep it easier for everyone to understand the automated test so that we were not dependent on a specific person's knowledge.
- Achieve easy maintenance.
- Keep a well-structured and clear overview.

We had a document that described the best practices and standards that had to be kept through the whole project period. If we chose not to follow the best practice, we had to have a sound reason, which was also written into our best practice document so we knew where we had deviations. Because we wanted to have a good explanation of them, we had very few deviations, but when we had one, it was necessary.

Good Point

Define standards but allow exceptions when needed.

6.4.4   Application Structure and Test Case Structure in QC

We adopted the structure from the application to QC by transferring the application flow structure to QC folders. Consequently, the structure in QC was exactly the same as the structure in the application. We had focused on the importance of always being able to find and compose the right components in a test case. (At the end of the project, we had 300 components and we could find and understand every single one.)

Tip

Your application should drive the structure in the tool, not vice versa.

The size of the components had to be suitable according to the test case composition so that it was possible to incorporate the components in test cases.

- Too big components would sacrifice the flexibility of using components because we would not be able to reuse them.
- Too small components would result in long test cases composed of many components, and the overview would be missing. Furthermore, there are performance issues that occur when components are executed, because when each component is launched into the test it takes time.
- The naming standard for components and test cases was done in a business-oriented way to ensure easy location of the cases and to maintain an overview.
- Test cases composed of general and specific components ensured that we did not have multiple components with the same purpose.

Good Point

A standard approach to testware architecture aids ease of use and long-term survival.

Well-arranged test cases ensure that every test case can be recognized and maintained. We are never in doubt what the test case does and which test case to use in a specific test scenario. Furthermore, it aids with test case maintenance.

Data used in the test cases is also well organized. The inputs and outputs from the components, which are called parameters, were adapted to as many test cases as possible. Therefore, we had a few functions added to the standard. The use of parameters made it possible to create data-driven tests, thus minimizing maintenance. Examples are given below; see Chapter Appendix for implementation details.

- We had a function called skip that allowed us to skip unused parameters. We could thereby use the parameters in any combination we wanted, no matter how many components were used—a few or all of them.

Tip

Define your own useful functions and conventions that can be used in many situations.

- We set up a standard for when we wanted to verify results. For example, every test should have a verification of the premium calculated so that the actual premium matched the expected premium.
- We had a wait function included because the performance response time on the application was very variable.
- We had a Citrix environment, so we planned to design the test cases to be executable on any Citrix environment. For example, a lot of the test cases were about creating an insurance policy, which meant that we were independent of existing data.

To explain how we adopted the structure from the application to the structure in QC, an example is given in Figure 6.3. By the way, there are also components in the areas of Pension and Private, and more components in the Business area, but they are not shown here.

Application structure

Test case structure

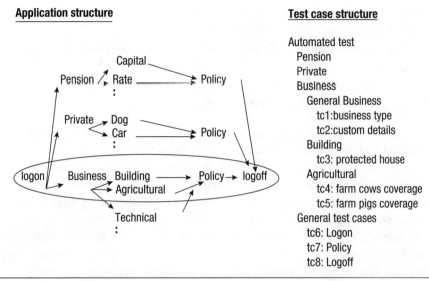

Automated test
  Pension
    Private
    Business
      General Business
        tc1:business type
        tc2:custom details
      Building
        tc3: protected house
      Agricultural
        tc4: farm cows coverage
        tc5: farm pigs coverage
  General test cases
    tc6: Logon
    tc7: Policy
    tc8: Logoff

FIGURE 6.3   Example overview

To explain how business components are incorporated in a business process test, an example of two test cases is shown in Table 6.5. A test case is the same as a business process test.

Table 6.5   Two Example Test Cases

Test Case: Agricultural Farm with Cows and Pigs	Test Case: Building Protected House
Logon	Logon
Customer details	Customer details
Business type	Business type
Farm cows coverage	Protected house
Farm pigs coverage	Policy
Policy	Logoff
Logoff	

Five components are general (logon, customer detail, business type, policy, logoff) and therefore used in more than one test scenario. When a component is modified, the modification is reflected in all the test cases where this component is incorporated.

6.4.5 Go/Do Not Go after 3 Months

After the first 3 months of work on the pilot project, we had an automated test for an insurance product. We could show the automated test to all the stakeholders, and they could see it function in a real setting. It is easier to understand what automated test means and what the benefits are if you can see it at work. Further, we could plan and estimate the entire project, which convinced the managers that it was a good solution to continue the automated test for the rest of the products.

So at the end of the 3 months, we had an automated test for the application based on a well-documented strategy, and it was done properly. We did a qualified estimation for the whole automated project and also described its benefits.

There was no doubt, it was go!

6.4.6 Real Project after the Pilot Project

On the basis of all our learning, findings, and experiences from the pilot project, we started the real project. Each team member chose a product to automate that had a high priority from the business perspective. The entire project team was still doing agile testing work toward demonstrable quality through weekly deliveries. The structure in QC and QTP was created according to the application structure. The design of the components was created according to the best practice and standard description, and all the test cases were designed as end-to-end tests. We still did not have many deviations, and when they were necessary, they were documented. The philosophy of keeping it simple ensured a visible structure and an easily maintained solution. We frequently reported the status of the project's progress and thereby kept management support. We didn't collect metrics about the automation, but in this way, we made the benefits visible to managers.

6.4.7 The First Automated Test Used in Real Releases to Production

As soon as one product had its test automated and approved for use in the regression test, we used the test in the ordinary releases to production. In that way, we had the benefit of the automated test as soon as possible. We did not wait to use the automated test until all the products were automated. We used the automated test in the regression test whenever it was possible during the project period. The benefits were as follows:

- We extended the automated test whenever a new product was approved ready to test.
- We learned how to maintain the components for real.
- We had a test report that showed the test cases that had passed or failed, so the automated regression test was now visible in a quality report.
- The organization soon came to depend on the automated test because it was quick and the test result was visible in a test report.

The example test report in Figure 6.4 shows two test cases that failed and others that passed.

Execution of the automated test gave benefits to many people. Sometimes the developers wanted us to execute the automated test in the development environment, and other times the testers wanted us to run an automated test in a test environment

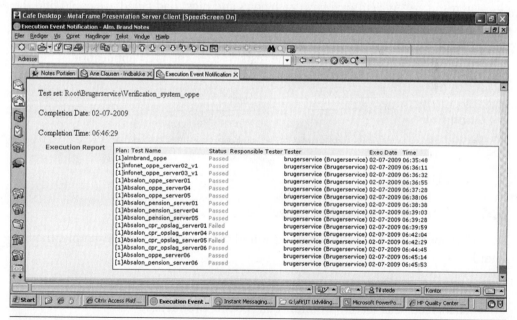

FIGURE 6.4   Example of a test report showing passed and failed test cases (two test cases failed)

before the real regression test was executed. We always performed the automated test in the preproduction environment before a release.

The process was working really fast in the project, and in another 6 months after the pilot project, all the insurance products were automated in test scenarios.

Before setting the automated test to production, we made agreements with the stakeholders:

- Developers must describe functionality and changes in GUI in the change management system so that the test automation team knew what to maintain.
- Delivery manager agrees on time for the schedule a long time before the automated regression test should be executed.
- Automated regression test takes 3 days to execute, including bug fixing and retesting.
- Business wants more test cases. A process for the work to continue is confirmed.
- Visible quality to managers. Every automated test ends up with a test report showing test coverage with passed or failed test cases. When a test failed, we could see which components caused the failure. In the example from Table 6.5, if test case "Agricultural farm with cows and pigs" had failed, we could find the component that failed. If, for example, the component Farm_cows_coverage failed and the test stopped, then we had not tested Farm_pigs_coverage. The components showed us where the tests were in the GUI application.

Good Point

Set realistic expectations and agree on what everyone needs to do and when.

6.4.8 The Whole Automated Test in Production

We experienced that the automated test found serious defects. For example, the test found:

- Links that were dead.
- Incorrectly calculated premiums on specific products.
- Nonexistent functionality, such as tariff calculation.

It would have been bad for the organization if these defects were found in production because:

- Many insurance agents depend on the system because it is their sales tool.
- The customer can rely on the system, and it provides positive publicity, helping the company retain our existing customers and win new customers.
- The system is now more stable and reliable, and also, according to the customer, we now have a validation on the premiums calculated, so we know that the insurance is right.
- The organization has the opportunity to earn more money when the system is more reliable and useful.

6.5   Conclusion

Although we never went back and calculated whether or not we achieved our projected ROI, we know that our automation was very successful. These are the main benefits that we now have:

- The automated test was in production with limited scope after 3 months and in full operation after 6 months.
- Small success motivates. When there are many small milestones, it is easier to achieve the goal and thus achieve success.
- Automated tests help to ensure quality.
- Automated tests find serious defects.
- Tests can be executed in many environments (Citrix).
- Tests can be scheduled when desired.
- The same regression test can be performed every time.
- Significant acknowledgment was received both inhouse and outside. Automated test is popular, and testers, developers, production team, and business team are happy with this test.
- Reports showing the test coverage are automatically generated.

During my 2 years of work with automated test, I found five success criteria, which, if adhered to, will give you a good chance to achieve success.

- Tasks and responsibilities must be agreed on and known in the organization.
- Make a pilot project and define clear goals.
- Ensure common understanding and knowledge; document best practice and standards.
- Understand the whole business application to ensure the right structure and size of test cases.
- "Keep it simple."

Finally, good luck with your automated test!

Chapter Appendix: Ensure flexibility in the components using "Skip" functionality.

To be able to combine data regardless if data is available (empty) or not you must code "skip-" functions in QTP. These functions are used in QC Components.

Example: Component "Customer Details" with data:

Customer Name	Customer Address	Country	Telephone	Email
Chris Schmith	6015 Dove, San Diego	USA	004412345678	SKIP
Mary Larsen	Ringvej 5, 3450 Lynge	SKIP	SKIP	mary@mx.dk

When it says "SKIP" in the data sheet the data is empty and therefore data is skipped.

Skip function "SetSkip" is coded in QTP like this:

```
'@Documentation Sets the value for the selected object or jumps over the field
Public Function SetSkip(test_object, Vaerdi)

  If  Trim(UCase(Vaerdi)) <> "SKIP" Then
    test_object.set Vaerdi
  End If
End Function
RegisterUserFunc "WebEdit", "SetSkip", "SetSkip", True
RegisterUserFunc "WebCheckBox" , "SetSkip", "SetSkip", True
RegisterUserFunc "WebFile" ,"SetSkip", "SetSkip", True
```

You can also code "skip" functions for other objects such as:

- Public Function SelectSkip(test_object, Vaerdi)
- Public Function ClickSkip(test_object, Vaerdi)
- Public Function VerifyPropertySkip(test_object, Vaerdi)

CHAPTER 7

AUTOMATING THE TESTING OF COMPLEX GOVERNMENT SYSTEMS

Elfriede Dustin

Elfriede Dustin, well known in the test automation world, shares her experience of developing an automation framework for real-time, mission-critical systems for the U.S. Department of Defense. Because of the particular type of software that was being tested, there were specific requirements for a tool solution, and Elfriede and her colleagues needed to spend some time searching for and experimenting with different tools. Their clear statement of requirements kept them on track for a successful outcome, and their eventual solution used a mixture of commercial, open source, and inhouse tools. They met with some unexpected resistance to what was technically a very good system. This story covers hundreds of testers and tens of automators, testing millions of lines of code, over a period of 4½ years. See Table 7.1.

7.1 Background for the Case Study

The company I work for, Innovative Defense Technologies (IDT), received a small-business Department of the Defense (DoD) contract in 2005 and with it was given the arduous task of "speeding up DoD software delivery to the field." The founders of IDT, having a combined 40-plus years of software delivery experience in the DoD industry, knew that one of the biggest challenges preventing speedier software delivery was the DoD testing bottleneck: leading-edge software technology could

Table 7.1   Case Study Characteristics

Classification	This Case Study
Application domain	Real-time mission-critical systems running heterogeneous multicomputer environments (cross-OS, i.e., Windows, Linux, Solaris)
Application size	Millions of lines of code
Location	United States
Lifecycle	Agile, continuous development and integration
Number on the project	More than 20 projects
Number of testers	100s
Number of automators	10s
Time span	4½ years
Dates	2006– 2011
Tool type(s)	Open source, commercial, and inhouse developed
Pilot study undertaken	Yes
ROI measured	Yes, reduced five testers to one; 100 times more scenario tests executed
Successful?	Yes
Still breathing?	Yes

be implemented by brilliant developers at exceptional speed, yet the rigorous DoD testing and certification processes, taking years, would bring efficient fielding of solutions to a screeching halt.

In 2006, I was hired as IDT's first contractor to help solve that specific testing bottleneck. As one part of the solution, IDT's founders had concluded that the mostly manual DoD testing process needed to be automated. Here began the long journey of trying to find an automated testing solution to be applied to some of the most complex, heterogeneous DoD programs.

7.2 Our Requirements for Automation

After gaining further understanding of the unique DoD automated testing challenge, we came up with the following seven major requirements for an automated software testing solution used on a typical DoD system under test (SUT).

Good Point

Start by identifying the requirements or objectives for the automation to ensure that your solution is directed toward the right things.

The automated testing solution:

- Can't be intrusive to SUT.
- Must be OS independent (compatible with Windows, Linux, Solaris, etc.).
- Must be GUI technology independent (i.e., should be able to handle GUI technologies written in Motif, C#, etc., and handle any type of third-party noncustom GUI control).
- Must be able to handle display- and non-display-centric automation (i.e., handle test operations on SUTs with GUI and handle operations on the SUT's backend, such as various messages being sent).
- Must be able to handle a networked multicomputer environment (i.e., multiple servers and multiple monitors/displays interconnected to form one SUT).
- Nondevelopers should be able to use the tool (testers in the DoD labs were subject matter experts but not necessarily software developers who could use an automated testing tool efficiently).
- Must support an automated requirements traceability matrix (RTM).

Our diligent automated testing tool research determined that while various tools on the market exist that meet one or more of these seven requirements, none existed that met all seven requirements in one solution.

This chapter describes the background of these requirements and how we at IDT evolved an automated software testing framework and solution, which we call Automated Test and Re-Test (ATRT), that ended up meeting all seven major requirements listed here, among others. It describes our initial approach to implementing this ATRT solution via reuse of existing open source solutions, along with a vendor-provided tool, and the challenges we ran into and had to overcome. It describes how we initially relied on the vendor-provided tool but how and why we ultimately adopted a hybrid automated software testing solution that is now a combination of vendor-provided, open source, and inhouse-developed tools.

> **Good Point**
>
> A combination of tools may provide an overall solution that no single tool can give; don't be afraid to mix and match, including open source, commercial, and your own developed tools.

7.3 Automated Test and Re-Test (ATRT), Our Automated Testing Solution—What Is It?

This section describes how we tackled each of the seven automation requirements one by one and how we solved each challenge.

7.3.1 Can't Be Intrusive to SUT

Originally, we set out to reuse any applicable vendor-provided automated testing tool as part of our automated testing framework. Before knowing the detailed requirements, I thought we'd be using tools such as IBM Rational Functional Tester, Hewlett-Packard's Mercury QuickTest Pro and WinRunner, TestComplete (then by AutomatedQA and now SmartBear).

However, given the requirement "can't be intrusive to the system under test," I knew immediately I had to cross these tools off our list of potentials. While some partially met the requirement, none met it 100 percent, meaning portions of the tool actually had to be installed on the SUT. Our customer would not be happy with the tool being even *partially* intrusive.

My continued search for tools that met this requirement led me to VNCRobot, which at the time was a freeware tool. The tool uses virtual network computing (VNC) technology to connect one computer to another. VNCRobot is the "VNC client" and can access and control the remote computer running a VNC server via the RFB (remote frame buffer) protocol. Figure 7.1 illustrates this setup.

When I got in touch with the VNCRobot author, I determined that he was the sole developer working on this project. Did we want to hinge the success of our project on that one developer? Not necessarily.

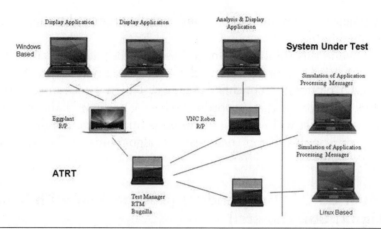

FIGURE 7.1   VNC and capture/playback tools

We decided to continue our search for additional tool options that allowed for nonintrusive automated testing and discovered eggPlant, which at the time was owned by Redstone. eggPlant had great potential: Like VNCRobot, it uses VNC technology and met our requirement of "can't be intrusive to the system under test." After a 3-month period of evaluating eggPlant and VNCRobot, we decided that egg-Plant had features we needed that VNCRobot didn't have. For example, eggPlant provided an image-collection feature, which allows for inclusion of various similar images in one test case for it to pass and, during test execution, allows for image searching and comparison of those similar images. This feature was useful because we knew that images could be in various states (selected, nonselected, highlighted, not highlighted). We realized the image-collection feature was important to allow for increased stability during test execution.

This evaluation was in 2007. In the meantime, in 2009, VNCRobot was acquired by T-Plan and renamed T-Plan Robot (www.t-plan.com/robot/). T-Plan Robot now also comes with the image-collection feature. Also, a reduced-feature version of T-Plan Robot is available as open source using a GPL license. I reevaluated T-Plan Robot and still feel our choice of using eggPlant was the better one for various reasons at the time, such as eggPlant's feature-rich solution and being available for numerous platforms.

Since my original evaluation, eggPlant had been acquired by TestPlant (2008) and in 2011 was awarded a patent that "pertains generally to computer systems, and more particularly to methods and techniques for monitoring, testing and controlling the operation of one or more computers through communications links."

How eggPlant behaves and fits into our overall automated testing framework is further described in the next sections.

Note that while this solution is image-based testing, it is not coordinate-based GUI test automation. Coordinate-based GUI automation is practically useless whenever a GUI element's coordinates change. I highly recommend that people avoid any type of capture that's coordinate based because if the location of the image changes, the test will fail. This solution is image based, independent of the coordinates, using sophisticated image-search algorithms to find the image anywhere on the screen.

7.3.2 Must Be OS Independent (Compatible with Windows, Linux, Solaris, etc.)

We also had to be sure the tool we selected as part of our ATRT framework was operating system (OS) independent. Our client uses every type of OS imaginable, but initially we wanted to set out our proof-of-concept on Windows and Linux. eggPlant ran only on a Mac, but at the time, they were working on a Windows appliance. However, with the Windows appliance, we still would have to use a Mac and the Windows appliance would have to be connected to the Mac. We were looking for a much less complicated setup for OS compatibility. In 2008, we (IDT) agreed with Redstone that they would develop a Linux eggPlant version in exchange for us in the meantime purchasing and using a set of Mac eggPlant licenses. After the acquisition, we worked closely with TestPlant on Linux requirements and actually became their Linux eggPlant beta testers. Ironing out the bugs in the Linux version was a lengthy process, but now we had a pretty solid Linux eggPlant license, while TestPlant also released their official Windows license in 2010.

We had now met the second requirement, that the solution must be OS independent (e.g., it can test Mac, Linux, Windows, Solaris, Symbian, BlackBerry, Windows Mobile, and KVM [keyboard, visual display unit, and mouse switches]). Not only is eggPlant OS independent, but it can also test different interfaces, such as iPhone applications, various screens, point-of-sale (POS) devices, command and control systems, air traffic control screens, smartphones, mobile devices, and more.

7.3.3 Must Be Independent of the GUI

Our solution should be able to handle GUI technologies written in Motif, C#, and so on, and to handle any type of third-party non-custom GUI control.

eggPlant works by using VNC to interact with all GUI elements of the SUT as images, independent of the GUI technology used. Many of the current vendor-provided automated software testing tools are GUI technology dependent. That means that if proprietary programming languages or third-party controls are used in the SUT GUI, the automated testing tool often is not compatible, which presents automated testing problems.

7.3.4   Must Automate Tests for Both Display-Centric and Non-Display-Centric Interfaces

Our solution needs to be able to handle test operations on systems through their GUI but should also be able to handle operations on the system's backend, not through a GUI, such as various messages being sent.

While eggPlant met previously discussed GUI automation requirements well, our customer also needed to be able to test various backend (non-GUI) interfaces using various protocols. eggPlant did not support this requirement. We had to develop an inhouse solution for this backend "interface" testing ourselves. The task was a complex undertaking because first we needed to understand the protocol requirements, which sometimes were proprietary, plus the makeup of the backend system. Our biggest challenge was the message data. Each SUT used a different protocol (TCP/IP, User Datagram Protocol [UDP], Common Object Request Broker Architecture [CORBA], proprietary, and more), and all used different message data formats. We developed an approach whereby all protocols and data could be tested via our ATRT framework. Our ATRT development effort was born.

7.3.4.1 Eclipse

We decided to use the open source Eclipse development environment. We chose the Eclipse rich client platform because it could simply be expanded on the base environment for ATRT to allow for configurability/extensibility via a powerful plug-in framework, which allowed us to integrate eggPlant into that framework. Other new feature sets and tools can be integrated, and plug-ins (see next section) can be added, removed, or modified easily through the Eclipse framework.

Eclipse provides various design elements that have to be considered for the various features required when developing and adding to an automated testing framework. Eclipse is an open source community whose projects are focused on building an open development platform comprising extensible frameworks and tools for building, deploying, and managing software across the lifecycle. A large and vibrant ecosystem of major technology vendors, innovative startups, universities, research institutions, and individuals extend, complement, and support the Eclipse platform. Eclipse is much more than just a Java integrated development environment (IDE).

Eclipse projects can be conceptually organized into seven different "pillars," or categories:

- Enterprise development
- Embedded and device development
- Rich client platform
- Rich Internet applications
- Application frameworks
- Application lifecycle management (ALM)
- Service-oriented architecture (SOA)

The exciting thing about Eclipse is that many people are using Eclipse in many ways. The common thread is that they are building innovative, industrial-strength software and want to use great tools and frameworks to make their job easier.

> **Tip**
>
> Use a flexible development environment so that you can tailor the tools and utilities to your specific needs.

7.3.4.2   Plug-ins

Eclipse comes bundled with a Plug-in Development Environment (PDE), which is a plug-in itself that streamlines plug-in development. Because the Eclipse framework is written in Java, the plug-in code ideally is written in Java as well. Other languages can be used in the plug-in development, but that would limit the multiplatform support you get with Java.

How is a plug-in integrated with Eclipse? The Eclipse IDE is built with a workbench that describes *extension points* from which external developers' code extends the functionality. Extending the IDE makes a tool's integration seamless to end users. For example, the *org.eclipse.ui.popupMenus* extension point allows for adding customized plug-in functionality to a view or editor popup menu. Each plug-in can be self-contained. This autonomy allows users to customize their workbench environment with the suite of tools necessary to perform their tasks by installing the appropriate plug-in. Additionally, updates to a plug-in can be installed independently. This gives developers the flexibility to package and release new versions easily and users the flexibility to install newer plug-in versions and/or revert to prior releases.

We created an extension point that defines an interface for our framework, giving the framework user a way to interact with an external tool in a standard way. Support for various protocols was developed, and ATRT can now test message data sent over TCP/IP, UDP, CORBA, proprietary, and many more.

We had zeroed in on the most efficient development environment; we now also needed a way to develop test message data. Although we could reuse samples of "live" message data (i.e., message data that was actually used in the SUTs), it would not give us the data coverage we were looking for. We needed a tool that would allow us to measure test data coverage so we could cover a broad range of test data. We initially evaluated FireEye, developed by the U.S. National Institute of Standards and Technology (NIST) for an orthogonal-array approach of data generation, but it didn't allow for the complexity of data interactions and relations required. We determined that MATLAB was the solution for our complex test data generation (www.mathworks.com/products/matlab/).

ATRT Test Manager now provides GUI- and message-based testing capability for SUTs.

7.3.5   Must Be Able to Handle a Networked Multicomputer Environment

While the commercial world mainly seems to focus on web-based applications and web testing, in this DoD world we are working in, systems consist of networked computers (i.e., multiple servers, systems of systems, multiple monitors and displays interconnected to form one SUT). eggPlant with its VNC use handles the interconnected systems well, and we developed ATRT in such a way that it can support this networked mesh of environments. For example, it can handle distributed and concurrent testing over a network: Automated tests can be executed concurrently over a network for the test case where various GUI- or message-based outputs are dependent on each other over a network or have to run in parallel. As long as a VNC server is installed on any of the networked computers, ATRT (which now also serves as a VNC client) can connect to them.

7.3.6   Nondevelopers Should Be Able to Use the Tool

One of the main requirements was that nondevelopers should be able to use the ATRT framework. Testers in the DoD labs were subject matter experts but not necessarily software developers who could use an automated testing tool efficiently. Nondevelopers generally don't want to be bothered with developing automated testing scripts; they want to be able to use the tool with the simple click of a button. We therefore developed a semi-keyword-driven approach. I call it semi-keyword-driven because our solution allows the testers to click on an icon that matches any mouse feature (left click, right click, middle click, mouse down, etc.), and via that icon click, ATRT generates the respective code behind the scene. Possibly a better term for our approach is "icon-driven" automated software testing.

Additionally, we added a model-driven automated testing capability that allows test flows to be generated via a simple point-and-click model-driven interface. We wanted to provide a solution whereby testers could model a test before the SUT becomes available and be able to see a visual representation of their tests. See Figure 7.2 for a data pool test example.

Figure 7.2 is an example of a test flow at the "action" level. The ATRT hierarchy consists of the following:

Projects
> Test cases
>> Test steps
>>> Actions

Sample actions that make up the test are depicted in this figure. To conduct the test, the user captured left clicks on the image, which were then captured and baselined inside the box labeled "Go To . . Ctrl+G." Next, the dataflow points to a file from which the test data is being pulled, called "Tests 'goto' expected results." The next step depicts a conditional flow; that is, if data is available, continue to left click on the next image Fix Point and continue to enter the data using an Input Type Text Action into the SUT at Fix Point and continue the actions described here (not all actions are shown due to space limitations, but you can see the parameter flow coming back into the data file), else end the loop and click on the image to end the test, which here is the X button on the upper-right corner of the tab.

Our goal was that a tester should be able to focus on test design and new features. A tester should not have to spend time crafting elaborate automated testing scripts. Asking manual testers with no development background to do such work places them at risk of losing focus on what they are trying to accomplish (i.e., verify the SUT behaves as expected).

Good Point

The purpose of automation is to serve testing. This can best be done by tailoring the automation so that the testers find it as easy as possible to use.

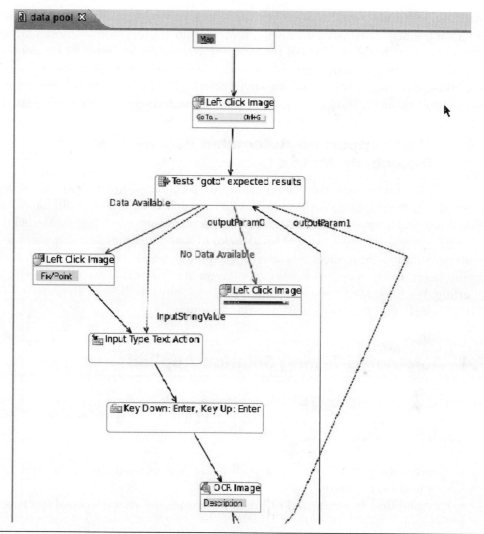

FIGURE 7.2   Visual test flow representation (note: "Tests 'goto' expected results" represents an image; "Test Go To" represents a data file)

GUI capture and modeling is described here, but the tool also allows for non-GUI message-based testing whereby messages can be sent over various protocols and also can be modeled by nondevelopers.

In summary, we met the requirement, that nondevelopers should be able to use this framework. ATRT provides the tester with every GUI action a mouse will provide in addition to various other keywords. Our experience with customers using ATRT for the first time is that it provides a very intuitive user interface, and interestingly enough, we find that some of the best test automators are younger testers who have grown up playing video games, coincidentally developing eye–hand coordination. Some of the testers even find working with ATRT to be fun, which alleviates the monotony of manually testing the same features repeatedly with each new release.

7.3.7 Must Support an Automated Requirements Traceability Matrix

We needed a framework that could allow for test management and automated requirements traceability. We developed ATRT in such a way that it could handle all related test management activities, including documenting a test case in the ATRT manager, along with a hierarchical breakdown of test cases into test steps and test substeps. Additionally, to meet this latest requirement, we allow users to import their requirements and to map test cases to requirements. From this, we allow for RTM reporting. We integrated the open source Business and Intelligence Reporting Tool (BIRT), which is an Eclipse-based reporting system.

7.4 Automated Testing Solution Applied

We successfully applied our ATRT solution to various DoD programs and have shown return on investment. We developed a complex ROI matrix that allows us to measure as accurately as possible and includes measures for things such as:

- Nonrecurring costs such as original setup and connection in the labs and required workarounds.
- Cost and time to create and maintain the automated versus manual test cases.
- Learning curve.

ROI includes not only time savings (e.g., on one program for a 48-hour endurance test, we were able to reduce the number of testers required from 5 to 1), but also increased testing coverage (i.e., our backend message-based testing allows a 100-fold increase in test scenario testing and analyzing, testing that manually would be time prohibitive).

Although we showed ROI on all programs, our biggest challenge for bringing automated testing, ATRT, or any such type of framework into the DoD labs was often the testers themselves who have done manual testing for years and often feel their jobs are in jeopardy. After demonstrating ATRT on their test systems in labs, more often than not we hear the comment, "Why don't you just put up a sign on these computers that says 'You have been replaced!'?"

Well, not quite. Our main goal is not to replace testers but to make them more efficient. Our goal with bringing automated testing to the DoD systems (old and new) is to increase the speed of the testing certification process, which is currently mainly a manual process, and hundreds of thousands of dollars are spent on inefficient testing processes. Often the mantra we hear is "This is how we have been doing it; don't rock the boat." ATRT is a new and more efficient way to implement testing on systems—it is not a silver bullet. For now, we have shown initial savings, but we will continue to enhance ATRT to be even more effective. The good news is that each day, our entire development and testing department is focused on developing a better automated testing solution. With each application to different systems, we learn more and add features accordingly.

> **Lesson**
>
> When introducing automation to manual testers, you may meet with unexpected resistance.

One of our additional challenges is testing of ATRT. We need to make sure that ATRT behaves flawlessly. How can we claim to have an automated testing solution that will save you time and make you more efficient, if there are problems with the ATRT solution? We have a rigorous ATRT development process in place that includes software development using continuous integration with code checked in daily to the source control tool (such as Subversion), nightly builds (using tools such as Hudson), and automated unit tests (using tools such as nUnit). Automated unit and integration testing is required to continuously add to the automated ATRT unit and integration testing framework. The more interesting testing part here is that we use ATRT to functionally test ATRT (a technique known as "dog-fooding" or "eating your own dog food"). Along with the nUnit tests, we have automated functional ATRT tests in place that test all of the ATRT requirements in a nightly build. A subset of automated tests of results reporting have been created, and a build is not considered complete until it is successfully built and passes all automated unit and automated functional tests.

Good Point

The automation itself must be tested so we can have confidence in it. This is also known as dog-fooding, meaning "eating our own dog food."

7.5 Conclusion

I am excited to work at a company that is funded by the government to develop an automated testing solution. It allows me to see the testing challenges that testers face and to help create and provide automated solutions to the unique challenges while continuously evolving in effectiveness. It also made me realize that there is no need to reinvent the wheel: An automated testing framework can successfully be built by reusing open source, vendor-provided, and inhouse-developed code. Just make sure the manual testers don't feel threatened by a solution that will make them 10 times more effective, and make sure to understand the limitations of the currently available vendor-provided tools. To solve the automated testing challenge, there is much more to be done and much better solutions to come.

CHAPTER 8

DEVICE SIMULATION FRAMEWORK

Alan Page

Alan Page from Microsoft tells a story of discovery: how to automate hardware device testing. We all take for granted that our USB devices will work with our computers, but the number of different devices that need to be tested is very large and growing, and it was difficult to automate such actions as unplugging a device. However, a simulation framework was developed that has enabled much of this testing to be automated in a way that has found widespread use inside and outside of Microsoft. The chapter includes numerous examples showing both the problems encountered and the solutions implemented. This story is from the United States and was an inhouse development now used by hundreds of testers. See Table 8.1.

8.1 Background for the Case Study

For as long as computers have had peripheral devices, it has been a challenge to test the massive amount of available devices in an efficient and cost-effective manner. Testing the interactions between unique combinations of physical devices is nearly impossible because of the combinatorial explosion of different configurations. For the device testing combinations and configurations that are attempted, the cost of the space required for labs, as well as power and cooling for those labs, is expensive. Moreover, the cost of paying skilled testers to sit at a computer and perform activities like plugging and unplugging a device probably doesn't seem cost-worthy to the bean counters in any software organization. The physical hardware is also often expensive, especially at a large scale; on top of all this, the Windows team at Microsoft often

Table 8.1   Case Study Characteristics

Classification	This Case Study
Application domain	Devices and device drivers
Application size	Not counted; likely over 100,000 LOC
Location	United States
Lifecycle	Traditional
Number on the project	
Number of testers	Hundreds
Number of automators	Hundreds
Time span	9 years
Dates	2001–present
Tool type(s)	Inhouse and available in the Windows Driver Development Kit
Pilot study undertaken	No
ROI measured	No
Successful?	Yes
Still breathing?	Yes

faces the challenge of writing (and testing!) device drivers for physical hardware that isn't even available yet.

Testing error paths in driver code is also a significant problem. Because most drivers run in kernel mode, where software has direct access to all hardware resources, errors in driver code—even a simple unhandled message—can cause a system fault (also known as the dreaded blue screen of death). Driver code contains a huge proportion of error-checking code. As much as 70 percent of the code in a driver only runs when encountering error conditions. Testing these error paths has traditionally been extremely difficult. Diligent developers will step through each of their error paths in the debugger, but a large number of error paths remain untested . . .

until someone—usually a customer working on something unbelievably important—reproduces just the right environment to trigger that error, crash his or her machine, and lose that work.

Testing devices is a huge challenge, one that has been addressed in the past (albeit somewhat inefficiently) via the brute-force method of a vast number of physical devices and large numbers of creative testers running manual tests. For many years, in fact, this was the only way to test a reasonable number of devices and configurations. At first glance (and at second or third glance for many), automating devices seems nearly impossible, but over time, an elegant solution appeared.

8.2 The Birth of Device Simulation Framework (DSF)

In late 2001, a Microsoft developer named Peter Shier first heard of the quandary faced by the Windows driver test team through his manager and thought it was an extremely intriguing (and challenging) problem. At this point, Peter had been a software developer for 16 years but had never thought much about the challenges of software testing. This particular challenge, however, was too fascinating and thought-provoking to pass up. Peter and other interested developers spent the next few weeks talking to the device driver test team in hopes of gaining a wider understanding of the problem space and the challenges of this area. They learned that the testing matrix was huge and continually growing! They learned that fault injection—the process of simulating errors in hardware in order to test error paths—was nearly impossible and that testers would never test most of the failure paths. Moreover, they learned that the testers had a huge amount of specific and valuable knowledge about testing devices that was difficult to quantify. For example, they knew exactly when unplugging a USB device was most likely to produce an error and what combinations of devices were most prone to expose unique problems.

The driver-testing problem space and Peter's experience in software development led him to the notion of creating simulations of hardware with software. If implemented correctly, the operating system would not be able to tell the difference between a simulated device and a real device, and this would enable execution and automation of testing scenarios never before possible. Peter also knew that for maximum effect he would want to take advantage of the domain knowledge of the test team. He decided that the simulation framework he was building should be easily programmable via common scripting languages such as VBScript and JavaScript. Many testers were already familiar with these scripting languages, which enabled them to easily transfer their domain knowledge to effective automated tests.

Good Point

Seek to use suitable languages for which there are plenty of skilled people available.

Finally, Peter knew he couldn't just build a framework and expect teams to use it. Outside of an executive mandate, the *Field of Dreams* "Build it and they will come" quote seldom works for software solutions. The Device Simulation Framework (DSF) had to be something compelling to anyone testing device drivers and something that would prove the value of DSF in terms of tester effectiveness and efficiency. In parallel with development of the framework, they built samples for USB controllers and devices. That sample ended up being the USB controller and USB device simulation kit that is now part of the Windows Driver Kit (WDK).[1]

8.3 Building the DSF

To simulate real hardware devices with software, DSF needed to redirect hardware access at the kernel level. To do this, the team would embed the core of the framework within the guts of the operating system. They soon identified a set of items that were common to all devices and began to build an extensible framework based on those items. They also separated the simulation of the *bus* and the *device* into two different simulators.

A device on the system *bus* has a direct hardware interface with its controlling device driver using input/output (I/O) ports, registers, direct memory access (DMA), and hardware interrupts. Examples of devices that have a direct hardware interface are controllers such as USB, 1394, SCSI, IDE, and CardBus. Devices on external buses are not controlled via a direct hardware interface. They connect externally to the system bus via a direct hardware interface device and are controlled by a higher-level driver that communicates to the device via the direct device's driver. Figure 8.1 shows an overview of the framework architecture.

Architecturally, it made sense to build a driver and simulation in parallel. A prototype device driver was in development at the time and made a logical candidate. Development of the simulator and the driver therefore was done at the same time, *before physical hardware was available*, based on the public specifications. When it

---

1. www.microsoft.com/whdc/devtools/wdk/default.mspx

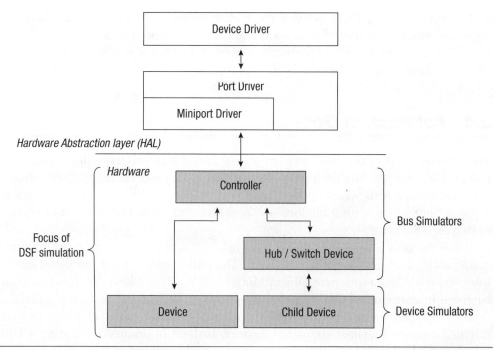

FIGURE 8.1 DSF architecture

was time to share the driver with the controller hardware manufacturer, the manufacturer was delighted and said it was the first time anyone had ever had such a high-quality driver so early in the hardware development. Rather than the waterfall of building a device, then writing a driver, then testing it, DSF enabled parallel development of the driver, test suite, and actual firmware.

Because of its relative simplicity, the earliest simulation target was a PS/2 keyboard (which also ended up as a key test vehicle for DSF itself). Because one of the key uses of DSF was to simulate devices that may not exist yet, the intent was to write the simulated device from the specification rather than based on any of the current driver implementations. While PS/2 seemed like a good choice, tracking down an actual specification for PS/2 was a bit of a challenge. After a good amount of searching for a software version of the specification, Peter eventually found a developer in Microsoft who had a hard copy of the PS/2 specification and went to work. His goal was to produce a simulated device based purely on the specification (this is how users of the DSF typically create their simulated devices). Although he did use the existing driver code as a reference, he soon discovered that if you write the simulation directly from the public specification, you get a different story than if you look at the driver code—it turns out that the PS/2 implementation in wide use today has some variations from the original specification. In the end, the in-use implementation wins, but the standard specification proved to be a valuable resource in this effort and helped prove the validity of the project and how it would be used.

8.4 Automation Goals

The primary goals of the DSF were to enable creation of programming models that imitated real life, to enable testers who primarily focused on manual scenarios to write automated tests when needed, and to allow them to document and automate some of the "device testing folklore" or "oral tradition" they had built up in years of testing experience.

Over the next few months, the framework began to come together, and the programmability features began to take form. The entry points of the simulated drivers were based on the Component Object Model (COM). This allowed testers to use any language that supported COM (including VBScript, JScript, or C#) to use simulated devices to rapidly create automated driver tests. Testers could now begin to write simple automation against simulated devices. Instead of manually inserting a USB cable from a keyboard into a computer, a tester could write something like:

```
Set DSF = CreateObject("DSF.DSF")
Set Kbd = CreateObject("SoftKbd.Kbd")
DSF.HotPlug "USB", Kbd
```

The scripting interface also became a quick way to explore unusual scenarios, for example, to discover what happens when multiple keyboards or other devices are connected and disconnected in arbitrary orders. Of course, when used to verify that every key press worked with a specific driver, a script-based approach was also a much more efficient use of time than paying a tester to press every key and key combination on the keyboard. Automation also helped with other unexciting testing tasks, such as opening and closing a cover on a scanner or unplugging a device during a storage transfer.

Good Point

Automation works well for things that are boring for people to do.

In addition to the more obvious goals of automation, such as basic functional testing or stress tests, simulators can expose objects that model the physical tests performed by many manual device testers today. For example, a manual test of a device may be to unplug the device in the middle of a particular operation. With DSF, this action can be automated—and repeated! DSF remains a framework in which non-programmers can learn to become script programmers because it allows them to learn a simple language and then to use a programming model that corresponds to the work they already know. For example, USB testers know how to create scenarios with various devices plugged into a hierarchy of hubs. The USB simulator could give the tester a scriptable object model that allows describing that scenario in words.

```
Set ExternalHub = CreateObject("USB.Hub")
RootHub.Ports(1).HotPlug ExternalHub
Set Mouse = CreateObject("USB.Mouse")
Mouse.ButtonCount = 3
ExternalHub.Ports(0).Connect Mouse
Mouse.RightClick
```

There were also some unique challenges in creating a simulation framework. For example, one of the challenges of simulating a peripheral component interconnect (PCI) controller is that it has a CPU doing work in parallel, but simulated devices had to run on the same CPU. The simulator had to juggle its workload so it *seems* like it's running in parallel. By partitioning the work, executing a piece of work, and then yielding control to the CPU, DSF could get quite close to *appearing* to run the PCI bus in parallel. It wasn't a perfect solution because it's always slightly behind parallel processing, but it was never so far behind that a driver or simulated device would know.

At this point, DSF was already in use in several teams in the Windows organization, and Peter began to share the framework with other Microsoft teams and with hardware vendors at external conferences.

8.5   Case Studies

This section describes a few test automation successes with DSF within Microsoft.

8.5.1   USB Firmware

From a USB perspective, infinite combinations of hardware topologies can potentially be tested. At any particular time, there can be up to 50 different flavors of

USB host controller firmware in use on consumer PCs and thousands of unique USB devices in wide use. The challenge of discovering issues with device and controller interaction without an automated solution is almost entirely hit or miss. The USB test team had previously tried a market share approach, but market changes over time made this tactic expensive and inefficient, but they discovered that *simulation* of a USB host controller through DSF worked well for their purposes.

The team had a list of several customer-reported bugs in the host controller driver, so they began to add fault injection and vendor-specific behaviors to the USB simulator to reproduce problems they were seeing in the field. This quickly grew into a regression library that has been increasingly valuable over time.

> **Tip**
>
> A way to build a regression test library is to start with bug fix tests.

Before creating this regression library, the team had no idea early on about how devices and simulators would interact (often, not until a Microsoft executive attempted to plug a new printer or scanner into a desktop computer). The Windows USB driver stack[2] also goes through a fair amount of churn to enable new functionality or to find opportunities to save on power usage. Changes like this usually work on the developer's machine but often also lead to several other people asking why their USB devices no longer work. The regression library enables the USB team to quickly and automatically evaluate the device impact of any change to the driver stack.

The USB team now has accurate simulations of the top six host controllers on the market and frequently conducts deeper analysis of controllers to make improvements and enhancements to the simulator. They also have a generic simulated controller that emulates properties of a variety of different host controllers. By emulating many of the quirks of different host controllers at once, the team can quickly create automated tests that "connect" a USB device of interest to a simulated controller and quickly discover any unintended interactions.

8.5.2   USB Storage

In a modern operating system, testing hardware manually is impractical and virtually impossible. The ability to automate hardware testing through simulated devices has

---

2. A driver stack is the hierarchy of device drivers used to enable a device. The USB driver stack, for example, includes a generic host controller driver, a "miniport" driver for the particular USB implementation, and a USB hub (or bus) driver.

great cost savings (far fewer devices to purchase) and allows for more complete testing in a reasonable amount of time. Without simulated devices, a storage test team could quickly spend tens of thousands of dollars on storage devices in an attempt to get wide coverage on a driver. With DSF, a single simulated device can cover nearly all of this testing. Plus, simulated devices don't get lost or broken, saving even more money in the long term.

USB storage devices include a variety of hard drives, optical disks, and flash drives. Before using DSF, testing these devices was almost entirely a manual process. Testers plugged in the devices, wrote files, read files, and removed the devices in a variety of sequences. Testing of a physical optical drive, for example, is a largely manual procedure. In one typical scenario, a tester needs to insert the disk, ensure that the disk is readable, and then eject the disk. Other common tests include unplugging the device during a read (conducted via the tester yanking the cable during the read operation). Simulated devices gave testers the opportunity to automate all of these tasks and enabled several other cost-saving scenarios (the least of which was replacement costs for broken cables).

The firmware of most computer DVD drives allows changing of the *region code*[3] up to five times, after which the latest region code becomes permanent. This means that you can test the boundary conditions of this scenario, testing whether lockout occurs correctly after five changes, exactly once per physical drive. With simulated drives, this testing scenario is simple to automate and extremely cost effective.

Simulators also enable more accurate performance scenarios, such as measuring the time it takes for a driver to load and unload when adding or removing a device. More importantly, it greatly reduces the number of cables and ports that go bad due to constant inserting and removing of a USB cable.

The team has recognized significant cost savings in other areas. The price of fiber channel storage devices and switches, for example, makes the cost of extensive testing of many real-world scenarios prohibitive. With simulation, however, this turns into an easily automatable and worthwhile test scenario.

The biggest success so far in the area of USB storage was the Windows 7 support for IEEE 1667, a protocol for authentication of secure storage devices. The protocol documentation was available long before actual devices were available, and although Microsoft announced that Windows 7 would support IEEE 1667 (aka Enhanced Storage), it was unclear if a significant number of physical devices would be available in time for testing before product launch. Without a single piece of hardware, however, the driver stack was fully tested. In parallel, as the protocol specification

---

3. The region code is a firmware implementation designed to prevent playing of media in a different country than it was produced or marketed in.

changed, updates were made to the simulated firmware. This enabled Microsoft to have a fully tested driver for hardware that didn't exist and to confidently ship that driver to millions of Windows customers.

8.5.3   Video Capture

Another challenging testing task is automating the testing of video capture. There are a huge number of video cameras in the market (and many more older cameras are used regularly but are no longer for sale). Furthermore, each of these cameras can implement any combination of hundreds of different features—but no camera implements every possible feature. Because it is cost-prohibitive to test every single physical camera, the traditional testing approach is to test cameras with high market share and top off that testing with cameras that implement the remainder of the possible feature set, keeping in mind that there may be *some* potential features not implemented in any camera shipping today.

While it is possible to simulate any real-world physical device with DSF, the simulated video capture device developed and used by the Windows video capture test team implemented *all* available USB video device features. This enabled easy automation and allowed the team to ship well-tested features that are not available on any currently shipping cameras. Code coverage increased by as much as 50 percent because code paths previously unreachable could now execute and be tested thoroughly. This enabled the discovery (and resolution) of new bugs, including several driver crashes in areas tested for the very first time.

> **Good Point**
>
> When automation enables tests of previously untested areas, new bugs may be found.

8.5.4   Other Applications of DSF

It's also possible to take advantage of DSF even if you don't write drivers. Hardware vendors can write a simulator to see how well their devices would work with the Microsoft class drivers before they burn any silicon. The typical approach in this situation is to use a field-programmable gate array (FPGA), but simulated devices are much faster and easier to modify.

Simulated devices also facilitate testing unique scenarios never before possible. For example, tests that randomly insert, use, and remove simulated devices for extended periods are a great stress test for driver subsystems. Simulation allows the creation of unknown devices or devices with multiple firmware issues that can ensure that the operating system handles these negative scenarios well. It's also possible to mimic user tasks that are not humanly possible, such as hundreds of plug and remove operations per second. Simulators and creativity enable a huge number of unique and effective tests that explore scenarios and functionality that are not possible via manual testing efforts.

8.6   No Silver Bullets

The DSF solves a big challenge in device testing, but it's not a replacement for all device testing. Many manual tests that require physical repetition may be good candidates for automation using a simulated framework, but replacement of some tests is not practical or possible via simulation. Electrical or timing issues with physical devices or end-to-end integration testing, for example, remain excellent candidates for human testing, which provides a degree of randomness that is difficult to achieve with simulators.

> **Good Point**
>
> Manual testing is better than automated testing for some tasks.

It's important to keep in mind that the framework is implemented in software and, as such, is subjected to the same issues that face any other software project. DSF has had its fair share of problems and issues over the years, but full support and quick responses from the framework authors have kept the framework popular and valuable at Microsoft.

Simulators enable earlier testing of device drivers and allow driver developers to practice test-driven development (TDD) if they choose by writing tests for device functionality that doesn't yet exist (but exists in the simulated firmware), and then writing the driver code to make the test pass. Finding a bug early is a common goal of any mature software team, and DSF enables many teams at Microsoft to achieve this goal.

8.7 Conclusion

DSF is continuing to gain popularity both inside and outside of Microsoft. Aditya Mathur, the department head of Computer Science at Purdue University, has used DSF as a teaching tool in his class on software testing. It's a straightforward, accessible way to walk students through drivers and help students learn how they work. Other companies use DSF to simulate a variety of devices to aid in product and driver development.

Within Microsoft, teams use simulated devices extensively. Use spans the Windows organization and beyond. Some examples include the bus simulators for PCI, USB 2.0, and USB 3.0, and device simulators for USB video, and infrared remotes. The solid design and extensibility of the framework is enabling usage of simulated devices in a wide variety of areas, often in areas not even thought of in the early days of DSF. The surface team uses DSF to simulate their multiple touch input, and the office communicator team uses DSF to simulate phone hardware. Teams at Microsoft continue to use DSF to increase the efficiency of their testing by enabling complex scenarios to be easily automatable. Teams at Microsoft using DSF are finding bugs sooner, many of which they may not have found using other testing methods. Through the use of fault injection and "fake" devices, testers continue to find bugs in areas where they never would have found them otherwise. More teams are using simulators for device testing and continue to see improvements in product quality and substantial cost savings.

8.8 Acknowledgments

Special thanks to Peter Shier, Rudy Opavsky, Bruce Campbell, Robbie Harris, and Art Trumble for taking the time to relate their experiences with the Device Simulation Framework.

CHAPTER 9

MODEL-BASED TEST-CASE GENERATION IN ESA PROJECTS

Stefan Mohacsi
Armin Beer

Stefan Mohacsi and Armin Beer describe their experience in using model-based testing (MBT) for the European Space Agency (ESA). Their team developed a test automation framework that took significant effort to set up but eventually was able to generate automated tests very quickly when the application changed. This chapter includes an excellent return-on-investment calculation applicable to other automation efforts (not just MBT). The team estimated break-even at four iterations/releases. The need for levels of abstraction in the testware architecture is well described. The application being tested was ESA's Multi-Mission User Information Services. The multinational team met the challenges of automation in a large, complex system with strict quality requirements (including maintainability and traceability) in a waterfall development—yes, it can work! If you are thinking of using MBT, you will find much useful advice in this chapter. A mixture of inhouse, commercial, and open source tools were used by the team. See Table 9.1.

9.1 Background for the Case Study

The members of the Atos Test Competence Center have many years of practical experience in testing large and safety-critical projects. In cooperation with Siemens

Table 9.1 Case Study Characteristics

Characteristics	This Case Study
Application domain	European Space Agency earth observation services
Application size	>500,000 LOC
Location	Vienna, Austria; Frascati, Italy; Darmstadt, Germany
Lifecycle	Traditional
Number on the project	>100 working for various contractors of ESA
Number of testers	5
Number of automators	3
Time span	Test automation for SCOS-2000 started in 2004, for MMUS in 2008; both projects are still ongoing.
Dates	2004 onward
Tool type(s)	Inhouse, commercial, open source
Pilot study undertaken	No
ROI measured	Yes, projected payback after 4 cycles
Successful?	Yes
Still breathing?	Yes

Space Business, they created a test automation framework for the European Space Agency (ESA) that has been successfully applied in a number of projects.

Key areas of our experience include:

- State-of-the art processes, technologies, and methods for testing complex systems.
- Automated testing technologies and tools—commercial, open source, and inhouse.
- Process improvement projects in software testing.
- Research software testing techniques in cooperation with universities.

In this case study, the application of model-based testing (MBT) and a test-case generator (TCG) in projects of the European Space Agency (ESA) is presented. This chapter has four main sections. Firstly, we examine MBT and TCG and their application in software development. The next section describes the nature of the project, the challenges, and the applied framework. This is followed by an outline of the experience and lessons learned after the application of the framework in ESA projects. The final section presents a summary and brief outline of future plans in the areas of MBT and TCG.

9.2   Model-Based Testing and Test-Case Generation

In our experience of developing complex systems, test cases are mainly created manually and are based on experience rather than systematic methods. As a consequence, many redundant test cases exist and many aspects of an application remain untested. Often, the effort for the implementation and maintenance of these test cases is higher than expected, and test completion criteria are too coarse. MBT and TCG helped us to improve the quality of the system specification and its associated test cases and made it possible to complete the project on time and within budget.

Issues to be solved in this area are as follows:

- Which kind of model notation can be used as a basis for deriving test cases?
- Many specifications using popular notations like Unified Modeling Language (UML) are not formal enough for automatically generating complete test cases because a lot of information is contained in plain text annotations. While UML can be extended to achieve the required level of formality, this approach typically aims at code generation rather than test generation and involves considerable complexity and effort.
- Formal models like finite-state machines are often very large and difficult to apply.
- A trade-off between formalization and practical suitability needs to be found.
- Which modeling and test-case-generation frameworks are available, and how useable are they?
- How efficient is test automation in terms of reducing test costs, and how effective is it in assuring high product quality?
- How effective are the test cases in detecting defects?

As depicted in Figure 9.1, the requirements are the source for the construction of both the system and the test models. The two models have to be separate because no deviations would be detected if both the code and the test cases were generated from the same model.

The test model's required level of detail depends on the requirements of the TCG and the planned types of test (e.g., functional or randomized tests). This approach guarantees the traceability from the requirements to the test cases, which is a prerequisite for an objective assessment of the test coverage and the product quality.

9.2.1 Model-Based Testing with IDATG

MBT and TCG are implemented by the tool IDATG (Integrating Design and Automated Test-Case Generation). IDATG has been developed since 1997 by the Siemens Support Center Test (now Atos) in the scope of a research project in cooperation with universities and the Softnet Austria Competence Network. Over the years, the functionality has continuously been expanded and the tool has been applied in numerous internal and external projects. Today, IDATG is a commercial tool also known as TEMPPO Designer and closely integrated with the Atos test management tool TEMPPO Test Manager.

IDATG consists of a set of visual editors for MBT specification and a powerful TCG that produces complete test scripts for various tools. Within the IDATG notation, we can distinguish different layers of abstraction that significantly increase the maintainability of the tests. The workflow for IDATG is shown in Figure 9.2.

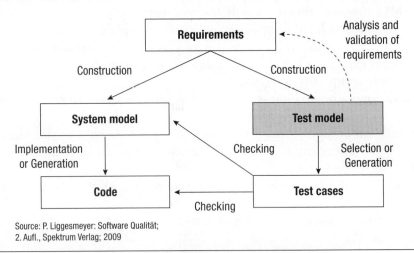

Source: P. Liggesmeyer: Software Qualität;
2. Aufl., Spektrum Verlag; 2009

FIGURE 9.1 Construction of a test model and generation of test cases

The IDATG Methodology

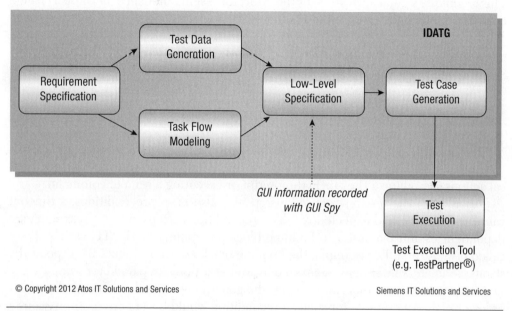

FIGURE 9.2   Workflow for using IDATG

9.2.1.1   *Task Flow Models in IDATG*

In IDATG, the following types of objects are organized in a hierarchical tree:

- Use case tasks that represent typical use scenarios or any other test scenarios that might be of interest.
- Building blocks that represent frequently used sequences of test steps and can be used as parts of a use case task. Similar to functions in a programming language, building blocks can be parameterized. Furthermore, building blocks may comprise other building blocks.

The *task flow model* of a task or building block is a directed graph that shows the associated sequence of steps. If there is more than one possible way to fulfill a task, the graph has multiple paths.

The steps of a task flow model may either represent *atomic actions* or refer to a *building block* that is itself composed of several steps.

In this way, it is possible to define a complex task as a sequence of simpler ones. This technique significantly reduces the effort for test maintenance, because a change only affects one building block instead of every single test case.

> **Good Point**
>
> Well-structured testware has layers of abstraction to keep different types of change restricted to as few elements as possible.

For example, for GUI testing, an atomic action can be the user input applied to a GUI object (clicking a button, entering text into a field). For non-GUI testing, typical actions are calling a shell or Python script or executing a remote command.

Apart from the test instruction, a step may also have preconditions, a timeout value, a criticality, and expected results. Preconditions are used to express semantic dependencies and may refer to building block parameters or IDATG variables (so-called designators). For example, the building block `Login` in Figure 9.3 expects the string parameters `User` and `Password` as well as a Boolean parameter `Anonymous`. Depending on the value of `Anonymous`, the generation algorithm chooses the upper or lower path. An example for such a precondition would be `(#Login:Anonymous#` `= FALSE) AND (#Login:User# != "")`.

It is also important to define the effects of each step. For instance, the value of a variable may change and thus affect the precondition of a subsequent step. For example, after the Login block, there might be a step with a precondition `#UserRole#` `= "Admin"`. In this case, it is necessary to specify to which value the variable `#UserRole#` is set in the `Login` block.

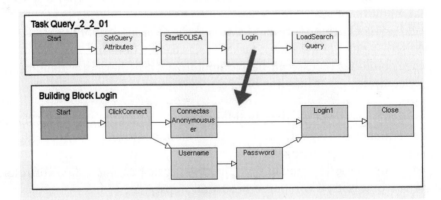

FIGURE 9.3 IDATG task flow (example)

Before the GUI is available, the task flows can already be modeled, with the assignment of the GUI objects at a later stage. As soon as a GUI prototype is available, the GUI layout, including the properties of all GUI objects, is recorded with the built-in IDATG GUI Spy directly from the screen. The steps of the task flows can then be assigned to specific GUI objects simply by pointing at the recorded screenshot. IDATG also offers a semiautomated auxiliary function for reassigning the steps after changes.

9.2.1.2 *Test Data Generation*

Apart from test sequences that can be expressed with a graph, it is also important to define the input data that should be used for the tests. Because it is usually impossible to test a component with every possible input combination, various methods are used to reduce the number of test inputs while still revealing a high number of program defects. IDATG provides a number of powerful features for creating this input data as well as expected results and for including it in the task flows. One example is the CECIL (cause-effect coverage incorporating linear boundaries) method, a powerful combination of the cause and effect, multidimensional equivalence class, and boundary value methods.

9.2.1.3 *Test Case Generation*

IDATG generates valid test cases based on the task flows and semantic conditions defined by the user. The test cases include the expected results and steps to check them against the actual results. The user can adjust the test depth by choosing between several coverage criteria (e.g., coverage of all steps, connections, data). Once a set of test cases is generated, it can be exported in various formats, such as XML; scripts for QuickTest Professional (QTP), TestPartner, SilkTest, or WinRunner; or as plain text. The produced test scripts do not require any manual processing but are immediately executable.

9.3 Our Application: ESA Multi-Mission User Services

ESA's Multi-Mission User Services (MMUS) infrastructure provides services for earth observation (EO) users for satellite planning, cataloging, and ordering of EO products. Supported services include user and project management, product catalog search and ordering, mission planning, online information, and documentation services. Various interfaces are available to the user, such as a Java standalone application (see Figure 9.4) and a web interface.

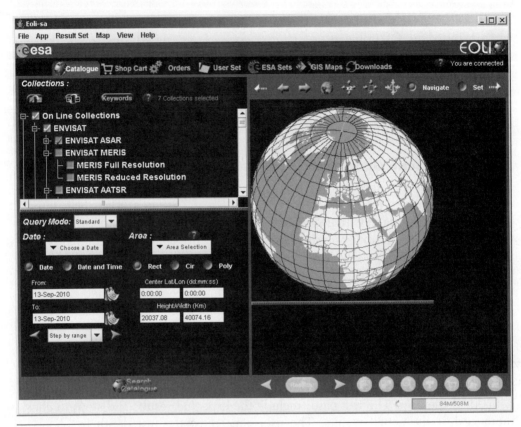

FIGURE 9.4   GUI of Multi-Mission User Services

Apart from the development and maintenance of the operational system, an important activity is the assembly, integration, and operational validation (AIV) of MMUS for major software versions ("evolutions"). The main tasks of the AIV team are:

- Setup and maintenance of an offsite integration and validation environment that is representative of the operational target environment.
- Installation and configuration of the MMUS applications in the AIV environment.
- Creation and maintenance of test specifications.
- Integration testing and system testing of software deliveries, changes, and related documentation.

- The responsibility of the AIV activities has been outsourced to Siemens. An objective of ESA was that the services should improve over time in order to continue to satisfy existing and new requirements. The analysis of key performance indicators (KPIs) and the technology evolution in the marketplace had to be taken into account. Innovation and use of advanced technologies, particularly for test automation, were major issues. An explicit goal of ESA was to reach a test automation level of at least 75 percent, meaning that 75 percent of all test steps had to be executed by an automation tool. In this project, a number of test steps, for example, editing database entries on a distant system, must be done manually.

9.3.1   Testing Approach for MMUS

A number of challenges were encountered in testing the MMUS applications:

- High complexity of the distributed MMUS system.
- Reducing the effort for test maintenance and regression testing.
- Poor testability—many GUI objects could not be properly identified by automated test tools.
- Lack of experience with virtualization required for the setup and maintenance of multiple test systems with different configurations.

9.3.1.1   Key Strategies

The following list gives the key strategies that were adopted to meet the challenges:

- Early involvement of the AIV team in document reviews to ensure early detection of requirement and design defects.
- Systematic test case design and generation using the model-based IDATG approach to guarantee an adequate level of test coverage and reduce the effort for test maintenance.
- Good cooperation with the developers resolved the testability issues. Following a clear naming convention, a unique ID was assigned to each GUI object by the developers.

Good Point

Developer cooperation is needed to build in automatability and testability.

- Strict test entry and exit criteria. An efficient integration test can take place only if the components have reached a certain quality level. For instance, a quick incoming inspection of the most important functions ("smoke test") was introduced, and one of the test entry criteria was "No 'critical' or 'blocking' defects are discovered during the smoke test." Likewise, the test of the completed system is only possible if the integration has been successful. An example for a test exit criteria is "All test cases with priority 'high' or 'medium' have been executed with result 'passed.'"
- Compliance with International Software Testing Qualifications Board (ISTQB) standard terminology (e.g., to avoid using the same terms with different meanings).

9.3.1.2 *Test Framework*

The software environment for the test activities consists of a set of powerful yet affordable tools. It is the result of testing experience in numerous projects at ESA, such as automated regression testing for the Spacecraft Operating System (SCOS)-2000 (see Mohacsi 2005 and 2006) as well as in the telecommunications, railway, insurance, and banking domains. All of these were complex projects where distributed teams worked together to deliver multiple releases of software systems to their clients. Figure 9.5 gives an overview of the AIV environment.

- For the crucial task of storing mission data and test management information, the commercial tool TEMPPO Test Manager (http://at.atos.net/temppo) is used. It is not only used for ESA projects but applied in a wide range of domains, such as automotive, health care, and the public sector. Its flexibility and adaptability to new missions is a valuable advantage.
- The main component for designing the test model and generating test cases is IDATG. From the abstract model defined in IDATG, the tool produces scripts both for GUI testing and for testing over other interfaces.
- For GUI testing, *MicroFocus TestPartner* is used. Test scripts are generated by IDATG and imported automatically into the TestPartner database.
- In the course of ESA's SCOS-2000 project, we recognized the need for a generic test execution tool that can perform tests over arbitrary interfaces (e.g., Common Object Request Broker Architecture [CORBA], TCP/IP). Because no such solution was available, Siemens developed the tool *Test Commander*, which receives test scripts generated by IDATG and executes them by sending commands over a set of test drivers and checking the results. The tool has a simple user interface, is written in Tool Command Language and employs the GUI toolkit (a combination called Tcl/Tk), and is therefore completely

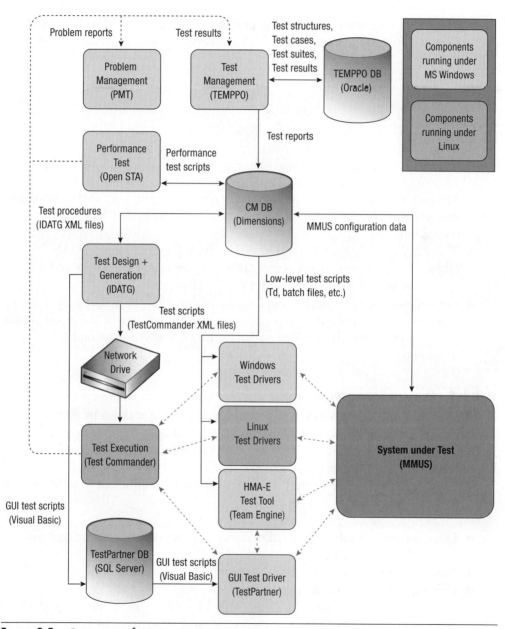

FIGURE 9.5   Overview of AIV environment

platform independent. About one person-year was spent on its development. Because the tool belongs to ESA and it is very easy to plug in new test drivers, the tool could easily be adjusted and reused for the test of MMUS.

> **Tip**
>
> Implement levels of abstraction by making reusable elements that are as generic as possible.

- The only system-specific parts are the *test drivers* required by Test Commander and *stubs or simulators* to replace parts of the system that have not yet been integrated.
- The ESA-specific tool *Team Engine* is used for generating SOAP (Simple Object Access Protocol) messages. The tool can either be used standalone or run automatically via its web GUI using TestPartner.
- For performance testing, finding an affordable tool is particularly hard. In our experience from previous projects, a reasonable solution is the open source tool *OpenSTA*, which provides sufficient functionality for an end-to-end performance test.

9.3.1.3 Typical Test Scenario

One of the core functions of MMUS is the search for images taken by EO satellites. The user not only can search the catalog for existing images but also may issue queries for "potential" ones (i.e., images that could be taken in the future when a satellite passes over a certain area).

The main challenge for testing has been the huge number of possible search options:

- Large number of satellites, most of them carrying various sensors that support different image modes
- Date and time parameters (both for past and future)
- Geographical parameters (search area)
- Satellite and sensor-specific parameters like orbit, track, swath, and cloud coverage

To handle this complexity, our goal was to model the basic test sequence to be as flexible and maintainable as possible. The general scenario of a catalog search test case is shown in Figure 9.6.

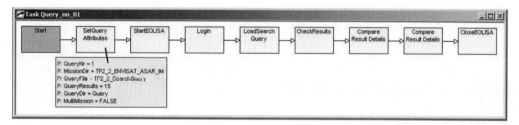

FIGURE 9.6   Test scenario catalog search

The block `SetQueryAttributes` is used to define the parameters of the test case. These include the directories and files for the test data, the number of expected query results, and a Boolean attribute indicating whether the query covers more than one mission. A previously prepared query file containing the search options is loaded from the path specified by the test case's parameters. From the set of query results, some representative items are checked in more detail, including an image comparison. The block `CompareResultDetails` appears once for each compared item and receives the index of the item as a parameter. In our example, we are comparing two items.

During the generation, the blocks are expanded and replaced by atomic steps. The average length of a completed catalog search test case is about 120 steps. The basic scenario can be reused with different parameters very easily:

- Create a copy of the scenario.
- Change the parameters of the first step and the `CompareResultDetails` blocks.
- Prepare the query file and the expected results (reference data).

In this way, a large number of test cases could be created in a very short time. In case of changes to the system (e.g., different login process), only a building block had to be adapted for generating a complete set of updated automation scripts. The same approach was used for other test scenarios, such as the ordering of high-resolution satellite images.

Good Point

Use a standard template to add additional automated scenarios with minimum effort.

9.4   Experience and Lessons Learned

The experience of using MBT has been very positive. In this section, we describe the benefits achieved and the return on investment (ROI) calculations for MBT, as well as some problems and lessons learned.

9.4.1   Benefits

The benefits of this solution have been the following:

- Implementing MBT with reusable building blocks significantly improves the maintainability (details can be found in Section 9.2.1.1).
- Traceability of requirements throughout all test-related documents (test model, test cases, test reports, defect reports) allows an objective assessment of the test coverage and the product quality. If neglected, important aspects of the system could remain untested.
- High defect detection potential of advanced TDG methods like CECIL. A number of case studies have shown that by applying the CECIL method, up to 30 percent more defects can be detected than with ordinary cause–effect analysis.
- Gaps and defects in the system model are discovered at an early stage because of the early involvement of the test team in reviews and the creation of a formalized test model.

9.4.2   ROI of Model-Based Testing

In this section, we focus on the ROI activities for test case creation, maintenance, and execution and compare the necessary efforts for a manual versus a model-based approach. Our study covers a basic set of 180 test cases for the catalog search and ordering scenarios. The total number of test cases created for MMUS was much larger. The values for the manual approach are based on experiences from testing previous MMUS versions and have been extrapolated accordingly.

> **Tip**
>
> Calculating ROI is important to do but doesn't have to be exact or complete to be useful and valid.

9.4.2.1 Test Creation

In the context of the MMUS project, the aim of test case creation was to achieve 100 percent requirements coverage and to include all satellites and sensors in the tests.

The textual description of a *manual* test case in a document, including the preparation of appropriate test data, took about 1 hour. The basic test set consisted of 180 test cases, so *180 hours* are required.

On the other hand, the creation of a *test model*, including building blocks, variables, conditions, and so on, took about 2 weeks (80 hours) for each of the two main scenarios. However, once a scenario exists, it can easily be copied and reused with different parameters (1 hour per test case, including test data preparation). Thus, the overall effort for the creation of the test model was 2 × 80 hours + 180 × 1 hour = *340 hours*.

Note that there were more usage scenarios than these, but we decided to start the automation with the two most important and promising ones.

Good Point

It is important to start with a limited set of tests but ones that will give real value when automated.

9.4.2.2 Preparation of the Test Automation Framework

Apart from the test case creation, several additional activities were required for automating the tests:

- Acquisition, installation, and configuration of test tools: *60 hours*
- Tool training for testers: *40 hours*
- Testability analysis of the user interface, solving testability problems: *200 hours*
- Obtaining all necessary information required to create a detailed test model: *160 hours*

All in all, about *460 hours* were required to prepare the test automation framework.

9.4.2.3 Test Execution

The average time required for executing a test case manually is about 45 minutes, most of which is dedicated to checking details of the actual results against the expected ones. In each test case, about 100 individual data checks have to be performed.

The total *manual* execution time of a complete test cycle is 45 minutes × 180 test cases = 8100 minutes = *135 hours*.

Automated execution with TestPartner is much faster, because checking the data is a matter of a few seconds. Even if we take into account that sometimes the test execution is halted by unforeseen events and has to be repeated, the average execution time does not exceed 4 minutes for any one test case.

The total *automated* execution time of a complete test cycle is 4 minutes × 180 test cases = 720 minutes = *12 hours*.

9.4.2.4 *Test Maintenance*

Maintaining textual test case descriptions can become quite tedious because changes of the system under test often affect a huge number of test cases. This is particularly difficult if the semantics have been changed and make it necessary to adapt the sequence of the test steps. On average, about 15 minutes are required per test case for maintenance before each test cycle.

The total *manual* maintenance time of a complete test cycle is 15 minutes × 180 test cases = 2700 minutes = *45 hours*.

While the maintenance of automated test scripts for a capture/replay tool can be a nightmare, the maintenance of an efficiently designed *test model* is far easier. Instead of having to adapt every single test case, only a few details of the model have to be changed. Subsequently, all test cases are generated afresh from the updated model. The whole process takes no longer than *5 hours*.

9.4.2.5 *Overall Effort*

The overall *manual* test effort can be calculated as follows:

Creation + Execution + Maintenance = 180 hours + (135 hours × number of test cycles) + [45 hours × (number of test cycles − 1)]

(Note that maintenance is only required on the second and subsequent test cycles.) Likewise, the overall test effort for *MBT* automation is:

Creation + Automation + Execution + Maintenance = 340 hours + 460 hours + (12 hours × number of test cycles) + [5 hours × (number of test cycles − 1)]

For the first test cycle, we get 315 hours for the manual approach and 812 hours for the model-based one. After about four test cycles, we reach the breakeven point of ROI with 855 hours versus 863 hours. In the course of the project, the difference becomes increasingly significant: The effort for 20 test repetitions reaches 3,735 hours versus 1,135 hours. This is summarized in Table 9.2 and Figure 9.7.

9.4.3 Problems and Lessons Learned

No matter how good an approach is, problems are encountered and lessons are learned along the way. These are some of the things we learned through our experience.

- Creating a test model requires detailed design documents. However, such documents often do not provide the required level of detail. Involvement of the test team in early reviews can help to mitigate this problem.
- Testability issues should be considered at an early stage. All test objects have to provide appropriate interfaces that allow automated test tools to identify them, send commands, and verify the results. "Design for Test" is already state-of-the-art in hardware development but very often neglected in the software domain.
- The creation of the test model requires considerable effort. If only a few test repetitions are planned, MBT might not pay off. On the other hand, MBT can significantly reduce the effort for each new test repetition. Therefore, it has to be calculated for each project when and if the ROI can be reached.

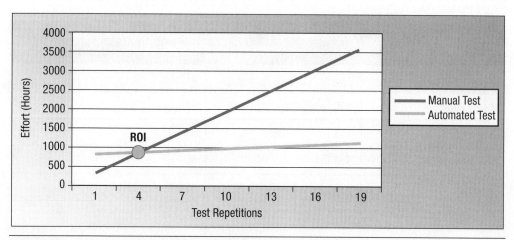

FIGURE 9.7   ROI of model-based test automation

Table 9.2   ROI Calculation

Activity	Manual Hours	Model-Based/Automated Hours
Test creation	180 test cases @ 1 hr: 180 hr	Creation of 2 scenarios @ 80 hr: 160 hr 180 test cases @ 1 hr: 180 hr
	Manual test creation total: 180 hr	Automated test creation total: 340 hr
Preparation of framework	N/A	Acquisition and installation of tools: 60 hr Tool training: 40 hr Testability analysis and improvement: 200 hr Obtaining information for test model: 160 hr
		Framework preparation (automation) total: 460 hr
Test execution (per cycle)	180 test cases @ 45 min: 135 hr	180 test cases @ 4 min: 12 hr
Test maintenance (per cycle)	180 test cases @ 15 min: 45 hr	2 scenarios @ 2.5 hr: 5 hr
Total Effort	**Manual Hours**	**Model-Based/Automated Hours**
1 test cycle	315 hr	812 hr
2 test cycles	495 hr	829 hr
3 test cycles	675 hr	846 hr
4 test cycles	855 hr	863 hr
5 test cycles	1035 hr	888 hr
10 test cycles	1935 hr	965 hr
20 test cycles	3735 hr	1,135 hr

- The creation of the test model requires advanced skills and should be done only by experienced test analysts. We strongly discourage any expectations that MBT or test automation could be efficiently performed by nontechnical staff or end users.

> **Good Point**
>
> MBT, like other technologies, can give great benefits, but only if the conditions are appropriate for its use.

9.5 Conclusion

In this section, we summarize our experience and give an idea of where we will be going in the future.

9.5.1 Summary

MBT and TCG can play an important role when it comes to improving defect detection and reducing quality costs. The prerequisites for the application of MBT are detailed requirements and skilled test case designers.

Experience from ESA projects has shown that the IDATG method is a useful approach for model-based test design. The building-block concept and the separation of sequences and data in the IDATG model help to reduce test maintenance costs significantly.

The automation framework presented here also incorporates tools for test management and defect tracking in order to allow traceability from the requirements to the test model, test cases, and defect reports. The framework is suited for testing complex applications such as MMUS and facilitates testing in the maintenance phase significantly. The efficiency of MBT and TCG is manifested by an ROI after four test cycles in the case of the MMUS project.

9.5.2 Outlook

9.5.2.1 Random Test Generation

In terms of the outlook for the future, the IDATG method presented in this chapter covers the functional test of typical use scenarios. However, reliability testing is also an important issue in respect to the development of dependable systems. To further enhance the IDATG approach, random testing has recently been added. In our experience, random testing should not be used as a substitute for systematic testing but rather as an important supplement that is likely to discover defects that are hard to detect by other methods.

When building blocks are used as a starting point, the new method creates randomly chosen paths through and between these building blocks while still observing the semantic dependencies. In a first step, each building block is converted into an extended finite-state machine (EFSM). Then, transitions are added between all the EFSMs. Guard conditions are automatically determined from the required state of the GUI elements in the start steps of the corresponding blocks. For creating randomized test cases (or "random walks"), these sequences are used rather than completely random inputs. The conditions for these steps are checked during TCG. The generation algorithm uses a hybrid approach combining a simple depth-first search strategy with refined constraint-satisfaction mechanisms. First results indicate that this hybrid approach seems to be a reasonable trade-off between good test coverage and acceptable generation times. A working prototype has already been completed and evaluated in the course of a pilot project (see Mohacsi 2010).

9.5.2.2 Latest News

To better support the user workflow and to avoid duplication of effort, IDATG was recently integrated into the test management framework TEMPPO. Accordingly, IDATG will henceforth be known as "TEMPPO Designer."

Siemens IT Solutions and Services and Atos Origin merged in July 2011 to become Atos. The rights to the TEMPPO tool suite, including IDATG, are also owned by Atos. Information about the test services of our new company can be found at http://atos.net/en-us/solutions/business_integration_solutions/test-and-acceptance-management/default.htm.

9.6   References

Beer, Armin, and Stefan Mohacsi. (2008). "Efficient Test Data Generation for Variables with Complex Dependencies." IEEE ICST 2008, in Lillehamer, Norway.

ESA Earth Observation Link. (no date). Available at http://earth.esa.int/EOLi/EOLi.html.

Fraser, G., B. Peischl, and F. Wotawa. (2007). "A Formal Model for IDATG Task Flows." SNA-TR-2007-P2-03.

IDATG and TEMPPO homepage. Available at http://at.atos.net/temppo.

Mohacsi, Stefan. (2005). "A Unified Framework for API and GUI Test Automation." *Proceedings of the 6th ICSTEST*, Düsseldorf, Germany.

Mohacsi, Stefan. (2003). "Minimizing Test Maintenance Costs through Test Case Generation." *Proceedings of the 4th ICSTEST*, Köln, Germany.

Mohacsi, Stefan. (2006). "Test Automation in Space Projects." *Proceedings of the 5th QA&Test*, Bilbao, Spain.

Mohacsi, Stefan, and Johannes Wallner. (2010). "A Hybrid Approach for Model-based Random Testing." *Proceedings of the 2nd International Conference on Advances in System Testing and Validation Lifecycle*, Nice, France.

Softnet Austria Competence Network homepage. Available at www.soft-net.at/.

9.7 Acknowledgments

The authors want to thank their partners at ESA, in particular Andrea Baldi and Eduardo Gomez, for the excellent cooperation and the opportunity to work in this fascinating domain.

TEN YEARS ON AND STILL GOING

Simon Mills

Simon Mills updates his case study from our previous book, *Software Test Automation* (Addison-Wesley, 1999). Still automating 10 years on is a significant achievement! The original story is included in full and contains excellent lessons and ideas. The success and continued growth of this automation is a testament to the sound foundation on which it was built more than a decade ago. The case study describes many lessons learned the hard way and some amusing observations on Simon and his team's first automation attempts. Their automation architecture separated their tests from the specific tools they were using—a wise move as was proved later. They devised a reliable way to document their tests that has stood the test of time. This story takes place in the United Kingdom, uses commercial tools, and covers about 15 years. See Table 10.1.

10.1 Background for the Case Study: "Before"

This story was first written and published in 1999's *Software Test Automation* and was based on our experience to that date. However, our journey has continued, and we describe "what happened next" later in this chapter, which represents a 17-year journey altogether.

Ingenuity, the testing practice, was born with the specific intention of providing business and risk management focused, independent testing with a bias toward using robust and reliable automated testing methods. Our main target then was the insurance industry, which was placing an increasing reliance on electronic trading, a trend that continues.

Table 10.1 Case Study Characteristics

Classification	This Case Study
Application domain	Insurance
Application size	Multiple applications (roughly 20)
Location	United Kingdom
Lifecycle	Chaotic and variable; some testers impose a recursive V model experience in problem resolution
Number on the project	Scores
Number of testers	Between 2 and 14
Number of automators	2
Time span	~17 years
Dates	1994–1999 for original story, updated to 2011
Tool type(s)	Commercial
Pilot study undertaken	No, but began small scale
ROI measured	No, but now running 5 million tests per month
Successful?	Yes
Still breathing?	Yes, and the client base is still growing every week

Because the following text was created at a point in the evolution of what has become a successful business, it seems best to leave the original text virtually unchanged, as a reflection of the "early days" of a technical evolution. After all, we all start somewhere, based on beliefs and experience to date, and then, inevitably, refine our thoughts and processes based on experience. At the time the chapter was first written, the processes were already standing up to rigorous use and did form the basis of a growing business.

Here's how it all started.

10.2   Insurance Quotation Systems Tested Automatically Every Month

© Copyright Simon Mills, 1999

This case study deals with a test automation project, from the reasons for its inception, through some of the critical milestones to the present day, some 4 years after its beginnings.

10.2.1   Background: The UK Insurance Industry

In the UK there are many ways by which individuals and businesses can obtain various types of insurance, so that on paying an annual premium they may have financial support in the time of a disaster. In the case of motor insurance, there is a legal requirement to have some form of recognized insurance.

The most common way in which insurance is obtained is by an individual approaching an insurance broker, or agent, who will offer them a selection of insurance "products" from different insurance companies. The job of the insurance broker or agent is to locate the most competitively priced premium for the client. The broker collects many details about them and about the situation they wish to insure (e.g. home, business, motor car, boat etc.), to search for appropriate alternatives. All brokers have access to the products of hundreds of insurers, who themselves often offer many different insurance products. All insurers have varying "underwriting cultures", meaning that they will accept certain kinds of risk in preference to others. Certain insurers will offer products to attract various target groups, such as lady drivers.

Insurers maintain very accurate records about what is more likely to result in a claim. This may be certain types of vehicle, parts of the country, age groups and many other factors. It is based around these details, as collected by a broker, that any given insurer will have a view towards a risk. It is critical to the insurers that their requirements are adhered to in order to minimize their risk.

During the 1980s a number of PC-based quotation systems became available that made the selection of competitive and appropriate insurance products much easier for the brokers. There are approximately 20 such systems in the UK covering personal lines of insurance. These systems were written by third party software providers who were entirely independent of the insurance companies.

Having input all of the details into whatever system the broker is using, a series of quotations are presented. For the insurance product selected, the broker will have a series of proposal forms and other documents (specific to that product) which are then completed by the individual. The broker collects a premium and the individual is then insured. The broker then sends the proposal to the selected insurance company.

In the past, this final step was done on paper. However, in the mid-1990s, the quotation systems enabled the proposals to be sent electronically over a wide area "value added" network, using Electronic Data Interchange (EDI).

Up to this point in time, insurance companies had taken little or no notice of the quotation systems, but the emergence of EDI technology presented a whole new arena for selling products, and one where administrative effort was minimized. The major insurance companies, of which there were eight to ten at the time, all joined the race to have quoted products being transacted by this new EDI technology.

As time progressed, these quotation systems became more regularly used. For example, one system grew from being used by tens of brokers to having nearly 2,000 users. At the same time, the number of products and insurers being represented on the quotation systems was increasing, from 78 to 298 in 5 years for one quotation system. Certain insurers have seen their annual premium income from this source grow from less than 1 percent to upwards of 25 percent of their annual new motor insurance business; that is nearly 10,000 new motor policies per month! This electronic trading rapidly became a business force to be reckoned with.

Unfortunately, when the amount of business presented was small, the insurers had taken little or no notice as to the quality of all of the decisions being taken on their behalf. All of a sudden, they had a large job on their hands to bring the quality under control.

This change in technology had a significant effect on the insurance business. One particular insurance company decided to use "text book" system testing as the necessary discipline to progress the business in this new area. This is the story of that company and our involvement with them. There were many testing issues as well as automation issues that needed to be addressed in order to meet this new challenge.

10.2.2 The Brief, Or How I Became Involved

The first meeting was between the tester (me) and representatives from a major UK insurance company: one from the marketing department and several business managers. This company had a number of products for motor insurance that were accessed by a dozen or so quotation systems and used by thousands of insurance brokers.

The marketing representative explained that the company wished to improve the volume of sales generated through the quotation systems. In order to do this, they would have to provide lower rates, better discounts and, by far the most important, a "Guarantee". The guarantee would be the marketing equivalent of the Holy Grail; every premium quoted would be stood by, even if in error.

This idea was not well received by the business managers, who were insurance underwriters. It was only the business managers who could authorize this "Holy Grail", since they were responsible for all costs and discounts, and ultimately for ensuring that the company remained in profit.

However, the experience of the business managers with the quotation systems was almost entirely negative. Of course, they had only ever been involved in the erroneous quotations that had been accepted by a client, generally because they were priced well below any one else in the market, and often with business unacceptable to the company at any price. Their assessment of the quotation systems was therefore highly subjective and mostly expressed in non-technical and unprintable forms of words.

Enter the tester, on the invitation of the marketing department, an unusual association in itself. The "marketers" thought that the subjective assertions of the business managers could be turned into measured assessments from which reasoned judgments could be made, based on an objective view of the quotation systems as a whole. This would involve extensive testing of the quotation systems using this company's insurance products. Specialist testers were required, because previous attempts to test thoroughly had failed due to the sheer volume of the testing required.

It was agreed that we would design tests, execute them, devise strategies for correction of problems, and re-test after they had been fixed. Most importantly, we would produce a way of presenting the findings to the business managers, hoping one day to sway their opinions.

10.2.3 Why Automation?

The reason to embark upon an automated approach from the outset was influenced by two basic factors. Although there were only two different products to test, they were represented across approximately 15 different quotation systems and were updated at least every month. There were known difficulties in the past, which had arisen following monthly releases, even when the insurer had not requested any changes to how their product should work.

It was quite obvious that we would be required to test each system every month for quite some time, during which we would hope to track the fixes we had suggested and prove that matters were becoming no worse. Our first job was to establish that the systems were performing correctly; then we could build the monthly regression tests.

10.2.4 Our Testing Strategy

Clearly, we could not test all of the quotation systems straight away, so we chose to concentrate upon one system, as a model. We would then work our way through the other systems after we had confidence that our test plan was good. We started with the system producing the most business, the one that was used by the majority of insurance brokers.

Good Point

Start small by focusing on a single but important part of the system.

We knew that we were going to have to set up a series of "test quotes" based upon the underwriting rules for each insurance product and apply them to the system under test, as if they were real input. These tests would have to reflect the many rules that are applied by underwriters when they determine whether or not to accept a particular risk and when they do, what they will charge for an annual premium.

The two products we were to test were quite different from one another but were to be treated in exactly the same way by each quotation system. So, our test strategy became "insurance product based".

Before commencing serious work on the first system, we had to know something about how the various other systems behaved, as our test strategy was going to involve us in setting up a number of test conditions that would have to be applied to each system. Could this be done?

Good Point

Don't lose sight of the bigger picture even though you are focused on one part of the system.

There was not a lot on our side. The systems all looked different, ran on a variety of PC Platforms (DOS, UNIX, XENIX, TRIPOS etc.), and asked 50 to 100 or so questions in different ways. At least the questions were roughly the same!

The answers, on the other hand, had to be delivered in a variety of differing ways. Name and address were no problem; after all there are only so many ways of expressing them. However, other issues were less straight-forward. For example, there are three types of motor insurance cover to chose from: "Comprehensive", "Third Party Fire & Theft" or "Third Party Only". If the test demands that "Third Party Only" is to be selected, in one system the users select "item 3" on a drop-down list, in another they would enter "O Enter", and in yet another "TPO Enter" and so on. We were looking at interesting times ahead.

These various questions have two fundamental results for a given insurer's product, when they are input to a quotation system.

1. Placement in one of 20 areas, 20 vehicle groups, 15 age groups, 3 cover types, a group for age and value of vehicle and so on. From these groups, the basic premium can be calculated from tables.
2. Placement in a risk category, based on questions about the proposer's accident history, previous claims, convictions, period driving, occupation, health, etc. The proposer may be unacceptable to this particular insurance contract or may require adjustments to be made to the premium, by way of loadings or discounts.

For our product-based strategy this allowed us to concentrate on the types of rule and the kinds of treatment they dictated. We devised a "Test Category" structure, and we also established the concept of a "Standard Quote".

The testing effort was broken down into both simple and combined test categories, which would determine the tests for particular elements of the product. For example, "Category 05 - Age of Vehicle", would carry tests for just this element and STRICTLY no other. This category list therefore became the detail behind the test strategy.

The Standard Quote was to be a proposer whose profile would result in an acceptable quote but one that would not attract any special attention from the labyrinth of validation going on. He was a 39-year-old museum curator, with a Fiat 126 BIS, with a full driving license for 17 years, no claims, accidents or convictions and not the merest hint of any physical infirmities in the last 10 generations.

The Standard Quote concept allowed us to "swap in" only the characteristics required for a particular test, and to correctly predict what our outcome would be, for example if our museum curator were 78 years old or had a bad claims history.

Our second Standard Quote was based up two drivers (partners). Our museum curator gained a 39-year-old museum-curating wife!

Our next task was to work out how many tests there should be within each category of test for each insurance product. Then the tests had to be run and analyzed.

10.2.5 Selecting a Test Automation Tool

We were making strides in terms of the strategy we were aiming to employ but we had yet to firmly decide how all of these tests were to be applied, manually or using a test execution tool. Just before reaching for a copy of The CAST Report (*The CAST Report*, Third edition, Dorothy Graham and Paul Herzlich, Cambridge Market Intelligence, 1995) which I can assure you we did, we took stock of our situation. We had done this type of thing before. (My company, Ingenuity Unlimited, is a specialist testing company providing testing contractors and testing services to a number of UK businesses).

These are the requirements that we took into consideration first:

1. We were going to keep our test case requirements outside of any test tool environment. We were not going to lock ourselves in to any particular CAST tool vendors' methodology.
2. (Of equal priority to 1.) We were going to run each test system as though it came from an insurance broker, as far as possible. Then we would know we were emulating the native environment of the system under test. I feel that this is a pivotal element to any testing process. Any "unnatural" test must have some impact on the credibility of the test itself.

Good Point

These automation requirements show farsighted wisdom of 10 years ago: keeping the structure of the automated tests separate from the tool's architecture and making test inputs as realistic as possible.

3. Because of 2, we were going to have a number of different machines, due to the variety of platforms we would have to accommodate when eventually testing across all systems.
4. Although all the current quotation systems were all character based; we would probably end up having to test GUI systems.
5. The normal operating circumstances at an insurance broker's office usually had some form of "network", even if it was simply 3 terminals connected serially to the UNIX "main machine".

We had previously gained some experience of Automator QA but had a look at "the opposition" anyway. The strengths we were seeking were robustness and track record, together with pertinent, timely and informed technical support. Direct Technology (now Compuware) offered all of these. We therefore settled upon Automator QA but purely as a means of applying our test cases by automation. Our test scripts and actual results, as obtained from our automated runs, would be held in files entirely of our design and under our control.

We had a test strategy, a DOS based system to test, a testing tool, and a plan for how we were going to forge ahead, but there was not a test script in sight. It was time to get started.

10.2.6   Some Decisions About our Test Automation Plans

We had a number of decisions to make about our test automation; all of them stood us in good stead, as matters turned out.

We hoped to run Automator QA resident on the same machine as our DOS based test systems. On the other platforms, we would substitute a dumb terminal with a PC (running Automator QA and a suitable terminal emulator) and the system under test would not know the difference.

Our chosen tool was feature-rich and quite able to assist us in handling all matters related to test data generation, test data maintenance, results handling and comparison. However, as with any broad spectrum tool, there are often better ways of doing certain jobs and we had experience of a few. We were also about to embark upon a huge amount of regular testing which, once underway, simply had to produce results month on month for a long time. We were not prepared to load all aspects of our testing into one basket.

The next decision we made was based on some past experience and partly, I must admit, because we were limited by the number of people who could work on this project. We decided to separate the disciplines of "Testing Technician" and "Automation Technician". There were two of us—it could work.

Good Point

Keep the roles of testing and automation distinct (even if one person undertakes both roles).

Immediately, we set about defining the roles of the two disciplines, which proved important.

10.2.6.1 The Tester's Job

The tester's responsibility is for the tests themselves. He or she is responsible for the quality of the tests and the effectiveness of the testing. The tasks are:

1. Define what is to be tested by producing test plans and test scripts that contain a number of Test Quotes.
2. Create the test scripts, execute them manually, analyze the test outcomes, and prove that each test has merit. This manual "proof" was to hold a great benefit later in the process.
3. Supply the data required for each automated test run in a form suitable for and dictated by the automation technician.
4. Define the expected outcome for each test case; this would be a financial sum and/or a message or messages.
5. Supply the expected outcome in a form to be compared with the actual results.
6. Execute and preside over the results of the later comparison between expected and actual outcomes.

10.2.6.2 The Automation Technician's Job

The automation technician's responsibility is for the efficiency of the testing. He or she creates the automated process by which the manual operation of keying in of input data is replaced. The basic tasks were expected to be:

1. Produce a "map" of each system to be tested.
2. Produce a script to apply each Test Quote as supplied by the tester.
3. Write a script to reliably collect the outcome from a final screen and write it to a file of actual results.
4. Produce an audit trail of some type, to indicate that what the tester dictated should be input had been reliably applied.
5. Become "expert" at running the automation tool without "tripping up" the system under test or the terminal emulator. We had gained enough experience to realize the importance, and relative specialism, of good memory management. Before you ask the question, we used QEMMTM (a memory management tool) and we always have the latest version on account of the fact that each version appears to assist in finding a few more useful bytes for the automation tool to use.

These two disciplines meant that the tester would remain very close to the "user", and would present test cases for review by a Business Manager. The automation technician was going to be far away from the business perspective and deeply involved in making highly technical things happen; nearer to a developer mentality. By and large we still maintain the same separation of disciplines on a day to day basis as this works very well in practice.

It is worthwhile pointing out that much of the scripting and the languages that are encountered among the different automated testing tools require a skill in programming coupled with great discipline in the manner with which they are used. The writer has experimented by using pure programmer skills as a way of preventing good test planners from becoming bogged down in the technicalities of automation scripting, but the developer-versus-tester divide always shows its head and takes quite a degree of managing. This mixture is found to work when a focus is maintained on the reason for using automation—it is to reliably and regularly execute the tests as demanded by the tester.

10.2.7   The Test Plan

We analyzed the insurance products and created a comprehensive list of "Test Categories" encompassing all of the facets of each product's decision making. One test plan would be written for each category—this was considered satisfactory to cover each facet of the products.

This was going to be a long job and we were eager to prove some automation. "Category 01 ~ Simple Premium Accuracy" was as good a place as any to start.

What other tools did we use? Our test planning tool was already a hit from the past—Lotus 123, now with multiple worksheets. Our test case generator? No such luck, no silver bullets here. When we got to Claims, Accidents and Convictions on one of the systems to be tested, there would be over 5 million permutations to decide from. Anyhow we were purists: the test case generator was to be a human being. The final selection of tests, of the order of 1200 for Convictions alone, was based upon a pure analysis of permutations coupled with much input from an expert in this field of insurance, as provided by our client. By this means, we ensured a user focus, but kept control of the number of potential tests.

While the "mapping" and some trial scripting were pressing ahead, the Category 01 Test Plan became an embryo. Several worksheets were set out in a format to be adopted for every Test Plan. The Test Plan contained the following information:

1. Development Notes: The scope of what was to be tested and what was to be disregarded were all noted here, signed and dated.
2. History Notes: Who did what to this Test Plan and when.
3. Shared Information: Lookup tables etc., some of our own design and some as supplied with the product information.

4. Test Data: The big one, see below.
5. Export For Test System: to be populated with the data to be exported for the automation run, and to be repeated for each Test System, for example "C" for Comprehensive or "item 3." for Third Party Only.
6. Expected Results: A resume sheet with expected results set out ready for export to the comparison tool.

At last, Test Case No. 01/10001, the first one (Category 01/Test 1) was about to be written out. For premium accuracy we had to set up our Standard Quote and then create areas 1 through 20, vehicle groups 1 through 20, and all of these permutations for each of 3 types of insurance cover. Lotus 123 has always been a magnificent tool for drafting out all of this information.

Our lookup tables contained all the information for the test. The left most column described the test condition, the next column contained the postal code for the selected area, then we had various details describing the vehicle (we had chosen one for each rating group).

The next set of columns collected the rating factors for each permutation, ending with a premium calculation and our expected outcome. Having finally created Test Case 1 and checked the calculation as being accurate to the penny, "copy down" comes as such a relief. At this point we were grateful for the printer that could print onto double-sized paper!

Our test data worksheet was capable of being presented to a business manager as the means of describing the tests which would be performed in this category, all 20 x 20 x 3 of them. Already we had created, albeit limited in terms of test coverage, a list of scheduled and reasoned tests. The client had never done this to this extent before.

Our test data worksheet described in literal but understandable terms " I want area 1, vehicle group 1, cover type comprehensive". It then showed the data that had to find its way into the quote system and reasoned out exactly what the expected result should be. The quote-specific information then had to be mapped into the "Export for Test System 1" worksheet, in order to appear in a form understandable by the system under test and the automation. This mapping task is very straightforward, and yet another good use of a spreadsheet.

The automation was ready, so we fed it the input file and ended up with a result for each case. The automated run was complete long before the manual execution and so we compared the actual results with the expected. One of them was wrong! After some perseverance, a good number of the manually executed results were available and they didn't agree with either the Test Plan or the automated results!

We had all permutations to consider. The result of the analysis? The automation had flaws, the Test Plan had calculation errors and the system under test had its fair share of "undocumented program features" (bugs) also.

The worst thing had happened. Our automation and the methods used to drive it had created an unreliable set of test results much quicker than ten humans could do working flat out. We returned to traditional methods. Tests were scheduled out carefully, reviewed and checked by us and, when necessary, the business managers. They were executed manually and the results reconciled before any automated run results were taken seriously. Only when we know that the only differences are due to errors in the system under test do we go with automated test results.

Lesson

Establish true confidence in the automated tests before relying on them in practice.

An exact match of a set of results from an automated run, compared against a fully reconciled set of manual results, allows only limited trust to be placed in the automation results, whether there are faults in the system under test or not. It is easy, unless your procedures allow for it, to place too much trust in an unproven automated process.

In that "first run" the audit trail highlighted mis-keying on the part of the automation scripts. It also pinpointed where it occurred and assisted with rapid debugging of the automation scripts.

Gradually, we built each test plan and executed it manually, dealt with the errors in the systems and followed up with the automation.

10.2.8 Some Additional Issues We Encountered

We used a statistical package, SPSS, to perform the comparison of results. It enabled the building of straightforward scripts, which pulled together the expected results and actual results files, performed the comparison and produced a report sorted by magnitude of error. These reports formed the basis for detailed viewing of malfunctions.

Tip

Use different tools to help with more effective comparison of results.

Many of the test plans have information that varies from year to year or month to month, not an uncommon circumstance. We anticipated this and spent much time in seeking ways to reduce the maintenance of test plans. Many of the tests were based around events with implied dates. For example, a test may require a driver aged 19 years and 11 months. As the test would be run every month, the date of birth would have to be altered every time the test case was used.

As we had many thousands of similar circumstances to consider, together with the likelihood of rating table changes and such like, the spreadsheets containing the test plans and the look up tables were built with a variety of mechanisms which would allow for updating from a "Master Shared Information" spreadsheet. Without this facility (yet another virtue of the humble spreadsheet), the maintaining of such Test Plans would be a logistical nightmare and would be open to all types of clerical error.

With up to 90 Categories and of the order of 30,000 test cases per insurance product, maintenance is a serious issue.

Good Point

Maintenance is a big issue that requires serious design effort early on to minimize costs.

Our early experiments included an attempt to justify the use of automation. We timed all manually input runs and compared them against the automated equivalent. A single test quote took a well-practiced operator, on average, 1 minute 50 seconds. This effort was found to be impossible to sustain for long periods whilst maintaining any dependable accuracy. In automation, 30,000 test quotes could be input at a rate of one test per 11 seconds without tiredness or inaccuracy. The difference is truly astounding, the accuracy impossible to equal in a manageable way!

At least once a month, we have to produce a set of files to be collected by the automation procedures when they run. These files contain the test data, adjusted where necessary, following any Test Plan maintenance (there will be many dates that needed to step on one month if nothing else). To cater for this we have built automated procedures which "make ready" all of the automation input files upon receiving a request from the tester to produce an automated run. This request is made after any Test Plan maintenance.

Good Point

Automate the processing around the automation as well, such as updating test inputs.

10.2.9   A Telling Tale: Tester Versus Automator

On one occasion we put the tester versus automation technician issue to the test with interesting results.

One category of test was seeking to prove that premium loads were being correctly applied for higher value vehicles. A flat additional sum of money was to be applied for each extra £5,000 in value over a threshold of £25,000 and up to a limit of £75,000, beyond which insurance should be refused for the product.

The automation technician built a script with a parameter table, using a test case generator method.

The tester built a formal Test Plan creating a boundary test from the threshold across each break point and some mid-range points up to the limit, where a refusal to insure was expected. The values tested were therefore £24,999, £25,000, £25,001 then £29,999 and £30,001 and so on up to £75,001 (not forgetting a £100,000 test!)

The tester created a "lean and mean" set of about 32 test cases, giving reasonable coverage from which to detect errors. The automation technician caused around 1600 test cases to be generated, at values starting from the threshold of £25,000 at £30 intervals, thereby missing the threshold boundary, missing many of the intervening boundaries and stopping at the limit, hence the "over limit" refusal was also missed.

Why did the automation technician do it this way? We concluded after much analysis, "because he could". This is most definitely a cautionary tale and cements our ideology that you do not replace the tester with automation, you augment the process by building the ability to readily re-apply proven tests in a manner which is both quick and accurate.

Lesson

Don't get carried away with "automation for its own sake." It must support good testing.

10.2.10 Summary

There were many stages where, if we had not been seasoned testers with some automation experience, a number of the hurdles we faced would have been enough for us to give up.

As it is, several years have passed since Test 01/10001 was written and the motor insurance testing is still being run every month. Now, for a number of insurance companies, we run tests containing around 30,000 test cases per product on 14 quote systems. The number of products has increased and we test between 6 and 16 products depending upon the quote system.

In addition to the private motor insurance, we also test commercial vehicle products, together with the hugely more complex household insurance and commercial products currently being traded by these electronic quote systems.

As we anticipated, we are now testing certain products on both character based and GUI (Graphical User Interface) quotation systems. This has caused the need to use an additional testing tool but the test cases and the method of supplying the automation technician with input files remains the same, vindication enough for our earlier decision to keep our Test Plans in an environment totally within our control.

The Holy Grail changed hands, for our original clients, once the performance of the systems was corrected and proven stable, following many months of repeated tests in certain cases. The level of reliable testing performed for that client alone, in the time frame in which it has to be completed, could not be conducted by wholly manual means.

As this is being written, the writer is heavily involved in making use of what has been learned to provide reliable repeated application of tests in many types of circumstance. The early lessons alluded to in the above paragraphs are constantly acting as a reminder of how to cope with a variety of automation issues.

10.2.11 Acknowledgments

The writer would like to thank the Commercial Union Assurance Co and particularly Urszula Kardasinska, Alan Dilley, and Neil McGovern of that Company for their initial faith and subsequent support and commitment. Without them this significant automation effort would never have been given the opportunity to flourish. I would also like to acknowledge my professional and business partner Bill Gribble. Without him, and the hours of toil, experimentation and arguments, we would never have formed the basis for Ingenuity.

10.3   What Happened Next?

More than 10 years on, and our automation runs on so many systems for so many insurers that we have between 12 and 36 machines running 24/7, executing in excess of 5 million tests each month, and still it grows. Mainly, though, it still "works" as testament to many of our original rules and design criteria being well considered at the outset.

> **Good Point**
>
> Set off on the right foot for long-lasting benefits from automation.

Needless to say, tools have changed, grown in number, and changed in ownership. Our original Automator QA gave way to adoption of the Rational Tools, now IBM Rational. Otherwise, our philosophy of using the most suitable application for the job has remained a mainstay.

10.4   Conclusion

Would we do anything differently? With 20:20 hindsight, who wouldn't? The following few paragraphs set out some of the observations and refinements that our experience has very firmly taught us.

10.4.1   Separation of Tester and Automator?

Originally, our rule was to have the automation technician quite separate from the tester to ensure that the testing and the emulation of human input were never clouded or cross-contaminated. At our testing practice, we still do this wherever possible, as it helps in ensuring that the two disciplines remain just that, "disciplined."

On reflection, what we were really recognizing at the outset is that you must first have "tests" and that those tests are delivering to notions of "quality," providing sufficient confidence that a "fit-for-use model" was being achieved in the software under test. Clarity of purpose is sufficient to arrive at the independence of purpose of the two disciplines; using separate individuals is a relative luxury.

Since 1994, we have been called in to a number of struggling automation projects, and there are always two significant threads contributing to the failure to thrive of the projects we see. First, a lack of "tests" and, second, a belief among management that the box states "Automatic" Software Testing Tool and not "Automated."

In our relative naivety, at the outset, we had no lack of clarity that we were try-ing to foreshorten execution times of otherwise "lean and mean" sets of tests. Time was our only enemy, and it still is. Our advice, always, is "If you do not have the tests, leave the automation tool in the box."

> **Good Point**
>
> Good tests come before automation. Automate only tests that are worth investing in.

10.4.2 Management Expectations

At client organizations, management, always on the hunt for a silver bullet, have to be restrained from any belief that the purchase of an expensive tool is the way to better quality. The best form of restraint is to set out what the testing is supposed to accomplish and how much person-effort is required to accomplish it. Add to this the argument that the testing is expected to be accomplished within, usually, crimi-nally short time constraints and, hey presto, the arguments exist to demonstrate the potential efficacy of using automated methods.

We have recognized that there is the need to manage an understanding of the relative maturity of the quality management, test strategy process, system specifica-tion, the test plan, the system under test, and the test automation suite before true success can be accomplished in deploying automated testing.

All of these components have to work in unison for a test automation process to be dependable. If any two of these components lack maturity (are still settling out), there is a huge risk that automation will produce bad testing and very quickly! This was the subject of my presentation to the World Congress on Software Quality 2009 ("Appropriate Timing for Deployment of Software Test Automation in Operational Environments," Fourth World Congress for Software Quality, September 14–18, 2008).

When undertaking our own automation projects or helping others with theirs, we always have to go to great pains to ensure that everyone concerned is aware of this critical harmony.

10.4.3 Independence from Particular Tools and Vendors

Another early decision that remains entirely unaltered and for continually demon-strated good reason is our nonreliance on any particular vendor or tool set. Instead, we always use the best tool for the job. Whether it is test case design/test repository, automated application of tests, comparisons of expected versus actual results, or problem reporting logs, we have never used a suite of tools from one vendor. This has allowed us to remain flexible and able to rapidly respond, especially when we have toxic cocktails of systems to automate and there is a need to become quickly adept at executing tests using a previously unused automation tool. With every other aspect of the process using safe and known methods, our response times and effectiveness remain high.

Good Point

Design your automation so that you can swap to different tools when needed—preserve your tool independence.

In the same vein, especially as the number of tools has proliferated out of all recognition since this chapter was first written, we continue to favor tools only from reputable and established creators/vendors. Our testing has to be businesslike, and we cannot risk being vulnerable to fad-driven, open source offerings that may be the product of folks indulging in an interest rather than being there 24/7 to provide support, however well intentioned their motives.

So, over 10 years after our first chapter was written, we are "still running," and that is something of which we are justly proud.

CHAPTER 11

A RISING PHOENIX FROM THE ASHES

Jason Weden

Jason Weden tells a story of initial failure leading to later success. The failure of the first attempt at automation was not due to technical issues—the approach was very sound. However, it was a grassroots effort and was too dependent on its originator. When he left, the automation fell into disuse. But the phoenix did rise from the ashes, thanks to Jason and others who had the wisdom to build on what had gone before, making many improvements to ensure that it was more widely used by business users as well as technical people. Their "test selector" for choosing which tests to execute gave the test engineers flexibility, and they ensured their legitimacy by keeping stakeholders informed about bugs found by automated tests. The small team that implemented automated testing for home networking equipment is based in the United States. See Table 11.1.

11.1 Background for the Case Study

Much has been written about how to improve various aspects of the lifecycle in software development projects in order to increase the chances of success and to avoid failures. But many times these failed projects can subsequently lead to great software and successful projects as we learn from our mistakes and build on them. My experience in one company on a software test automation project certainly took this route.

Table 11.1   Case Study Characteristics

Classification	This Case Study
Application domain	Networking equipment
Application size	30,000–40,000 LOC
Location	United States
Lifecycle	Traditional (waterfall)
Number on the project	25
Number of testers	9
Number of automators	1–2
Time span	3 years
Dates	2003–2006
Tool type(s)	Inhouse
Pilot study undertaken	No
ROI measured	No
Successful?	Ultimately, yes
Still breathing?	Yes

Though this project for an inhouse software test automation framework was a complete failure in the beginning, it created the foundation for a successful test automation framework that ended up challenging me and others and eventually made us better software test engineers along the way. The metaphor for this experience is aptly portrayed by the ancient myth of the phoenix:

> *A phoenix is a mythical bird with a colorful plumage and a tail of gold and scarlet (or purple, blue, and green, according to some legends). It has a 500- to 1,000-year life-cycle, near the end of which it builds itself a nest of myrrh twigs that then ignites; both nest and bird burn fiercely and are*

reduced to ashes, from which a new, young phoenix or phoenix egg arises, reborn anew to live again. The new phoenix is destined to live as long as its old self.[1]

11.1.1 The Organizational Structure

Nine test engineers and 16 developers were roughly split between the east and west coasts in the United States. The entire test engineering team had one manager; the development team had one as well. Though the software methodology used in the lifecycle across all of our projects was the traditional waterfall model, the close relationship between developers and testers often resulted in the test engineering group receiving informal, early releases with short feature descriptions in order to begin creating test cases and perform actual testing of new features earlier in the process.

11.1.2 The Business Domain

The system under test (SUT) was a home gateway used for a home's Internet connection. Included within the SUT were dozens of features such as firewalls (of various types), parental controls, routing, switching, Network Address Translation (NAT), virtual private networks (VPN) of various types, and support for various Internet protocols used for administration and configuration. The SUT had various administration interfaces, such as Simple Network Management Protocol (SNMP), web interface, command-line interface (CLI), and various flavors of XML interfaces requested by customers. The SUT also came in various hardware configurations where the WAN (wide-area network or Internet-facing) connection was Ethernet or digital subscriber line (DSL) and the local area network (LAN) had Ethernet interfaces (one or several), wireless (of varying speeds), and other types as well.

11.2 The Birth of the Phoenix

As many automation frameworks begin, so did this one—organically as an effort of one employee (we'll call him Jeff) working on it when he could as a background task. Jeff was my peer, another senior test engineer like me. It was called *APD*, an acronym for *Automated Perl Driver*. In many project lifecycles for software test engineers, there are times when test cycles ramp up and ramp down. Without a doubt,

---

1. http://en.wikipedia.org/wiki/Phoenix_(mythology)

software test engineers are busy. But if a test engineer takes advantage of some of the downtime or judiciously takes time away from tasks that have a due date pretty far out, a lot can be accomplished.

Jeff, then, took advantage of such time to build an automation framework. He built a harness into which tests for various features could easily be plugged. It was run from the command line and comprised lots of reusable code given that it was built using an object-oriented design in the Perl programming language. The framework required just two steps to add tests for a new feature. These steps are summarized in Table 11.2.

Figure 11.1 shows a schematic of a VPN test and also provides an indication of how APD, in general, sends and receives data to determine whether tests pass or fail.

As shown in Figure 11.1, APD interacted with both the Linux OS and the SUT. In the 3DES VPN tunnel test, for example, APD would send commands to the SUT CLI over a telnet connection to configure and start a VPN tunnel and run other SUT commands to verify the tunnel was up. APD would then send a network probe

Table 11.2   Steps for Adding a Test to the Original Automation Framework

Steps for Adding a Test of a New Feature	Explanation
Create `NewFeature` class	The test itself. This class inherited from the `TestCase` class, which itself had methods to run one or more test cases for a single test feature, log test results, and determine test success or failure. Also, the `NewFeature` class could construct and operate on objects of other reusable libraries such as the `TelnetConnection` class (to telnet to the SUT) and the `SystemCalls` class (to send commands to the Linux OS on which the test program ran).
Harness `NewFeature` class in `TestExecutor` class	The harness used to run the tests and collect results. Inside of this class, one needed to create the command-line flag to run the test, construct the `NewFeature` object and call methods to run the test, log test results, and determine test success or failure (i.e., call the methods on the `NewFeature` object that were inherited from the `TestCase` class). This was about 20 lines of code.

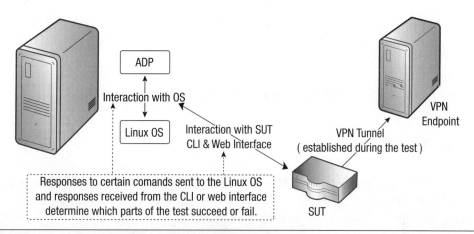

FIGURE 11.1   Schematic of the APD 3DES VPN tunnel test

request using the ping and traceroute utilities built into the Linux OS to verify network reachability from the APD server to the VPN endpoint and beyond.

Once the steps in Table 11.2 were completed, the user could run the TestExecutor script from the command line. This command would include the newly added flag such as --des3_test, which would run the test cases for the new feature in the newly added NewFeature class, perhaps named something like *DES3VPN*. (3DES is a type of encryption used in VPNs.) Therefore, an APD installation could test one or more features depending on how many flags were passed in by the user on the command line when running APD. Tests for a feature were self-contained in that each of these features was responsible for proper teardown so that any subsequent feature test could operate from this teardown state. This not only eliminated problems with test failures that could prevent subsequent feature tests from being run but also reduced confusion whereby an automation test engineer didn't need to keep track of dependencies across separate test features.

In summary, the object-oriented design allowed Jeff to plug into a test harness in a standard way and reuse existing components to test new features, thereby minimizing the amount of code needed to automate various test cases.

This solid foundation allowed tests to be added at a good pace right from the start. It wasn't long (about a month of Jeff's time) before solid bugs were being found by the automated tests. The effort to create this inhouse automation framework, APD, was well worth it here because an off-the-shelf product didn't exist to test the myriad of features of our SUT. Furthermore, the SUT was configured via proprietary commands sent through the CLI, web interface, or some XML-based interface. Having our inhouse automation framework eliminated these problems and gave us full control over our test case design and execution. It also allowed us to use what open source code—many of which were standalone Linux utilities—we deemed helpful along the way (NMAP for network testing, Apache to serve up the APD web interface, SendMail for email notifications, Net-SNMP for SNMP testing, hacker scripts for security testing, etc.). *The phoenix was born!*

11.3   The Death of the Phoenix

How could such a phoenix die? There was so much investment in building a solid architecture for a very functional yet extensible automation framework, and it was finding valid bugs. What could possibly go wrong?

> **Lesson**
>
> Initial success is no guarantee of long-term success. Technical aspects are not the only factors that influence a project.

All applications have two kinds of architecture: a technical architecture and a business architecture. Certainly, this automation framework had technical prowess; its technical architecture truly exemplified the software engineering education and experience of its creator.

What about the business architecture? The automation framework certainly fit the business domain, as real test cases were being automated and bugs (very good ones) were being found. But an application exists within the context of a business: It is a function of the expertise of those who own the application and maintain it; this maintenance function exists not only to fix bugs in the application (i.e., the automation framework) but also to make it more efficient and effective for a business's goals.

The business architecture for the automation framework actually never existed. The phoenix flew alone. Only its creator understood the automation framework and maintained it. *Therefore, the automation framework was a part of only one employee's workflow: Jeff's.* The problems here were as follows:

- There was no manager pushing for others to learn about the automation framework, to add to it, or even to use it; the manager had no experience with running a test automation project.

> **Lesson**
>
> Starting automation "bottom-up" is difficult; management support is needed for long-term success.

- The program's creator was not given the time or encouragement to share his knowledge and expertise about this program with others.
- Most of the other employees had no programming skills with the exception of one other (we'll call him Barry) who was taking some programming classes and just starting to get on the better side of the learning curve in this area (more on him later). Barry was also my peer, another senior test engineer.
- Though employees were just starting to realize this new automation framework was finding good bugs and running important test cases, the overall effectiveness of the automation framework was not being officially tracked in any way.

The program therefore existed in a business vacuum. Without a business architecture to support the automation framework, it died when Jeff left to pursue an opportunity at another company. This happened just as the program was starting to find good bugs and increase its coverage of more complicated features of our SUT. The program lay dormant for many months. The technical architecture (the bird's nest, if you will), which at first amounted to everything, was ultimately reduced to ashes because the business architecture on which it should have been predicated didn't exist. *The nest of myrrh twigs was ignited, and both bird and nest burned fiercely and were reduced to ashes.*

11.4   The Rebirth of the Phoenix

11.4.1   (Re)Starting the Automation Project

Remember Barry who was taking programming classes? Well, he started to dust off the automation framework, also as a background project, and used his growing software engineering expertise to learn Perl and understand how object-oriented design worked in the program. For Barry, who was always a tinkerer of sorts anyway, it was the natural thing to do and a chance to apply a lot of what he had been learning. Furthermore, test fatigue from manual testing also motivated him. As Barry looked over the framework, he found a lot to learn from and reuse.

In parallel with this, I took a second stab at learning Perl. My first efforts in learning Perl were wholly unsuccessful because I was using a poorly written book on the subject and didn't realize it. When I, at a much later point, came across a much better book that presented material in clear, concise lessons, it was a whole new world. This book was *Perl by Example* by Ellie Quigley (now in its fourth edition; Upper Saddle River, N.J.: Prentice Hall, 2008). From this one book, I learned PERL (and basic programming concepts for that matter).

By the time I reached the latter parts of this book, I was learning about object-oriented design in Perl, a skill that transferred well to learning about our automation framework. By this time, Barry had single-handedly resurrected the automation framework and started running and enhancing it. We sat inches from each other in the test lab, which facilitated knowledge transfer as we taught each other things about Perl and about the automation framework; from time to time, we did some pair programming as well. I was soon automating test cases using the automation framework as well as enhancing the underlying test harness.

11.4.2   Increasing Ease of Use

We helped to flatten the beginner's learning curve in two ways: first, for just running existing feature tests in APD and, second, learning how to add new test cases to APD for a new or existing feature. How? I created documentation on setting up the automation framework on a test machine; I also conducted training that taught others not only how to use the automation framework but also how they could automate test cases as well. Barry created a web interface for APD to facilitate ease of use of the automation framework by others. Figure 11.2 shows only a handful of the dozens of different features it actually tested.

This web interface also allowed us to better track, at a high level, the scope of the automation framework, because we could more easily identify which features were being automated by simply viewing the list of features that were listed on this web interface page.

There was now a third step to creating a test in addition to those listed in Table 11.2: Add the test to the web interface (as part of a later version of APD). But this just involved another few lines of code that needed to be added to the Perl script used in the web interface.

11.4.3   Increasing the Visibility of Our Automation Efforts

I also requested that test engineers flag all bugs found by the automated tests in our bug tracking system. Because the method was so simple (just creating a flag in the

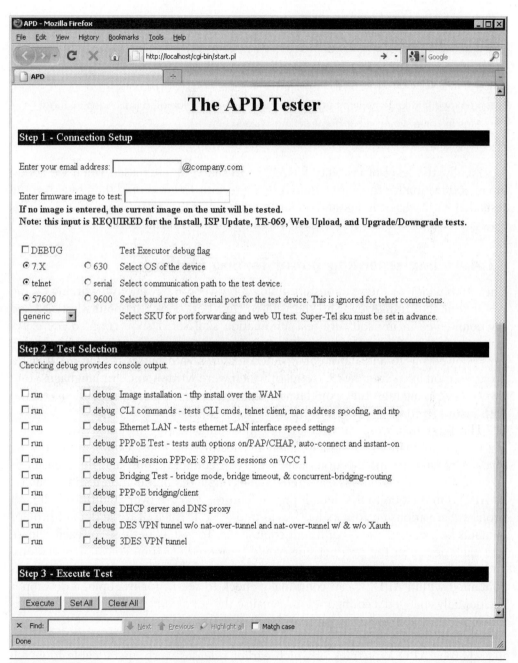

FIGURE 11.2   APD web interface screen

subject line of the bug entry), others were willing to engage in this small level of effort to help us track bugs found specifically from the tests run by APD.

> **Tip**
> If you want to know which bugs were found by your automated tests, identify those bugs in some way in your bug tracking system.

Finally, the level of visibility for APD was markedly increased when we added email notification for the automation test run results. Others could then see all of the tests that APD was running (and obtain a nice feel for its test coverage) and any bugs it might have found. A strong business architecture was finally being created.

11.4.4 Implementing Better Testing Methods

The combination of the relationship-building between Barry and me working on the test automation framework and the well-written Perl book exponentially increased my confidence in my software test automation skill set. I soon coupled my experience with formal education, a software engineering program at a nearby college. This allowed me to add more complicated features with better testing methods to the test automation framework (some of which were written in other languages) that assisted in finding bugs that would have been very hard (or incredibly tedious) to find with manual testing.

The bugs that were difficult to find in manual testing included those resulting from combination testing and boundary testing methods. Combination testing involves testing the intersection of multiple test configurations, and for each intersection, a certain outcome is expected. One example of combination testing enabled by APD is in relation to the default profile feature; we have over 20 different default profiles that various customers have used in our SUT. Each of these default profiles contains between 10 and 50 different commands. To test all of these for each release and each device in the product line would be incredibly time consuming, tedious, and, due to testing fatigue, error prone. If each of these known configurations is contained within APD, it can continually check to see if, for example, a developer accidentally changed a configuration. Because the set of such test configurations was finite, we were able to automate tests for all of them.

Another similar example of combination testing with our SUT is upgrade testing whereby APD kept track of which earlier releases were upgradeable to which later releases (another fairly large matrix); APD performed all combinations of such upgrades and ensured configurations remained intact and operational.

Boundary testing is where one tests the known lower and upper limits of a specific feature. Our SUT, for example, could have only 100 firewall rules for each rule type. (There were different firewall rule types, such as rules for inbound traffic, rules for outbound traffic, and rules of other types as well.) A looping data structure in our feature test could easily create such a configuration whereby we enter 100 and even 101 rules for a certain type (the latter being a negative test, of course); then, a much smaller amount of code could be added to attempt the same test with a different firewall rule type.

11.4.5 Realizing Benefits: Return on Investment

Eventually, we reached a point where a complete APD run against a release on a single device was 11 to 14 hours and spanned hundreds of test cases across dozens of features. An educated guess is that a single APD run performed the amount of testing it would take two full-time test engineers 6 weeks to run manually. Furthermore, this estimate does not take into account that APD (installed on other test servers) could be simultaneously launched against SUTs that were on other devices in the company's product line; and, yes, APD would every now and then find bugs specific to just one of these products.

And this is where we saw the power of regression testing. Not infrequently, new feature work would result in an unintended breakage of an existing feature. Running APD on every release allowed us to zero in on such bugs very quickly without the need to assign a test engineer resource dedicated to continual regression testing.

APD's strong technical architecture allowed someone with the right expertise to resurrect the automation framework and to greatly enhance it; and along the way it served as a great learning tool. As we started to support it with the right business architecture, the project stood on much firmer ground. The old phoenix set in motion these events leading up to the most important part of the phoenix myth, the rebirth. *At last, the phoenix was reborn.*

11.5 The New Life of the Phoenix

Contrary to the phoenix myth, we were determined to have the new phoenix outlast its old self. With our efforts in building the business architecture as described previously, we were successful. During this time (about 2 years), the following things came to light: focusing on knowledge sharing, tracking of automation framework test run results, and designing for speed and ease of use.

11.5.1 Focusing on Knowledge-Sharing

Due to the stronger technical and business foundation for the automation framework, its effectiveness increased such that my automation efforts took up 80 to 90 percent of my job role. Because more benefits were seen in spending time on working with automation as opposed to manual testing of the same functional areas, more and more of my job role became that of a test automation engineer. However, this did not eliminate manual testing. Manual tests were performed in some cases to initially define the test case to automate. Exploratory manual tests were also periodically performed by another QA engineer who did not do any automation. These exploratory tests helped to provide some initial quick feedback to the QA and development groups about how some of the earlier versions of the newer features functioned.

We realized that the close proximity afforded by the lab benches (as opposed to a cubicle setup) allowed for freer flow of communication such as engaging in ad hoc pair programming to resolve troubling areas in the program. Informal presentations within the group and with other groups enhanced this knowledge sharing. Such knowledge flows allowed the automation framework to be resilient when Barry eventually moved on to the development group.

11.5.2 Tracking of Automation Framework Test Run Results

11.5.2.1 What We Tracked and the Two Main Benefits

The tracking of the APD test run results had two main benefits. The first benefit was that others became increasingly aware of the work the test engineers were putting into automation. Though we still lacked solid management backing for this work, we could empirically demonstrate the effective use of our time on the automation project. Because we could track the number of bugs found and their priority via a one-click query in the bug-tracking system, because we could demonstrate the scope of the automation in terms of which features were touched by reference to the listing on the new APD web interface, and because we could demonstrate real-time test coverage from the daily email notifications of test runs that went out automatically from APD, we could summarize the effectiveness in weekly summary reports to management and in more official yearly performance evaluations. For example, in such reports we could include statements such as "x, y, and z test features have been automated," and this could also include a guesstimate of the percentage of test cases automated if previous test cases were undocumented, which in fact was common; a hyperlink to the bug-tracking system showing APD bugs could also be included in these weekly summary reports. This visibility resulting from our tracking efforts ensured legitimacy—a much-needed workaround for the lack of management direction for our automation efforts. Though the legitimacy of our work on APD was never questioned, we always made it a priority to justify the time we as test engineers spent on APD as it became an increasingly larger part of the job role.

> **Tip**
>
> Tailor your automation and information reporting to meet your objectives (here to find increasing numbers of important bugs).

The second benefit was that it allowed us to see patterns in the results of our test automation runs. For example, in a cursory glance at the bugs found by APD in our bug-tracking system, we realized that more bugs were being found when we took a *breadth-over-depth* approach to test case automation. New features were being added rapidly to our SUT. We found that if we judiciously used our time to automate just a few of the higher-priority test cases across *each* of these new features (a breadth approach) rather than spending the time to automate most or all of the test cases for *one specific* feature (a depth approach), more bugs were found and more important bugs were found. The lesson learned here was to balance the breadth—whereby each feature was in some way touched by the automation framework—with enough depth—whereby we knew we were going "deep enough" in terms of automating test cases for one specific feature. In this latter scenario, we knew we were testing a feature with enough *depth* when APD found problems that were tangible and replicable enough such that these problems could be considered bugs that could be entered into the bug-tracking system. An example here was that if we performed the most basic and higher-priority tests for different features (VPN feature: setup most common configuration and verify operation; DNS feature: verify DNS works [no negative tests]; firewall feature: set up one simple rule and test), we would be more apt to find a bug than if we automated all of the test cases that encompassed all of the different kinds of configurations for just the VPN feature.

11.5.2.2   *A Threat to Our Work from Another Part of the Company*

Such legitimacy was also very important when another competing and overlapping inhouse test automation project emerged—a by-product of this lack of management direction. This was a background project that the testing group in the office on the opposite coast started (i.e., not part of any formal project). Our group could never figure out why this was started in light of the maturity of the APD automation framework and the fact that we had visits from the West Coast group where we demonstrated and trained them on the use of APD. In our opinion, the other project was built on a much less solid technical foundation. However, unlike our automation framework, its effectiveness was never tracked and a case could never be made to devote resources to it (an issue that emerged when more than background cycles needed to be spent on it), ultimately resulting in its demise.

11.5.3 Designing for Speed and Ease of Use

Other people are more likely to use an automation framework if it is easy to use and if it is fast. And the more people who use the automation framework, the more tests will be run, and therefore the more likely it is that existing bugs in areas covered by the automated tests will be uncovered. An automation framework's tests can have wonderful test case coverage, but if the automation framework isn't run or run enough, its benefits can never be fully realized. Furthermore, since APD automated some of the more tedious and lengthy test cases, test fatigue related to these tests was markedly reduced with increased use of APD because these tests didn't have to be run manually anymore. The following attributes were found to lead to an increase in the use of APD.

11.5.3.1 Ability to Launch a Variable Number of Tests

A good automation framework should allow any combination of features to be tested. This was designed into our program by our web interface by having checkboxes next to each feature that a user desired to test. (Refer to Figure 11.2.)

> **Good Point**
>
> Set up a "test selector": a way to select which tests to run on the basis of changes to the software.

This came in really handy late one day when the development group was making last-minute changes to a feature for a customer. We were aware of what features could be impacted. Because we were able to have a last-minute mini-regression run with just those features, we found an unexpected but major bug that would never have been found by a manual tester, given our time window for customer shipment that day. (More on the importance of regression testing shortly.)

11.5.3.2 Debug Logging Options

Good debug logging options allow users to view details about a test that can markedly reduce the time needed to distinguish between a real bug and an error caused by the automation framework itself. That's the difference between output such as:

```
12-Jan-2006, 11:40PM: The vpn configuration failed
```

and (a hint that the VPN feature test should take into account default profiles when testing the VPN feature):

```
12-Jan-2006, 11:40PM: vpn configuration command failed:

SUT-CLI>configure vpn
SUT-CLI-vpn>set vpn 3des on
* Error: this default profile does not allow VPN configurations

12-Jan-2006, 11:40PM: The vpn configuration failed.
```

This scenario highlights a problem with the test itself (i.e., the tester forgot to enable the correct profile for testing VPN) rather than a real bug in the VPN feature. This debug option could be easily turned on by checking the "debug" checkbox next to the desired test, as shown in the web interface in Figure 11.2.

11.5.3.3   User-Friendly Interface

Other people probably would never have used the automation framework were it not for the web interface that allowed the user to easily plug in everything needed for a test run. This definitely lowered the barriers for adoption because the web interface was almost entirely self-explanatory. It was very easy to use and easy to remember how to use. In a pinch, the web interface could be brought up, configured, and executed—this was important in situations where tests needed to be performed quickly.

11.5.3.4   Automation of Test Setup

The user should have to do as little as possible in setting up an automation test run. We built test setup and teardown into each test to reduce the effort needed to set off an automated test. Our automation framework required the SUT to be hooked up to one or two cables used by the test server as the only manual step. The automation framework did everything else: It downloaded the build off the build server that the user specified via the web interface, installed it, started the user-specified tests, and automatically emailed the test run results.

Good Point

Automate pre- and postprocessing activities, or you will need manual effort to set up your automated tests.

11.5.3.5 Regression Testing

As the tests accumulated along with the design changes described previously, the ability to regression test emerged. This is one of the strengths of automating within a test harness and one that is user-friendly—regression testing is an emergent feature. Regression testing therefore involved merely running any number of previously automated tests; no extra manual effort was involved in creating the specific ability to regression test. Therefore, once a new build was released to the test engineering group, all that was needed was to put the name of the build in the web interface and, because all of the tests were enabled (checked) by default, just click "Execute." As stated earlier, the sum total of the tests ran 12 to 14 hours, so it was quite easy to run a daily regression test and wait for the email of the results the next day. The one thing we didn't build into the architecture was the ability of one physical test server to test more than one SUT. This didn't end up being a major problem. There were always extra older servers lying around that could easily be repurposed as test servers. (An aside here: I've learned that a test engineering group can be the ideal place to dump old hardware for use in test architectures.) So we always had at least one or two test servers for regression purposes and a few others for use by anyone wishing to either develop more automated tests or to just execute a variable number of tests for some particular purpose. Soon, even developers who knew nothing about the test architecture could bring up their web browsers and perform regression testing to ensure they didn't break anything because of some new functionality they had added.

> **Tip**
>
> Offer to take old hardware from other groups—it could be useful for testing!

11.6 Conclusion

The phoenix myth teaches us that what looks like a complete failure, what looks like a death, is not necessarily a really bad thing. In fact, such a failure can lay the foundation for a successful endeavor, a new life, a new phoenix. Lessons can be learned; old projects can be built upon and learned from; and more resilient, effective infrastructures can result. The following are some of these more important lessons that have been learned in this case study.

11.6.1 Use Time to Automate

Automation is one of the best ways to fill time between manual testing cycles. Constructive use of time is always important, and an automation project is something that can be started and worked on incrementally as time allows. After a while, these pockets of well-used time can only save time later because routine automation runs of test cases mean that what was previously time spent on manually executing these tests could now be time spent elsewhere.

11.6.2 Enhance Automation Skills and Share Knowledge

Skill sets in automation need to be fostered. This not only helps in getting people to work with the framework but keeps everyone thinking about automation; this engenders a unified automation strategy that can be built into every project lifecycle. (Though this can sometimes result in differing opinions as to how to proceed with a strategy for automation, it is important to realize [especially at our company] that to begin serious conversations about automation was a big step in and of itself.) Skill sets can be fostered through knowledge sharing, which can occur in three ways:

- *Bottom-up:* Self-motivation is a quality we all need to work on. We all have off-days and we all have job roles where at times we feel stuck in a rut. We need to be tenacious and continually try to find creative ways to overcome our obstacles and look for new avenues of growth. For example, finding the right book on Perl allowed me to see everything about that complicated technical topic from a different perspective. Tenacity paid off.
- *Laterally:* Knowledge sharing among coworkers is very important. This is especially true when you are working on an automation framework with other test engineers. An automation framework is no easy feat, and being able to discuss weaknesses and capitalize on each other's strengths will keep an automation test engineer on the right path. Lateral knowledge sharing can happen with documentation, hallway (or in-the-lab) conversations, informal presentations—I conducted learn-at-lunch seminars—and pair-programming.
- *Top-down:* In this case study, the automation project never received what we eventually came to understand should be the next step: management goal-setting for automation efforts built into job roles and performance evaluations. (However, this never amounted to any major problem, given the general laissez-faire approach management took to our automation project anyhow.) We came to this realization after seeing the success of our efforts, and it was our focus on the other two ways of knowledge sharing that allowed us to make up some ground here.

11.6.3 Acquire Formal Education

The right formal education can widen your perspective on automation projects. The rebirth of the automation project happened because its technical foundation (attributable in large part to its creator's education) was so solid to begin with. Would we have been successful the second time if we had to start again from scratch? (Answer: probably not as successful because reading the existing code and learning about the framework was so educative itself.) Additionally, the software engineering program that I finished allowed me to take a step back and gain skills from quite different technical projects that were part of the curriculum. Nevertheless, such skills transferred very well to my day-to-day challenges as a test automation engineer. Furthermore, to have skills that allow one to properly design reusable components lowers the barriers to entry for others to automate test cases because there is so much less code to then write. So an automation framework design can have a direct impact on how much the program is used and enhanced by other test engineers.

Good Point

Education is useful. Good software design practices apply to automation as well.

11.6.4 Track Progress

Track the progress of your automation framework. A lot was already stated on this topic (see Section 11.5.2), but two points are worthy of reiteration here. First of all, tracking the effectiveness of your automation framework allows you to gauge your own effectiveness as an automation test engineer. This can be communicated to the managerial level. Second, such tracking gives your project visibility and greatly increases the chances of your automation framework being used by others.

11.6.5 Assess Usability

Assess your automation framework for usability: How does it fit in with the workflow of others? Is the automation framework easy to install, configure, and use? If your automation framework has very few manual pre-setup tasks and is easy to use (e.g., has a nice web interface), it will be more usable and therefore used much more. One good rule of thumb here is to watch a test engineer who is not an automation test engineer install, configure, and use the automation framework. What is the engineer's feedback?

> **Tip**
>
> Learn how usable your automation really is by watching a tester try to use it.

11.6.6 Tailor Your Automation to Suit Your Organization

Inhouse automation frameworks provide lots of control. And having control of your automation framework is a very good thing. For example, we were able to tailor usability of the tool to our test engineers' needs, thereby increasing its use and visibility.

11.6.7 And Finally . . .

Let's have both a business and technical perspective for our automation projects. Let's learn from failures only to increase our success. Let's take full advantage of what we know and have. Let's truly learn from and create what we don't yet have built. Let us be taught by the myth of the phoenix.

AUTOMATING THE WHEELS OF BUREAUCRACY

Damon Yerg (A Pseudonym)

Damon Yerg (a pseudonym) tells of experiences in automating large systems for a government agency, over more than 10 years, with hundreds of developers and testers and more than a dozen automators. After some uncertain starts, external pressure brought the right support to move the automation in the right way. The tests to be automated covered diverse applications from web-based to mainframes, all with environmental factors. This story brings home the need for automation standards when many people are using the automation. Damon and his colleagues organized the regression library into core and targeted tests to enable them to be selective about which tests to run, and they related the automated tests to risk factors. The basic design of the automation supported business expert testers and offered technical support as needed. One of the most powerful things they did to ensure continuing management support was to develop a spreadsheet describing the benefits in a way that communicated effectively to stakeholders. This is a very successful large-scale automation project from Australia. See Table 12.1.

12.1 Background for the Case Study

12.1.1 The Organization

The organization (which we'll call "the Agency") is a large Australian government service provider. As a government statutory agency attached to one of the country's

Table 12.1   Case Study Characteristics

Classification	This Case Study
Application domain	Government service provider; mainframe and web-based
Application size	An enormous mainframe and web-based applications of varying size, some very large
Location	Australia
Lifecycle	V model
Number on the project	Hundreds of developers (numerous systems and applications)
Number of testers	300–500
Number of automators	2–17
Time span	11 years
Dates	1999–2011
Tool type(s)	Inhouse
Pilot study undertaken	Yes
ROI measured	No, but comparable manual effort calculated
Successful?	Yes (peaks and troughs)
Still breathing?	Yes, thriving and forging ahead to new heights

largest departments, our role is to provide a range of payments and services to customers. This means working with the government of the day, via legislation, policy, and ministerial direction, to deliver payments and services to those Australians who need them.

In size and turnover, the Agency is in the top 100 Australian companies. We distribute 86.8 billion Australian dollars per year in customer payments on behalf of our client departments.

Our mainframe customer database comprises nearly 7 million customer records, each of whom receives any number of payments and services. Our Model 204–based mainframe has a number of different discrete but interactive systems within it, depending on payment/service type, of which there are many. We also have a number of web-based midrange applications that interface with the mainframe and the systems of various other agencies and departments. Our systems record more than 6 billion customer transactions per year.

Our information and communication technologies (ICT) divisions work in an environment of high governmental expectations of modern, useable, and cost-effective systems and applications that are easily adaptable. Frequent policy amendments and new legislation and initiatives make for a challenging demand to keep pace with constant business change.

12.1.2 The Agency Testing

The Agency's two testing centers are based in the charming and picturesque city of Adelaide in the South and beautiful, balmy Brisbane to the North. During each quarterly major software release testing exercise, each site may have anywhere from 150 to 300 system testers, some permanent and many brought in from the service network around the country just for testing that one release.

The Automation Services team is now spread across both sites with two managers and six engineers based in Brisbane, and another four engineers based in Adelaide. We currently have an IT graduate recently recruited under the Agency's graduate intake program. We also often host graduates from other teams for short placements on our team as part of their induction and probation programs.

12.2 The Agency Automation

I came to the Agency automation team as a business analyst in the antipodean winter (which I think is equivalent to the Northern Hemisphere summer on both the calendar and the thermometer) of 2008. A small part of the research for my assigned tasks involved delving into the history of automation in the Agency, and what I uncovered turned out to be an extraordinary journey of discovery, ingenuity, and perseverance.

The team had begun in 1999 when a member of our testing executive became increasingly aware (via a variety of sources such as testing magazines, external testing conferences, and staff who had also researched automation) of benefits achievable through test automation and obtained agreement, with limited funding, to investigate if and how this could be beneficially implemented in the Agency.

12.2.1 Enhancing Record and Playback

A small process improvement team was established in Brisbane to investigate and demonstrate what could be achieved. Two very clever and IT-savvy testers began investigating what could be done with our current shelfware record and playback (R&P) tools. They undertook industry research via the web, special interest group presentations, and testing magazines to familiarize themselves with automation principles and practices, and they procured guidance on test/automation interface from a tool vendor. While vendor guidance experiences in ensuing years have sometimes had less than positive outcomes, we must have been lucky on this first occasion, because the vendor's help was quite valuable. Of course, our guys were pretty knowledgeable from having read other published experiences.

> **Good Point**
>
> A lot of good information about automation is available, so make use of it. Don't forget that tool vendors can also be helpful.

In these first months, we identified the possibilities for automation of change and regression testing, and there were some early attempts at using web-based R&P tools to execute regression. By and large, these attempts were unsuccessful. The test cases were not of high design quality or necessarily of high value, they were too complex, or the functionality was new and subject to continual code change (unstable).

We determined that pure R&P tools were not suited to most Agency testing but could be useful if they were modified by adding some programming for variable workflow management. Agency workflows are seldom linear in nature, more often resembling a complicated web of possible alternative workflows, depending on variable input options at each screen. We also realized that production-derived data used in manual testing has too much historical "baggage" that increases the potential for script failure. It was clear that purpose-made customer records were required for testing.

> **Lesson**
>
> Simply translating manual tests may not give the best automated tests.

Our self-taught developers went about building this new framework, using not the web tools but an existing mainframe-based tool known as Hyperstation (a

Compuware product) that was being used (and is still in use today) in manual testing. Its language is third-generation REXX (Restructured Extended Executor), much better suited for building on the two additional aspects of customer record generation and variable workflow management. Our developers recognized the potential to tap into the enormous power of our leviathan mainframe.

This also meant that automated suites could be run as a mainframe batch, parallel to normal network use, thereby avoiding the usual network traffic and resulting in zero network latency (no send/receive time). A whole day's work for five manual testers could potentially be completed in 1 hour.

12.2.2   Health Checks and Smokers

We determined that many of our test environment health checks could be automated, so the team went ahead to develop and execute limited suites of business-process health check tests. The result was savings of hundreds of man-hours each release, as environmental issues could be identified and resolved more quickly, usually before our hundreds of testers wasted their time trying to test in unstable environments.

Of particular value among these new automated health checks was the type we dubbed "Smokers" because they're a form of smoke testing. The term *smoke testing* comes to software testing from a similarly basic type of hardware testing in which the device passed the test if it didn't catch fire the first time it was turned on. Another way of looking at it is "where there's smoke there's fire"—discovery of high-level bugs often means more deeply embedded problems. Our Smokers are daily high-level, nonexhaustive tests of our mainframe systems, checking that the most crucial functions are working but not bothering with finer details. This high-level testing is sometimes also called *breadth testing*.

Many of these original health checks and Smokers are still in use today, and many more have been implemented.

Good Point

Smoke tests are a good place to begin with automation because they are run often and can be boring and error prone when run by human testers.

12.2.3   Challenges and Lessons Learned

Attempts at automated regression testing had met with limited success. The available/expanded tools didn't cater effectively for the level of maintenance required and weren't suitable for emerging midrange applications testing. The early tool design had not fully resolved multiuser capability, thereby failing to meet the management requirement for high productivity rates. They lacked the framework to manage the high complexity of Agency process workflow variation.

Governance over test design quality, what functionality should be automated, and availability of resources were also important factors. Therein lay our first major lessons in automation:

- Successful implementation is a by-product of good process. Tests must be of high design quality before attempts are made to automate them, so work on test inputs and process before automating. "If you automate chaos, all you get is faster chaos."[1]
- Don't try to automate complex tests too early—learn to walk before you run.
- There is less value in automating tests for unstable functionality because maintenance overheads will be higher. It's better to focus your efforts where highest reward can be reaped.

Lesson

Beware of automating poor or complex tests, especially on unstable functionality.

The positives taken from this experience were as follows:

- Suites of high-value test environment health checks and smokers were developed and are still in use.
- Issues with test design, process, practices, and tools were identified.
- Objectives were identified: Reduce manual labor costs, improve product quality, increased testing flexibility, free manual testing resources for testing of changes (with a higher bug-discovery rate), and reduce strain on network resources as fewer temporary testers were required.
- Strong support from senior management continued with the assurance that issues such as funding and test design quality, originating from outside the team and affecting our ability to progress, were being addressed.

---

1.   Dorothy Graham, *The CAST Report* (Uxbridge, UK: Unicom Seminars, 1991).

12.3   From 2000 to 2008

From 2000 until 2008, automation fortunes fluctuated between achievement and lessons learned (some of them hard ones). Formal funding came from various projects in which automation featured as a significant contributor and in a couple of cases were specifically aimed at leveraging mainframe test automation capability. But these were limited and sometimes abandoned before completion for various reasons. In the main, the automation team survived through the astute and optimistic support of a minority of farsighted executives who provided the necessary sponsorship.

12.3.1   Benefits from the Mainframe Tool

Gradually over the period to 2008, real benefits began to be achieved from the automation of regression testing using the new mainframe tool. The team began to expand in numbers (including some with formal technical skills and qualifications) because of the increase in demand for our services from test teams throughout the organization. We began to locate some new team members at our sister site in Adelaide to better service the accounts tested from there.

Further development on the mainframe automation tool ceased in about 2004, though it is still in broad use today and continues to provide substantial capability for Agency automation now and into the future.

12.3.2   The Web Way

In the early 2000s, the Agency had begun its first ventures into web-based customer applications that interfaced with our mainframe and the systems and applications of other agencies and departments. This direction was broadly forecast to be the way of the future (and it certainly is in terms of user interface), and there was even speculation that web would soon replace our beloved M204 mainframe. Time has told a different story, and it's now clear that our mainframe is far from reaching redundant senescence. However, we still had a pressing need to automate the testing of the new web applications, so we needed to focus on development and use of a web-based test automation tool.

In late 2003, a large government initiative made funding available to upgrade IT throughout the Agency. Testing was assigned funds to enable a formal and comprehensive initiative to develop a web-based automation framework. Experienced IT managers were engaged to manage the project and the development, along with a number of formally qualified application developers.

12.3.3 Our KASA

Thus a formal project to develop capability to automate tests for both mainframe and midrange applications was initiated. The Keyword Automated Software Assurance application (KASA, not its real name) was conceived. This inhouse Eclipse plug-in tool, which, as its name suggests, uses the keyword-driven test automation approach, quickly became our tool of choice. We can employ a web-based mainframe "emulator" in order to also use it for mainframe testing. It also incorporates other industry-accepted techniques such as modularization and the use of variables, helping to simplify the script-development process and achieve "one-point" maintenance. Because scripts reference the modules from a central library, any necessary changes can be made to the central module rather than to every script containing it.

> **Good Point**
>
> Standards become more important as more people use automation; getting feedback from potential users of the automation is important for later acceptance.

The new automation framework was built, and this is essentially the same framework in operation today.

Toward the end of the development of KASA and in preparation for implementation, work also commenced on designing, documenting, trialing, and refining the necessary test writing and automation methodology and process. We assiduously consulted Fewster and Graham's book *Software Test Automation* and successfully implemented many of its concepts and tips with great success.

12.3.4 More Challenges and Lessons Learned

Organizational issues around processes and practices continued to impact the quality of inputs and resultant progress and outcomes. Resourcing proved to be a significant barrier to resolution of these issues. Unfortunately, initial resources assigned to provide automation inputs and development were also assigned to mainstream development and testing, and this work took priority as the software release deadlines loomed large.

> **Lesson**
>
> Taking test automation development seriously involves dedicated resources. (There is no such thing as a free lunch.)

From early 2006, with KASA development now completed, the team (now expanded to about 10 members with solid backgrounds in testing and significant technical aptitude) continued making progress to identify and rewrite suites of high-value tests to a level of design quality needed for effective automation. A variety of workarounds were used to address gaps and issues with existing test processes and other aspects. This approach was critical to demonstrating potential benefits and ensuring the ongoing survival of the automation services team. This effectively reinforced the need for organizational processes and practices to be standardized and modernized in line with recognized software testing industry good practice.

Lesson

Don't automate poor tests; effort put into automating high-value, high-quality tests will provide greater payback.

Positive results of this experience were as follows:

- In testing KASA during its development, a variety of trials with different test teams pinpointed relevant process and practice issues. It became apparent that standardized and change-managed quality processes and practices were essential across all test teams to ensure the long-term success of automation.
- We had developed a keyword-driven test automation application designed to check and provide real-time detailed reports for each testing environment.
- The new automation framework could interface with the existing core testing tool set and could also be used standalone, as is current practice in the Agency.

12.3.5   Selling Automation

One of the big challenges we faced was facilitating a realistic management understanding of what automation can and can't do. This is something we still haven't resolved fully, and we continue to chip away, using various marketing strategies, including presentations, demonstrations, and invitations to application-specific discussions on what we can do. If I had to sum up our strategy in three words, they would be "Engage! Engage! Engage!" An important component of this is clearly articulating the answer to "What's in it for management?" Of course, the most convincing argument is dollars, preferably expressed in terms of return on investment (ROI).

In a huge organization like ours, with so many different teams, sections, groups, branches, and divisions all interacting with each other, accessing the kind of data we need to accurately demonstrate real ROI is a huge challenge, one we are still working on. In the meantime, we use what seems like quite an effective alternative approach. It involves showing the cost of developing and executing automated test suites (Figure 12.1), and comparing that cost with what it would have cost to achieve the same outcomes manually (Figure 12.2). This has proved to be a powerful selling tool, as shown by the summary in Figure 12.3.

> **Good Point**
>
> It is essential to communicate the benefits of automation to high-level management. Comparing automation to manual testing can be effective.

The "silver-bullet syndrome" is something I'm sure all automators have or will encounter occasionally. Yes, we can leap tall buildings and see through walls, but to what purpose? Superman is a show-off. We can automate just about anything, but there must be some benefit in the outcome. For example, some change testing can be automated to great effect, but if the functionality is still being tweaked and likely to change considerably in the future (is unstable), we're unlikely to make much long-term gain because of the effort required to continually amend the tests to account for the changes.

Test managers have busy, demanding roles, particularly in our organization. An ongoing challenge we face is getting enough of their attention to discuss what we can do to save them some time. They're so busy sweeping with their brooms, they don't have time to talk to the vacuum cleaner salesperson! Obviously, that's an over-simplification and maybe a little unfair (apologies to test managers, and apologies to automators for the door-to-door salesperson comparison), but I'm sure readers can relate to the analogy. Both time and cost can be saved, but only if you take the time now to put in place things that will pay off later.

12.4 An Alignment of Planets

In late 2008, three fortuitous events roughly coincided to give the Agency automation team the essential elements it needed to ensure its journey would lead to more lasting success.

| | AUTOMATION | | | | | | | |
| | Framework A | | | | Framework B | | | |
Accounts	Tests	Runs	Total	Effort (mins)	Tests	Runs	Total	Effort (mins)
Account 1			0		89	8	712	106
Account 2			0		103	8	824	0
Account 3			0		78000	4	312000	3600
Account 4	100	25	2500	750			0	
Account 5	45	10	450	15			0	
Account 6			0		180	17	3060	150
Account 7			0		5	1400	7000	420
Account 8			0		330	17	5610	200
Account 9	190	1	190	1			0	
Account 10			0		249	25	6225	1341
Account 11	45	10	450	15			0	
Account 12	179	2	358	3670			0	
Account 13	100	15	1500	750			0	
Account 14	45	5	225	15			0	
Account 15	125	2	250	5020			0	
Account 16			0		249	25	6225	300
Account 17	60	6	360	592			0	
Account 18	21	11	231	180			0	
Account 19	30	8	240	10			0	
Account 20	29	5	145	1259			0	
Account 21			0		2279	6	13674	10
Account 22			0		180	17	3060	150
Totals	969	100	6899	12277	81664	1527	358390	6277

FIGURE 12.1   Human cost for automated testing for two frameworks

| | AUTOMATION TOTALS | | | COMPARABLE MANUAL | | |
Accounts	Total Tests	Total Executions	Automation Effort (days)	Manual Effort Tests/day	Manual Effort (Days)	Single Run Savings (Days)
Account 1	89	712	0.2	4.8	148.3	18.3
Account 2	103	824	0.0	4.8	171.7	21.5
Account 3	78000	312000	8.0	60	5200.0	1292.0
Account 4	100	2500	1.7	48.6	51.4	0.4
Account 5	45	450	0.0	200	2.3	0.2
Account 6	180	3060	0.3	50	61.2	3.3
Account 7	5	7000	0.9	5	1400.0	0.1
Account 8	330	5610	0.4	424	13.2	0.3
Account 9	190	190	0.0	150	1.3	1.3
Account 10	249	6225	3.0	65	95.8	0.9
Account 11	45	450	0.0	500	0.9	0.1
Account 12	179	358	8.2	4.8	74.6	29.1
Account 13	100	1500	1.7	48.6	30.9	0.4
Account 14	45	225	0.0	224	1.0	0.2
Account 15	125	250	11.2	4.8	52.1	14.9
Account 16	249	6225	0.7	320	19.5	0.1
Account 17	60	360	1.3	8.6	41.9	5.7
Account 18	21	231	0.4	6.4	36.1	2.9
Account 19	30	240	0.0	200	1.2	0.1
Account 20	29	145	2.8	5.6	25.9	2.4
Account 21	2279	13674	0.0	150	91.2	15.2
Account 22	180	3060	0.3	424	7.2	0.1
Totals	82633	365289	41.2		7527.5	1409.2

FIGURE 12.2   Cost comparison of manual and automated testing by account

SUMMARY	
Total Tests	82633
Total Executions	365289
Total Effort Saved (Days) for a single run.	1409.2

FIGURE 12.3   Summary of savings for a single run of automated tests for all accounts

12.4.1 Gershon Review

In April 2008, the Australian government minister for finance and deregulation engaged Sir Peter Gershon to lead an independent review of the Australian government's use and management of ICT. Gershon provided the minister with his report on August 28, 2008, and the minister released it on October 16, 2008.

Gershon's report provided a comprehensive and detailed analysis of wide-ranging issues affecting the government's use and management of ICT. It also outlined a phased plan for the implementation of recommendations. In November 2008, the government endorsed in full all the recommendations of Gershon's *Review of the Australian Government's Use of Information and Communication Technology*[2] and initiated an ICT Reform Program.

In his accompanying letter to the minister, Gershon summarized his key findings and recommendations, including "ensuring the enablers of change are properly resourced, not only in funding terms but also with skills of the right calibre." These few words and the manner in which they were reflected across Gershon's recommendations were the most powerful enablers of automation in the Agency that had occurred to date. And so I coined our new team slogan: "Automation—Enabling change through more efficient Quality Assurance."

Good Point

An outside view can provide the strongest support for internal change.

12.4.2 Independent Testing Project

In October 2008, the Agency's deputy CEO of IT endorsed the implementation of the independent testing project (ITP). Its charter was to provide an independent testing service that optimizes resource availability and provides standardized methodology and quality. Previously, test analysis, design, and specification had been within the domain of the application development teams.

This meant that for the first time, an enterprisewide approach to test coverage, design, quality, and techniques (including automation) was under the control of a centralized and independent governing body. This enabled the provision of an

---

2. Available at www.finance.gov.au/publications/ict-review/docs/Review-of-the-Australian-Governments-Use-of-Information-and-Communication-Technology.pdf.

independent process that verifies product quality at release by more effectively minimizing defect risk against predefined requirements. This huge independent testing framework has been implemented in a phased approach over 3 years.

What this meant for automation was, first, that mainstream test methodology, design, and specification were on the same risk and requirements–based testing (RRBT) page as we were. Also, where necessary, we were more able to influence the quality of the inputs (i.e., test cases) we received via our common governing body.

Second, because a component of the ITP charter was to drive initiatives delivering more efficient use of resources through improved techniques, they began working closely with us and test managers to maximize the beneficial use of automation. We still have some distance to go in this endeavor, but significant inroads have been achieved.

12.4.3   Core Regression Library Management Methodology

This new methodology is based on the development of a regression test library divided into two parts, core and targeted, and better, more structured and traceable use of RRBT methodology. Its purpose was to help modernize Agency testing methods in line with current industry good practice and to encourage maximization of the automation of core regression tests. Some other organizations have achieved about 80 percent automation of their core regression libraries.

The same core suite scripts (covering the core functionality of the application identified mainly on the basis of objective analysis of use frequency and criticality) would be run for every testing exercise (preferably on each new version of code), whereas the targeted test scripts executed for each release would vary depending on the change that was being introduced, covering areas where defects were more likely and/or expected.

> **Good Point**
>
> Structure the automated tests for most efficient execution; don't assume you always have to run them all.

The purpose of the core suite is to validate that core application functionality still works (risk assurance), though tests must be designed to find defects should they exist. The purpose of the targeted suite is to test code that would potentially be of higher risk to regress and to find defects based on the change(s) being introduced.

Regression testing historically finds a relatively low percentage of total defects during a testing exercise but has proven itself essential in helping to provide the level of confidence and assurance required to release change. Our automation of regression testing is about efficiency, assuring that the system still works, and freeing manual resources for testing that reaps a greater proportion of defects such as change, exploratory, and the more complex regression testing that is not suitable for automation. In the end, it's all about risk and traceability of requirements and coverage.

Good Point

The main benefit of regression testing is confidence and assurance, not defect discovery.

Under our methodology, if automation is applied to clearly defined core functionality and processes via documented coverage and design quality of the highest and stringently assured specifications, any defects should be discovered before release into production. If some automated scripts are continually not finding defects, test managers may determine, again using objective risk analysis, whether it's appropriate to retire them.

In late 2008, completion of a fully detailed, documented, trialed, and refined end-to-end methodology and process for automation of core regression tests, extendable to cater for targeted regression and change testing where clear long-term benefits are apparent, was completed and implemented across all test teams. The process commences with objective and traceable test coverage analysis based on risk; continues through identification and design of test cases, test specification, and referral for automation; and finishes with test maintenance. It also prompts consideration (by both manual and automation test management) of continuous improvement across the integrated process. An associated methodology training package was also designed, developed, and delivered in both sites.

12.4.4 Our Current Location on the Journey

These three roughly coinciding initiatives (Gershon's review, independent testing, and core regression methodology) made the importance of automation clear at an organizational level and provided the driver, the direction, and the fuel we had been seeking for our automation engine. This was the definitive alignment of events that allowed us to turn onto the road signposted with destination "Success."

12.5   Building Capability within Test Teams

12.5.1   The Concept: Combine Script Development and Business Knowledge

In general, industry experience indicates that having manual testers also doing automation work has been unsuccessful—largely due to trying to get nontechnical testers to do engineering-level work. In this model, we built our tools and framework in such a way that the less technical aspects of automation script development and execution may be done with technical support.

Using our current process for the automation of discrete business workflow test cases, there are two levels of script development. The first, module (usually per screen) development, is the level applicable to the automation engineer role. Maintenance of these screen modules is also in the engineer domain. The building of the script by dragging and dropping premade modules from a library into the KASA script panel is where mainstream test analysts can be involved. As business workflow experts, they know which screens to load and in what order. If the modules are created by the engineer to replicate the required inputs for the screens they relate to, and are named according to screen and input, building the script by dragging and dropping modules in the correct order is a task that can be achieved by testers with limited technical skills.

> **Good Point**
>
> Have the engineers (test automators) construct elements that can be used with ease and no technical know-how by testers at the business knowledge level.

To complete the script, a number of other contextual modules and variables must be added, and some setup conditions must be applied. This requires some training, but for any test analyst with some technical aptitude, this is entirely achievable. We therefore developed an effective training package and enhanced our tools to optimize their usability by less technical staff.

This change is not viewed as a rollout. The skills required are dependent on the trainees having the necessary technical aptitude and successful training, so a prerequisite for providing the service is having the necessary inhouse technical capability. There is also the risk of skills developed within one team being lost to staff movement, which could result in complete loss of the capability or the transfer of capability to another test team. Our strategy for mitigation of this risk is threefold: (1)

An effective and quickly deliverable training package is provided; (2) test teams are encouraged (with reinforcement by governance) to have trained backups available; and (3) in the event 1 and 2 fail to resolve an issue, the automation team may provide a resource if available.

While the service may be provided for one release exercise, if prerequisites are not met, it might not be available for the next. We also insist that test team resources assigned to automation focus on that task as their priority.

> **Tip**
>
> Keep technical knowledge requirements to a minimum for business-level testers, but provide training and support for any technical tasks they need to do.

The organizational advantages of this approach are that the business knowledge and the less technical automated script development (dragging and dropping of modules, etc.), execution, debugging, and reporting capability are incorporated in the same person. This is a powerful combination.

Test automation (script development, maintenance, execution, and reporting previously always done centrally within the specialized automation services team) is now a part of the mainstream testing regime in a number of test teams, with the service take-up expected to expand to most teams in the next financial year. The automation services team will continue to provide the tools, frameworks, infrastructure, training, and support for this to continue. We'll also continue to provide a holistic automation service (including script development, maintenance, execution, and reporting, as well as the tools infrastructure) as required.

12.5.2   The Tools: KASA Meets DExTA

To complement our new supported test team automation service, we recently developed a client/server agent controller application to manage the execution of our mid-range and browser-based functional tests. The use of this tool eliminates the need to run all the scripts for each suite sequentially. The controller manages the execution of the suite on our client machines to facilitate concurrent execution across multiple machines, greatly reducing our execution time.

The idea for this tool originated inhouse through the abstraction of a math problem: If one person can execute 100 tests an hour, how long will it take 10 computers to execute 100 tests?

The idea to execute on multiple machines was implemented via a tool that "remotely controlled" the process of receiving and managing schedules provided by the user. The remote control is achieved by running programs called agents that communicate with the scheduler and receive a signal to execute tests.

The scheduler and agents are built on existing proven technologies (Internet communication and control mechanisms). The scheduler waits for the determined date and time before dispatching jobs to the agents and keeps track of the agents while jobs are progressing. Agents act like members of a work crew who request a job from the scheduler, execute the dispatched job, and come back when ready with the results. The process repeats until all jobs are completed.

The team named the new product by holding an inhouse competition. The name "DExTA," which stands for Distributed Execution Test Agent, was the winner. It was connected to the title and theme of the television series *Dexter* for splitting up large test suites into smaller pieces. Although I've never seen the series, I understand it involves a "likable" serial killer who has a charming habit of distributing body parts around the city!

In a recent pilot, trained manual testers first used only KASA to execute automated suites. The same manual testers then used DExTA and KASA to execute the same suites. The resulting data showed that automated execution using only KASA achieved up to 85 percent savings in effort compared to manual execution. However, when DExTA and KASA were used in conjunction, effort savings increased to up to 97 percent.

During a review of the pilot, testers involved commented that using DExTA was far easier and less technically challenging than not using it. A significant reduction in the level of technical support they required was noted when they used DExTA.

12.6   Future Directions: The Journey Continues

12.6.1   MBT Solutions

We developed a model-based testing (MBT) implementation for one of our applications, and we are now investigating an improvement to this process such that any change to the source document will automatically build applicable new test cases, execute, and report results. Once we have this working effectively on our pilot application, the intention is to adapt and apply it to others.

12.6.2   Embedded Automation Engineers

Our preferred business model of assigning and co-locating automation engineers with manual test teams has now been implemented and is proving its inherent value. Taking this approach enables greater collaboration between test designers and automators; facilitates better, faster identification of the highest value areas/tests to automate; and exposes testers with some technical aptitude to automation tools, principles, and processes.

12.6.3 Organizational Approach to Regression Testing

Currently, each application area has its own library of regression tests. This means considerable duplication of regression testing because of the many commonalities and overlaps among the functionalities of the various systems and applications.

The concept being promoted by automation services is for the development of an overarching regression library based on core processes and functionality of the systems and applications of the whole organization. These would be risk-based suites covering the critical functionality that must work in order to effectively deliver services to customers, not based on any changes being introduced. They would be run every time new code is deployed, avoiding much of the duplication that currently occurs.

The result will be an organizational regression suite based on risk that validates the essential business process, including any surrounding process for systems integration testing (SIT), and lower level functional tests for product integration testing (PIT). Naturally, such a suite should be automated to the maximum, an estimated 80 percent of the total suite.

12.6.4 Automate Early

Consider:

$$\text{If } A = C \text{ and } B = C, \text{ then } AB = C^2$$

Now transpose:

A = Test early, test often
B = Maximize beneficial automation
C = Savings

It's a simple enough equation and, I'm sure, makes perfect sense to any right-minded tester. Put early testing and automation together, and the savings and benefits are increased exponentially. Getting it to happen requires a much deeper level of engagement and convincing demonstration of benefit outside the traditional testing forum, which has often historically been that bit tacked onto the end of development and is done as thoroughly as the budget allows.

At the moment, we have a large testing exercise each quarter during which many network experts are sourced to perform our SIT testing. Much of this so-called SIT testing is actually PIT testing that can and should be performed earlier, and most of it can be automated. Our goal is to use continuous integration principles and automation to perform this testing.

To achieve this objective, some changes aimed at improving environment and test capability and compatibility must be made. For example, we may have to stub out interfaces and create harnesses, and so on, but the resulting benefits should far outweigh the cost of these modifications. This would have the added benefit of allowing our expert system testers to focus purely on SIT testing.

12.7   Conclusion

Automation in the Agency has had its setbacks and its spurts of progress. Thankfully, overall, it's been more of two steps forward, one step back than the reverse. I think what we've been able to accomplish to date is remarkable when considered in the context of our enormous public service organization and its inherent methodical and conservative approach to change.

As you may have gleaned, I see the climax or turning point of our story as being the alignment of planets in late 2008. Although it's in no way smooth sailing from here, we've reached the point of no return, and automation in the Agency is here to stay.

AUTOMATED RELIABILITY TESTING USING HARDWARE INTERFACES

Bryan Bakker

Bryan Bakker tells of automating testing for medical devices, an area with stringent quality requirements and difficulties in accessing the software embedded in devices such as X-ray machines. Bakker and his team's starting point was simple tests that assessed reliability; functional testing came later. The automation was developed in increments of increasing functionality. The chapter contains many interesting observations about management's changing views toward the automation (e.g., management was surprised when the testers found a lot of new bugs, even though "finding bugs" is what management expected of them). The team developed a good abstraction layer, interfacing through the hardware, and were even able to detect hardware issues such as the machines overheating. The results in the test logs were analyzed with inhouse tools. The reliability testing paid for itself with the first bug it prevented from being released—and, in all, 10 bugs were discovered. Subsequent functional testing was smoother, resulting in cutting the number of test cycles from 15 to 5. This story is from the Netherlands, and the project had excellent success using commercial and inhouse tools with just two people as the test automators. See Table 13.1.

Table 13.1   Case Study Characteristics

Classification	This Case Study
Application domain	Medical device (with embedded software)
Application size	500,000 LOC
Location	The Netherlands
Lifecycle	V model
Number on the project	50
Number of testers	10
Number of automators	2
Time span	1.5 years
Dates	2008–2009
Tool type(s)	Commercial, open source, inhouse
Pilot study undertaken	Started on one project, later spun off to other projects
ROI measured	Yes, based on defects found and test cycles reduced from 15 to 5
Successful?	Yes
Still breathing?	Yes

13.1   Background for the Case Study

Sioux Embedded Systems supplies trend-setting services in the area of technical software that is subsequently embedded in equipment. At Sioux, we focus on added value. We continuously look for new skills and expertise, new ways to increase our productivity, new ways to do business: We are driven to create innovative solutions for our customers. Testing is one of the ways to ensure the high quality of the systems we deliver. Our team of testers specializes in test design and execution as well as test-consulting services. Sioux strives to provide these testing services in close cooperation with development in order to have short feedback loops to the developers.

One of our customers manufactures medical X-ray devices for patient diagnosis and patient surgery. The application described in this case study is used during all kinds of surgical procedures. The system generates X-rays (called exposure), and a detector creates images of the patient based on the detected X-ray beams (called image acquisition). The image pipeline is in real time with several images per second, so the surgeon can, for example, see exactly where he or she is cutting the patient. During an operation, X-ray exposures are performed several times. The frequency, duration, and characteristics of the beam can be adjusted and optimized for the type of surgery being performed. The X-ray exposure should be as small as possible but should still result in sufficient image quality.

In the R&D department of this specific customer, new devices are being developed—the software as well as the hardware, electronics, and mechanics. Quality is of utmost importance in these applications because failure of the system can have negative consequences. Testing is a critical part of each project and consumes about the same amount of effort as the development tasks. All testing activities are performed manually, resulting in a developer–tester ratio of about 1 to 1.

My role was to improve the test process by finding ways to introduce automated testing. The focus of automation included but was not limited to software testing.

13.2 The Need for Action

Although testing is considered important in the customer's organization, existing systems at customer sites had reliability issues. The system was always safe, but the functions executed by the customer (e.g., transfer of acquired images to external devices) now and then failed to perform as expected, resulting in crashes of the system. The development department had devoted a lot of money and effort to fix these issues and release them to the field. This necessary effort greatly impacted other projects that were working on new functionalities and other systems. These projects had to delay their milestones because of restricted resources, both development and test resources.

When a new project was started with new functionality to be developed on comparable systems, reliability was one of the attention points of the project. Senior management demanded action to increase system reliability. Several improvements were considered: FMEA (failure mode and effects analysis), reliability requirements, reliability agreements with suppliers, design measures to increase robustness, and (automated) reliability testing.

To avoid long discussions about requirements that were not yet fully understood, we did not try to define reliability requirements early on but would address them once the notion of reliability became clearer. Therefore, we focused on automated reliability testing first to demonstrate that some problems could be addressed before the product was released. The other ideas would be tackled in future projects. Our rather small reliability team consisted of a hardware engineer, a developer, and a tester, all also working on other projects. Because the available effort was very small, we decided to develop a "quick and dirty" solution at first. The idea was that with a first increment of a test framework, we could run simple test cases repetitively in order to execute duration tests focusing on the reliability of the system. The test framework would not need to schedule test cases or evaluate and report the pass/fail criteria in a nice way. In fact, the test cases would not have pass/fail criteria at all. The test framework would only deliver a log file provided by the system under test (SUT). Test case maintenance was not yet important. The only requirement was that the system would be "driven" via hardware interfaces, so no special test interfaces were implemented in the software.

The expectation was that the first few test cases would identify several reliability failures, which would need to be analyzed and fixed. This would create awareness in the project, freeing up more resources.

Good Point

A small-scale start can help to raise awareness of the benefits of automation.

13.3   Test Automation Startup (Incremental Approach)

The first increment of the test framework consisted of hardware interfaces from the system (such as buttons on the keyboard, hand switches and foot switches to start the X-ray acquisition) that were accessible from LabVIEW by simulating hardware signals. This approach was chosen because it was not the intention to change the embedded software of the system. The software development crew was busy with the implementation of new features. New feature requests from the test team would certainly be rejected. LabVIEW was chosen because it was already used by the hardware development team to perform measurements and tests on different hardware components. The architecture of our first increment is shown in Figure 13.1.

The first few test cases were designed in LabVIEW using the graphical language that is part of the tool. We focused on duration tests because they are small and quick to implement but can be executed for several days on the system. They require little effort but result in a lot of testing time and such test cases can reveal some nasty defects. Within several weeks of development, the first test cases could be executed at night and over the weekends when the systems were not used. In the first weekend of testing, several different startup problems were discovered. In the following weeks, the test cases were slightly extended: More X-ray acquisitions were performed before the system was switched off again, and more defects related to the increased system usage were found. The development crew was busy analyzing and fixing the problems, and as a consequence, the next milestone (an internal delivery) was delayed. Some bug-fixing time had been scheduled in the plan, but it was by far not enough to fix all the issues. Senior management was not pleased about the missed milestone, but they also realized that the quality of the delivery was being improved, which is exactly what they asked for in the first place.

Lesson

Don't forget to include time to fix defects and retest.

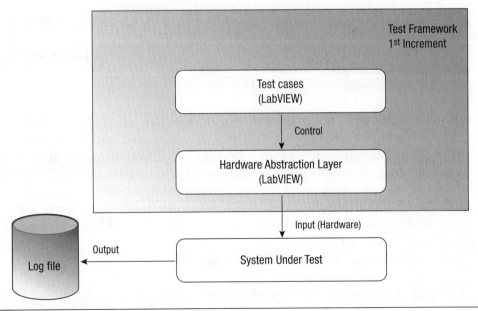

FIGURE 13.1   Architecture of the first increment

The chosen framework could only perform actions on the SUT, but no verification of whether the system indeed performed as expected was done at this time. The system generated a log file containing all kinds of information, both for service engineers and development engineers. This log file was analyzed for failures after the test ran. This, of course, took some extra effort but also provided evidence of failures for the development department.

13.4 Buy-In from Management

Now it was time to get some buy-in from management. Management heard about defects being found by the "new way of testing" but they still did not thoroughly understand what was going on. Some defects looked like duplicates of defects already communicated by end customers using old versions of the system. It seemed that the reliability tests detected several issues already known to be present in the field and also present on the yet-to-be-delivered system. These defects were not yet reproduced in the development department, so no solutions were available yet. With the automated testing, these issues were fairly easy to reproduce. As we all know, reproducibility is very important to fixing defects.

> **Good Point**
>
> Automated tests are reproducible, which is essential for knowing that a defect has been correctly fixed.

Several presentations were given to senior management, project leaders, and product managers about the approach taken with automated testing and the most recent results, mainly the number and the kinds of defects detected. It was also clearly communicated that the test cases developed and to be developed focused on reliability only, not on functional or other nonfunctional items.

A definition of reliability for our system was specified on the basis of the primary functions of the system. Failures that impact the (defined) reliability are called reliability hits (see Figure 13.2).

Following are some examples to illustrate the different categories:

- Primary failures (problem in primary function):
  - System startup results in a nonworking system (failed startup).
  - Running acquisitions are aborted.

- Secondary failures (problem outside primary function but impacts primary function):
  - Viewing old/archived images was not defined as a primary function, but when viewing these images results in a nonworking system (e.g., due to a software crash). This does count as a reliability hit.
- Tertiary failures (no direct impact on primary function):
  - Not all images are stored correctly on a USB medium. This is not a primary or secondary failure because USB storage media are not considered to be used for archiving. For archiving of medical images, other independent and more reliable systems exist. Thus a failure in this storage function does not count as a reliability hit.
  - X-ray images cannot be printed due to an internal failure.

Defects detected by our reliability tests would almost always be critical defects because they affected one of the most important characteristics of the system. On the other hand, the automated test cases did not eliminate the need for manual test cases; they were performed in addition to manual tests. As a consequence, the contents of the upcoming test phases (system test and acceptance test) remained the same.

Management demanded action toward increased reliability but had no idea how to address the challenges—nor did the quality assurance department, under whose purview reliability fell, know how to approach the issues. The ideas came from engineers (lower in the hierarchy) and focused on the short term.

The early solution showed senior management that the project team was making progress. Even with the first increment of the test framework, the added value was evident.

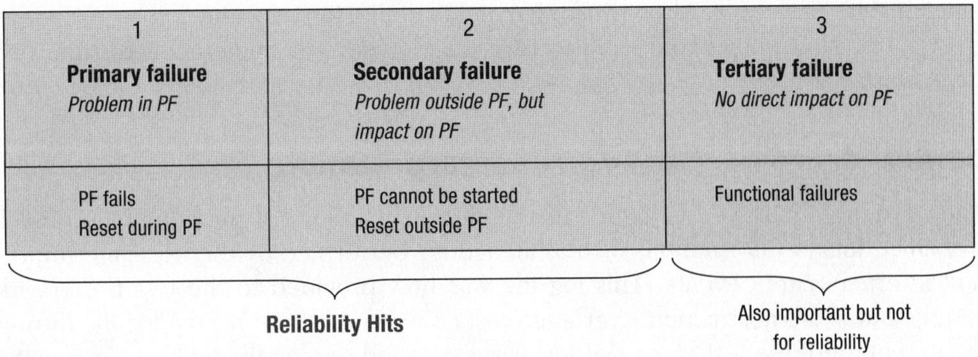

1	2	3
Primary failure *Problem in PF*	**Secondary failure** *Problem outside PF, but impact on PF*	**Tertiary failure** *No direct impact on PF*
PF fails Reset during PF	PF cannot be started Reset outside PF	Functional failures

Reliability Hits — Also important but not for reliability

FIGURE 13.2 Definition of a reliability hit related to Primary Function (PF)

With our definition of reliability, it was also possible to define measurable reliability requirements. Because of the chosen focus on automated reliability testing, developing measurable reliability requirements was postponed and defined as an improvement opportunity for the future.

13.5   Further Development of Test Framework

13.5.1   Increment 2: A Better Language for the Testers

After management were convinced that the test automation approach was the road to follow, the team received resources and funding to further develop the test framework (the test framework, consisting of dedicated hardware and LabVIEW, was not cheap). The next step (increment 2) was to abstract from LabVIEW because its programming language was unsuitable for defining test cases. LabVIEW turned out to be difficult for our test engineers to learn, and we expected that maintainability of the test cases would be an issue in LabVIEW. Our test engineers had only basic programming knowledge, so using the same programming language as the software developers used was not an option. We decided to use a scripting language for its flexibility and ease of use. Ruby was chosen because it is a dynamic open source scripting language with a focus on simplicity and productivity. It has an elegant syntax that is natural and easy to write, lots of support information was available, and Ruby interfaces well with LabVIEW. The hardware abstraction layer was still programmed in LabVIEW, but the test cases could be programmed in Ruby now, hiding the complexities of LabVIEW. Standard functionality of the test cases was implemented in libraries, so the test cases were straightforward, and maintainability of the test cases increased. Because we intended to use the framework in the future not only for reliability tests but also for functional tests, we were already taking maintainability into account.

Figure 13.3 shows the architecture of the second increment of the test framework.

13.5.2   Increment 3: Log File Interpretation

The third increment added log file interpretation. The log file provided by the SUT contained lots of information, such as all actions performed by the user, and important internal system events. This log file was now provided to the test framework (via the hardware abstraction layer), and test cases could interpret the log file during the execution of the test case. The test cases scanned the log file looking for specific regular expressions and could thereby implement pass/fail criteria. In the first two

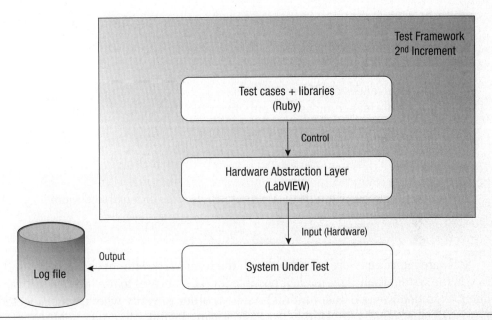

FIGURE 13.3   Architecture of second increment

increments, test cases consisted only of actions; now the corresponding checks were added to the test case.

Analyzing the log file also allowed the test case to follow different paths based on the information in the log file (although this makes the test case more complex).

This also enabled us to test much more efficiently. When testing the system extensively, as is done during reliability testing, certain parts of the system become too hot, causing the system to enter a cooling down period. In this state, no X-ray exposure can be performed. Most test cases would fail because of a hot system. Now it was possible to detect this condition, and in the cooling down period, power-cycle tests were performed. These tests switch off the system and switch it on again, and then check via the log file whether the startup was successful. The framework monitors the system temperature, and when the system is sufficiently cool, it executes other duration tests. Efficiency was improved because other valuable test cases could be executed during the cooling down period.

Part of the evaluation of the test results was now performed during the test execution by checking the pass/fail criteria. However, the log files were still manually analyzed afterward for undetected error conditions and unwanted behavior. (For example, hardware failures are not detected by the test cases but should be detected in the subsequent manual analysis.) Several different small, home-made log file analysis tools were developed to scan and parse log files from the SUT. It was possible to:

- Detect errors in log files.
- Count occurrences of different errors.
- Derive performance measurements from the log file (such as the number of images acquired per second).

> **Tip**
>
> Nonintrusive tests drive the system from external interfaces so that the software is not affected by the test.

Software interfaces were integrated with the framework without changing the software in the system itself. This made it possible for the test cases to use internal software functions to determine certain internal states in order to verify whether an expected state equals the actual state. During test case design, the following rules hold:

- For test case actions, use the external interfaces as much as possible to simulate a real user as closely as possible. Using internal interfaces to trigger actions should be avoided.
- The internal interfaces should be used only to check certain states or variables when they cannot be derived from the log file.

With this approach for the framework, other kinds of test cases could be implemented, such as smoke tests, regression tests, functional tests, and nonfunctional tests. Because of resource restrictions, these tests were not yet implemented. Focus remained on the reliability tests, but nevertheless the framework also supported these kinds of tests.

A test scheduler was implemented to facilitate the definition and execution of test runs. A facility to generate a report that gave an overview of the executed test cases and their result was also implemented. The test cases (scripts), the test framework, and the test results were stored in a central repository, the same as used for the software and documentation of the project. This ensured that the set of test cases was consistent with the software and the documentation and prevented incorrect versions of the test cases from being used to test the software and the system. This was a further step into professionalism.

Other improvements to the test framework were already defined, such as reading in hardware signals and retrieving images from the image pipeline. The implementation of these improvements would be performed in upcoming increments.

Reliability is not a binary characteristic. You cannot say, "The system is reliable." It is a quantitative characteristic expressed, for example, in mean time between failures (MTBF). We wanted the new system to be more reliable than the legacy system, so we needed to measure the reliability on these legacy systems with the same set of test cases. Because these test cases use hardware interfaces to trigger actions on the system, the test cases could also be run on older versions of the system, as these hardware interfaces were never changed. We could do so without altering the framework or the test cases. Now it was possible to clearly compare the existing (legacy) system with the newly developed system with respect to reliability.

Good Point

Reliability is not binary but a characteristic measured by a scale of varying values. A good comparison point is the previous system.

Figure 13.4 shows the architecture of the third increment of the test framework.

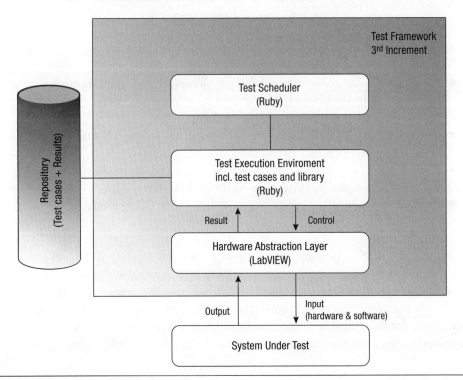

FIGURE 13.4   Architecture of the third increment

13.6   Deployment and Improved Reporting

During the development of the different increments of the test framework, a return on investment (ROI) calculation was performed to further convince the management of the added value of this reliability test approach and to justify further investments into it. An overview was made of all the defects found with the reliability tests. Together with a service engineer and a systems test engineer, an analysis was performed to identify the defects that would not have been found by later test phases but would certainly be noticed by end customers. The management team was asked how expensive one such defect would be (including costs like penalties, development costs, release costs, service costs). Of course, the real damage would be greater than such a dollar amount—just think about a dissatisfied customer or the impact on the brand of the company. But these are difficult to measure, so we decided to only take the "hard" costs into account. On the other hand, we did calculate the expenses for hardware equipment and resources. Here is our ROI equation:

$$\frac{(\text{NumberOfDefects} \times \text{CostOfDefect}) - (\text{CostEffort} + \text{RemainingCost})}{(\text{CostEffort} + \text{RemainingCost})}$$

where,

- *NumberOfDefects:* Number of defects detected by reliability tests that would not have been detected by later test phases but would be encountered by end customers and would require field updates.
- *CostOfDefect:* Average (hard) costs of resolving a defect found in the field and re-releasing the product to the field.
- *CostEffort:* The total cost of the effort spent on the development of the test framework and the development of the test cases.
- *RemainingCost:* Other costs such as hardware purchased, hardware developed, and licenses.

When this equation becomes larger than 1, the added value of the test framework has exceeded its costs, so we have positive ROI. In our situation, that was already the case when only one defect had been found, because the solution of defects in the field is very expensive. The fact that 10 potential field problems had been prevented was positive for the visibility of the test framework in the organization. This was communicated to the entire organization by means of mailings and presentations.

Good Point

Make the benefits of automation visible. For example, show how defects were prevented from escaping to the field (and to customers).

To improve communication about the results of the tests to management, reliability growth plots were generated that depicted the growth (or decline) of the reliability of the system over time. The Crow-AMSAA model for reliability measurements was chosen because the test results contained different kinds of tests on different system configurations with different software versions installed. Other models are more applicable for test results on fixed system configurations.

A fictitious example of a Crow-AMSAA plot is shown in Figure 13.5. The X-axis represents the cumulative number of startups of the system. The Y-axis shows the MTBF of the startup behavior of the system. Each triangle in the plot depicts one test run, and the solid line is the line with a best fit through all triangles. This line can be used for reliability predictions by extrapolating it to the future. The exact meaning of this plot is not related to this case, but it can be seen that these plots are fairly

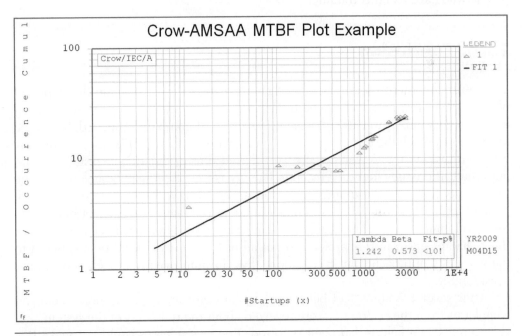

Figure 13.5   Crow-AMSAA plot

easy to read and very understandable, even by nontechnical personnel, after some explanation. Management can monitor the reliability trend in the project and take corrective actions when needed.

All the information needed for these plots was automatically extracted from the log files, which are stored during the reliability tests overnight and over the weekends.

Good Point

Automate the reporting of test results in a way that is easily understood by managers.

Several different plots were designed, not only for the reliability of the startup behavior but also for the reliability of the exposure functionality and the reliability of mechanical parts that can be moved.

A pitfall with these graphs is that people who do not understand them may draw incorrect conclusions from them. We avoided this problem by offering several training sessions to explain how to read the graphs. The graphs are distributed only to people who have had this training.

13.7 Conclusion

The results for the project were clear. The test phases following the development phase (system test and acceptance test) ran a lot smoother than on previous projects. A comparable project with respect to size and complexity needed 15 system test cycles to reach the exit criteria. In the project described in this case, it took only 5 system test cycles. Fewer defects were found during the system test, but more important, the issues found were nonreliability issues. Reliability issues tend to be really nasty and can take quite some effort and lead time for analysis and solution. This effort and lead time were still needed, not at the end of the project but during the development phase, and we know that fixing defects earlier is cheaper. Other things had changed in this project, so not all of the benefits could be attributed to the reliability approach, but it is evident that the improved approach contributed considerably.

After several systems had been used by end customers for several weeks, no complaints from the customers were received about the reliability of the system, and not even a single failure had been reported. Previous releases could not make this claim. Also the product managers who had regular contact with customers were very positive about the stability of the system. The product managers became so enthusiastic that they wanted to add a feature to the sales points of the system: improved reliability. After some discussion, it became clear that doing so was not a good idea because it would have a negative impact on older systems being used in the field and that could still be bought by customers. It was decided that customers should experience that stability for themselves.

Good Point

Benefits are both quantitative (5 instead of 15 cycles) and qualitative (happier customers). Both are clear benefits from the automation approach.

Other projects also noticed the improvements and asked for reliability tests. More test setups were purchased, and dedicated test cases were implemented for other projects and products (including legacy products that needed maintenance). The decision to interface with the product at the hardware level made the conversion to other products fairly easy; although the software of these systems is different, the hardware interfaces are the same.

Good Point

The best way to spread automation practices inside the company is for other groups to want what you have!

All issues identified with the test framework were indeed failures. No false negatives were identified. The fact that no failures were related to the test automation approach was mainly due to the use of hardware interfaces that interacted with the product. This results not only in high coverage (not only software is part of the test, but also hardware, electronics, and mechanics are used during the test execution) but also in a very low probe effect. A probe effect is an "unintended alteration in system behavior caused by measuring that system" (http://en.wikipedia.org/wiki/Probe_effect). When too many false negatives are reported, the confidence in a test approach (whether automated or not) quickly declines.

As a result of the awareness in the organization about the importance of system reliability, a critical aspect of milestone reviews became the reliability. The reliability team became an important player during these milestone reviews during which it was decided whether or not milestones were passed.

The contents of the reliability test cases were chosen by best guess and in close cooperation with product managers. Future plans include an analysis of log files from the field to define real user behavior. This information can be incorporated into the test cases to improve the simulation of the end user.

For the success of this test automation approach, the following points were crucial:

- Choose the right project at the right time.
- Develop the test framework incrementally in order to show the added value as early as possible.
- Communicate the approach and the results by frequent presentations.
- Use clear, simple, and understandable reporting of the reliability growths (e.g., Crow-AMSAA plots).

What's nice to notice is that none of these points handles technical approaches or tool choices.

Good Point

The tool is not the most important part of automation.

CHAPTER 14

MODEL-BASED GUI TESTING OF ANDROID APPLICATIONS

Antti Jääskeläinen
Tommi Takala
Mika Katara

Antti Jääskeläinen, Tommi Takala, and Mika Katara tell how they used model-based testing (MBT) in a substantial pilot study, testing smartphone applications—specifically Messaging, Contacts, and Calendar—on the Android platform. They used domain-specific tools rather than generic testing tools and a mix of commercial, open source, and inhouse tools, including two MBT tools. Testing in a huge state space was quite a challenge, but they give clear examples of the types of tests they were automating and good explanations of the algorithms used. They include many helpful ideas for making testing easier, such as using correct syntax for keywords and converting testware to more usable formats. This story covers a pilot project in Finland. See Table 14.1.

14.1 Background for the Case Study

In this chapter, we describe a case study on model-based GUI testing of Android applications. Android is a new Linux-based open source smartphone platform by Open Handset Alliance. The purpose of this case study was to evaluate how well model-based testing (MBT) works for GUI testing on this platform. Moreover, we

Table 14.1   Case Study Characteristics

Classification	This Case Study
Application domain	Android applications (smartphone)
Application size	Three applications, size unknown
Location	Finland
Lifecycle	Functional GUI testing
Number on the project	2
Number of testers	None
Number of automators	2
Time span	6–8 months
Dates	Autumn 2009–Spring 2010
Tool type(s)	Commercial/open source/inhouse
Pilot study undertaken	This is a pilot study
ROI measured	No
Successful?	Yes
Still breathing?	Yes

wanted to compare the use of our MBT tool and test model library, originally developed for GUI testing on the S60 smartphone platform (Jääskeläinen et al. 2009; Jääskeläinen, Kervinen, and Katara 2008) to traditional manual testing, which is still very much in use in smartphone application development.

We chose three applications—Messaging, Contacts, and Calendar—created test models for them, and generated tests that were executed online on a real device.

For modeling, we used two different open source tools, Model Designer, developed inhouse, and ATS4 AppModel, a part of the Nokia ATS tool family. For the Messaging application, we were able to reuse test models created for the S60 platform. For accessing the system under test (SUT), we used A-Tool by Symbio, which is a more conventional test automation tool for smartphone GUI testing. The results of the case study were promising. One of the greatest benefits seems to be the ability to automatically create complicated tests that can be run using A-Tool for regression testing purposes.

In this chapter, we first introduce the background of our work, including our MBT approach and the associated toolset. Then, we present the case study in detail. Finally, we discuss the lessons we learned.

14.1.1 About MBT

Model-based software testing has been an active research topic in academia for more than a decade now. Due an increase in both commercial and open source tool offerings, it has also become a viable option for industrial testing projects. The main benefits of MBT include its ability to automate the test design phase and facilitate the test maintenance phase; tests are automatically generated from a high-level description of the SUT called a model. In the test maintenance phase, after the changes are updated to the models, the tests can be regenerated automatically.

The main obstacles to the wider industrial deployment of MBT have been the lack of both modeling skills and easy-to-use tools. Although newer tools are considerably easier to use than some of the previous ones, there is still the problem of modeling skills. However, we think this problem can be alleviated by proper training and expert modeling services.

> **Tip**
>
> MBT requires not only good tool support but also the right skills.

14.1.2 Our Experience: Using TEMA on Android Applications

This case study describes the use of MBT on Android applications. Android is a new Linux-based open source smartphone platform by Open Handset Alliance. System-level testing of smartphone applications is very challenging, given the availability of a wide variety of configurations, languages, operator settings, and so on (Harty 2010). Manual GUI testing is very much in use in this domain.

Automation would be helpful in many types of testing, such as regression, performance, and robustness testing. However, the fast pace of product creation often hinders the use of automation because the platform must be sufficiently stable to make automatic test execution viable. Time-to-market and feature-richness are the top priorities in this domain, so seldom is time sufficient to prepare support for automated test execution in the platform unless a roadmap exists for similar future products justifying the investment. This calls for efficient reuse of test models across the product family.

In the background of the case study is the TEMA[1] toolset for MBT of smart-phone applications. To make the toolset as easy as possible to use, it is domain-specific for smartphone applications. The tool is based on long-term research into MBT at Tampere University of Technology in Finland. The first version of the tool was targeted for the S60 platform based on the Symbian operating system. Although we had some prior experience in using the tool for testing on the Linux platform, one of the aims of the Android case study was to reuse as much as possible the models developed for S60. For the actual test modeling, we used two different open source tools: Model Designer from the TEMA toolset and ATS4 AppModel, a part of the Nokia ATS tool family. For accessing the SUT, we used A-Tool by Symbio, which is a more conventional test automation tool for smartphone GUI testing.

> **Tip**
>
> Try to reuse models in different environments where possible; don't assume you need to start from scratch.

14.1.3 The Rest of This Chapter

The structure of the rest of this chapter is as follows: In Section 14.2, we review the TEMA toolset. In Section 14.3, we discuss the test modeling process, and the associated tools are explained in detail. The test generation is discussed in Section 14.4, and the connectivity and adaptation issues in Section 14.5. The results of the case study are discussed in Section 14.6, and Section 14.7 concludes the chapter with lessons learned.

14.2 MBT with TEMA Toolset

14.2.1 Domain-Specific Tools

As already mentioned, TEMA is a domain-specific tool. We believe that domain-specific tools are easier to use than more generic ones, which is important for the wider deployment of MBT technology. What this means in practice is that we have been able to hide much of the complexity inherent in this technology behind a simple

---

1. The toolset was originally developed in a project called TEMA (Test Modeling using Action Words).

web GUI that can be used by testers without expert knowledge of the models and algorithms used.

> **Tip**
>
> Domain-specific tools can be easier to use because they can assume knowledge about the domain.

14.2.2   Roles in TEMA

The architecture and the associated roles are described in Figure 14.1. There are three roles:

- *Test model execution specialist:* Resembles a regular test engineer role. The person in this role orders tests from the web GUI and oversees the test execution.
- *Test modeler:* Responsible for creating and maintaining the models based on informal or formal specifications, reverse engineering, and so on.
- *Test manager:* Responsible for ensuring that the objectives are achieved and adequate metrics are produced.

14.2.3   What the TEMA Toolset Does

The toolset generates tests from behavioral models, specifically state machines called *labeled state transition systems* (LSTSs). The toolset allows us to assemble several models into one with *parallel composition*. In practice, this means that the test modeler can create small *model components* to depict different smartphone applications or their parts, and these can be combined into a single *test model* according to predetermined rules. In this way, the individual model components can be small enough to remain comprehensible, yet we can still obtain complex test models necessary for the creation of diverse and comprehensive tests.

The model for a typical application might contain one or two dozen model components and hundreds or thousands of states; as new applications are added, the number of states grows exponentially.[2]

---

2. The estimated number of states in the composed S60 model library is at least 10^{19} states. In practice, such huge state spaces must be generated on the fly because they cannot fit into the memory of any computer. This also calls for a redefinition of conventional coverage metrics based on model elements, such as covering all states.

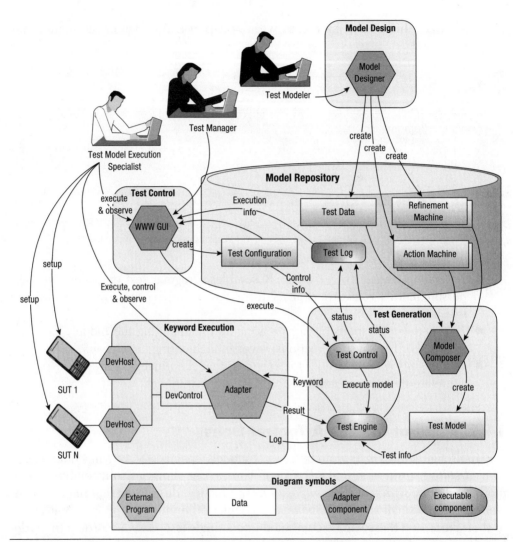

FIGURE 14.1   The architecture of the TEMA toolset with DevHost and DevControl attached

14.2.4 Action Machines and Refinement Machines

The model components are divided into two categories: *action machines* and *refinement machines*. Action machines are used to model the functionality of the system at an abstract level. They are abstract in the sense that they contain no UI-specific information, but only general descriptions of functionality expressed in *action words*

(Buwalda 2003; Fewster and Graham 1999). Action words express user actions, such as launching the Messaging application or beginning the creation of a Short Message Service (SMS) message. The high level of abstraction allows us to use the same action machines for several different phone models, even on different platforms.

In theory, action machines alone could be used to generate abstract tests for manual execution. In practice, however, the automatic execution of tests is immensely valuable; because of that, we need refinement machines.

A refinement machine defines the implementation of the action words of a single action machine for a single phone model. The implementation consists of *keywords*, which correspond to GUI events, such as pressing a key or checking whether a certain text is on the screen. Typically, implementations for action words are simple keyword sequences, such as beginning the creation of an SMS message by opening the menu and selecting the appropriate item. Branching and looping constructs are possible but more likely to occur on the action word level.

14.2.5 Defining Test Data

Apart from the various state machines, we need a method for defining data. A simple form of data is provided by *localization tables*, which can be used to convert a symbolic text string into a GUI-specific one. They allow the use of symbolic names for GUI items in the models that are converted to texts in the specific language version under test.

However, many applications require more complex data, such as the name and phone number of a contact. For these we use *data tables*, which contain information in arrays of structured elements. Data tables can be accessed in the state machines via *data statements*, which consist of simple Python statements. The data statements can also be used to access other Python functionality, such as the date-time library for modeling real-time properties.

14.2.6 Test Configuration: Test Model and Testing Modes

Once the models are ready, tests generated from them can be ordered through the web GUI shown in Figure 14.2. This is done by creating a *test configuration* that defines the test model and the goal of the test based on one of three testing modes:

Test model

- What types of phones are included in this test run
- What model components are included for each phone
- What kind of data is used

Testing mode: What kind of test is generated

- Use case mode
- Coverage mode
- Bug hunt mode

In the use case mode, the test model execution specialist defines a combination of action words that must be executed.

Good Point

Tests, including automated tests, should be driven by the test objectives.

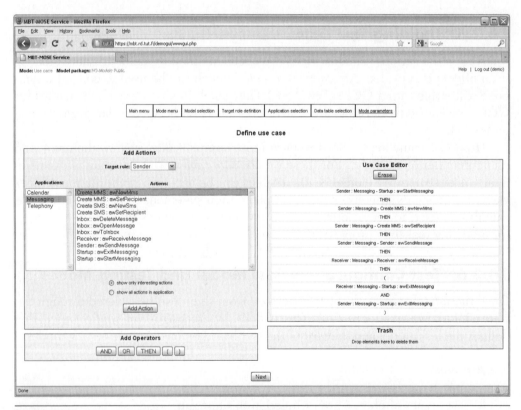

FIGURE 14.2   Use case editor in the TEMA web GUI

The coverage mode offers options such as executing all action words in the model.

Finally, in bug hunt mode, the test is generated with no specific direction or ending criterion, with the goal of traversing the test model in a way likely to uncover potential bugs.

To generate a test from a configuration, one more detail is needed: the specific phones used in the test. The configuration refers to each phone with an arbitrary symbolic name in order to remain usable with different phones; only the types of the phones are fixed.

The prepared configuration can be launched directly through the web GUI, or it can be downloaded as a script that can be executed separately as part of a larger test automation system, for instance.

14.2.7   Test Generation from the Model

Once a test configuration is created and actual phones are attached to it, the test generation can begin. First, the test model is composed from the model components defined in the configuration. Once the test model is ready, the test engine can begin exploring it, looking for ways to fulfill the goal of the test. The exact algorithm used depends on the goal and the specifications of the test configuration.

As the model is traversed, the encountered keywords are sent to the phones for execution. The results of execution can be used to further guide the test run. For example, a keyword could be used to verify that the Contacts application has at least one contact; if the verification fails, the test run must create a new contact if it seeks to handle one. This approach is called *online* testing in contrast to *offline* testing in which test generation and execution phases are separated. All executed actions are written into a test log, which can be used to examine test results and for debugging or repeating the test.

14.2.8   An Example: Sending an SMS Message

As an example of ordering and executing a test, let us consider a case of sending an SMS message. We include two Android devices, which we name Sender and Receiver. For Sender, we include the models for the Messaging and Contacts applications, and for Receiver, just the Messaging application. Because we have a specific sequence of actions in mind, we select the use case mode. We define the use case with the following sequence of actions:

1. Launch Messaging on Sender.
2. Create an SMS message on Sender.

3. Receive a message on Receiver.
4. Close Messaging on both phones.

A use case test is generated with an algorithm suited for seeking out specific actions within the model. Such an algorithm does not need to be told all of the actions involved in the test. For example, creating and receiving a message imply that it must also be sent. Explicitly defining steps makes the task of the algorithm easier, however. That may be useful if the model is large and the test generation correspondingly difficult.

Here the test generation algorithm has some leeway in reaching the third step, because there are two ways to define the recipient: writing the phone number into the message or selecting the recipient from the Contacts application, which we included on Sender. Had we desired, we could have defined the method by adding an appropriate step into the use case.

Finally, the fourth step in the sequence consists of two actions whose order is left undefined; the test generation algorithm may elect to perform them in either order. A similar use case is shown in the web GUI in Figure 14.2.

14.3 Modeling Application Behavior

14.3.1 Modeling with TEMA Model Designer

The modeling tool included in the TEMA toolset (available at http://tema.cs.tut.fi) is TEMA Model Designer, developed for the creation and maintenance of test models. It is based on the concept of a *model library*, a collection of model components from which an actual test model can be generated. Such a structure allows us to obtain different test models as needed, for example, for different smartphones or their combinations, without having to model them all separately. A screenshot from Model Designer is shown in Figure 14.3.

The domain view on the top left shows the contents of the NG Models[3] smartphone model library. It includes several different platforms (such as Android), which in turn contain phone models for which there are various applications (Messaging and Contacts). The same application can appear beneath several different phone models.

---

3. NG stands for Next Generation. The First Generation library only supported S60.

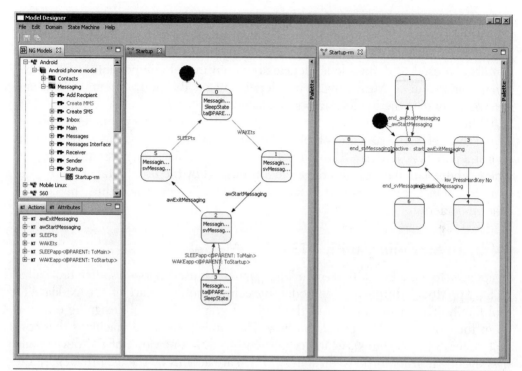

FIGURE 14.3   TEMA Model Designer

Each application is divided into several action machines (such as Main and Create SMS under Messaging), which model the different parts of the application. Under each action machine is the corresponding refinement machine (marked with –rm) for the phone model under which the application appears in the tree.

Model Designer is used to create models directly conforming to the TEMA semantics. Although it offers some features to aid the creation of models, its modeling interface is a straightforward state machine editor. Figure 14.3 shows two editor windows in the middle and on the right, with supporting Actions and Attributes views at the bottom left. The creation of data is likewise simple, with localization tables defined for products and data tables at the top level of the domain, available for all the models.

Most of the modeling effort on Model Designer goes to the creation of the action machines. This is natural because the tested functionality is contained in them. Once action machines are ready, refinement machines and test data are generally easy to create.

More important than simple modeling is Model Designer's ability to maintain the model library. The most obvious maintenance feature is the domain view and its tree structure, which shows how the model components are related to each other. It can also be used to define dependencies between model components (such as the Main component of Messaging being dependent on the Startup component) and what kinds of data the model components need.

When the models are ready for use, they are exported into the model repository where the web GUI can access them. The export can encompass the whole domain or just a part of it, as desired. In partial exports, Model Designer essentially creates a new subdomain that includes the elements desired by the user. Total or partial, the exported models can be imported back into Model Designer and thus shared with other modelers.

14.3.2 Modeling with ATS4 AppModel

In addition to modeling with the Model Designer, we used an open source tool called ATS4 AppModel (http://ats4appmodel.sourceforge.net/), a part of the Nokia ATS tool family. The main function of the tool is a graphical model designing environment for modeling GUI application flow. The models are state machines that contain system events (states), which correspond to different views of the device, and user events (transitions between states), which are actions by the user that cause the device to move into a different view. The tool enables users to define a kind of use case based on the models and to automatically generate test automation scripts and test specification documents from those. In addition to running use cases, the tool allows running through the models using the Chinese postman algorithm. The tool also enables users to simulate their models and use cases and has a plug-in interface for test execution tools, making it possible to directly execute tests on the SUT. A screenshot from the tool in the model designing view is given in Figure 14.4.

Similar to our system, the test execution in ATS4 AppModel is defined with keywords. When the modeler is creating a transition between states, he or she can specify an event description that contains some of the predefined phrases to express what actions cause the transition to occur. For example, a music player application could have a transition with the following description: *The user presses softkey "Play" to start playback*. The tool automatically detects the defined phrase inside the description, and once a test case that contains that transition is created, the tool includes a keyword *kw_PressSoftkey "Play"* in the script. While writing the description, the application automatically suggests phrases that fit to the text. The states in the models can also contain actions, typically verifications, which are executed once the state is entered. The phrases and their corresponding keywords are configurable, making it possible to adjust the tool for multiple domains.

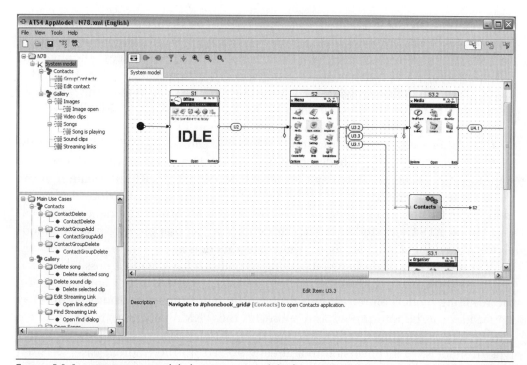

FIGURE 14.4   ATS4 AppModel showing a model of an S60 device. Screenshots from the SUT can be used to specify model states.

Good Point

Build an environment that helps testers create automated tests; for example, suggest correct syntax for keywords.

Models in ATS4 AppModel can be made more dynamic using a flag mechanism. Flags allow the modeler to enable or disable other transitions while executing a transition. This enables modelers to restrict certain areas in the model until some actions have been executed first.

The main difference between ATS4 AppModel and TEMA is that ATS4 AppModel is an offline tool. For example, ATS4 AppModel modeling formalism does not support branching transitions based on the results of the previously executed keywords. Because of this, the state of the device must be strictly known beforehand, and modeling nondeterministic behavior is restricted. In contrast, TEMA models can check the state of the device and adapt the test run on the basis of that knowledge. Moreover, ATS4 AppModel cannot switch between applications without being explicitly told to do so. The same goes with models that use multiple devices. Although this is supported by ATS4 AppModel, all changes to other targets are explicit. In TEMA, the modeler can define specific states where the active application or the target can be changed to any other application or target included to the test. Finally, defining test data such as inputs to the SUT is more versatile in TEMA.

The differences between the tools are mostly caused by their different goals: TEMA models are specifically designed from the testing perspective, whereas ATS4 AppModel is meant for designing GUI flow, and including such information in the models is not relevant for that purpose. The advantage of ATS4 AppModel is that the models can be easier to understand and create without former experience in modeling. Also, if ATS4 AppModel is used during the GUI design process, resulting models are a good foundation for more detailed test models later.

The similarities of these two modeling formalisms have made it possible to convert a model created with ATS4 AppModel into a TEMA model and to execute the resulting models on our system. In fact, the modeling formalism used in ATS4 AppModel can be interpreted as a subset of the TEMA modeling formalism. We have used this possibility before to convert the former type of models to the latter type of models, so a conversion tool already existed. In the Android case, we used ATS4 AppModel to model the Calendar application and then converted the model into a TEMA model before execution. We were also able to compose models created with ATS4 AppModel and TEMA and execute them concurrently, although the composition required some manual adjustments.

Good Point

If something isn't directly suitable, automate the conversion of it into a form that is.

14.4 Generation of Tests

14.4.1 Function and Choice of Guidance Algorithms

Test generation in the TEMA toolset is based on graph search algorithms. Without going into the theory, we now briefly describe the basic principles behind the different types of test generation algorithms, with emphasis on the ones we used in this case study, because they are essential for any MBT solution.

The quintessential part of test generation is performed by the guidance algorithm. The algorithm's task is to examine the model and the goals of the test as stated by the test configuration and, based on those, decide the best way to progress in the model. Different goals call for different kinds of algorithms.

An important question in the choice of algorithm is how densely the sought-after target elements (actions, states, etc.) occur in the models. The goals of a coverage mode test tend to involve densely packed targets that appear regularly everywhere in the test model, at least initially. Conversely, a use case test can often only progress with the execution of a single specific action, making the targets extremely sparse. Finally, a bug hunt has no specific targets at all, and the guidance algorithm must base its decisions on other criteria.

14.4.2   Guidance Algorithm Trade-Offs

The simplest of guidance algorithms is the completely random one. The greatest advantage of the random algorithm is its speed: With minimal calculations needed, the tests can generally progress as fast as the SUT can execute keywords. The disadvantage is, of course, that the actual guidance is minimal, making random a bad choice for seeking out sparsely appearing targets. However, random is quite efficient in finding densely appearing targets, such as in initial coverage mode tests. It is also a solid choice for a bug hunt.

One smarter algorithm is a breadth-first search, which seeks out the target closest to the current position in the models. A breadth-first search is the best choice when seeking sparsely appearing targets. It is also generally a fair all-around choice for any test with specific targets because it can always be counted on to find some way to make progress.

A weakness of a breadth-first search is that it always executes the first target it finds, regardless of the consequences in the long term. A fixed-depth search algorithm does not have this problem. It searches the model in every direction up to a fixed number of transitions, and then makes a choice between all the routes found. A variant version continues to search until a time limit is reached, typically until the previous keyword has been completely executed. Where a breadth-first search may be lured into a useless area of the model by a single appealing target, a fixed-depth search can choose an initially weak but ultimately valuable direction and can generate excellent tests with densely packed targets. However, small search depths fare ill when targets are sparse, whereas large depths increase the time consumption significantly, making the choice of depth a delicate balancing matter.

The algorithms designed for bug hunt are a different matter entirely. With no specific targets defined, the algorithm can only base its decisions on the general features of the model. One example is an algorithm that seeks frequent switches between applications in the hope of uncovering concurrency issues. In practice, a random algorithm works quite well, possibly with some minor tweaks such as avoiding recently visited actions or states.

14.5   Connectivity and Adaptation

14.5.1   The Adapter Executes Keywords

The test execution level in TEMA models is defined with keywords. The phase wherein the abstract keywords are executed in the target device is called an adaptation, and the system that performs this phase is called an adapter (refer to Figure 14.1). In this section, we describe how the adaptation was realized in the Android environment.

The adapter communicates with the test server using either socket or HTTP/HTTPS connections. The adapter runs in a loop, receiving a keyword from the server, executing the keyword on the SUT, and finally reporting the result of the keyword back to the server. The communication protocol between the test engine and the adapter is simple, thus new adapters can be attached to the system with relative ease. The main difference from other test automation tools is that in our online system, the test execution needs to work together with the test engine, when in many existing test automation systems, the test execution is based on running predefined test case scripts offline.

14.5.2   Action Keywords and Verification Keywords

Keywords are roughly divided into two different categories:

- Action keywords typically cause the state of the device to change. These keywords define user actions that can be performed on the device, such as tapping a touch screen or pressing a button.
- Verification keywords are used to verify that the state of the device corresponds to the expected state in the models, that is, making sure that expected texts or bitmaps can be found on the screen. The verification keywords typically do not affect the state of the device in any way.

14.5.3 Challenges in Implementing Verification

The experiences we gained in the Android domain and in the previous domains we have tested have shown that implementing the adaptation is often considerably more difficult in the case of verification keywords than action keywords.

Performing state verification with bitmap comparison would often be technically simple, but maintaining a large set of bitmaps becomes tedious. Therefore, our verifications are based on finding specific texts from the screen. However, searching for these texts on the device can be more complicated than bitmap comparison.

Typically, there are two ways to facilitate text-based verification. If the target platform supports API access to its GUI resources (for example, Accessibility APIs), the texts can be searched through that API.

However, in many situations, the only way to search texts is to observe the screen in the same manner as the user. To automate the verification in such a situation, optical character recognition (OCR) technologies can be used.

Both of these methods have their own problems. Although API access is often a fast and reliable way to find texts, it sometimes provides a slightly different view of the application than the user can actually see. This could lead to false-positive results where according to API, the text is visible to the user, but in reality it cannot be seen on the screen, for example, because some other window obscures it.

> **Good Point**
>
> Checking the results of a test may not be straightforward.

In addition to performance issues, the main problems with OCR are related to its reliability. Especially if the color themes in the device are complex, or the fonts are too decorative, OCR algorithms often have problems identifying texts from the screen.

14.5.4 Using A-Tool and Changes Needed to Use It

Adaptation in the Android case was founded on a test automation tool called A-Tool from Symbio (www.symbio.com/products/a-tool/). A-Tool is based on running predefined test scripts that are written with a specific A-Tool scripting language. The tool consists of a UI application for designing, running, and monitoring scripted test cases (A-Tool scripter), a library component used to communicate with the devices from the PC running A-Tool (DevControl), and a host driver application installed in the device (DevHost). The communication between DevControl and DevHost can be handled by Bluetooth, USB, or socket connection. DevHost executes actions on the device and is specific for each different device type. At the time of writing, the tool supports testing in S60, Android, Maemo, Windows Mobile, and Windows desktop. The A-Tool UI and the DevControl components support Windows operating systems.

The script-based testing in A-Tool was incompatible with the online approach of the TEMA model-based system, which is the same problem we encountered in other domains as well. That is why the A-Tool UI could not be used. Instead, only the DevControl library was used to communicate with the DevHost in the devices.

On top of DevControl, an online keyword-based interface was built. In addition to the A-Tool components, the Microsoft Office Document Imaging (MODI) component was used to perform OCR on the device screen captures acquired with DevControl. The MODI component is delivered with the Microsoft Office tools since version 2003 and can be programmatically accessed through a COM interface. The structure of the adaptation and its relation to A-Tool is shown in Figure 14.5.

Performing basic actions such as pressing keys, launching processes, and tapping touch screen coordinates was easy to perform with the interface provided by DevControl.

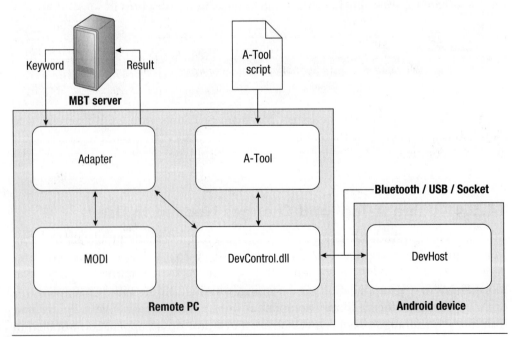

FIGURE 14.5   Android adapter

However, to make models easier to maintain, using exact coordinates of GUI components in the refinement machines is best avoided. Instead, whenever possible, the keywords should be specified so that some text is used to find the component from the screen. This enables minor GUI rearrangements without needing to maintain the models.

Good Point

Avoid verifications that are tied to fixed points on a screen, such as coordinates or bitmaps, because they require more maintenance effort in the long term.

The DevControl component did not provide such services; therefore, OCR was used to find coordinates for texts from the device screen capture. As just described, text verification was also used to identify different states of the device.

14.5.5   Additional Problems

In most cases, the MODI OCR performed well with the Android screen and fonts, but some images were problematic. These included screens that had complicated color themes, such as fading colors, or fonts that were slightly transparent or otherwise did not resolve well from the background. However, it was found that by trying OCR on multiple images that were processed in different ways, more reliable OCR results were gained. For example, if the OCR did not find a searched text from the original image, we created inverted color and monochromatic images from the original screen capture and double-checked the result with these images.

Tip

Problems with optical character recognition (OCR) in a complex visual environment may be overcome by additional manipulation of the image.

Another problem with the test execution was caused by technical problems in getting the current image of the device. This problem forced us to run tests extremely slowly to make sure the device screen was updated before executing any actions that required information from the screen. In such a situation, we used a delay of over a minute when normally a few seconds is enough. Even such a long delay did not completely remove the problem, although it became rarer when measured on the number of test steps executed. Unfortunately, the actual cause of the problem was not found, though the prototype hardware in the device used was suspected. With an older Android phone model on which the test automation was first tried, this problem did not exist.

> **Good Point**
>
> You may never solve all the technical problems, but that doesn't mean test automation will not be worthwhile.

14.6   Results

In this section, the results of the case study are discussed. Some of the details have been omitted for confidentiality reasons.

Concerning the modeling effort, adapting the Messaging models from a phone model of another platform and creating the Contacts models from scratch took roughly a day of time. Calendar modeling took likewise about a day from a modeler who had little previous modeling experience with ATS4 AppModel. In addition, configuring ATS4 AppModel (adding phrases and keywords for the Android domain) and debugging the models for all three applications took some additional time. While the configuration took perhaps 1 hour, model debugging was more tedious because it involved running a test until a modeling bug was found, fixing that bug, starting a new test, and so on. This is usual in MBT, but after the models become mature enough, the bugs found are problems in the applications instead of the models, which is the real purpose of testing. In the case of the Calendar application, for instance, the debugging of the models took about 1 day. As usual, first the test runs fail fast, but after some time, failures occur much less frequently.

Combined models of the three applications were run mostly with random guidance algorithm (as explained earlier). After the modeling bugs had been fixed, problems with OCR and the screen update issues were the typical problems that caused our long-period tests to stop unexpectedly; the target duration of such tests is at least some days. However, we were able to run multiple tests that lasted dozens of hours, with the longest one over 40 hours—such a random test would have been very unpleasant to execute manually. In addition, the models were run with a guidance that aimed to produce switches between the applications. The goal was to find out if alternating between applications that share resources (such as Contacts and Messaging) introduces problems.

As usual in MBT projects, most of the bugs were found during the modeling phase, and some issues were revealed using test execution also. During the modeling, four bugs or instances of inconsistent behavior were found in the applications. In addition, two bugs were found in nonmodeled applications with a bit of exploratory testing. Two of the bugs were found while executing the models. One of them can be reproduced every time. The other has been encountered twice, but any pattern that exactly causes this bug has not been found at the time of writing. The first bug is concurrency related and occurs only if the user presses a button in a specific moment, while the application is performing background operations. The second bug caused the application to crash.

14.7 Conclusion

The purpose of this case study was to evaluate MBT on the Android platform. The platform is new, and there is a large application developer community. Enabling MBT on this platform would enable third-party developers to test their applications in the context of preinstalled applications, including interaction testing producing switches between the applications. Some lessons we learned during the case study are discussed here.

First, the modeling effort needed was much less than anticipated. Reusing some of the high-level models from the S60 domain helped in this respect. Moreover, the modelers were familiar with the tools and had previous experience in test modeling. Considering the adapter development, it took much more time, but it is still reasonable effort because the adapter can be reused in the future projects. The reliability and performance of OCR-based solutions is problematic, but this was something we anticipated.

The number and type of bugs we found were satisfactory. As usual in this kind of industrial case study, the applications were well tested before our pilot started. In the case of the Messaging application, for instance, it had been tested manually using hundreds of test cases revealing hundreds of bugs that had been fixed before our case study started. The manual tests had involved both functional and nonfunctional test cases. Nevertheless, the case study revealed issues that could have been found in manual tests, but a more detailed comparison with manual testing is left for future work; such a study would require additional considerations on how to set up the experiment and how to define the metrics used for comparison.

Unfortunately, we were not able to repeat the bug that crashed one of the applications. Based on our experience, some of the bugs observed with MBT can be "corner cases" that depend on the exact timing and similar factors. Such bugs can be tedious to locate, but application crash is always worth investigating and reporting. Moreover, while the number of bugs was moderate, by running thorough tests, our confidence in the quality of the applications increased.

In the future, the adapter must be developed to be more reliable. From the modeling side, the models could be improved to test performance issues, such as whether it takes too long for a menu to open after a key is pressed. In this case, the interaction testing becomes handy because the response time is affected by the other applications running concurrently. However, this approach needs to be supported by the platform and the adapter to make such testing reliable enough. Moreover, because model debugging takes considerable time, static analysis tools should be developed and integrated into the modeling tools to catch at least those modeling bugs that can be found this way.

14.8 Acknowledgments

The authors want to acknowledge partial funding from Tekes, Nokia, Ixonos, Symbio, Cybercom Plenware, F-Secure, Qentinel, and Prove Expertise, as well as the Academy of Finland (grant number 121012). Special thanks to the other members of the TEMA team and to Symbio and Riku Henriksson for enabling this study. In addition, Julian Harty helped by commenting on a draft version of this chapter.

14.9 References

A-Tool by Symbio. Available at www.symbio.com/products/a-tool/.

ATS4 AppModel. Available at http://ats4appmodel.sourceforge.net/.

Buwalda, Hans. (2003). "Action Figures." *Software Testing and Quality Engineering*, 5(2): 42–47.

Fewster, Mark, and Dorothy Graham. (1999). *Software Test Automation: Effective Use of Test Execution Tools*. Harlow, UK: Addison–Wesley.

Harty, Julian. (2010). *A Practical Guide to Testing Wireless Smartphone Applications*. San Rafael, CA: Morgan & Claypool.

Jääskeläinen, Antti, Mika Katara, Antti Kervinen, Mika Maunumaa, Tuula Pääkkönen, Tommi Takala, and Heikki Virtanen. (2009). "Automatic GUI Test

Generation for Smart Phone Applications—An Evaluation." In *Proceedings of the Software Engineering in Practice Track of the 31st International Conference on Software Engineering (ICSE 2009)*, pp. 112–122 (companion volume). Vancouver, Canada, May 2009. IEEE Computer Society.

Jääskeläinen, Antti, Antti Kervinen, and Mika Katara. (2008). "Creating a Test Model Library for GUI Testing of Smartphone Applications." In *Proceedings of the Eight International Conference on Quality Software (QSIC 2008)*, pp. 276–282. Oxford, United Kingdom, August 2008. IEEE Computer Society.

Tampere University of Technology. TEMA toolset site. Available at http://tema.cs.tut.fi.

CHAPTER 15

TEST AUTOMATION OF SAP BUSINESS PROCESSES

Christoph Mecke
Melanie Reinwarth
Armin Gienger

Christoph Mecke, Melanie Reinwarth, and Armin Gienger tell how automation is used in testing major application areas of SAP, specifically banking and health care. Because SAP applications are deployed in many client sites and have a long life, the test automation is on a large scale, with over 3 million automation lines of code and 2,400 users of the automation. The testware architecture of the tool they developed is very modular. The standards and guidelines put in place ensure the automation can be used in many areas and in many countries, and the tool can be used by SAP customers as well. The automated tests must be ready to go as soon as new software is delivered to enable the testing to help speed delivery rather than slow it down. Some of the problems they encountered concerned testing parallel versions and multiple releases, consistency of test data environments, setting of customized parameters, and country-specific legal issues. One particularly good idea the authors relate is to have a tool do static analysis on the test automation scripts. They also warn about ending up with "zombie scripts": dead automation code in a script. This story takes place in Germany and India over several years. See Table 15.1.

Table 15.1   Case Study Characteristics

Classification	This Case Study
Application domain	Enterprise resource planning (ERP) systems
Application size	Health care: 2,907 KLOC; Banking: 2,208 KLOC
Location	Walldorf, Germany and Bangalore, India
Lifecycle	Traditional
Number on the project	
Number of testers	
Number of automators	Health care: 1; Banking: 7
Time span	Health care: Creation, 1 month; execution, 3 hours Banking: Creation, ~3 months; execution, 10 hours
Dates	Health care: 2007–2010; banking: 2009–2010
Tool type(s)	Commercial/inhouse
Pilot study undertaken	No
ROI measured	No
Successful?	Yes
Still breathing?	Yes

15.1 Background for the Case Study

One of the lessons we learned at SAP over the years was very simple: Test automation is nothing but software development. This statement, of course, sounds contradictory to the message some test tool vendors would like to send to the market: Test automation is easy, no programming skills are required, and it is best done by end users.

At least for us, we can say that any test automation project that did not follow software development processes and standards failed or ended up with huge maintenance efforts. Proper test specifications, reviews, coding standards, and—probably most important—a strict reuse principle have been proven as key success factors.

This chapter gives insight to our best practices in automating SAP Business Processes of SAP Banking and SAP Healthcare. We focus only on test automation at the system level.

15.1.1 Special Requirements of SAP as a Software Company

15.1.1.1 Numbers

For integration and UI testing at the SAP Business Suite, we mainly use our own test tool, eCATT, which comes (for free!) with each SAP product developed in SAP's own programming language, Advanced Business Application Programming (ABAP; see tool description in Section 15.1.2). To provide some numbers, we can say that we own about 38,000 automated test scripts (usually valid for several releases of each product). On average, one test script has about 10 variants, each using different input data.

The test scripts are compiled out of about 130,000 different modules, which means an average of three to four modules per test script. In terms of thousands of lines of code (KLOC), this means a total size of about 3,600 KLOC for our test scripts (without counting comments or blank lines). This number probably demonstrates best why well-defined processes and standards are crucial for our test automation. With respect to execution, we produce about 140,000 logs per month. The number of users creating or executing these scripts is about 2,400. The lines of test code on a unit level (developer tests using unit test frameworks) are not considered in this case study.

15.1.1.2 Software Releases and Test Script Versions

As a software company, SAP has some special requirements for test tools and processes that might be different from the situation in other projects. The most important difference we see is that we maintain different releases of one product in parallel. Because our maintenance strategy ensures that our customers can rely for many years on first-class support and maintenance from SAP, it takes a long time until a release runs out of maintenance and therefore regression testing is no longer required.

Good Point

The longer production software is in use, the greater the use of automated regression tests can be.

Our SAP Business Suite also allows the combination of older product releases of one product with the newest release of another product, which generates a new dimension of combinations that have to be covered. If the test case stays the same for these combinations from a functional point of view, we of course do not want to generate another copy of the corresponding automated test script even if some screens have been changed slightly. We therefore expect that a test tool can identify the release we intend to test and select the appropriate test script version automatically.

Good Point

Automating configuration management tasks can prevent many costly mistakes.

15.1.1.3 Technology

Because SAP also develops its own development environment and technology (e.g., ABAP), we have to ensure that the test tools stay up to date in this respect. We therefore have to ensure that our test tools are developed in parallel to the development of the technology so that the products that make use of the new technology can be tested before the product and technologies are released to our customers for the first time. To do this with an external partner would be quite difficult and would generate a dependency that is not desirable for us.

15.1.1.4 Distributed Development

SAP has several development labs worldwide working closely together, so we also need to ensure that a worldwide cooperation regarding testing is (tool) supported. This includes a reliable mechanism for access and authorization, locking control, support of different languages, and so on. Because these requirements are the same as our customers expect from our products, it is another good reason why SAP decided long ago to go for its own test tools using the same technology as for our products.

15.1.2 Test Automation Tools at SAP

15.1.2.1 Introduction to eCATT

eCATT stands for *extended Computer-Aided Test Tool*. The word *extended* comes from the fact that eCATT is the successor of the older CATT tool. eCATT is SAP's own automation test tool and provides comprehensive capabilities for testing SAP solutions in an automated way.

By automating the user behavior, eCATT enables both component-based functional tests and integration tests based on business processes that run across different components and system boundaries. A typical use scenario of the latter is the automated regression test, which is performed after extending the system or installing support packages for example.

15.1.2.2 *Advantages of eCATT*

Now let us have a look at the advantages the use of eCATT offers (the following list is just an overview):

- eCATT is included in the basic component of SAP applications as of SAP Web Application Server 6.20. Therefore, it is *free of charge*. Our customers and partners therefore do not need to acquire any extra license if they want to use it. It comes with the package.
- eCATT can access all layers of the SAP system, which means presentation layer, application layer, and database. For example, you can execute a transaction in SAP GUI (the graphical user interface of SAP) and check later if the correct values have arrived in the database.
- eCATT is remote-enabled. This means that eCATT is managed and maintained in one central system. And out of this central system, you can run tests in a complex system landscape.
- eCATT offers maximal reuse of all kinds of test and system data because this data is also treated in a modular way. What is meant by modular? Just imagine that you have written a test script and you write the system information, where the test should run, and the test data (the data sets with which the test should run) as fixed values in the script. There won't be much reuse. But eCATT uses the concept of system and data containers. Instead of writing the data in the test script, you write them in containers, and then many different test scripts can use or reference a subset or partial quantity of this container data.
- eCATT can integrate external tools for extending reach to non-SAP applications.

15.1.2.3 *Limitations of eCATT*

As with any tool, eCATT has some limitations and things that can be improved. Actually, one of the authors acts as the product owner of eCATT and maintains a list of requirements coming from our users (internal and external). These requirements get implemented step by step. Some of the major limitations we see at the moment are as follows:

- eCATT is intentionally limited to SAP UI and API technologies in the ABAP development environment (SAPGUI, ABAP Web Dynpro). Other UI technologies, such as HTML, are not supported. In this case, SAP has an official API where other test tools can be integrated (BC-eCATT).
- eCATT is clearly a tool which addresses power users. Programming experience is a must. End users or business users will find it hard to use.

15.2   Standards and Best Practices

As with all big organizations, it is also a challenge for SAP to agree and implement one widely accepted approach to standards and best practices for test automation. We accept that a one-size-fits-all approach is not feasible throughout the whole company. But we do want to use a common standard in test automation for some clusters of products that have some common characteristics. The SAP Business Suite is such a cluster for which we have started in an iterative way some initiatives during the last several years to achieve this.

> **Good Point**
>
> Automation standards are needed when many people will use the automation; however, exceptions should also be allowed when justified.

We would like to outline some of the most important standards that have been worked out by test architects over the years. These standards are documented and stored in a central place. Some standards are supported by templates. In all cases, it is important to describe good examples in detail. The rollout was always done onsite via our test automation network. From time to time, we check whether the standards are executed and, if they are not, we find out why. In some cases, these compliance checks can be done automatically.

15.2.1   Regression Test Process

This general guideline gives an overview of the whole system regression test cycle. It starts with the definition of our test scope. The test scope is broken down into our test objects and a process of how to prioritize tests based on a risk management process. The priorities are set from 1 (highest) to 4 (lowest). Priorities 1 and 2 are the main candidates for test automation. These priorities are subject to change based on feedback by support, customers, and others. As a basis for our test objects, we use the use cases and requirements and link them to test objects and test scripts so that we can build up a complete traceability chain.

Other topics in this guideline are the general test concept (with focus on test automation) describing execution frequency during development and maintenance phases and the way our reporting is done.

15.2.2   Specification and Design

Once we have identified the test objects as a first step, it is crucial to get the right understanding of the expectations and requirements of a test case. Because SAP software is highly dependent on customizing and existing data on the database (state driven), the main part of a test specification is about the preconditions for the test case. Then all the execution steps have to be described and reviewed. We still see room for improvement by getting the widely accepted black-box test design techniques better integrated in this process of describing the goal of our test cases more clearly. We see it as a general risk in test automation that the focus is sometimes too much on tools and all the technical traps and pitfalls connected to them. This happens especially when inexperienced people are on the team and the tasks of test case design and test automation have to be done by the same person (we have seen specification documents describing perfectly the preconditions and steps but without any description of an expected result).

For reasons of simplification, we have a chapter in our template focusing on test script architecture and design within the same document. The main focus of this chapter is to ensure reuse.

For reasons of stability, we generally prefer API-based testing instead of UI testing on a system level (using eCATT) as long as the test goal can be achieved and the APIs needed are available.

15.2.3   Coding Guidelines

Most test automation tools offer a scripting language open for freestyle programming. But it does not always make sense to use this flexibility if aspects like maintenance and reuse come into play. In our coding guideline, we therefore give clear dos and don'ts.

Spaghetti code is clearly something we want to avoid. Modularization and stable interfaces are a key success factor. It also makes sense to parameterize as much as possible in order to avoid costly rework even if the actual test case you are going to automate does not require all the fields as parameters. Other best practices are the use of the correct data types per parameter (most test tools just use a default "text" parameter). This will lead to more stability if scripts are reused (the most famous examples of this are date and currency fields).

Other "softer" standards are the way we comment our code as well as the naming conventions we use for scripts and parameters, which make it easier for everybody to reuse other scripts.

Many other things are proprietary to the tool we use and are therefore not described here.

15.2.4   Code Inspections

A process we also copied from product development is code inspections, which we apply to our own test automation (eCATT) code. We found that it is very useful to have somebody who is a test automation expert from a closely related area review the test script. This person has to prepare for the code inspection meeting by walking through the code beforehand on his own. In the meeting, he presents to the author on what he understood and where he had problems. We found that, through such feedback, the discovery of possible issues that can lead to stability or maintenance problems in our test scripts is much higher.

> **Good Point**
>
> Inspections and reviews are very effective on automation code, scripts, and documentation.

15.2.5   Reuse Guideline

The key success factor in our test automation projects has always been the strict reuse of the same scripts. In a big organization, this is a never-ending struggle. The reasons consolidation and refactoring activities are necessary from time to time are always the same: New people come on board; sometimes it is a challenge to find the reuse modules; and sometimes, from a short-term perspective, it seems easier to create your own script to perfectly meet your expectations instead of extending an existing script. Nevertheless, we know of no example where a test automation project was successful in the long run without strictly following this rule.

Note: In the last several years, keyword-driven test automation has become popular. We had a close look at this concept and found it similar to our reuse approach (if the names of the reuse scripts are clear and understandable).

15.2.6   Checkman for eCATT

One of the most interesting tool improvements in test automation at SAP was a tool called Checkman for eCATT. The idea was to find weaknesses and defects in our test script code itself. Because static checks are a best practice in all modern development environments, we found that it was worthwhile implementing the same for our test scripts, keeping in mind the enormous number of test scripts at SAP.

As for other static test tools, not all kinds of code problems can be found with static checks, but the same arguments for doing it anyway are also valid here. A static tool can do many routine checks on a regular basis with high accuracy. This is also the easiest way in a big organization to monitor if the agreed standards are followed where they can be translated into a static check.

> **Good Point**
>
> Static analysis is useful for any kind of code, including test automation scripts. After an initial implementation cost, it offers virtually free defect finding for those defects that are statically detectable.

Again, we took advantage of the fact that our test tools and scripts are fully integrated in our ABAP development environment, so we could simply extend the existing framework (Checkman) for static checks in our product development to our eCATT test scripts. Features like direct navigation from issues into the code, reporting, workflow integration, and exception handling have simply been reused for our purposes.

Ideas for the checks we wanted were collected and prioritized by the test automation community. Not all of them turned out to be feasible, and some would have been very costly from a performance perspective. Most checks focus on efficiency and maintenance. Examples of these are checks on the reuse principle, proper attribute settings, naming conventions, and so on. Our favorite checks are on test script modules that are not being used anywhere and test scripts with no code at all. You might have doubts if this is really relevant and why we even bother with these checks, but we found that this is really an important and unfortunately existing issue in practice: What sometimes happens is that a test script runs into a problem and it turns out that the problem is not on the product side but in the test script itself. Unfortunately, sometimes the erroneous code in the test script is commented out for whatever reason (e.g., to correct it at a later time). If this code is forgotten, you have created a "zombie" test case. From now on, it appears in all test reports with a nice green status (but actually doing nothing). Because nobody usually looks into a test script that is running fine, the test case becomes completely invisible. This can lead to a dangerous situation and might even result in wrong release decisions. A static check on this brings this script back on our radar screen so that it can be fixed.

> **Tip**
>
> Beware of "zombie" test cases in your automation suites!

Not surprisingly, we now face the situation where we have a huge number of issues from all of these checks (average is three problems per script!). It is also interesting to compare test teams by the results of the checks. Currently, we have to work toward reducing these high numbers of script issues. On the other hand, we are always working on new ideas for checks; this makes us a learning organization in test automation but also increases the number of issues we find.

15.3   eCATT Usage Examples

In this chapter, we present two examples of test automation for business processes. The examples are from different application areas (health care and banking) and use different approaches for the automation frameworks that are used.

15.3.1   Data-Driven Automation Framework for Health Care Processes

When doing software testing, you often must deal with a huge number of test cases derived from combinations of your import parameters. This is just as true for testing business processes inside SAP with its wide variability in configurations and characteristics.

We illustrate this challenge with an example of a regression test for a business process in the area of health care (using the SAP for Healthcare solution).

Our to-be tested health care process consists of the five process steps shown in Figure 15.1.

The underlying software is mature and in use by many customers for many years. However, because lots of different country versions exist and frequent legal changes have to be implemented down to even very old releases, we decided to do very thorough regression testing for this process and execute these tests with a high frequency in several releases. For each of the process steps, so-called BAPIs (business application programming interfaces) are available. A BAPI is a standardized programming

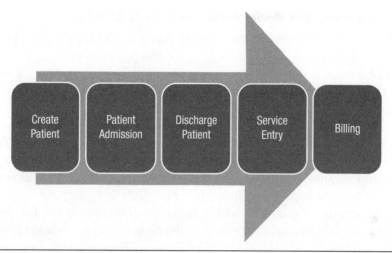

FIGURE 15.1 Health care process

interface that facilitates external access to business processes and data in the SAP System. They are implemented and stored as RFC-enabled function modules in the Function Builder of the ABAP Workbench and therefore can be called by eCATT. Using BAPIs, automated tests can be performed without using the UI.

We automate the process test by creating an eCATT for each step that

- Calls a BAPI that executes the step in the system under test.
- Checks for successful execution of the step.

To understand the complexity of the test scenario, we need to consider the input parameters in our test scenario:

- Import parameters of the BAPIs
- Systemwide settings

The goal of our test is to cover as many combinations as possible of the parameters to check if the interaction of those parameters will have negative effects on the processes' expected behavior.

We use the test technique of *all-pair testing* for this, a method that focuses on all pairwise combinations.

15.3.1.1 Defining the Model for All-Pair Tests (APT)

Before we can apply the method, we must define a model for the right parameters. It does not make sense to put variation on all the parameters (e.g., a patient's last name should not have any effect on the process behavior). Therefore, it is essential to choose the parameters that really have an influence on the program flow. For each BAPI, we did this with the help of experts from development. Out of the 50 to 100 parameters per BAPI, 5 to 10 of those "essential" parameters were identified.

In addition, we chose the systemwide setting Country Version (health care software includes a lot of country-specific legal requirements) and the Business Function (an enhancement concept introduced with Release ERP 600, which allows the customer to switch on additional functionality optionally).

The next step for the APT model is to define the value range for each of the parameters—we did this again with help of developers and application experts. The value range reaches from binary values (like Business Function switches on or off) up to 10 different values for a configuration parameter. Other parameter value ranges needed to be segmented using "equivalence classes" (i.e., representatives for all values that have similar behaviors).

All in all, our model contains 43 parameters with about 1.4×10^{15} combinations!

15.3.1.2 Computing the Test Cases

For the APT model, we use a tool called PICT from Microsoft, which calculates the pairwise test cases based on a list of parameters along with the value ranges that are provided in an input text file. The PICT tool now computes the test cases, and creates the output. Fifty-two different test cases were computed by this method. Out of about 1.4×10^{15} possible test cases, we restricted ourselves to 52, making sure to test each "combination of two" at least once.

15.3.1.3 Designing the eCATT

The eCATT design is quite simple: For each process step, we call a BAPI that executes the process step, and then we check if this process step was successful—that is, no error messages were thrown and all expected values were created in the database tables.

With the nice feature in eCATT of having test scripts and test data stored in different objects, the various test cases can be created in a very efficient way: You either upload or copy and paste the test cases produced by the PICT tool to the eCATT's test data containers.

Effort considerations include the following:

1. *Defining the model:* Because of the comparably simple structure of the test, the right APT parameters could be quickly found. On average, the developers spent 2 hours for that task per process step (i.e., 10 hours overall).
2. *Creating the test script:* Creating an eCATT that calls a BAPI is easy. For stable eCATT design, though, you need to implement preparation steps and postprocessing steps like checks as well. On average, the creation time per eCATT for one process step was 1 day.
3. *Creating the test cases:* Entering the APT parameters together with the values into the PICT tool, calculating the test cases, and copying the test cases to the test variants in eCATT took about 1 hour.
4. *Executing the test:* For one test case, the eCATT execution time was on average 3 minutes (i.e., all test cases were executed in about 3 hours).

15.3.1.4 *Results and Outlook*

The most important aspect for these tests is the detection of regression defects that might be introduced by our own corrections and enhancements to the existing software before it is shipped. Several of those unwanted side effects were found and corrected just in time. We successfully reached the goal to increase the level of test coverage (which can be seen by an increased code coverage) and thus increased the trust in the quality of our software.

The test project is still going on, and we plan to extend the test scenarios. We want to test more processes by combining different process steps from other customer use cases. For some of the processes, we will then need to combine the API tests with UI tests, because BAPIs are not available for all steps.

15.3.2 Test Automation Framework for Banking Scenarios

The next example shows the implementation of test automation in the SAP for Banking solution.

For testing banking processes, we have the following main challenges:

- Many processes span over a long time frame (e.g., several weeks).
- Within the process lifecycle, parallel processes may be interdependent on each other.

We show this implementation with two example processes, as shown in Figure 15.2.

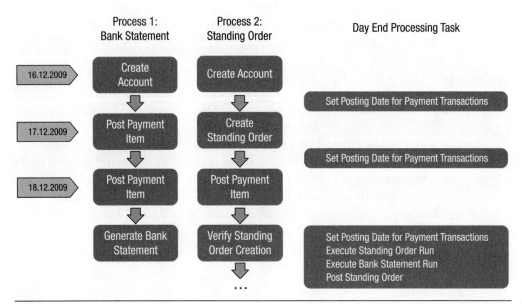

FIGURE 15.2 Banking process

Our test objects are processes structured in *elementary functions* (EFs). An EF is the smallest building block of a process that is independent of other process steps. In Figure 15.2, there are two processes shown: Bank Statement and Standing Order; the chained boxes such as Create Account and Post Payment Item are EFs.

In addition to the elementary functions, there are the *day end processing* tasks (DETs; the last column of Figure 15.2); these are tasks that need to be executed at the end of the business day.

We implemented the automated test cases for these processes in the following way:

- For each EF and each DET, reusable eCATT modules were developed, along with checks that verify the successful execution of each task. This modules are implemented by calling either a BAPI, an ABAP report, or a dialogue from eCATT.
- For a simulated real-time bank process, a framework was developed that controls both the per-day EF execution (in an inner loop) and the DETs in an outer loop.
- The tests are thus designed by entering the right EFs and DETs in the matrix shown in Table 15.2.

Table 15.2   Control Matrix for Test Automation Framework in Banking

Days	Process 1	Process 2	Process n	Day End Process Tasks
Day 1	EF1, EF2	EF1		DET1
Day 2	EF3	EF4, EF6	EF2	DET2, DET3
Day 3	EF4	EF5	EF3	DET3
. . .	EF2, EF6		EF4	DET4
		. . .	. . .	. . .

Currently, per release, about 400 processes are automated with a total execution time of 10 hours.

15.3.2.1   Benefits of the Framework and Outlook

Because of the generic nature of the framework, extension of the test coverage can be achieved with low effort—we need to do new recording or scripting only in the case of new elementary functions. The high reuse of the modules guarantees a minimized maintenance effort. The way the framework is designed also ensures a higher quality of the test compared to standalone execution of single processes, which would not embrace interdependencies between them. With the capability to start processes in parallel, we also achieve a benefit with respect to execution performance. Automation of banking processes is an ongoing task in SAP; with new functionalities, the test coverage of the framework is enhanced permanently.

Good Point

The more reuse you have of your automated testware, the less you will need to spend on maintenance. The DRY principle ("Don't' Repeat Yourself") leads directly to reuse.

15.4   Conclusion

For test automation of most SAP applications, eCATT has proven to be useful, especially taking into account SAP's special requirements, such as the simultaneous maintenance of several releases per product and the allowable combinations among them. The close integration into the ABAP development environment allows direct access to database tables and APIs. This not only is valuable for checking data at the point where it really matters but also makes test scripts more robust because many test steps can be implemented without using UIs. Sometimes the use of these technical possibilities is a trade-off between robustness of test scripts and effective testing from an end-user perspective. If the business logic is the focus of the test, it is greatly beneficial to reduce maintenance. The extensive eCATT scripting possibilities allow creation of robust and reusable scripts.

We learned that test automation in a large organization requires clear processes and standards similar to any software product development. Most attempts to do test automation as a "hobby," by people whose "real" job responsibilities lay elsewhere, failed because of a lack of guidance and sustainability. A tool like Checkman for eCATT can help here by doing static checks on the test script code, thereby supporting a high test script quality in large and distributed organizations. In addition, it turns your project into a learning experience. Because many test tools make use of standard development environments and languages, it should not take much effort to implement those static checks by reusing existing static check frameworks. For us, especially, the high reuse factor makes the difference for successful test automation.

For the banking processes, we ensured effectiveness by making the test scenario as realistic as possible (e.g., by simulating lifecycles that span over several weeks within one test run). By using this framework, we achieved the additional benefit of reuse, stability, and especially extensibility of the test cases with new functionality or new processes in an efficient way.

In health care, there is a high test demand generated by the many legal changes that have to be implemented frequently into many releases and for many different country versions. The biggest challenge for this test project was to cover the most important combinations of parameters. The all-pairs method helped us to design the test cases effectively, and eCATT's architecture principles allowed implementing the automated test cases very efficiently.

We know our customers would love to get our eCATT scripts so they can use them as well. Unfortunately, we found in some pilots where this was done that this is a good idea only at first glance. Our experiences show clearly that our customer' environments are usually quite different from ours due to customer modifications and customizing, so most of our scripts would run only after some adaptations. Overall, sharing our scripts resulted more in frustration on both sides than in real benefits. Therefore, the question of how to ship test content remains a challenge.

eCATT code examples for the scenarios in this chapter can be obtained on request from the authors.

15.5   Acknowledgments

We owe a big thank you to our colleagues from Business Suite Test Center in Bangalore who implemented and executed the tests and to all our colleagues at SAP who contributed to improving processes, tools, and test scripts over the years.

CHAPTER 16

TEST AUTOMATION OF A SAP IMPLEMENTATION

Björn Boisschot

Björn Boisschot tells how he developed a generic framework based on his observations while setting up automation for various clients. He explains how he used the framework and extended it in the automation of the testing for two SAP applications in the energy sector. The groundwork for the project is well laid, with a proof-of-concept forming the basis of the go/no-go decision. Björn gives good examples of communicating with managers, explains why capture/playback does not work, and emphasizes the importance of setting realistic expectations. The framework, now a commercial product, used good automation and software development principles to construct a modular structure that successfully scaled up. The layers of abstraction are well implemented, separating the automated tests from the tool and giving users access to tests without having to program. He ends by showing how multilingual tests were implemented through a translation table and some of the challenges of that project. This case study takes place in Belgium and is the origin of a commercial framework. See Table 16.1.

16.1 Background for the Case Study

As a test tool consultant since 2004, I did a lot of test automation projects in different companies situated in different sectors (from public, energy, mobile, financial to

295

Table 16.1   Case Study Characteristics

Classification	This Case Study
Application domain	SAP applications in the energy sector
Application size	80 SAP SRM end-to-end flows; SAP modules covered MM, PM, FICO, SD, and PP
Location	Belgium
Lifecycle	Traditional
Number on the project	12
Number of testers	1
Number of automators	3
Time span	6 months
Dates	2009–2010
Tool type(s)	Commercial
Pilot study undertaken	Yes
ROI measured	No
Successful?	Yes
Still breathing?	Yes

medical). After a few projects, I realized I was creating the same functionality over and over again. Even for different projects in different environments, there were a lot of similarities that reoccurred for each one (structure, multiple environments, data management, versioning, documentation). As a good IT person (read: lazy one), I started thinking about how I could make my life a lot easier by combining all the knowledge from previous projects and building a framework that would tackle these issues.

I started by looking back at the different test automation projects I had done in the past and focused on the reasons for their failure or success.

The goal of the initial investigation was to find the key factors that resulted in the failure or success of a project and implement those that contributed to success into a new framework and avoid those that contributed to failure.

I came to the following conclusions:

- Best approach for most cases was a mixture of keyword- and data-driven approaches:
  - Keyword-driven automation, good for nontechnical users to create automated test cases.
  - Data-driven automation, good for easy regression testing of multiple data sets.
- It is important to divide the work between two types of profiles:
  - Functional profile: People who know the application and how to create the best test cases (functional testers, business analysts, and others).
  - Technical profile: The test automation specialists who understand the tool and know where the possible problem areas are situated.
- Implementation of test automation should be a structured process:
  - Put in place a mechanism to select the possible automation candidates (multiple solutions here based on complexity, ROI, criticality, and more).
  - Define who is responsible for what.
  - Decide on which platforms to run the automated tests.
  - Define when to execute tests, when to retire them, who is responsible (e.g., based on a RACI [responsible, accountable, consulted, and informed] matrix).
- The change process is one that is often forgotten:
  - Set clear expectations.
  - Business needs some time to get used to the automated test cases.
  - Functional testers are sometimes reluctant because they fear for their jobs (reassure that automation will only replace the boring regression tests so they can focus on the more important and challenging tests).
  - Sometimes small development adaptations (e.g., extra IDs in HTML) to the application are needed to make it more automation friendly.

Enlightened by these insights, I started developing my framework, now called FASTBoX, in 2007. FASTBoX became a standard in CTG test automation implementations. During the 2-year-long creation phase of my framework, we ran into different issues that we hadn't anticipated, which resulted in the refactoring of part of the code.

> **Good Point**
>
> The more you know about both successful and unsuccessful automation efforts, the more likely you are to succeed next time.

When you read between the lines, you may already have seen some keywords from the world of programming (*develop*, *refactor*, etc.). As you read through this chapter, you will see that the approach for this test automation project is closely linked to different development best practices.

This chapter describes a SAP project that provided a challenge for the framework and in which we were able to fully use its strengths and remediate the possible weaknesses.

16.2   Project Overview

The test automation project covered in this chapter was started in 2009 because the SAP system at the company was becoming increasingly complex and integrated with other SAP and non-SAP applications, which made it difficult to manage manually. The IT department only had one tester who needed to test all these new SAP projects (eight developers) and if possible also test the integrations with other tools. On top of this, the SAP updates needed to be tested.

Why did the IT team want to automate the regression tests?

- There weren't enough resources to execute the regression tests manually.
- They wanted to start security role testing (very work intensive).
- They needed to make sure the critical SAP data transfers were working well on most of the environments.
- They wanted end-to-end tests (business flows covering a complete business process).

In the first instance, this was an IT project, and the IT manager was the sponsor for this project (never forget who is financing your project and why).

The first step of this IT project was to find the best tool for the job. To be able to do this, the IT team gathered all the different requirements for the test automation tool, including:

- Ability to cover the different technologies (SAP GUI, SAP Web, .NET, MS Outlook, Adobe Interactive Forms, Web Services).
- Ease of use for the technical scripters as well as the business people.
- Ability to input Excel data.
- Critical mass using the product (easy to find people with knowledge in the market).
- Open/nonproprietary scripting language.
- Maturity of the test tool and supplier.

You might think SAP's eCATT would be the ideal tool for this kind of test automation project, but due to the lack of support of technologies other than SAP GUI, it was ruled out. The company chose Hewlett-Packard's QuickTest Professional (QTP) on the basis of the preceding criteria and the attributed scores (the most important one being the support of technologies such as Web Services, Java, Adobe, .NET, and others). Because nobody in the IT organization had any experience with test automation or QTP, they started their search for an integrator. They didn't want to start from scratch and create their own framework, so they were looking for an integrator with an existing and proven framework. This is where CTG came into the picture. During this project, I have implemented the first version of our framework and have further enhanced it.

The project was divided into two phases. First, a proof-of-concept (POC) would be done to show that the chosen tool (QTP) and our framework could handle all the different technologies used by the client.

After this POC (10 days), the management expected us to give a presentation on what we were able to do with the tool and framework in this short period, what bottlenecks we had encountered, and the expected number of test cases we would be able to automate during a given period of time. After this presentation, they would decide whether or not the second phase of the project could start (go/no go meeting).

The second phase of the project was to extend the test cases from the POC and automate extra regression tests.

16.3   Phase 1: Proof of Concept

16.3.1   Define the Scope of the Project

The first thing to do was to check that the scope defined in our proposal for the POC (signed by both the client and our company 2 months before this meeting) was still what they actually needed.

As with many of the starting IT projects, the enthusiasm and expectations at the start of a project are so high (called uninformed optimism in the cycle of change) that the initial scope is forgotten and the new scope of the project becomes larger, technologically more complex, but still expected to be delivered within the same time constraints (preferably even faster).

Luckily for them and me, I like a challenge and tend to work better under a fair amount of stress. After the first meeting, the tone of the project had been set: Try to work as fast as possible but still deliver a structured setup that can be used as a foundation for phase 2.

I had a number of days to implement our test automation framework in the company and to create end-to-end automated test scripts on two of its main SAP applications:

- Supplier Relationship Management (SRM, application that automates, simplifies, and accelerates procure-to-pay processes for goods and services)
- Time Registration (application used to handle the generation, retrieval, and calculation of timesheets for all workers by using Outlook, Adobe Interactive Forms, and SAP R/3)

These two SAP applications were chosen for the following reasons:

- To cover all the SAP technologies used at the company
  - SRM: Standard R/3 GUI + Web Dynpro + PI + XI
  - Time Registration: Web Dynpro + Adobe Interactive Forms + MS Outlook
- Importance of the applications
  - Applications used by a large group of users
  - Applications with high financial impact
  - Business-critical SAP transactions will be tested
- Applications that are still being developed
  - A lot of regression testing will be needed
- End-to-end flows for applications where possible
  - Same end-to-end flows that business users test on the acceptance platform
- Technical complexity of the application flows
  - Combination of actions in the applications, batch jobs, XML interfaces, and so on

I met with the functional specialists of both applications. We went through the different end-to-end scenarios, and they provided me with some data sets, explained how the application handles errors (a lucky break for me was that both applications always handle errors in the same way, making it easier for me to capture the errors and process them).

After this meeting, we set the new scope and communicated to the project manager what test cases we would automate in the time span given to us (communication on the test automation progress is very important in order to keep all involved parties interested).

Good Point

Define the scope of what you plan to automate in a time box, and set realistic expectations.

The only thing that remained for me to do on the first day was to install the testing tool and explore the two applications to try to identify possible problem areas.

16.3.2 Set the Expectations

The next day on the project, I had a chat with the project manager about the SAP test automation project. The idea was to figure out why he wanted to automate the test cases (why not spend more time in manual testing?), what he thought was important, and where the company saw the most benefit for test automation. I also asked about some of the general pitfalls, such as data management and stability of the application.

The goal of this conversation was to set the expectations right (don't forget that sales and tool vendors have promised them heaven on earth: "Just click on record, execute the business flow, and your test case is automated").

Good Point

Sometimes, your task is to disillusion a manager who has been oversold by a tool vendor.

- I explained to the project manager that test automation is more than record and playback.
  - I used the example of buying a new AC/DC recording from iTunes by selecting the album from a web table on the iTunes site. If you record your actions in any testing tool, the tool will capture the row number in the web

table that you selected. When you try to replay your actions (test) the next day, the tool will select the row *number* it recorded, whatever is now in that row. It will not search for the AC/DC mp3 file but will select the nth row. Instead of the AC/DC recording you wanted, you might have inadvertently purchased an mp3 file from the newest boy band in town.

- ■ I tried to convince him that a structured, well-documented, and standardized way of working will ultimately generate more benefit than a quick and dirty approach. I did this by comparing spaghetti code and structured programming. In the early years of programming, spaghetti code was one of the main reasons that some IT projects were failing and were considered not maintainable. Then the switch to structured programming was made, and to some extent this problem was solved. But even with structured programming, you could start to write spaghetti code, so it is very important to stick to the rules defined in your structured approach.

■ I showed him that record and playback is probably the fastest approach to set something up, but the maintenance issues caused by this approach ultimately will kill the automation project. I explained this by showing him an example of one of the company's own applications (lucky for me, I had an inside informant who shared this information with me). In the last version of this application, the company had added a Captcha verification to the login process. I explained to my project manager that if record and playback had been used, we would have to adapt this piece of code in every script we created (suppose 100 scripts). If we had used function calls, only one function would have had to be changed. I explained that, theoretically, every test is automatable, but you must look at the ROI and time needed to automate a test case.

To summarize, I explained that we would have a higher startup cost and would not automate every regression test, but all of this would contribute to the ROI of the project.

I also explained to him the cycle of change we would be going through during the test automation project. The previous point was more about aligning the technical expectations, and now it was all about people issues.

This cycle of change, or progress path of change (see Figure 16.1), indicates that at the start of a project, everyone is in the uninformed optimism phase: Everyone is feeling certain about what they are going to do; there is a lot of enthusiasm; and so on.

After a while, during the new project, the mood starts to shift. People are not informed about what's going on in the project, they become disappointed because it is taking longer than expected, they start to have doubts about the success of the

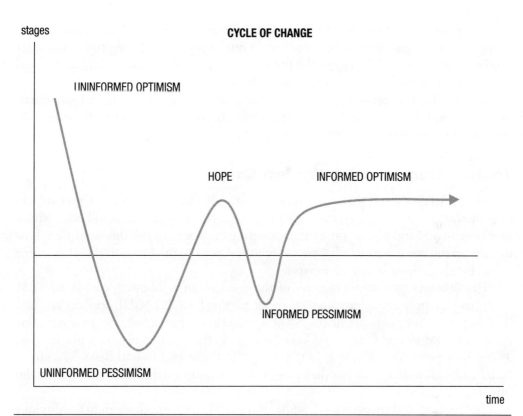

FIGURE 16.1   Cycle of change

project, and the enthusiasm wanes: Everyone is sliding into the uninformed pessi-mism phase.

Then, when the first tests are delivered and seem to work, everyone starts feel-ing hopeful again. It seems the project is going to be successful after all: Everyone is moving up to the hope phase.

After a few releases, some of the test cases need to be rewritten, there are some false negatives, people get stressed and start working on their own parts and stop communicating: They are slipping down to the informed pessimism phase.

Once the false negatives are fixed, the scripts are made more robust, the whole test automation process runs smoothly, everyone knows what their responsibilities are: We are now entering the informed optimism phase, which should bring us sta-bility in the long run.

The reason we always try to explain this up front is because we know we are going to go through these phases anyway. In our experience, if the project manager knows about the cycle of change, the pessimism phase will not be as long as it would be if the project manager weren't prepared for it.

At last, after two whole days of setting the expectations, gathering test case documentation and data, getting to know the applications, and bothering everyone with my questions, we started on the scripting part of the POC project.

16.3.3   Start Scripting the Test Cases

By using FASTBoX and the many functionalities it already provides, I was able to directly start automating the test cases I received. No need anymore to bother about how to structure the whole test automation project, where to put the input files, how to start up the applications, what recovery to use, and so on, because these concerns were already defined in our framework.

The first test case was a mixture of the creation of a shopping cart in an SRM (web-based) application, creating an order in the SAP R/3 GUI application, and finalizing the shopping cart in the SRM application. The fastest way to create this automated end-to-end flow would have been to do the "record/playback magic." But as our best practices state, it is better to create these end-to-end flows in a structured and well-defined way so they can be reused afterwards during the rest of the project.

The support and recognition for SAP R/3 by QTP was good; we didn't encounter any real issues when automating our tests. But we did have an issue with the support on Web Dynpro; as with most web-based applications, there wasn't always a unique identifier by which to recognize the objects. Not all elements have an HTML identifier (or any other unique identifier) and can be recognized only by their text property. The use of the text property was not ideal for us because we needed to be able to run the tests in multiple languages.

Because SRM is not developed internally (created by SAP), it wasn't possible to ask the developers to add some HTML identifiers, so the solution we needed was a multilingual object repository. Our first idea was to create an object repository for each language. The problem was that this approach goes against our methodology for implementing test automation. We are always preaching to centralize/generalize as many things as possible to limit the maintenance issues, and now we would be creating four object repositories for one application just to handle some multilingual objects! This meant that if something changed in the GUI of our application, we would need to change four object repositories. For me, as the creator of our framework, this was unacceptable, so I started searching for a better solution.

After looking at several ideas and at the capabilities of QTP, we came up with the following solution:

- We created a translation Excel workbook in which we filled in the translations for the different languages we supported. This is shown in Table 16.2.
- Using the QTP object repository parameters, we created the link between the translation items and the objects in the object repository (see Figure 16.2).
- In our global sheet from QTP, we indicated in which language we were working.

By implementing this solution, we needed only one object repository and one translation Excel spreadsheet to allow us to cover the four languages. It was even easier to update when labels in the application changed. We didn't need to open QTP and the object repository; we just needed to update the Excel workbook.

Table 16.2 Translation

QTPName	Regular Expression	NL	FR	EN
OpShortText	FALSE	Omschrijving operatie	Désignation opération	Description operation
Work	FALSE	Werk	Travail	Work
Workplace	FALSE	Werkplek	Poste	Workplace
Yes	FALSE	Ja	Oui	Yes
No	FALSE	Neen	Non	No
Print	FALSE	Printen	Imprimer	Print
Page	TRUE	Pagina [0-9]*	Page [0-9]*	Page [0-9]*

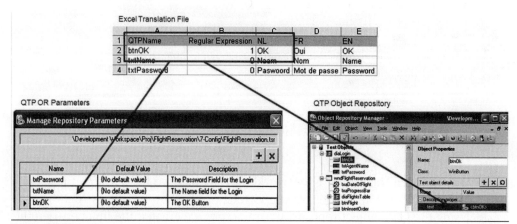

FIGURE 16.2 Object repository translation

The second problem we encountered was that the second application uses Adobe Forms sent out by email. Checking if the email arrived and opening the correct attachment wasn't a real problem (we already had these functions available in our framework), but we now needed to fill in data on the Adobe Form. Luckily for us, Adobe offers a QTP plug-in for its Adobe Forms (which is free of charge), so we only needed to download and install the plug-in, and we were able to fill in the forms and submit them to the system.

After 3 days of scripting fun, I was able to finalize the end-to-end flows and start working on the go/no go meeting. This meeting was held in front of a mixed audience of SAP project managers, business users, testers, and general IT management (at that time, the meetings felt like the Spanish Inquisition because of the skepticism and doubt that still surrounded the ROI of test automation). We explained all the steps we had taken so far, what benefits we saw in test automation, the possible problem areas, and what costs they could expect. We also showed them a live demo of how to create a script, how to execute it, and what the final results looked like.

During the demo, we were asked a lot of questions, such as the following:

- Will this still work when the application slows down?
- What if the screen is redesigned?
- How do you handle exceptions?
- Can we run the tests on a different platform without the need to rescript everything?
- How about multilingual testing?

- Do we really need to do regression testing?
- I have never seen test automation work on SAP, so why should it work this time?

After answering all the questions, defending our approach, showing the live demo, and losing a few pounds, we finally left the room so the remaining people could start their internal debate on what they found. Fortunately, they said GO!

16.4   Phase 2: Project Start

16.4.1   Approval

After the official go from the management, we started the second phase of the project. The work done during the POC served as a starting point for the remainder of the project. The structure, framework, code conventions, and ways of working were already in place.

The first extra factor that came into play was that I wouldn't be working alone anymore but that two of my colleagues would join me on this assignment. My assignment changed from setting up the framework and proving that test automation on SAP can deliver ROI to coaching and training my two new colleagues.

To do so successfully, I needed to leave my comfort zone (thinking out new ideas and scripting them myself) and risk myself in the rather unknown area for me of delegation, setting up a vision, and coaching.

16.4.2   Code Conventions and Documentation

The documentation standards and code conventions we used helped us to work as a team and understand each other's automation code. It was now possible for us to sit together and walk through a piece of code without needing to explain every variable and function used in it.

> **Good Point**
>
> Standards for automated testware, particularly code conventions and documentation, are important when scaling up.

It also allowed us to better reuse functions created by other team members (just read the documentation header or look at the function prefix to understand what it returns) and limited the maintenance time needed (easier to understand the function without going through each step).

For the code conventions, we didn't want to reinvent the wheel, so we examined the Microsoft VBScript code conventions and decided to implement them with the following conventions:

- Use descriptive names.
- Each word in a name starts with a capital.
- Classes, functions, and methods begin with a capital.
- Attributes, parameters, and local variables start with a lowercase.
- Attributes and parameters start with a prefix that indicates the type of the attribute or parameter (*int*, *str*, *bln*, *dbl*, and so on).
- Functions start with a prefix that indicates the type of the return value.
- Global variables start with *g*.
- Constants are uppercase.

We also included some general rules to make code more readable:

- No more than one statement on each line.
- Maximum 80 characters per line.
- Indent subitems.
- Use parentheses in case of more than one operator.
- Turn on Option Explicit (forcing you to declare your variables in VBScript).
- Parameters in the function definition are always preceded by `ByVal` or `ByRef` (indicating if parameter is passed by reference or by value).

Listing 16.1 is an extreme example to demonstrate that these coding conventions really add value. (Some of you will already have seen such a badly written piece of code.) Because of the nonexisting code conventions, it is almost impossible to understand the first example without spending a lot of time investigating it.

Listing 16.1   Example Code without Code Conventions

```
01 Public Function Calc (n)
02 If n <= 0 Then
03 Elseif n <= 26 Then
04 Calc = Chr(64 + n)
05 Elseif n mod 26 = 0 Then
06 Calc = Calc(n \ 26 - 1) & "Z"
```

```
07 Else
08 Calc = Calc (n \ 26) & Chr (64 + n Mod 26)
09 End If
10 End Function
```

This second example, shown in Listing 16.2, is the same as Listing 16.1, but code conventions are applied. This greatly improves the readability and understanding of the code.

Listing 16.2   Example Code with Code Conventions

```
01 Option Explicit On
02
03 Public Function StrGetColumnName(ByVal intColumnNumber)
04     If intColumnNumber <= 0 Then
05          StrGetColumnName = Nothing
06     Elseif intColumnNumber <= 26 Then
07          StrGetColumnName = Chr(64 + intColumnNumber)
08     Elseif (intColumnNumber Mod 26) = 0 Then
09          StrGetColumnName = _
10               StrGetColumnName((intColumnNumber \ 26) - 1) & "Z"
11     Else
12          StrGetColumnName = _
13               StrGetColumnName(intColumnNumber \ 26) & _
14               Chr(64 + (intColumnNumber Mod 26))
15     End if
16 End Function
```

The use of code conventions made our teamwork easier, but we still lacked a good way to reference all of the functions that existed in our framework. The key answer here was to document all our functions in an easily maintainable way that didn't clutter the code and, if possible, was also searchable. Putting a documentation header on top of each function wasn't too hard, but we needed to find a mechanism (tool) that would allow us to extract these documentation headers and put them into a useful documentation format. After searching the Internet, we came up with the tool TwinText, which we believed would allow us to do that. TwinText is a source code documentation tool that generates HTML and HTML Help documentation directly from code comments. It supports different programming languages such as VBScript, C#, Java, and Perl.

> **Good Point**
>
> Use searchable information in script headers, and devise or discover a good way to find what you need to know quickly and easily.

Listing 16.3 shows an example of the function header used in FASTBoX to document all our functions.

Listing 16.3   Example of Function Header

```
01 'Function StrGetColumnName
02 'Given a column number, this function calculates
03 'the corresponding Excel column name. <br/>
04 'e.g. 2 becomes "B", 28 becomes "AB", 105 becomes "DA", ...
05 '
06 'Parameters:
07 'intColumnNumber - number of the column >br/>
08    this number should be > 0
09 '
10 'Returns:
11 'The name of the column. If the column number was invalid (<=0)
12 'the function returns nothing.
13 Public Function StrGetColumnName (ByVal intColumnNumber)
```

By using TwinText, we are able to generate a complete HTML Help file for our framework that can be used as a reference document by anyone who uses the framework. Figure 16.3 shows an example of a generated HTML Help file.

16.4.3 Structured Approach

A structured approach to test automation is needed in order for a team to work together successfully. We had already defined our coding conventions and documentation standards. Now it was time to explain how to create a logical and easy way of structuring all of our test resources (Excel spreadsheets, scripts, test cases, configuration, etc.) in such a way that we could reuse everything at its maximum and still make changes for one specific project if needed.

We also wanted to be able to enhance our framework in the future without interfering with the tests that were running in our current QA environment (no

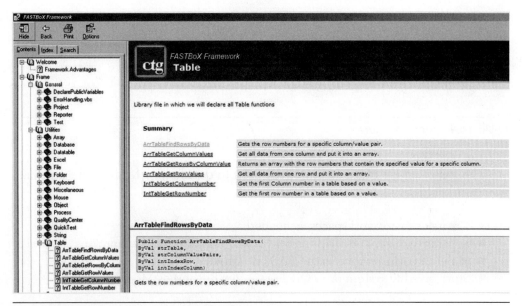

FIGURE 16.3   A generated HTML Help file

interference between running our tests and creating new functionalities for auto-mated tests).

It was also necessary for all our scripts to be executable in different environments (development, test, acceptance) without the need to change a lot of parameters, which would waste valuable time.

The easiest way to work with multiple run environments in QTP is to use the Relative Folder option, which is shown in Figure 16.4. We started with two workspaces, development and acceptance, which allowed us to run tests in the acceptance environment and at the same time develop our new tests and functionalities in the development environment.

Because we were working with three people on this automation job (most of the time writing scripts for different applications), we needed to share the functions we created between projects, so we needed a way to separate functions specific for one project (e.g., Buy train ticket) and functions that could be reused across applications (e.g., Select row based on data in a column). An important factor to remember is that all our team members were expected to create their functions to be as generic as possible, which is not easy for someone who is starting with test automation.

Figure 16.4 shows an overview of the main structure we created for the project. In the following pages, we explain the reason for the different folders and the structure we created.

FIGURE 16.4 Main structure

The following list of arguments were used to decide how to structure our main framework folder:

- Create as many workspaces as needed.
- Separate project-specific functions from general reusable functions.
- Make all paths relative to the FASTBoX folder.
- Store on a file system or in Quality Center Resources Module.

In the Frame folder, we also needed to separate code specific to one technological environment (SAP R3, web, Adobe) and the code written to support utilities (search Outlook, create .xml file, etc.).

Figure 16.5 shows the structure of the Frame folder, which has subfolders for

- *Docu:* Documentation of the framework
- *Gen:* Functions to initialize the framework
- *Lang:* Functions specific for each language

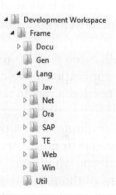

FIGURE 16.5 Frame folder structure

- *Util:* Functions to support the following utilities (and more):
  - XML
  - Outlook
  - QC
  - Databases
  - Strings

For each project, we then created a separate folder with a number of subfolders. This structured way of working allowed our team to be very flexible in sharing resources. Everyone knows how each project is structured and where to find what code, as shown in Figure 16.6. The subfolders for the SAP applications are:

- *InputFiles:* All input files used by your scripts
- *Libraries:* The function libraries specific for your project
- *TestScripts:* The QTP test scripts
- *Execution:* The test sets, utility to execute tests
- *Results:* All the results from the runs
- *Documents:* Documents specific for your project
- *Config:* All configuration resources for our project (object repository, recovery, and more)
- *Temp:* A temporary folder (if needed)

FIGURE 16.6   Project folder structure

16.4.4 Data-Driving Test Cases

One of the major goals of this test automation project was to make sure the regression tests covered the most critical data combinations foreseen in production. To test this in a manual way requires too much effort. The problem we had, as automators, was that we didn't know all these possible data combinations, and the business didn't have time to explain them. We needed to create our test cases in such a way that the business would be able to test all the data combinations without the need for additional scripting.

We tried to gather all the possible requirements for allowing the business users to input their own data:

- Ability for easy data input
- Possibility to add checkpoints and verification steps
- Ability to manipulate all possible objects
- Ability to extract data from the SUT
- Possibility to control iterations by users
- Ability to execute negative test cases

First, we chose Excel as the data input tool for business users (easy-to-use, well-known tool). We needed to create a mechanism that would data drive our test cases from Excel on the basis of the requirements defined previously.

We eventually created a mechanism that provides the business users with an Excel workbook to fill in. This workbook contains different worksheets (each worksheet represents a specific SAP tab page on a screen) with columns (each column represents an object on that tab page). For each test case they want to execute (test case that does something on this tab page), they must fill in a row of data.

In Figure 16.7, the business user wants to do the following:

- SAP window to work on: Vd_SalesArea (see worksheet name)
- SAP tab page: BillDocu (see worksheet name)
- For the TestCase
  - TC_001: Indicates test case number or ID

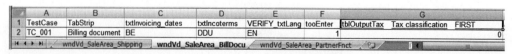

	A	B	C	D	E	F	G		
1	TestCase	TabStrip	txtInvoicing_dates	txtIncoterms	VERIFY_txtLang	tooEnter	tblOutputTax	Tax classification	FIRST
2	TC_001	Billing document	BE	DDU	EN		1		0

↿ ◄ ▸ ◖   wndVd_SaleArea_Shipping   **wndVd_SaleArea_BillDocu**   wndVd_SaleArea_PartnerFnct

FIGURE 16.7   A test case constructed by a business user

- Select the tab page Billing document
  - TabStrip: Billing document
- Fill in the following fields:
  - txtInvoicing_dates: BE
  - txtIncoterms: DDU
- Verify a value
  - txtLang field should contain value EN
- Click on the SAP Next toolbar (or press Enter key)
  - tooEnter: 1
- Fill in a value in a SAP table
  - tblOutputTax: The table to manipulate
  - Tax classification: The column in which to fill in data
  - FIRST: A keyword indicating user wants to fill in the data on the first row
  - 0: The value user wants to fill in the table cell

Note that the value 0 is just a value we need to enter into a specific cell in a SAP table. Each column in the Excel spreadsheet/data table stands for an object that can be manipulated. In this case, the object is a cell of a SAP table.

The advantages we have seen by using this approach are as follows:

- High flexibility for the users.
- Capability to add checkpoints and to extract data from the GUI and put them into the Excel spreadsheet (can be reused as data input later on).
- Less code written (by a factor 5) than in a normal record/playback QTP test.
- Users who have business knowledge can now drive the scenarios based on the data they use. Only one script is needed for all data combinations in an end-to-end flow.
- Creating a new test case (data) means filling in Excel instead of creating a new QTP test.

But as with everything in this world, it wasn't completely smooth. This approach had the following problems:

- The code conventions on all objects in the QTP object repository should be respected, which was not always the case.
- The creation of the Excel workbooks is a lot of work; for example, one screen with 50 input fields requires creating one Excel worksheet and copying and pasting the 50 input field names into the columns.

- Some end users want to have 100 combinations in which only fields in one specific window change, and they don't want to retype or copy and paste all data for the other windows. They need the ability to reference an existing row of data.
- When creating big end-to-end flows, the Excel workbooks tend to become too large, which results in some users losing the overview.

Because we heard from the users that this gave them a lot of freedom and, from a scripter's point of view, this was less work for us, we decided to stick with it and solve the issues instead of starting all over again.

We created a VBScript file that would apply all the coding conventions to the object repository and export a selectable number of windows/tab pages to an Excel file. We created the ability to reuse existing rows of data from other test cases in Excel files (this eliminates the need to recopy everything). We also created a new function to generate the whole Excel workbook based on a specific test script (of course, the user still must fill in the data).

The issue of Excel files getting too large still remains, but we had to choose between a small number of sheets with a lot of columns (with the risk of losing

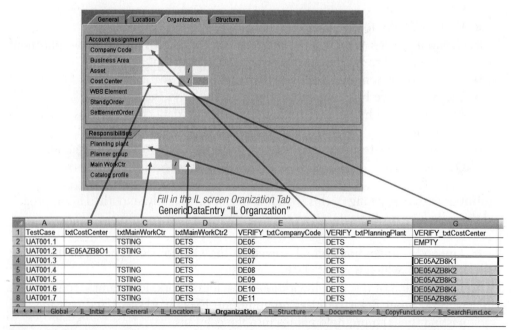

FIGURE 16.8   GenericDataEntry relationship between Excel sheet and the SAP tab

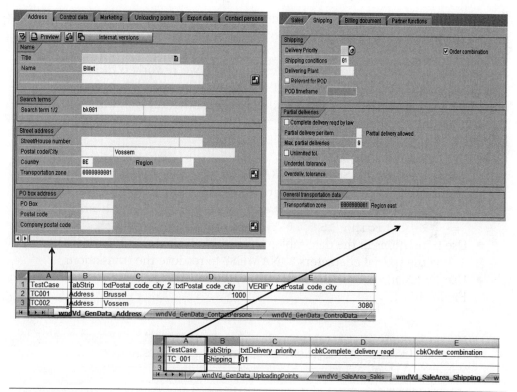

FIGURE 16.9   Skip screen entry for test cases

oversight per sheet) and a high number of sheets with a normal amount of columns (with the risk of losing oversight on workbook level). Figure 16.8 shows the relationship between the Excel spreadsheet and the SAP tab being filled in.

Figure 16.9 shows that it is not necessary that each of the tabs/screens is used by all transactions. If, for a specific tab, there is no TestCase ID in the Excel worksheet, the GenericDataEntry mechanism does not select that tab when executing this TestCase.

16.3.5   Multilingual

As previously explained, we needed to test the applications in multiple languages. For this, we had already created the Excel translation workbook linked to the QTP object repository. However, during the scripting phase, we encountered an extra problem concerning multilingual aspects:

- Checkpoints in code need to be multilingual.
- Column headers of tables need to be multilingual.

Instead of creating a completely new solution, we reworked the existing functionalities in the framework we created for the multilingual object repository problem. The result now is that, by using this Excel translation workbook, we can use translations in the following areas:

- Use translations in code:
  - Use the keyword StrProjectTRANSGet to retrieve the translation:
    ```
    Msgbox StrProjectTRANSGet("Confirmation") & " 15"
    => "Confirmation 15" if test case runs in English
    => "Bevestiging 15" if test case runs in Dutch
    ```
- Use translations in the data table: An example is shown in Figure 16.10.
  - Use the special characters $$NAME$$ to retrieve the translation.
- Use translations in the object repository: An example is shown in Figure 16.11.

	A	B	C	D	E
1	TestCase	TabStrip	txtPostal_code_city_2	txtPostal_code_city	VERIFY_txtPostal_code_city
2	TC001	$$Address$$	Brussel	1000	
3	TC002	$$Address$$	Vossem		3080

wndVd_GenData_Address   wndVd_GenData_ContactPersons   wndVd_GenData_ControlData   w

FIGURE 16.10   Data table translation

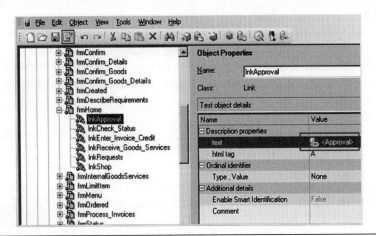

FIGURE 16.11   Object repository translation

16.4.6 Security Role Testing

Another big part of this project was testing all the different security roles together with all the data combinations. Until automation was in place, only a few of these tests were done because they required an enormous amount of manual labor. With test automation, these tests can be set up to run in only the time required to fill in a few columns in an Excel spreadsheet. Because we knew security role testing was important before we started scripting, we had foreseen the mechanism that would allow us to do this.

In our global Excel spreadsheet (the one that drives the test iterations), we created a few columns that allow us to start each test case with a different user. By just filling in the correct aliases, our end users can create an end-to-end flow that executes each test case with possible different credentials. This allows them to execute all possible security role tests on every platform. All they need to do is change the user and password settings that are linked to a role.

16.5 Conclusion

During this project, we saw that test automation on a SAP landscape is not very different from test automation in other environments. Most of the guidelines and principles of general test automation are also applicable in SAP.

The biggest difference between SAP's environment and others' is the high data dependency of all test cases in SAP—and that's also the biggest challenge. This challenge, combined with the frequent data refreshes, can make the work of a test automation engineer very difficult, so test data management is a crucial aspect that cannot be lost sight of. Test data management can be done in many different ways (tools can be used to do drop and restore, automated test suites to prepare data, SQL scripts to update data, and so on).

The knowledge (or lack of knowledge) of SAP is also a factor that may cause issues. In other test automation projects, knowledge of the application is usually not necessary (an easy learning path or well-documented flows can be enough for engineers to understand what needs to be scripted). In SAP, the large number of different transactions in different modules (from completely different worlds such as human resources and finance) makes it impossible for any one person to know them all. But a general knowledge of how SAP works (interaction between modules, data transfers, general transactions, and so on) is needed to be able to understand the difficulties of test automation on such a project.

SAP test automation is not only about SAP R/3 GUI testing—it goes much further than that. You need to script tests for web applications, Adobe Forms, .Net, Java, XML interfaces, Web Services, and so on. A suitable tool is needed that supports all of these different environments in a stable and extensible way (not only standard SAP transactions must be automated; the tool also must be able to handle custom Z transactions, modifications of standard SAP transactions made at the customer's request, and all the environments involved in the project).

It is also important to use a structured way of working with test automation from day one, which can be a commercial framework (like FASTBoX), a self-built one, or an open source framework to lower the danger of huge maintenance costs and to have a methodology that can be used in the whole organization.

Today's implementations of SAP are not practically testable anymore in a purely manual way, so test automation will be needed to test the releases in the limited timeframe and budget that is foreseen.

It is imperative to select the correct test cases to automate, set the expectations, and select the correct toolset and framework. The preparation of the test automation project is as important as (if not more important than) the scripting itself. To be able to do this in a structured and efficient way, a framework should be used together with the appropriate test automation tool.

As shown in this chapter, all the standard principles of test automation will be applicable in a test automation project for SAP. Everything that was designed and created for this SAP test automation project (all general non-SAP or project-related resources) can be reused for other test automation projects (Oracle Forms, Siebel, .NET, and so on). Of course, every technology will have its differences, but looking from a test automation point of view, they will have mostly similarities!

CHAPTER 17

CHOOSING THE WRONG TOOL

Michael Williamson

Michael Williamson tells the story of trying to use a tool (which he inherited) that he later realized was not suitable for what he was trying to test. He was trying to automate the testing of major functionality in web development tools at Google, where he was new to testing and test automation. Some assumptions that seemed obvious at first turned out to be not as they seemed. His approach to taking over the use of an existing tool seemed sensible, yet he encountered a lot of problems (which are illustrated), particularly in automated comparison. Michael found it was difficult to abandon something you have put a lot of effort into already, yet in the end, this was the best approach (and he was surprised when he discovered what had really been hindering his efforts). This story is of one person in the United States attempting to use a commercial tool. See Table 17.1.

17.1 Background for the Case Study

17.1.1 The Product

Webmaster Tools is a web-based product offered by Google that's free to use with the end goal of making Google search better. Webmasters can use the tool to control various aspects of their sites, such as what pages Google crawlers can access and what URLs will show up in the Google search index. Users can also see statistical measurements, such as how many people are linking to their site and what Google queries produce for their site in search results. For more information, look at www.google.com/webmaster/tools.

Table 17.1   Case Study Characteristics

Classification	This Case Study
Application domain	Web-based, distributed
Application size	>100,000 LOC
Location	United States
Lifecycle	Agile
Number on the project	15
Number of testers	2
Number of automators	1.25
Time span	6 months
Dates	February 2009–October 2009
Tool type(s)	Commercial, open source
Pilot study undertaken	Yes
ROI measured	No
Successful?	No
Still breathing?	No

From a technical perspective, when I was on the team, the Webmaster Tools frontend answered HTTP requests from a Java-based web server that employed small amounts of JavaScript and cascading style sheets (CSS). It provided approximately 20 different features, each with its own web page. Behind the scenes, the frontend was backed up by a handful of databases and other subsystems. Most of the actual data that users saw was not generated in real time but in separate jobs that ran periodically.

17.1.2 Development Team

Webmaster Tools employed between 15 and 20 developers, technical writers, and testers. Personally, I was a software engineer in test, and I held the position of technical lead in quality analysis. Our developers were split roughly 50/50 between the frontend and the backend. Half our team worked in C++ on projects that generated data, and the other half worked in Java, JavaScript, and CSS on the frontend.

17.1.3   Overview of Development at Google

Google is a very developer-centered company, and developers are expected to do a large portion of their own testing. For example, any code that is checked into the Google code base is expected to have unit tests. The Java code base that made up the frontend of Webmaster Tools maintained 60 to 70 percent unit test coverage (measured by lines of code covered), and all of those tests were written by developers.

Not only is all code expected to be accompanied by unit tests, but every revision also has to go through a fairly rigorous code review cycle. Having another person's eyes on one's code greatly reduces the frequency of careless mistakes. The lifecycle of a code revision is shown in Figure 17.1.

> **Good Point**
>
> A review (of code or anything else) is still an effective way to reduce bugs.

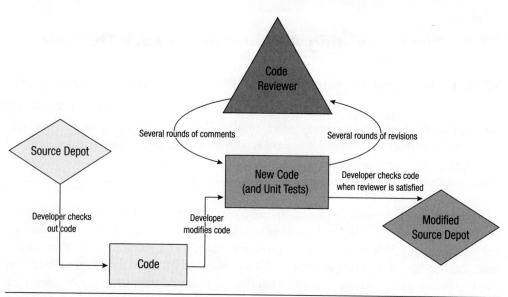

FIGURE 17.1   Lifecycle of a code review

17.1.4 Overview of Release Cycles

Google prides itself in being able to release software relatively quickly. Release cycles are quite short, usually at least one every 1 to 2 months, and they can be as short as 2 weeks. Webmaster Tools did a release roughly once every 6 weeks. A normal release cycle allowed for about 3 weeks of development time, followed by 2 to 3 weeks of quality assurance (QA) time. During the QA time, the code for the release candidate was frozen, meaning no code revisions could be checked into the source depot (for the release candidate, at least) unless those revisions were fixes for bugs found by testers.

Why did Webmaster Tools need such a relatively large amount of time for QA? Even though the development processes at Google were fairly strict, bugs still always found their way into the end product. As a result, it was a tester's responsibility to walk through the UI manually before every major release. We had scripts describing testing procedures for every major feature in Webmaster Tools. The manual tester followed the scripts and walked through the UI in every major browser that Google supported. Not only was the tester responsible for each of the major browsers, but also had to test the product for internationalization. At the time, Webmaster Tools supported 23 languages, and it was essential that the product displayed correctly in all of them, even those in which the text reads from right to left, such as Hebrew and Arabic.

17.2 Our Preexisting Automation (or Lack Thereof)

17.2.1 Manual Testing and the Need for More Automation

Even though Google was and is a very advanced company, Webmaster Tools still carried out most of its QA processes manually. This was becoming an increasingly unacceptable situation. We were always trying to reduce our release cycles, and we were incapable of reducing them further when we had to reserve a massive 2-week block for QA. As a result, automating our testing procedures was a huge priority for us.

When using the word *automation*, we mean a very specific type of automation. Yes, we had unit tests that automatically ran all the time, but this is not what we are talking about. What we mean is automation of the test specifications that, at the time, had to be carried out manually. These were end-to-end functional tests that tried to simulate the interaction of a real user with a real web browser. Figure 17.2 depicts what our automated system tests needed to cover. We didn't worry so much about the backend jobs that generated all of the data because these were mostly

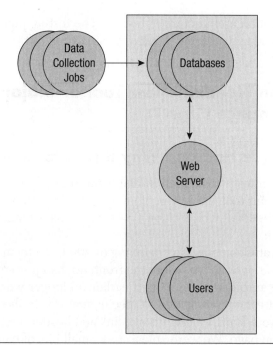

FIGURE 17.2   Webmaster Tools testing architecture with automation coverage highlighted

covered by unit tests. A very small percentage of the bugs we saw were related to data quality, the rest caused by functionality failures in the Java frontend. As a result, testing the functionality of our web pages was what the majority of our effort was focused on. We also didn't worry too much about testing the components that our frontend depended on to serve data to live user traffic. We tested that they interacted correctly with us, but we left the majority of the functionality testing to the Google teams that supported those components.

Good Point

A good automation strategy focuses on the most important objectives for the automated tests.

Of course, we didn't want to do our testing against live user data. Webmaster Tools has the power to remove sites from the Google index, and removing a site like www.amazon.com would be very bad! Luckily, we had the resources to completely duplicate our production architecture in testing. The testing pipeline was where the majority of the manual and automated testing was carried out.

17.3   Decision Needed: New Tool or Major Maintenance Effort?

17.3.1   What We Had and Why It Had to Change

Webmaster Tools had test automation in one form or another for several years. For a long time, a dominant tool within Google was eggPlant, a commercial testing package written by the TestPlant Corporation. There were many teams, Webmaster Tools included, that used it.

When I arrived at Google in the beginning of 2009, the team was at a crossroad. The user interface, along with the rest of the frontend, had just gone through a major overhaul. All of the automation developed earlier no longer worked because it had been written so that each test was tied to specific features in the user interface. For example, the tests would verify elements like link and header text, as well as their relative positions on the page. We were able to save small bits of common libraries, but we still wound up losing on the order of several thousand lines of test-specific code. The first major decision I had to make when I arrived was what to do going forward. Should we continue using eggPlant and rework all our current libraries, or should we start completely from scratch with a brand new tool?

> **Lesson**
>
> Depending on how test automation is structured, vast amounts of effort may be thrown away when major changes occur to the system under test (SUT).

When it came to testing, I was a complete novice. Before I joined Google, I had never done any sort of testing work, and it's definitely not something they teach you in school. What's worse, there was not a whole lot of information within Google comparing and contrasting the various tools. There were plenty of documents describing how to use each of them, but nothing that would give me a clear picture about which tool would best fit Webmaster Tools.

At the time, there were several main tools used within Google, most notably the open source project Selenium (which Google engineers contribute to significantly), an internal tool named TAU (Test Automation Unit) used by several major teams, and the third-party tool eggPlant. In addition to these were plenty of other commercial testing tools available on the market; however, as a relatively low-level and inexperienced engineer, I was not in a position to bring any of these tools into Google. I didn't even bother to explore any of them, instead choosing to stick with things that were already in use by other Google engineers.

Not knowing which tool to choose, I asked around. Because I worked in the Seattle office, most of the testers I asked were located there, and most of them used eggPlant in varying amounts. Overall, feedback about eggPlant was pretty neutral, while feedback on the other two Google tools was quite negative. The major problems were these:

- The project that developed and maintained TAU was in the process of dying. Google, as a whole, was moving away from it. The tool was written in C++, and there was a growing consensus that it was simply too hard to write tests using it.
- Selenium relied heavily on something called the Selenium farm. Because Selenium supports tests with all sorts of different browser and operating system combinations, Google had to maintain a pool of machines with those combinations. The Selenium farm filled that need. If a test needed a machine running Windows XP and Internet Explorer 7, it would make a request to the Selenium farm, which would hand back the address of the machine that would run the test. The problem was that the Selenium farm was greatly overused. It barely had any actual machines, and as a result, any tests that relied on it were extremely flaky. Most would just time out waiting for a machine to be allocated.

With this situation in front of me, my decision seemed like a simple one. In addition to the negatives that I found from my inquiries, we already had a fairly large common Google codebase in eggPlant that we could use to interact with the various operating systems, launch browsers, and so on. Because the tool had been so heavily used before, I figured it must have provided a reasonable amount of value. On the other hand, I never actually checked any return on investment figures, which in hindsight turned out to be a mistake. Regardless, I wound up meeting with my manager and other key players on our team, and we decided to move forward with eggPlant. Our goal was to continually shrink the release cycle of Webmaster Tools, and eggPlant seemed to be the tool that would allow us to do that. We would start by automating the manual test specifications for four or five features of Webmaster Tools, and if that experience turned out well, we would look into using eggPlant on more of the product. We had no idea how long and painful automating those 4 or 5 features would be.

Good Point

Start small. Tom Gilb says, "If you are going to have a disaster, have a small one."

17.3.2   Overview of eggPlant

eggPlant is a test package that uses image analysis at its core. The idea is simple: Compare the image of an actual user interface to an expected image and see if they are similar to within a user-defined tolerance for equality. The user interface doesn't necessarily have to be a web page; it can be anything that runs on one of the major operating systems. Everything must be tested using image analysis. Even when completing a simple task like comparing two strings, the tester writes code that causes eggPlant to generate an in-memory image of the expected text that it then searches for on the screen.

The actual eggPlant code is written in the language SenseTalk, and when we were working with it, it ran only on Macs. To function, an eggPlant test runs on the Mac while making remote procedure calls (RPCs) to an eggPlant server running on the system under test (SUT). In our case, the SUT was usually some flavor of Windows, and we would run our tests against an instance of Firefox or Internet Explorer that would be opened to a testing instance of the Webmaster Tools site.

17.4   Moving Forward with eggPlant

17.4.1   Development Experience

Working on the eggPlant code were two people: myself and a manual tester. The manual tester didn't work on automation full time; he spent a lot of his time getting Webmaster Tools ready for releases. Experience-wise, he was a hard-core tester, whereas I'm a hard-core programmer. Neither of us had much experience in the other's discipline.

In many ways, eggPlant is great for someone who does not have much programming expertise. SenseTalk is a very simple language, and it's geared toward someone who does not think like a software engineer. The technology behind it is also extremely cool. The idea that you can somehow retrieve meaningful test data just by checking how a web page looks is quite seductive. Just a few years ago, that sort of image analysis was science fiction (at least on personal computers). Even though the idea behind the tool was extremely attractive, we soon found that it didn't work so well in practice. Unfortunately, the majority of our experiences with eggPlant were negative. It wasn't that it was a bad tool; it was just that we used it in the wrong environment. I describe some of the most obvious issues next.

Good Point

Tool features that look great when you first see them may not be so good when you try to use them in earnest.

17.4.2   Using the Tool Language

Probably the largest problem we had was that the tool forced you to develop in the language SenseTalk. It wasn't like Selenium, where you could pick the language you were most comfortable with; the test package was *only* available in SenseTalk. The implications of this were far reaching and devastating:

- None of the developers on our team knew the language. The only people familiar with it were the people who actively developed in it, meaning only a handful of testers had ever even laid eyes on it. In an organization like Google, where code reviews are required before anybody can check in anything, this was not a good thing. Usually engineers choose their code reviewers on the basis of how much knowledge and insight those people can provide for their code. If the code reviewer doesn't know the language, it won't do much good for the engineer to send that person the code to review. That was the situation the manual tester and I were in. We could basically only send our code reviews to one another. At times, this resulted in a bottleneck. In addition, because the manual tester didn't have much industry coding experience, he was less likely to be able to point out my careless mistakes.
- Because eggPlant was written in SenseTalk, it didn't work with any of the other standard Google technologies we used to develop code. It had a completely different build system and a different source depot. Most Google code was written in Python, C++, or Java, and developers could invoke unit tests, compile code, or run programs using a single tool. Any eggPlant test had to be run from the eggPlant tool. The number of users of the test package were sufficiently few that integration with other standard Google technologies was not deemed necessary. Not only that, it would have been quite challenging

technically to make eggPlant work with other Google software simply because the languages are so different.

- At first glance, it might seem like eggPlant's not playing nicely with other Google technologies was only a minor annoyance, but it actually had far-reaching consequences. As I mentioned before, Webmaster Tools used a frontend written in Java. There was no easy way (or any way that I know at all, for that matter) for eggPlant code to call functions in Java, or vice versa. On Webmaster Tools, we already had vast Java libraries written for dealing with things like interacting with our databases and our other backends. There was no way to reuse this code from eggPlant to help setup and clean up our tests, and we had to write everything over again. For example, there was no easy way to do an RPC to a backend database from our test code.

- Another problem with SenseTalk is that the language is just plain hard to use for someone experienced in any of the other major languages. It might be fine for novices, but most people in engineering positions at Google have quite a bit of experience writing code. For example, the manual tester who worked with me didn't write much code, but he still had a computer science degree. To demonstrate how different SenseTalk is from other languages, I included several code fragments in Listing 17.1. Both implement a routine to look for the string `Michael` in the lines of a file, but the left is in Java while the right is in SenseTalk. To a layperson, SenseTalk seems like it would be easy to understand. After all, reading the code is like reading an English sentence. Like English, however, SenseTalk can sometimes be very imprecise. As one can see from the figure, SenseTalk has many more reserved words than Java does. As a result, it can be difficult to remember what each of the reserved words does and in which context each should be used.

Listing 17.1   Routine to Find the Substring `Michael` in the Lines of a File with Java (Left) and SenseTalk (Right)

```
String lineWithMichael = null;              set lineWithMichael to ""
for (String line : fileLines) {             repeat with each line of fileLines
    if (name.contains("Michael")) {             if "Michael" is in line then
        lineWithMichael = line;                     put line into lineWithMichael
    }                                           end if
}                                           end repeat
```

■ Finally, like most interpreted languages I've worked with, SenseTalk becomes increasingly cumbersome as the size of the application increases. These languages are good for small tasks, but when too many lines of code are involved, the smallest bugs, such as forgetting to initialize a variable, become a major burden. Languages like Java and the various flavors of C catch these bugs with the compiler. What's worse, usually when someone is writing code in an interpreted language, he or she has the opportunity to write unit tests that catch most of the things the compiler normally would. This isn't necessarily true when writing test code. We usually tried to avoid writing unit tests for test code unless it was going to be used in library code.

17.4.3   Problems with Image-Based Comparison

Another major problem we had with eggPlant was that it was an image-based tool, and we were using it to test a web application. Even though this was its biggest selling point, it also turned out to be its largest drawback. Image comparison is an especially slow area of computer science, meaning that our tests were much slower than they needed to be. Every time a test needed to search for a string, eggPlant had to look through every pixel on the screen for a possible match. eggPlant allowed the programmer to limit the search area, which helped some, but the tool would still be searching through a relatively large number of pixels.

Good Point

Image (bitmap) comparisons are inefficient at best and are better avoided if possible.

The speed wasn't the largest problem with the image comparison engine—it was that such tests were inherently flaky. As I mentioned before, eggPlant had to use image analysis for everything, even searching for text. This meant that if the size or font of text on a webpage changed, the test would break. It wouldn't signify a real bug, only a sign that the test needed to be updated. To complicate the situation, the image analysis forced us to take into account differences between various browsers. For example, Internet Explorer, Firefox, and eggPlant all render underlined text differently, as shown in Figure 17.3. As you can see, the different applications render the word *page* with different underline thicknesses and with different amounts of space between the letters and the underline. As a result, any test looking for the text

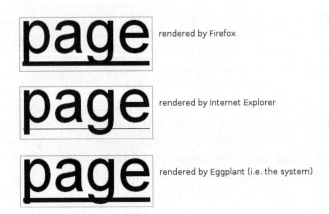

rendered by Firefox

rendered by Internet Explorer

rendered by Eggplant (i.e. the system)

FIGURE 17.3   Different renderings of the word *page* in Firefox, Internet Explorer, and eggPlant

page may work in FireFox, but it will break because eggPlant won't be able to find the text image in Internet Explorer, and it will think the text isn't there.

The eggPlant version of *page* is the image that eggPlant will search for on the screen. Because it is different from the images produced by Firefox and Internet Explorer, it will sometimes have problems finding the text, even though it may well be visible on the page.

A lot of these image comparison issues could be solved by tweaking the image tolerance used during searches. Unfortunately, the required image tolerance would usually change from search to search, so it was something we constantly had to tweak to get our tests to succeed. This was a recurring theme that we found everywhere when we were trying to develop eggPlant tests. Put simply, it was really hard to get our tests to pass even though we knew they should.

17.4.4   Test Maintenance Had to Be Done by Testers

Not only was it hard to get tests to pass, eggPlant also forced all of the test creation and maintenance onto the testers. On my team, where the tester-to-developer ratio was very small, this was not a good thing. Because all the code was written in a different language, none of our developers could easily understand it, and it probably didn't make sense in terms of ROI for them to learn. As a result, all of the test development was left to us. When a test broke, either because it needed to be updated or because of an actual bug, we were the only ones in a position to determine what went wrong.

17.4.5   Submitting Code Using Continuous Integration

In our system, all code revisions were required to go through a submit queue before they were allowed to pass into the source depot. In the submit queue, all the code affected by a revision was built and tested. If the test suite was comprehensive enough, the submit queue would almost be enough to ensure that the revision wasn't introducing any new bugs into the product. Granted, this was usually a very unrealistic goal, but the submit queue still had the ability to catch many bugs before they ever showed their ugly faces in the final product. Ideally, what we needed was for as many tests as possible to be running in the submit queue of Figure 17.4.

There were several technical challenges to getting all of our tests running in the submit queue. First, all the tests needed to be fast because the system couldn't place too much of an inconvenience on the developers. We typically used a benchmark of about 15 minutes as the maximum that a submit queue could take to run. This didn't necessarily mean that any test could take up to 15 minutes, however, because a lot of time was spent compiling code and running other tests. We tried to keep any test running in the submit queue to no more than 5 minutes. Second, any test running in the submit queue needed to be rock solid (in other words, not flaky). Again, this was for the sake of the developers who only wanted to see a submit queue failure if their new code actually broke something, not if some test was acting up for a random reason. Finally, any browser-level test needed to run against a version of the web server built from the version of the code that the developer was working on. It would do no good to run such a test against a server that was built from a version of the codebase

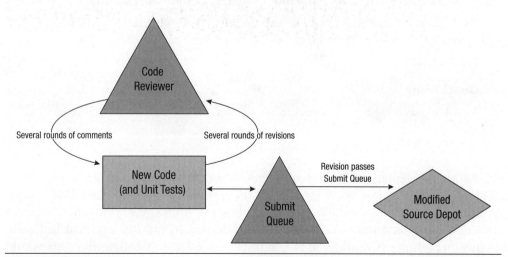

FIGURE 17.4   Submit queue system

from several days or even weeks before. If that test succeeded or failed, it would be absolutely meaningless because it would have no dependency on the code in the developer's workspace. As a result of this requirement, the test needed to be responsible for building and starting a version of the server that was the same as the version of the developer's codebase.

Unfortunately, eggPlant failed as a solution to any of these technical challenges. In terms of speed, we had eggPlant tests that took longer than 20 minutes. They weren't doing a whole lot; it was just that it took forever for the tool to do image validation on every single test condition. When it came to flakiness, eggPlant tests were as flaky as they come. The slightest modification in the way the browser displayed a web page would cause the image validation to fail. Many times, the page modifications were nothing that our developers had anything to do with. For example, if, for whatever reason, the browser window was smaller in different runs of a test, it was highly likely that the test would fail. Finally, because eggPlant tests were written in SenseTalk, and because SenseTalk did not work well with any other Google technologies, there were no hooks to kick off tests as part of submit queue runs.

17.4.6   What Would the Submit Queue Have Done for Us?

The submit queue is extremely valuable because it allows developers to catch bugs as soon as possible, often before their minds have shifted to another topic. Without something like the submit queue, most bugs are caught by testers doing test passes in preparation for a release, which can be weeks or even months after the code was originally written. By that time, the developer has no idea what he wrote, and it takes considerable time and effort to figure out what went wrong and how to fix it, not to mention the time and effort required to find and write up the original bug.

> **Good Point**
>
> Tests that give immediate feedback to developers are the most useful to them.

Another advantage of the submit queue is seen when new code breaks a test. It might not be a bug; instead, it means that the test needs to be updated. With a submit queue, it's the responsibility of the developer to update the test. When we were developing eggPlant tests, the best we could do was to run our eggPlant test suite nightly. Sometimes it would find actual bugs, but most of the time the tests would need updating as a result of code revisions that had gone in during the previous day.

It turned into a maintenance nightmare for the two of us to try to figure out why our tests were broken almost every night. Many times, the breakages had nothing to do with actual code changes; it was just that the test was flaky, and we hadn't known it before!

17.4.7 How Did Our eggPlant Automation Adventure Turn Out?

As you might imagine after reading about all the problems we ran into using eggPlant (I didn't even include all of the little problems we encountered), our automation attempt turned into a complete disaster, and we wound up having to throw out all of our code after 6 months. We periodically discussed the value of eggPlant during that 6-month period, but we didn't elect to throw everything out and start over with a new tool until the very end. Even though we knew that eggPlant had significant drawbacks early on (at least in the way we were using it), we were reluctant to give up all the work that we had spent so much time on. It eventually turned into a vicious cycle. We didn't want to throw out all our hard work, which lead us to wasting more time writing unusable code, which we eventually had to throw out anyway.

> **Good Point**
>
> When you are spending too much time on maintenance of the automated tests, it's time for significant changes, even if it means abandoning something you have put a lot of effort into.

17.4.8 A Surprising Twist to Earlier Assumptions!

Even though Webmaster Tools had used eggPlant for a couple of years before I started at Google, I didn't realize until later that it wasn't actually doing the team much good. The manual tester who worked during most of that period would run the automated tests during his manual test passes, but he didn't rely on them. He retested everything by hand, including the features that were already covered by the tests. It was no fault of the team for using eggPlant during this period because there was nothing for browser automation that was any better. One of the biggest reasons we finally moved away from the tool was that by late 2009, there were some serious competitors.

17.5   What Did We Do after eggPlant?

After our first automation attempt , Webmaster Tools began moving closer to the system depicted in Figure 17.4 with all of our tests running in the submit queue. One of the many lessons we learned was that image-based testing of a web application does not provide a good enough ROI to warrant consideration. We began employing the rule of thumb that if we found ourselves trying to test whether something "looked right," then we probably had a problem. Consequently, we switched to an open source tool known as WebDriver that was originally developed within Google.

Similar to Selenium (WebDriver will actually be a part of Selenium 2.0), WebDriver works by examining the HTML source returned from a web server and by manipulating JavaScript. Using it, we tested *only* the functionality, not the appearance, of our web pages with automated tests. We still checked the appearance manually, but once all the functionality had been verified with automation, this was a simple and fast exercise.

Most of the testing involved finding HTML elements within the page and then doing string comparisons looking for expected text. As a result, tests ran in a fraction of the time they had taken under eggPlant. For example, one test suite that took more than 20 minutes with eggPlant took less than 30 seconds with WebDriver. Not only was the tool much faster, but also we began handling most of the test setup and cleanup with RPCs that only took a couple of hundred milliseconds. Our tests were also much more stable. They no longer broke whenever the font or the size of the text changed, and because they were written in Java, they worked nicely in our submit queue system.

17.6   Conclusion

17.6.1   eggPlant as a Tool

Despite all the problems my team ran into with eggPlant, I haven't given up hope on it. It's still a neat testing package with an appealing set of features. The biggest problem we had was that we were using it for the wrong things. It is definitely not the best tool to test the functionality of a web application. I do wish it was packaged a bit differently. If it was written in a standard language, then maybe we could use it every now and then to test visual aspects.

17.6.2   Test Automation in General: Our Lessons Learned

Even though my team's experience with test automation was a little painful, I do not think automation in general is a waste of time. On the other hand, I do think it's necessary to closely examine what you're trying to automate before you begin. At Google, we have thousands upon thousands of unit tests that run in an automated fashion, and this works beautifully. By definition, a unit test does not access any external resources (such as a database), and it only tests a small fragment of production code. They're easy to write, and when they break, it's almost always because of a real problem.

By contrast, system-level tests, like those we were trying to do with eggPlant, are extremely difficult. Because they test so many live components, they're bound to be flaky. For example, our eggPlant tests depended on the browser, all of our frontend code (because the tests ran against a live server), and all of our backend databases. If any one of those dependencies broke for whatever reason, the tests would almost certainly fail.

The main problem we had when we started out was that we chose the wrong tool, but I'm still not sure that using the right tool would have alleviated all our headaches. Although WebDriver was dramatically better than eggPlant, we found that stable, maintainable tests were still surprisingly difficult to create. This seems to be the consensus with every browser-based automation tool I've ever heard of.

17.6.3   Current Problems with Automation

Unfortunately, browser-based automation seems to be one of those areas of computer science that isn't well developed yet. Ideally, we would have a tool that could hook directly into the browser and control it, without the need for any plug-ins or JavaScript hackery or anything. It would be supported natively in all the major browsers. To my knowledge, nothing like that currently exists, although WebDriver is slowly moving in that direction. Because we don't yet have such a tool, browser-based automation tools are left in an odd state. They have no way of knowing when certain events happen, such as when a JavaScript Ajax request returns or when the onload handler for a web page finishes running. The result is that the test writer is left to rely on a system of timeouts that leaves much to be desired.

As an example, take a scenario I was trying to test recently. The goal of the test was simple: select an item from a dropdown list in the user interface, and verify that a status message appears. This is trickier than it seems, however, because after selecting the dropdown item, the user has to wait a certain amount of time before the request goes through and the status message appears. If the user tells WebDriver to search for the status message immediately after he or she selects the item, the test will most likely fail because the status message will not have appeared yet.

So, what's the solution to this problem? The test writer has to tell WebDriver to sleep and then wake up at given intervals, polling the web page until a timeout elapses. How long should the timeout be? An easy solution would be to set a huge timeout that WebDriver would probably never get to. Unfortunately, a solution like this can mask other problems. For example, if it takes over 2 minutes for the request to go through, even in the testing pipeline, then there are probably some major problems that need looking into. As a result, we usually try to choose reasonable timeouts, anywhere between 10 and 30 seconds. The downside is that if the network is running particularly slow on any given day, the test will fail for a reason completely unrelated to anything that a developer did.

This scenario is all too common using any of the testing packages that are available today. It would be much more ideal if the test writer didn't have to worry about waiting at all. If the tool could somehow be aware of the fact that the browser is doing something and wait until that action completes, tests would be much simpler to write. The programmer wouldn't have to worry about telling the tool to wait; it would just happen automatically. Granted, it would still be a good idea to have a timeout on any of the browser actions, but the tool could set a default internally that would work in the vast majority of cases.

> **Good Point**
>
> Synchronizing tests with responses from the SUT can be difficult. Building the software for automated testability (for synchronization) is the best solution.

Because Google is one of the largest web-based companies in the world, I'm sure the problem of system tests and browser-based automation will continue to be a major priority well into the future. I trust that the quality of the tools, and also the knowledge of how best to structure automation infrastructure, will continue to improve.

CHAPTER 18

AUTOMATED TESTS FOR MARKETPLACE SYSTEMS: TEN YEARS AND THREE FRAMEWORKS

Lars Wahlberg

Lars Wahlberg gives an insight into his 10 years of test automation for marketplace systems, including the development of three automation frameworks. One of the key messages in this chapter is the importance of having the right abstraction level between the technical aspects of the automated tests and the testers. Lars describes how they addressed this issue in each of the different frameworks and some of the problems that occurred if the abstraction layer was too thick or too thin. As Lars and his team moved into agile development, they found the process worked best when they had people who could be both tester and test automator, but the role of the test automation architect was critical for smooth implementation of automation. The chapter illustrates the progression of a test from manual to automated and the automated checking of preconditions. Lars also includes an illuminating assessment of return on investment for automation based on how often tests are run, the costs of automating, and the number of tests that are automated. This work was done in Sweden using open source tools. See Table 18.1.

Table 18.1   Case Study Characteristics

Classification	This Case Study
Application domain	Financial industry, marketplace systems
Application size	3–5 million lines of code
Location	Sweden, but testing on products used globally
Lifecycle	From incremental development to agile
Number on the project	20 (typical customer project)
Number of testers	8 (typical customer project)
Number of automators	4 (of above testers)
Time span	Approximately 10 years
Dates	1998–2009
Tool type(s)	Open source
Pilot study undertaken	Yes
ROI measured	Yes, projected payback for tests run daily, weekly, or monthly
Successful?	Yes
Still breathing?	Yes

18.1   Background for the Case Study

This chapter describes my experiences of working with three automated test frameworks used to test three different software products for marketplace systems in two companies. The frameworks differ, but in general, they have many similarities. They have all been successful in automating test execution, allowing rapid deliveries with extensive regression testing (ranging from 15,000 to 50,000 tests). The discussion is on a general level around technology, costs, and people, explaining success factors and pitfalls that we experienced (some of which led to some delays). Real names are not used, and some simplifications have been made (i.e., not mentioning all details) to keep the chapter at a reasonable length.

18.2   Automated Test Frameworks

A simplified picture of our automated test framework is shown in Figure 18.1. The test engine selects the tests that are to be executed; summarizes test results; and provides methods for setup, cleanup, reporting, and assertions, and so on. A common test engine used today in Java development is, for example, JUnit. The abstraction layer is the interface or the API that a test engineer uses to write/implement the test scripts. It hides the test engineer from the technical details of the real system interface. Figure 18.1 illustrates that framework: The left side facing the test script is black, and the right side facing the system is white, where one could think about seeing the system as a black or white box (requirement or structural point of view). The test script uses the abstraction layer to enter inputs to and verify outputs from the system. The system configuration is available in some form, either via transactions from the system (such as queries) or in some readable form (e.g., a file exported from a database).

For us, a typical project doing adaptations from the base product of our marketplace software for a customer (such as an exchange for equities, options, or

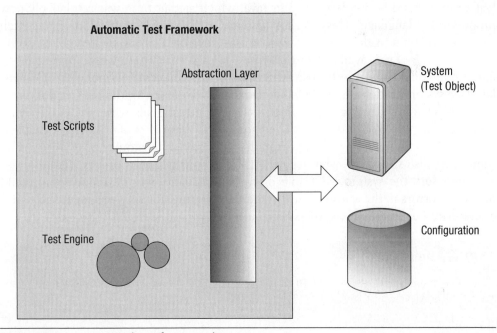

FIGURE 18.1   Automated test framework

commodities) had around 2,000 to 5,000 functional automated tests. To get a feeling of the size, this is approximately equivalent to 15 A4 binders (each containing around 300 pages) of detailed manual test procedures (using a level of detail in scripts that I expect is common in the finance industry). Having several customers for a product, a test framework may support from 15,000 to 50,000 tests (individual test cases). There are no technical or resource constraints to have more tests if needed. The number of tests varies with time depending on, for example, if a customer project closes down, an increase or reduction of tests when functionality changes, or a decision is made to use or not use automated tests for a specific customer project (maybe due to limited staff resources).

18.2.1   Framework A

The first framework, A, was developed in 1998 under much time pressure, because an external test firm had completely failed in automating the tests (they lacked the technical skills to automate and the domain knowledge of test design for marketplace functionality). There was no formal pilot project or analysis; two experienced developers (with some knowledge of automated tests from the telecom industry) convinced the management that they could solve it. One early decision was that the test scripts would be implemented in Java, which at that time was a relatively new programming language. This decision was made to encourage developers to switch over to the testing side. The test engine was developed from scratch, because no open source tool was available at that time. After 1 year, there were approximately 2,000 functional tests able to test most parts of the relevant functionality of a marketplace system (order matching logic, auctions, trade halts, trading schedules, etc.). The project was judged as a real success, and the test goals were achieved within time with an effort of about 2 to 3 person-years. After 4 years, the tests reached up to 15,000 automatic tests, supporting tests for several customer adaptations. The framework also supported what we called simulations whereby orders were entered randomly into the system. A simple oracle functionality was developed that could find some errors in the output, but the simulation's functionality was most successful at finding defects that caused the system to stop or crash.

> **Good Point**
>
> Choose a scripting language that will be popular and for which there will be plenty of skilled developers.

18.2.2   Framework B

The second framework, B, started development during 1999, mostly based on the inspiration and success from framework A (that could be regarded as the pilot project). It tested another marketplace product that was much more widespread with more customers. The test scripts were also implemented in Java. Lots of concepts from framework A were reused, but because the largest part of the framework lies in the abstraction layer, a major rework was needed. It was also hard to get resources from framework A to work with B because of an overall shortage of people at this time (the IT industry was really hot in 1999).

The development of the framework was ongoing for some years, rewriting parts back and forth—for example, switching to JUnit as a test engine. The framework got stuck in a forever improvement cycle with few tests, which was a problem. The team were constantly "tinkering" with the framework instead of expanding the number of tests. Another problem was that not enough resources were assigned for automating tests. One explanation could have been lack of interest from higher management.

Good Point

Get the balance right between working on the automation framework and creating tests.

Then, during 2002, heavy investments were made to create large regression tests for the customer projects, which finally pulled the framework into real use. This was partly thanks to a senior manager who had been responsible for the whole organization that worked with the product that was tested by framework A. He gathered information needed for the funding, set up clear goals, and followed the progress very closely. The goals included, for example, functional areas to be automated, number of tests (indication based on an initial test design), and progress per week. It helps to get attention from higher management! The number of tests increased rapidly during 3 years to over 50,000 test cases as a total for all customer projects. The reuse of tests was an important factor, and several analyses were done on cost and return on investment (ROI), which is discussed later on in this chapter.

Good Point

Having the support of a senior manager can make a tremendous difference to the automation effort.

18.2.3 Framework C

The third framework, C, was developed partly by some people who had experience from framework A, but there were also people with experience from other automated test frameworks. Again, it tested another marketplace product and in a completely different organization. The development started around 2003. JUnit was used as the test engine. A difference was the language used for implementation of test scripts; a test script language was invented using XML. It was still possible to write tests in Java, but this was not the preferred option (initially). It was assumed that our new test script language would make it easier for people lacking programming skills to write tests. There were about 1,000 tests initially, but it got stuck (stalled) at that size. The problems were related to the abstraction layer (test script language), which is explained in more detail later in this chapter. During 2007, the abstraction layer was simplified and changed so tests were implemented in Java instead. Today, this framework supports about 20,000 tests in various customer projects.

18.3 Test Roles

Tools and machines are great, but in the end, it is the people who matter. Putting together an effective automated test team requires lots of planning and skills. Some of the roles we used are discussed in this section.

18.3.1 Test Engineer

The (automated) test engineer is the frontline soldier. He or she has good technical skills to understand the system at an API level. The test engineer has knowledge of a programming language to implement test scripts and has test design training. It is possible to separate the work of script writing and test design between two people, but we have small, agile teams that require people with broader competence. The test design should also be reviewed by a senior test engineer (more than 5 years of experience in the domain). A recommended way to recruit is to train newly graduated students into the role. Converting manual testers may fail on needed programming skills. A good developer not interested in test methodology is not a good candidate. There has been a trend that developers write lots of automated tests, but the full-time test engineer is still in demand (by the team and the organization) to get a higher level of independence (from the implementation/design). The ratio between testers and developers has decreased from one tester and two developers to around 1:3 to 1:4 during a 10-year period.

> **Good Point**
>
> There are advantages to having the tester also take on the role of being the test automator (and there are also disadvantages).

18.3.2 Test Automation Architect

The test automation architect is a key player who is responsible for developing and maintaining the test framework. He or she defines best practice and coding standards to be used in implementation of the tests and trains test engineers to do minor changes in the abstraction layer needed by the customer projects (so the architect doesn't become a bottleneck).

18.3.3 Daily Build Engineer

The person in charge of the daily build ensures that the test batch is executed, makes the first analysis of the results, and distributes the work needed to analyze the tests. Some of the teams don't separate this role; instead the entire team takes responsibility. Test frameworks A and B used their own developed tools for daily builds, which was maintained by the daily build engineer. Test framework C now uses the open source tool Hudson for continuous build and test, which has decreased this maintenance work.

18.4 Abstraction Layer

The abstraction layer is the interface or the API that a test engineer uses to write/implement the test scripts. It hides the test engineer from the technical details of the real system interface. For example, to enter an order into a marketplace system requires about 60 to 80 fields to be considered in a specific order-insert transaction (or an enter-order dialogue in a test client GUI). Most tests on matching logic need to set only a few important fields (e.g., price, quantity, bid or ask side, order book ID); the rest can be set to default values, and not all are mandatory in all situations. An example of a simple test implemented in Java for framework A or B on the black-box side of the abstraction layer looks as follows (with a manual example first):

Manual Test Procedure

Pre-req:	Any order book that is open (ready for trading, not closed)
Action:	Enter an ask/sell order with price = 10 and quantity = 20
Verify:	Order is inserted into the order book, no trade occurs
Action:	Enter a bid/buy order with price = 10 and quantity = 40
Verify:	A trade occurs with price = 10 and quantity = 20
Verify:	A bid/buy order is in the order book with price = 10 and quantity = 20

Automated Test Script

```
public boolean Test1() {
        Orderbook ob = getRandomOrderBook;
        long price = getRandomprice(ob);    // tick size aligned
            price
        long quantity = getRoundLot(ob);    // allowed trading lot

        Trader1.enterAskOrder(ob, price, quantity);
        Trader2.enterBidOrder(ob, price, 2*quantity);

        boolean success1 = Trader1.verifyTrade(ob, price,
            quantity);
        boolean success2 = Trader2.verifyBidOrder(ob, price,
            quantity);

        return success1 & sucess2;
    }
```

Scenarios involving more order types (e.g., limit, market, stop-loss, or iceberg orders) and what information must be verified (public, private, consolidated information) makes the scripts in reality longer than in this simple case.

If the abstraction layer is too thin (e.g., too many fields are set in a specific test script), the tests can be cumbersome to maintain. If one field changes, several hundreds of tests may need to be modified. This also requires a more technical knowledge of the system (e.g., the real interface to the system).

On the other side, if the abstraction layer is too thick (too large or too advanced), the complexity of the layer itself can be a problem. There are several ways to deal with this problem.

For example, framework C initially used an internally invented test language implemented in XML. The first problem was that the test engineers needed to learn the test language, which required documentation to be created and maintained. Any maintenance to the abstraction layer (e.g., if some new fields were added to a transaction) required knowledge of modifying this inhouse-invented "compiler," which partly used code generation. It ended up that the test automation architects became a bottleneck; it was too difficult to increase the number of tests in the organization. The abstraction layer was later simplified and changed so tests were implemented in Java instead (which required more programming skills from the test engineers).

Lesson

Don't overlook the costs of learning, developing, and maintaining a custom scripting language.

But writing the tests in Java is no guarantee of solving problems with thick abstraction layers. All frameworks A, B, and C have from time to time run into problems where, for example, test engineers wanted to write very compact and object-oriented code using various design patterns (believed wrongly to give lower maintenance cost), which lead to a thick abstraction layer. On one occasion for framework A, there was a test suite that even the test automation architect couldn't understand! There may be several explanations for this. One could be that the test engineer is more interested in software design than in writing tests. Other explanations include different viewpoints on how to keep maintenance cost of test scripts low, what readable code is, and what language skills are required when writing tests.

We found that the use of coding standards, lots of good examples, and follow-up by the test automation architect are ways to handle this. Using object-oriented concepts in writing tests can also help. For example, both frameworks A and B suffered from having many different functions for entering orders and verifying results, depending on how many relevant fields there were for the test. Framework C uses a compact design pattern, allowing fields to be set arbitrarily as follows (each "set" can be skipped if wanted; it then is given a default value):

```
tTrader1.enterBidOrder.setObId(orderbook)
.setPrice(price).setQty(quantity);
```

Instead of having several functions (that need to be maintained) in the API, a single object-oriented method can be used for writing tests like:

```
enterBidOrder()
enterBidOrder(orderbook)
enterBidOrder(orderbook, price)
enterBidOrder(orderbook, price, quantity)
enterBidOrder(price)
enterBidOrder(price, quantity)
enterBidOrder(orderbook, quantity)
enterBidOrder(quantity)
```

Our success over the years has been in selecting the optimal thickness of the abstraction layer and its technology.

18.5   Configuration

The configuration used by the system under test is of course closely connected to the tests. Configuration in this case for marketplace systems are market setups, parameters for matching logic, allowable order types, user roles, user names and passwords, and so forth. The configuration varies for different customers and environments (test, production); frameworks B and C use a fixed configuration per test batch (all tests). This configuration is maintained and version controlled together with the tests. Each test states what it needs in the configuration, and if that is not available, the test is skipped.

> **Good Point**
>
> Check the preconditions for a test automatically, and don't run the test if they are not met.

Another strategy used by framework A was the use of so-called predicates, which could be applied to order books, users, and system. Code typically looked as follows:

```
PredicateList.add(new PredicateCurrency("USD"));
PredicateList.add(new PredicateRoundLot("100"));
PredicateList.add(new PredicateStopLossAllowed(true));

Orderbook ob = getRandomOb(PredicateList);
```

The code returns an order book that has currency in U.S. dollars, round lot size of 100, and allows entering of stop-loss orders (a special order type not allowed in some markets). The strategy of using predicates adds complexity but makes tests more robust to changes in configuration.

A good side benefit is that the tests can be used to test the configuration in an environment. Are correct tests skipped? For example, stop-loss orders may be allowed in a test system (so they can be tested) but not in the production stage environment. If all tests are executed against the production stage environment, then all tests that require stop-loss orders to be allowed should be skipped. If not, then something is wrong with the configuration of the market.

18.6 Cost and ROI

The large effort put into the automated tests needs to be justified. A lot of models were considered when trying to justify the large investment of automated tests for the product tested by framework B. (Even though framework A was successful, framework B would require a substantial investment because it was a new application area.) When considering the ROI, consider the worth of the tests:

- *The worth of each defect potentially found.* A typical value is maybe 10 to 20 hours for each defect found (cost in support, analysis, correction, test, maintenance release, project management, etc.) for this kind of application. A severe fault in matching logic or defects that cause the system to crash (downtime) can cost the company much more (potentially millions of Swedish Kroner) in fines, bad will, and such.
- *The worth of each passed test.* In the financial industry, there is a large demand on extensive verification (due to the importance of the systems).
- *The worth of rapid deliveries* (new feature, urgent defect correction).

Good Point

The value of automated tests is often in confidence and speed rather than defects found.

All this must be assessed by the organization for the specific product and customer requirements. A simple ROI calculation is to consider the worth of each passed test and compare the cost of executing tests (like a factory). The numbers given here are based on some measurements and assumptions made by experienced people. They were used for real ROI calculations, but do not copy them blindly into your organization!

Figure 18.2 shows this simple calculation on how much cost (time) is saved by automating tests versus numbers of tests executed daily, weekly, and monthly. For example, if executing 1,500 tests monthly, the saving in automating would be around –25 percent, which means it is more expensive to automate tests that are only run once a month. If executing 1,500 tests weekly, the saving would be around 40 percent (a significant saving). Finally, if executing 1,500 tests daily, the saving would be around 90 percent. It is most likely not feasible to manually execute them daily (would require about 150 man-hours per day, so 20 persons). For daily and weekly execution of 1,500 tests, the savings are significant, so automation is a very good solution in these situations.

Note that this calculation doesn't distinguish between test design and implementation for automated tests versus manual test procedures. The test design always needs to be done anyway, and the implementation is similar (as shown by the example earlier). The main difference is in the test framework maintenance versus manual execution cost. It is assumed that it takes about 2 hours in general to do the test design (split up per test case) and implementation. A test batch (all tests) contains 2,000 to 5,000 test cases and takes in effort around 8 hours to execute and analyze. It takes all of the daily build engineer's time if running tests daily, which we typically do. Running a manual test is assumed to take around 6 minutes per test. The automated test framework requires about 3,000 hours per year in maintenance. The rest is just arithmetic: The savings in percentage is how many hours are saved by running the tests automatically instead of manually. Figure 18.2 shows the percentage of savings compared to the number of tests, with three graphs for tests run monthly, weekly, and daily. We can see that monthly run tests never break even, daily run tests always give a benefit, and weekly run tests break even for around 700 tests.

The maintenance of the test tool can be further divided. It is important because the test framework in itself is an advanced program that requires considerable maintenance. For example, an internally developed test tool for a marketplace could be about 100,000 lines of code and the test scripts about 1 million lines of code (~10,000 tests) of Java code. Even if off-the-shelf tools are used, the abstraction layer must be developed anyway. The cost of the test framework should be paid by both the line organization and the specific projects that are using it. Table 18.2 shows an example of how costs can be divided.

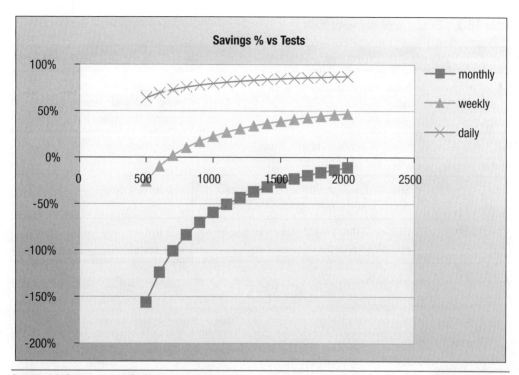

FIGURE 18.2   Savings by automating tests

Table 18.2   Example of Maintenance Cost

Description	Example	Paid By
Maintenance cost needed to ensure the foundation and technology of automated tests for a marketplace product	~600–800 hr/yr	Line/ product
Maintenance cost to update tool and test cases when adding or changing functionality of the product in a specific project	~200–400 hr/project (3-mo projects)	Project

Table 18.3   Example of Reuse of Tests

Category	Description	Effort (Example)
I	Same functionality area and configuration	~2 hr/test suite (time to copy, test and version control the suite)
II	Same functionality area but different configuration	~10 hr/test suite
III	Similar functionality area but tests need minor modification	~ 1 hr/test case
IV	Functionality area differs too much; complete rewrite of tests	~ 2 hr/test case (same as new tests)

Assumption: Test suite contains 50 tests.

Good Point

Automation should not be charged (only) to projects; the costs and benefits should be more wide ranging.

Another important aspect of costs is the ability to reuse test cases between different projects. It depends on how many adaptations the various customer projects have (e.g., similarity in functionality). An example of how to categorize the work needed is shown in Table 18.3. The entire test batch (all tests) that perhaps contains up to 100 test suites must be analyzed. Each test suite maps against a functionality area (a collection of requirements, e.g., iceberg order functionality).

18.7   Conclusion

Table 18.4 summarizes all the test frameworks.

Table 18.4   Test Frameworks

Name	Development Year	Tests (Max)	Still Used	Test Script	Open Source	Problems/ Concerns
A	1998	~15,000	Yes	Java	—	Predicates used to handle variable test data could maybe have been skipped (to make framework simpler)
B	1999	~50,000	Yes	Java	JUnit	Test framework got initially stuck in a forever improvement cycle with few tests
C	2003	~20,000	Yes	Java	JUnit Hudson	Initial abstraction layer using a test script language made it difficult to scale up tests; was abandoned for a simpler approach in Java

To summarize 10 years of experience of automated tests for marketplace software:

- The abstraction layer of the test framework is very important for success. It needs to have the optimal thickness. The technology, such as the scripting language, is also important. Using Java has been shown to work very well.
- The strategy of using predicates was impressive for framework A, but we found that large, maintainable test batches were achieved by using a fixed

configuration instead (test frameworks B and C). This made the test framework less complex.

- The number of tests for marketplace systems is typically around 2,000 to 5,000 functional tests per customer project (an adaptation made on a base product). The demand for extensive verification and rapid deliveries has forced the companies to automate tests to save money in test execution. This has been the case for the last 10 years. The technology and solution for frameworks A, B, and C are similar. Greater use of open source components has occurred during the 10 years.

- Test roles in automated testing have varied over the years from having many full-time testers to fewer, putting a larger demand on the developers to write tests. It is highly recommended to have a test automation architect who ensures that the abstraction layer doesn't become too complex.

CHAPTER 19

THERE'S MORE TO AUTOMATION THAN REGRESSION TESTING: THINKING OUTSIDE THE BOX

Jonathan Kohl

Jonathan Kohl takes us through a set of short stories, each illustrating a variation on the theme of automating things other than what people usually think of, that is, thinking outside the box. The stories together demonstrate the value of applying ingenuity and creativity to solve problems by automating simple tasks, or processes other than test execution. Full-scale automation is not necessarily a practical option in some cases, but small and simple tool solutions can provide significant benefits and savings. Jonathan shows that even devising "disposable" automation scripts can be very useful. These experiences from Canada cover small to large applications, from web-based to embedded systems, using commercial, open source, and inhouse tools. See Table 19.1

19.1 Background for the Case Study

We can reap the benefits of test automation using tools that are readily available with less effort than regression test automation. While simpler automation efforts are what I started out with as a rookie tester, I didn't take the ideas too seriously until I read Cem Kaner's paper, "Architectures of Test Automation" (2000), in which

Table 19.1   Case Study Characteristics

Classification	This Case Study
Application domain	Various: web applications, integrated embedded systems
Application size	From very large to very small
Location	Canada
Lifecycle	Agile, traditional, and combinations of both
Number on the project	From less than 6 to more than 60
Number of testers	From 1 to many
Number of automators	1 (me) but I had some help
Time span	Various experiences over the years
Dates	Late 1990s–2011
Tool type(s)	Commercial, open source, inhouse
Pilot study undertaken	Yes, in some cases
ROI measured	No
Successful?	Yes
Still breathing?	Yes, some of the automation is still in use

he introduced the idea of computer-assisted testing, and James Bach's "Agile Test Automation" (2003) presentation. Kaner pointed out that *test automation* is a misnomer because there is still a good deal of human involvement no matter what we are trying to automate. Bach had an even stronger idea that resonated with me: He called it "tool-supported testing," declaring that any use of tools to help our testing is a type of test automation.

In *Software Test Automation*, Mark Fewster and Dorothy Graham (1999) talk about pre- and postprocessing tasks that surround test automation. I've done the opposite: automated pre- and postprocessing tasks, leaving the test execution and evaluation up to a human user. This has led me to a lot of different automation approaches.

In our rush to automate regression tests, we often overlook simpler, yet effective types of automation:

- Task automation (automated build creation, product installation, data population)
- Using automation to aid exploratory testing (partial automation, workflow automation)
- Test data creation, data interaction
- Monitoring, reporting
- Simulation: Using automation tools to create real-world conditions

In this chapter, I show how automation helped testing in these five areas. (I first introduced these ideas in "Man and Machine: Combining the Power of the Human Mind with Automation Tools" [Kohl 2007].)

19.2 Two Tales of Task Automation

19.2.1 Automation Failed, and How Did That Tester Suddenly Improve?

This project involved a medium-sized software company/software as a service/application service provider.

I've seen a lot of test automation failures. Generally, the causes can be summed up as:

- A lack of clear goals over and above "automate tests."
- Not measuring whether automation is helping or distracting (especially without clear goals).
- Blind faith in record/playback, or "no programming required."
- Using tools without inhouse expertise in the underlying language.

19.1.1.1 Two Tools and You're Out

All of these came into play in one organization. After management and testing were sold an expensive record/playback tool, they found it didn't work beyond simple demos. They had to hire a contractor who had the technical knowledge to modify recorded scripts and work with the proprietary scripting language and window maps. This was costly, and with only one person working on the ambitious "automate our regression test suite" task, progress was slow. It took months to determine that a lot of money had been spent on a tool that just wasn't up to the job, in spite of what the marketing brochure said. Realizing that this was the wrong tool, management looked at competitor offerings and decided to switch to a similar tool from a different company. While initially it seemed to be an improvement, it was still poorly matched to the rapid application development environment (using a Scrum-like management system) and the different web technologies they implemented on products. After two tools, two years, and two automation failures (and a lot of lost money), "test automation" was practically a swear word in the organization.

> **Good Point**
>
> Failure with one tool doesn't mean you will succeed with another.

19.2.1.2 Reducing 3 Hours to 30 Minutes in 50 Lines of Code

I came in to help the testing team identify areas to optimize, but I didn't know the history of automation disappointment. One of the testers told me she was having a lot of trouble with repetitive work. Most of her days were spent like this:

- Get a new set of test data from the development team first thing in the morning.
- Test inputting the data sets in the application on two different web browsers.
- Go to the database backend and verify that all the test data was stored correctly.

She told me this was taking her anywhere from 3 to 4 hours per day. The datasets were entered into the application in exactly the same way, using the same workflow. She said she would get tired, enter the wrong data, or forget where she had entered data and get lost. She wondered if I knew of any sort of lightweight automation that could help her. I immediately thought of the scripting language Ruby and the popular Ruby library Watir that can drive both Internet Explorer and Firefox web browsers. In short order (under an hour), I wrote a basic script that automated some of the tasks she found difficult. It didn't automate everything, but it copied the test data from a source document, and then ran through the workflow, inputting each dataset into the application first in Internet Explorer, and then in Firefox. She had to monitor the tests, because I didn't add code to check for possible problems, so if something went wrong, she would stop the script and take over manually and report the problem to the development team. At the end of the script run, she would connect to the database and query to make sure all the data was stored correctly. We made a few tweaks to it, such as adding prefixes to the first and last entries so she could find them in the database more quickly and standardizing naming conventions of test inputs so they were easier to keep track of.

> **Tip**
>
> Automate the mundane repetitive tasks; leave the complicated assessment to the live tester.

After some improvement, I had a script that was about 50 lines long (including formatting) and used two Ruby libraries: one to read the test data from the source Excel document and another to drive the web browsers. I purposely left some things out, such as error checking and validation, because that would add a lot more code and complexity to the script. I wanted to have a script that could be thrown away and re-created in minutes when the application under test changed, and I wanted it to be maintainable by a novice programmer. Furthermore, it was more effective to have the tester do the verification with her own eyes, experience, and knowledge than to try to program the script to do that for her. She said that starting off the script and watching it play back through the various datasets was almost like "watching TV," and she started noticing minor problems with the application she hadn't noticed before. If the script crashed because of an error on a page, she just grabbed the error report and sent a bug report to the programmers. The end result was extraordinary: a 3- to 4-hour job was reduced to 30 minutes per day.

19.2.1.3 How Did This Tester Get So Much Better All of a Sudden?

As you might imagine, a tester who suddenly has 3 extra hours in the day to explore other testing activities gets noticed. The programmers were surprised at how much faster she was finding and reporting problems, not to mention the sudden increase in the number of defect reports. When the programmers asked her what had changed, she showed them the script and how it worked. They were excited—Ruby was a real programming language that was freely available, so they could rerun the script on development machines when investigating a defect.

One morning, the tester asked me if she could learn some programming basics so she could maintain the test script herself. After a couple of days, she was able to make simple modifications to the script and make improvements. She wasn't ready to start scripting from scratch, but she could read the code I had written and make changes when needed.

Soon, word got back to the other testers. "How come she has a cool automation script but we don't?" I wrote several more simple, small automation scripts to help them out, cautioning against being overly ambitious and taking on too much automation with the resulting maintenance burden. While none of the others had such an extraordinary effect as those 50 lines of Ruby, they all made testers' lives easier.

Good Point

Being overly ambitious can harm your automation efforts and prevent real but smaller-scale benefits.

About this time, management told me about their automation failures in the past. Comparing previous efforts to what I had done, they realized where they made a mistake. They had jumped into automation as an industry best practice without looking at specific goals and measuring automation effectiveness against them. They also had unrealistic and overly ambitious ideas about what automation could do for them. They were stuck on the idea of automating regression tests instead of looking at other areas that could help them for less cost. They decided to try test automation again, but with more careful planning, consideration, and an open mind.

19.2.2 Automating Around the Testing, Not Automating the Testing

This project involved a small systems-management company.

When I started out doing test automation work, most of the literature I read talked about regression test automation. At the time, I was working with older technology, and there were no automation tools available that were beginner-friendly. I was under pressure to deliver on a project with a tight timeline, and I knew that some sort of automation would help. Without a GUI automation tool or readily available test harness that I could purchase or use, I sat down with a colleague and began to brainstorm alternative ideas.

First of all, any automation effort we used had to help us save time. Without a lot of time or people, our automation development had to be done quickly, because we had very little time dedicated to this task. The technology and processes needed to be things I was familiar with and capable of executing and maintaining myself, and any test scripts needed to be small so they could be easily maintained or thrown away and rewritten in minutes. We couldn't afford to introduce anything that added a maintenance burden either.

With our efficiency goal in mind, we started identifying areas related to testing that were the most time consuming, felt frustrating or boring, and threatened efficiency. We identified:

- Copying and installing builds on multiple machines (this could take a couple of hours per build).
- Setting up and copying test data to multiple machines (this could also take an hour or two per build).
- Repetitive, similar GUI workflows required when running multiple tests.

Good Point

The best areas to automate are not necessarily the most obvious. Look for time-consuming and frustrating tasks that can be simplified or expedited by the use of tools.

We settled on the Unix Bash scripting language for copying and installing builds on multiple machines because we were familiar with it and it was available on most of our test machines. In short order, we had developed scripts that would copy and accurately deploy builds in minutes.

The test data management took more effort. We spent time pulling test data referenced by test cases into a central repository. We then created a script that would delete and copy over test data from the repository onto test machines. This took a few minutes to run, running in the background while testers were free to look into other tasks. This saved several hours a week of time-consuming manual work.

Finally, we looked at what we could automate through the GUI, which was where we spent most of our testing time. While we couldn't drive the application with a test tool, we had another option: The application could be launched into various states from the command line. It wasn't our ideal, but we developed scripts to partially automate tests or some of the steps to set up tests so we could take over manually. We didn't have the time to create a test harness to determine passes and failures, so we left that up to the tester. We were amazed at how effective this combination was as a time-saver and at the increased ability to discover important bugs. It was like rocket fuel for our manual testing: We could test a lot of scenarios much more quickly.

Defining goals other than "automate tests" helped us focus our efforts. Partially automating some tasks had a lot of merit. Completely automating them would result in a lot more coding and design effort, and the combination of automation and the observation of a skilled tester was powerful and quick.

> **Good Point**
>
> Combining good testers with appropriate tool support can increase their power and speed dramatically.

While our test automation effort wasn't a typical regression test suite, it was effective. Not only did we save time, we introduced a higher degree of accuracy in testing tasks. Small, strategic automation projects are less expensive but can be very effective in whittling time off a release.

With hindsight, we should have done some things differently. For example, the Bash shell wasn't available on all the machines, so we had to modify scripts to use native shell scripting languages like Korn shell (ksh), Z Shell (zsh), and others. This was time consuming and added an extra maintenance burden. A better option now would be to use a free and widely available scripting language like Perl, Ruby, or Python. It would also have been better to use a language and/or tools that the developers were using.

> **Lesson**
>
> Use tools and languages that many people are familiar with.

At the time (the late 1990s), I didn't realize how innovative our ideas were. Because we weren't using popular automation tools or techniques, we were almost embarrassed about what we had done, although we were pleased with the results. It took me a while to come full circle to revisit ideas I had learned early in my career after observing some regression automation failures. Thankfully, I had this early experience to turn to and build on when needed.

19.3   Automation to Support Manual Exploratory Testing

This project involved a large software development company.

Customer support called the quality assurance team to ask for help in repeating a bug that had been reported by an important customer. The customer was an administrator with a large client, and they were frustrated by an intermittent crash that was occurring in the system. Customer support couldn't repeat it, so testers were assigned to help. Support had a basic idea of the area of the application that was troublesome, but it could take several minutes to navigate to that area of the application; it was deep inside a complex workflow. The first thing I did was reach for my test automation scripts I had developed already and made a copy of one that navigated to that section of the application. I modified it slightly so that I could easily take over, and then I ran the script, watched it navigate, and took over manually, implementing dozens of exploratory tests that came to mind while monitoring the log files for anything interesting.

> **Tip**
>
> A combination of automated navigation and manual exploratory testing can be very effective.

After a couple of hours, I ran out of ideas, so I went back to customer support to get more information. One question I asked was if there was ever more than one administrator working on the application at a time. They said it was possible, because it was a large company with several administrators. With that new piece of knowledge in hand, I returned to my navigation script. I decided to try to emulate multiple users by using my automation script on one machine, with me testing manually on another.

I modified it slightly by adding an iterator that caused the script to navigate to the trouble spot, loop in the administration area for a few minutes, log out, and repeat. On another machine, I ran the navigation script and took over manually. In short order, the application crashed. I found out what was causing the failure by monitoring the server logs, modified the script, and reran it on both machines. The failure was now repeatable in every case. There is no way I would have found that by working in isolation without some of the testing steps being automated and used in conjunction with skilled exploratory testing. Completely automated tests wouldn't notice issues the way a human tester would, and a human tester can't repeat steps accurately or simulate multiple users at the same time because we can't be in two places at once. [Kohl Machine]

When I find I am repeating workflows in my testing, I like to quickly create disposable navigation scripts to set up my exploratory testing. I use scripting languages like Ruby and the Watir library for web browsers and capture/replay tools if the application user interface doesn't change very much. I like them to be disposable so I don't have to worry about losing time to test case maintenance, but they should be in areas that provide a lot of value for effort. In some cases, if I see something odd when watching the scripts play back, I like to be able to add variables and looping to help repeat something intermittent or explore an area of the application that now looks risky. It is also possible to easily change data values entered into the application by using programming language variables.

> **Good Point**
>
> Disposable scripts can have real short-term benefits.

A harmony of human and machine can bring about the best of both worlds: speed and precision from the tool and the rapid observation powers, not to mention the knowledge, experience, and curiosity of a human.

Other team members were expecting an ambitious, thorough GUI regression automation, so they were skeptical of this approach at first. They expected to see all the manual regression tests automated and a test harness that ran unattended, validated test outcomes, and reported results. It took a while to demonstrate how we could still get high value testing but with a far lower automation investment cost.

It was difficult to sell this approach to other team members. They believed that the automation would be inherently superior in every way to manual testing. It required a lot of education to show them that humans are superior to machines with certain testing tasks, and vice versa.

> **Good Point**
>
> Test automation education is often key because many people do not understand what is realistic and what is not.

19.4 Automating Data Interactions

This project involved a large corporate IT department.

I was called in to help a team that had a scheduling problem. They needed to upgrade a large database to a new release in a large business-mission-critical system. The programmers, database analysts, testers, and business analysts had determined how much effort it would require. Because it was a major release with a lot of risk, the team decided to run every single manual test they had. The trouble was, this came out to months of effort. The team didn't have months of effort available, so I was asked to see if there was a way we could use automation to help meet a shorter schedule.

I analyzed the system and created a model of it (see Figure 19.1). I then reviewed the test cases and determined that the tests wouldn't cover all the different kinds of database interactions, so a lot of that effort wasn't going to help the team much anyway. We strategically chose manual tests that would provide the most confidence that the system was working, and we decided to use automation to help augment that effort. This could significantly speed up testing, with the added bonus of covering far more test scenarios than possible with manual testing alone.

Using the model of the application, I determined a test data automation integration path: I decided to ignore both the user interface and web services layers of the application for automation. The GUI would be too time consuming and too slow to execute tests with, and the web services interface would require a lot of work to change for testing. Instead, I recommended creating a custom interface to talk with the part of the system that was responsible for processing data: the data access objects (DAO) layer. As you can see in Figure 19.1, data moves from there down toward the database, where it is processed, but it goes through two important transformations on the way there and on the way back. The Persistence Layer is a program that converts object-oriented code used by the programmer and application servers, such as Java or Python, into structured query language (SQL), which is the language the database uses. It is then transformed again through a database driver, which essentially works as an interpreter. Then it is processed and stored in a relational database, itself a complex system with programs and rules. In her 2007 presentation, *Functional Test Driven Development for Legacy Systems*, developer/tester Jennitta Andrea calls this approach "testing through the side-door." [Andrea] (The "front door" is the GUI, the "back door" is the database.)

Why would I want to do this? If I test the data integration path very heavily with test automation, I gain a lot of speed in execution. I don't have to worry about going through a time-consuming workflow; I can just test that path directly. Because I have speed and programming on my side, I can create far more combinations of test data. What would take weeks to do as a manual test can be done in seconds or minutes by automation. Also, because it can run quickly, we can run those tests frequently whenever there are changes in that integration path. When you update a database, you almost always end up with changes in the database itself, the driver, the object-relational mapper (ORM), and the code that interacts with the data.

For our custom test interface, we used a tool called FIT (Framework for Integrated Testing), which is ideal for creating custom automated test interfaces. We then created a program that would convert a production database snapshot and feed

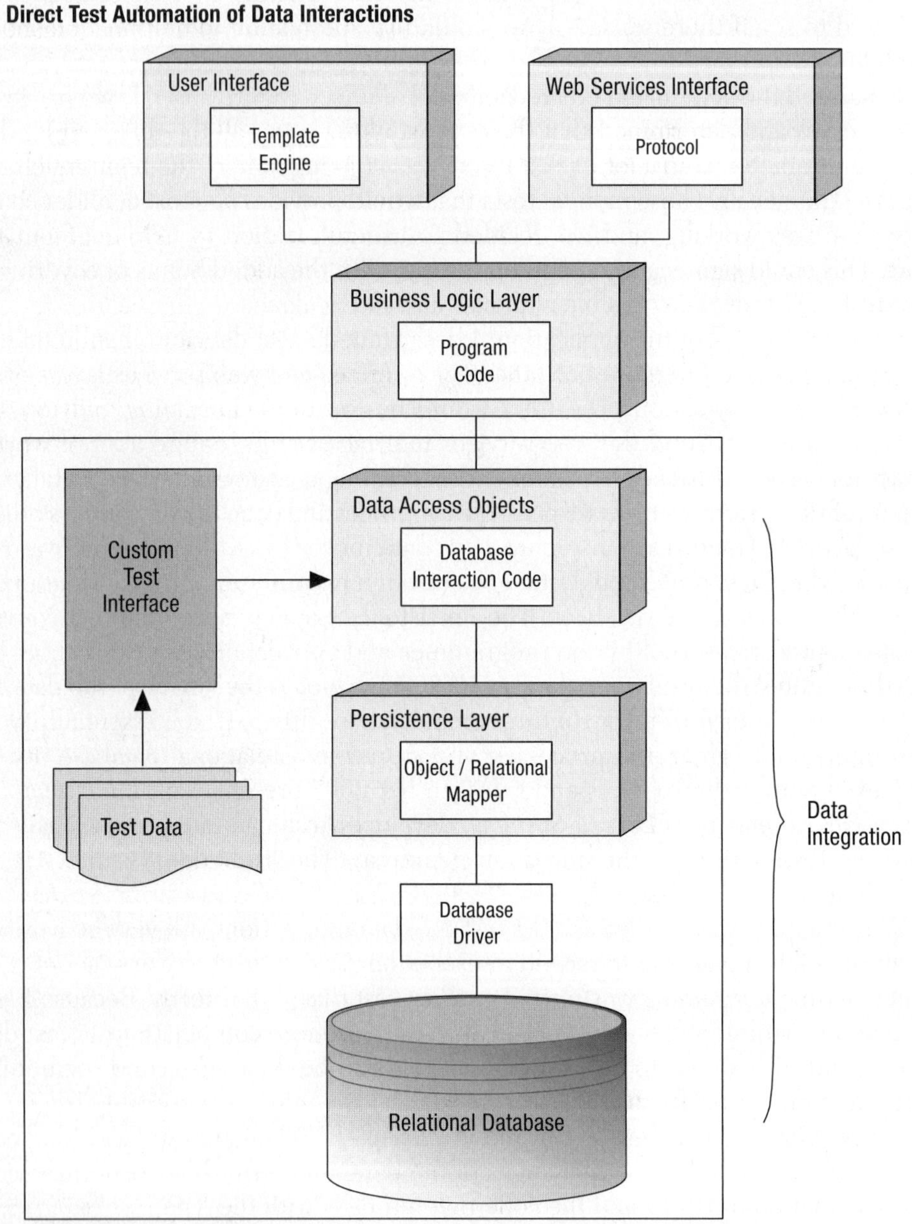

Direct Test Automation of Data Interactions

FIGURE 19.1   Data interaction model

the data through this custom interface. We also analyzed different kinds of problem data types that we dealt with using a combination of manual and automated tasks. We used a script to generate some data for us, and testers manually entered the remainder into delimited text files that the automation could read. (A lot of people prefer FitNesse, which has a wiki on top of FIT, but I've had more success with FIT.)

Our first test run was an eye-opener: The test failed spectacularly after a few seconds. The new database couldn't handle some data that the old one didn't have a problem with. We also found problems in our data access objects, the object relational mapper, and the database driver. Each problem area was addressed, and the test was used to find new problems. It took a few days before we had a clean run with this test, but we were able to find a lot of problems quickly that went unnoticed by the manual tests and acceptance test automation. Once the data and data integration issues had been sorted out, the testers refocused on risk areas and high-value manual testing. The testing cycle was reduced from months to weeks, and the whole team had much more confidence in this approach. With a little creativity, we were able to use automation in conjunction with manual testing to create a superior, faster, and more accurate test project.

We gained some additional benefits with this approach. One of the issues we had with our test environment was that the database was used by different groups and would end up in a nontestable state. To fix it required IT operations to schedule database administrator (DBA) time to clear and refresh the database. There isn't a lot of testing value in this effort—the DBA just takes a snapshot of production, alters it to remove any private information, and puts that image directly on our test database. Now we had a baseline to begin testing with. With our automation tool, we could refresh the database ourselves and get double duty out of the effort. Not only did we now have a refreshed database to accurately test with, but the test provided enormous testing value through integration testing. We were able to spot new problems quickly when trying out new database drivers, object-relational mappers, or minor code changes to determine if they had a negative impact.

After we had our test suite running reliably, we found it could take up to 30 minutes to run. We decided to ensure that a minimal amount of test data existed within the first 5 minutes of the test executing to support manual testers. Manual testers would then start working with the system as the test was running. We found some hidden benefits to this. Testers found or repeated production bugs related to timing or database locks that we weren't able to replicate previously due to the extra load on the system created by the test.

At first we relied too much on data quality standards and didn't move beyond that with invalid data types in our testing. A quick run with production data demonstrated that we assumed far too much about the system. We should have tried invalid data types earlier on. Certain invalid data types could not be injected into the system using this tool. We had to manually input them either into the database itself or through the GUI.

This type of automation can be time consuming to implement at first. In fact, on other projects at other companies, we have created a new development team project with the sole responsibility of creating a testing interface like this. If you decide to utilize this approach, make sure you understand the effort and time required. It needs to be a short-term pain for a long-term gain kind of project or it might not be worth doing. For higher-risk systems, this kind of automation can be well worth the effort.

19.5   Automation and Monitoring

This project involved a medium-sized service company with a small development team and a large customer base.

If you can't see what's happening behind the scenes, your automation may not be showing you the whole picture.

A small extreme programming (XP) team asked me to come in and help them with regression testing. They had thousands of automated unit and user acceptance tests, with an impressive regression test automation framework. They asked me to supplement their automated testing with manual exploratory testing. The product owner, a system administrator (who was also a fabulous tester), and I were to do the testing. I was supposed to find weak spots and work with the product owner to help them develop more testing skills. We didn't have a lot of testing documentation outside of the automated test cases, so I started there. We used the automated tests as our initial guidance for technical areas of the application that we were less familiar with.

19.5.1   The Tests That Passed Too Quickly

After reading the code and the comments in the code, I ran a complex user acceptance test. It returned with a green bar (meaning the test had passed) very quickly. I was suspicious—it seemed to run too quickly, too smoothly, and I wasn't exactly sure what it was doing. We ran it again two or three times, and it kept running quickly and returning a pass. The system administrator had a deep understanding of how the production system worked, so the three of us mapped out the application from a user's perspective (what goals are they trying to achieve by using the system?) and from a technical perspective (which code comes into play, which components are touched, and which machines/network infrastructure are used?). Once we had a better understanding of what was going on and what the tests were trying to do, we decided to use tools to help us see what was going on within the system.

The system administrator used a combination of scripts and monitoring tools to visualize what was going on within the production system and to alert him if there were any problems. We decided to borrow these and use them on the test system. We had custom scripts to read and gather data from test server logs, SQL scripts to count records in database tables, and other scripts to monitor inputs and outputs (I/O) and CPU and memory use on test machines. The system administrator used free, open source tools like Cacti and Nagios to analyze the data and to visualize it. Once we had that up and running (initially, it took a couple of hours), we reran the automated acceptance test.

19.5.2   If Nothing Is Wrong, the Test Must Have Passed, Right?

The difference between the test result "test passed" and the data we saw in the monitoring were at complete odds. It turned out that the automated acceptance test did not notice that data was being deleted. It wasn't making it to the database because another system was so overtaxed it was just ignoring data instead of processing it. The verification scripts in the acceptance test weren't working, but the defects that were occurring weren't making it up to the test harness. Because there were no recognizable defects reported to the harness, it automatically passed the test.

> **Good Point**
>
> Just because an automated test passes, it doesn't mean there aren't any problems. (You can't always believe those green bars.)

Using more powerful monitoring tools outside of an automation script and having skilled humans analyze the data using visualization tools brought a series of failures to light that were previously undetected by the automated tests. It turned out that this feature had not worked at all over the release, because the programmers had written the acceptance test first and added enough code to get it to pass. The product owner had relied on the acceptance test results to verify that the feature was working. These conflicting results were addressed, and the feature was improved so that it worked under close monitoring and scrutiny.

Now that we had more powerful tools for monitoring the system, we were able to trace intermittent issues to memory leaks, thread errors, configuration issues, and a whole host of issues that had been undetected at the GUI or unit test level in the past. Combining strategic manual and automated testing with good monitoring tools helped us track down issues that appeared intermittent at the GUI level and helped us pinpoint trouble spots.

> **Good Point**
>
> Use good monitoring tools to provide information that will help testers and/or developers identify and resolve problems.

(I described a similar story in "Exploratory Testing: Finding the Music of Software Investigation" [Kohl 2007]).

19.6 Simulating Real-World Loads by Combining Simple Tools

This project involved a different medium-sized service company with a small development team and a large customer base.

With powerful monitoring and reporting tools in a test environment that mirrored a production monitoring system, we were able to observe our test environment differently. One area we explored was the trends of traffic and the resulting behavior of our production servers, which we then compared with the test environment. We found that even with several testers working in the test environment daily, our test machines weren't reaching the same levels of CPU use, memory use, I/O, and so on. Because we couldn't have tens of thousands of users to use our system the way people did in production, we decided to take a different tack. Even though we had load testing tools, we couldn't physically generate that much load with the tools and with the network constraints imposed by the organization. What we could do was artificially create the same conditions with regards to CPU use, memory use, and I/O. At least we thought we could. With some experimentation, it turned out that we could indeed.

It required a combination of tools. We used a scripting language (Ruby), a web browser library (Watir), load testing tools (WebLOAD open source and JMeter), and a web services testing tool (soapUI). Here is how it looked:

- Automated workflow Ruby/Watir scripts ran in loops on a couple of machines using real web browsers. These had timers for page loads that were printed out for analysis.
- We used the Watir scripts to capture HTTP traffic in WebLOAD, and then used the tool to simulate many virtual users.
- SQL scripts were run to tax the database.
- JMeter scripts were used to simulate systems integration with a legacy system.
- soapUI web services automated testing was used to generate systems integration.

It looks like a lot, but all the scripts were small, simple, and could be rewritten in minutes if necessary. We included enough logic to add randomly seeded time delays to simulate the ebb and flow of production traffic. We ran it for an hour to test it out, and not only did it simulate the server conditions we saw in production, it also brought our test system to its knees. New database tables were filling up quickly, causing delays in the system as it tried to keep up with increasingly larger reads, and our legacy system integration would die after a few thousand transactions. Once development dealt with those problems, we ran the tests over the weekend and found similar problems. The difference between running tests on an underused system and on a system that was used similarly to production was incredibly revealing.

Tip

Use a combination of tools to achieve what is difficult or impossible to do with a single tool.

One area that was interesting was the performance impact the testers felt. "This feels slower when I run a report" was a common complaint. A programmer can't fix "this feels slow," so we used timing metrics from our Watir scripts and pinpointed bottleneck areas using our load testing and monitoring tools.

Because simulations aren't "the real thing," we faced a lot of resistance at first from other team members. We were artificially creating server load conditions, and some developers felt it was unfair. They dismissed many of the defects that were revealed through simulation because it wasn't a "true" representation of production. It took a while to build trust (and the odd panic caused by a similar bug in production) to help win them over.

Creating simulators requires technical skills and proficiency with multiple tools. It's a tough thing for beginners or people with less technical skills to tackle at first. There is more maintenance overhead than is involved in using one type of automation tool because this approach can require several tools and systems. The benefit is enormous, and I have learned that development teams for mission-critical systems use simulators for testing a lot.

19.7 Conclusion

Each of these stories is typical of experiences I have had in many projects over a number of years. I've had success with teams when we treat automation as a means to help us solve problems rather than as a solution to our testing problems. When we widened our view of test automation beyond regression test automation, all kinds of possibilities started to emerge. Sometimes they were simple adaptations of what we already had in place. In other cases, they involved including approaches like task automation as a type of automation to help speed up testing.

There's nothing wrong with regression test automation—it has its place. However, it's important to realize that other automation options can be used in conjunction with or instead of regression test automation. In my experience, once we decided to exploit automation to help our testing create value rather than treat automation as our solution, all kinds of creative, effective, and fun solutions started to take shape. More important, they demonstrated value by helping our manual testers do more with the tools they had at hand.

19.8 References

Andrea, Jennitta. (2007). "Functional Test Driven Development for Legacy Systems." Paper presented at Much Ado About Agile Conference, September 26–27, Vancouver, British Columbia, Canada.

Bach, James. (2003). "Agile Test Automation." Available at www.satisfice.com/presentations/agileauto.pdf.

Fewster, Mark, and Dorothy Graham. (1999). *Software Test Automation*. Harlow, UK: Addison-Wesley.

Kaner, Cem. (2000). "Architectures of Test Automation." Available at www.kaner.com/pdfs/testarch.pdf.

Kohl, Jonathan. (2007). "Exploratory Testing: Finding the Music of Software Investigation" Available at www.kohl.ca/articles/ExploratoryTesting_MusicofInvestigation.pdf.

Kohl, Jonathan. (2007). "Man and Machine: Combining the Power of the Human Mind With Automation Tools." *Better Software Magazine*. Available at www.kohl.ca/articles/ManandMachine_BetterSoftware_Dec2007.pdf.

CHAPTER 20

SOFTWARE FOR MEDICAL DEVICES AND OUR NEED FOR GOOD SOFTWARE TEST AUTOMATION

Albert Farré Benet
Christian Ekiza Lujua
Helena Soldevila Grau
Manel Moreno Jáimez
Fernando Monferrer Pérez
Celestina Bianco

Even if you are not working with medical devices, this chapter, written by Albert Farré Benet, Christian Ekiza Lujua, Helena Soldevila Grau, Manel Moreno Jáimez, Fernando Monferrer Pérez, and Celestina Bianco, has many interesting lessons for anyone in automation. For the safety-related applications they test, a strict, formal test process is used with a risk-based approach to the implementation of the automation. Their story shows how success can be mixed even across different projects in the same organization; attempts to resurrect previous automated tests that had fallen into disuse resulted in different outcomes in different projects. In some cases, unrealistic imposed objectives ("total automation") virtually guaranteed failure. However, they did progress, devising a good list of what they wanted to use automation for and what they wanted to avoid automating. The problems encountered included some that are unique to regulated industries (where test tools need to be formally validated before their results can be used in the qualification testing of the software), problems with hardware interaction, and problems with custom controls (overcome by an abstraction layer). Their honest description of problems, solutions, and lessons learned in the four projects described is as useful as it is interesting. These stories from Spain involve commercial and inhouse-developed tools and cover projects lasting a few months to 5 years. See Table 20.1.

20.1 Background for the Case Study

In this section, we describe briefly our company background, we present the projects under study, and we describe medical device software and its constraints and relation to software test automation (STA).

20.1.1 Medical Devices Background

Because software for medical devices is to be released into a regulated market, there are implications for the way the software is to be tested. Tests have to be formally planned, formally designed, formally executed, and the results formally reported. Under this "formal" approach, test execution requires a lot of repetitive tasks, so the first idea that comes to mind to many managers and testers is to automate software testing as much as possible.

It is still too common outside the automation teams to think that almost everything can be automated at a reasonable cost. But once you start working in this field, you realize that this is not the case and that automation is very time consuming. Furthermore, an automation project is a development project. That means you have to create an architecture, design, coding standards, and so on, all of which translate into a rise in estimated costs.

Many solutions we had adopted proved successful as soon as the first execution results were obtained. Others could not be evaluated until later, when the global situation was analyzed. Automation results and evaluation conclusions were varied. In some projects, the timing of automation may have been poor. In others, automation was introduced at an appropriate time, and STA has now been in use for a number of years. For some projects, the scope of STA has been expanded, and for others it has been suspended or discontinued.

Whatever the outcome, many lessons have been learned from our different experiences. Those lessons were shared within the team, providing new views and new ideas to improve effectiveness on future automations and projects. Although our

Table 20.1 Characteristics of Case Study

Classification	PHOENIX	MINIWEB	DOITYOURSELF	HAMLET
Application domain	Medical software	Medical software	Medical software	Medical software
Application size	Not available	Not available	Not available	Not available
Location	Spain/United States	Spain	Spain/United States	Spain/Italy
Lifecycle	Spiral with some prototyping	Hybrid waterfall-spiral	Spiral with some prototyping	Spiral
Number on the project	4–6 (variable)	2	17	6–8
Number of testers	1–3 (variable)	1	10	1–2
Number of automators	Up to 50% of a single engineer's effort	15–20% of engineer's effort	1–3 (currently 1)	Up to 50% of engineer's effort
Time span	5 years	1 year (part time)	2 years	Few months
Dates	2004–2010+	2006–2007 (part time)	2008–2010+	2009
Tool type(s)	TestComplete 3	SilkTest	Inhouse	SilkTest
Pilot study undertaken	No	No	No	No
ROI measured	Not numerically	Not numerically	Not numerically	Not numerically
Successful?	Yes	Yes	Yes (after changing the goal)	No
Still breathing?	Yes	Project is on hold; yes for next version	Yes	No

activities are focused on critical software, we think these experiences may be interesting for all members of the STA community.

> **Good Point**
>
> Automation is not always successful, even in the same organization. Identify the relevant factors and learn from experience, whether good or bad.

20.1.2 Company Background

Here at Systelab Technologies S.A. in Barcelona, we produce and verify software and provide independent verification and validation (V&V) services for other manufacturers of medical devices. The test team, as part of the quality assurance (QA) department, provides testing for all projects and is formed by test engineers who hold degrees at least in one of physics, engineering, or computer science.

In 2000, when the QA department comprised six people, we started our first steps with STA. Now the test team numbers over 20 quality engineers, and we have several experiences with STA. Test engineers assigned to a project are responsible for any test task, including STA, rather than counting on a specialized and fully dedicated STA team.

> **Good Point**
>
> The role of tester and test automator can be taken by the same person provided they have the relevant skills.

20.1.3 Medical Device Constraints and Specifics Pertaining to STA

Practices and procedures in the development of medical device software must comply with strict standards (addressing security, privacy, safety, etc.) mandated by such regulating agencies as the U.S. Food and Drug Administration, the International Standards Organization, the International Electrotechnical Commission, and others. Manufacturers of medical devices are also required to follow a quality system guided by set standards (manufacturers institute their own procedures that may even surpass the standards set by the regulating agencies). See Figure 20.1.

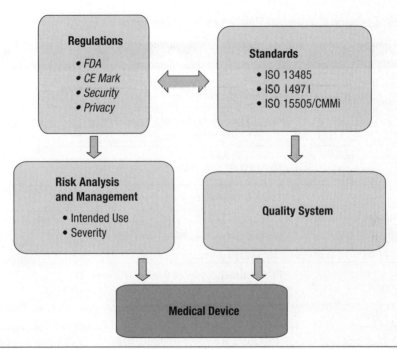

FIGURE 20.1   Standards and regulations for medical devices

Regulations concerning medical devices require the application of some type of safety risk analysis and management, which is basically driven by the intended use of the medical device. Additionally, the level of risk may require tighter or looser V&V measures and more or less documentation and paperwork.

The overhead that mandatory executions of risk-related test cases adds to each test cycle can seriously reduce the time for other testing. STA is often used to ensure broader test coverage by reducing execution time of some of the tests.

The preceding requirements result in a series of constraints applied to test automation. The rigorousness of medical device regulations can create conflicts with STA activities, constituting an additional cost to solve them. However, it is still possible to turn some specifics of STA to our advantage as STA engineers. A set of the most common constraints related to test automation are summarized in Table 20.2.

20.1.4   Different Projects, Different Scenarios

We describe the story behind four recent projects. We chose these projects to present a wide scope of different types of medical devices and automation techniques.

Table 20.2 Common Constraints Related to Test Automation

Constraint	Test Automatic Specific	Hindrance	Help
V&V tools must be validated for their intended use	Third-party STA tool to be validated and revalidated at each tool main version	X	
	Internal STA tools or customizations to be revalidated with every changed version	X	
Test protocols must be documented	STA scripts are the protocol		X
Input and outputs must be documented	STA log records all steps, input, and output		X
	An additional utility may be necessary to make test records readable if the tool does not provide it	X	
Test records need configuration control	STA scripts and logs are files under configuration control; logs must include trace of tested version and hardware/ software environment		X
	If configuration is controlled by the same STA tool, tool shall also be validated from the configuration control viewpoint	X	
Test results must be signed	If the STA tool includes electronic signature (very unlikely), no paperwork is required		X
	If not, signing procedures must be established for results	X	
Traceability: Document that each requirement is tested by at least one test case, with the coverage assigned by the risk	Automated tests may have to follow paths other than natural flow verifications of software requirement specifications, which makes them harder to trace	X	
	Some STA tools can be integrated into test tool suites that usually include test management and traceability utilities		X
Test cases must provide full coverage of risk mitigation features for each release	STA allows repeating that test at each release (ideally) with low cost		X
After a corrective change or an improvement or modification, test of the areas potentially affected and tests that provide risk coverage must be repeated			

Based on these projects, we can establish comparisons for the different stages of our V&V process with regard to STA. Automation was present in all of them, but it was not always successful and indeed was applied in different ways. Note that project names are purely fictional and are unrelated to their commercial names. Instead, they are named with regard to their relation with STA to ease identification.

The project PHOENIX case is the story of STA of functional test for software that controls an in-vitro diagnosis instrument used in a laboratory environment. The software basically deals with a robotic system that obtains data from human tissue samples. The software application also has significant subsidiary functionalities ranging from materials management to quality control and connectivity to laboratory information systems. In this project, the team inherited a test suite that required too much maintenance and seemed condemned to be abandoned.

Another STA experience closely related to hardware is project DOITYOURSELF, specifically, a critical care diagnosis instrument. The medical device under test makes whole-blood gas testing and provides immediate results. It can be used in a laboratory or at point-of-care. It can also be remotely controlled through a web interface. STA for a device that can work in different configurations (standalone, client/server, and web) was a challenge. This case is characterized by the use of a homemade STA tool.

Project HAMLET is an application that determines, using an expert algorithm, the next medication dosage for a patient with a chronic disease. A new interface was developed using new Ajax-related technologies. The new GUI, however, tried to maintain most of the original interface elements and behaviors. Records of earlier STA were present, but because it was discontinued some years earlier, the cost of reintroducing STA had to be evaluated.

Finally, project MINIWEB consists of a small web application developed for a limited number of end users such as laboratories with hemostasis-diagnostic analyzers. The application includes a feature to calculate and improve the accuracy of two parameters the analyzers need in order to calculate patient sample results. These parameters are especially critical to diagnose and prescribe drug dosages inside a therapy. STA was to help with the repetitive process that required a lot of manual insertions in the different scenarios to consider.

20.2 Comparison of the Different Approaches to Each Project

Now that we provided a short overview of the company, projects, and medical world, we describe the initial situations, planning, and considerations of different projects.

20.2.1   Defining Test Objectives: Focusing on Critical Features

As stated previously, before planning any STA activities or even manual test activities, it is necessary to analyze safety risks present in the medical device. After performing a safety risk analysis, we obtain an evaluation of which are the most critical areas and critical functions for the safety of the patient and the operator. We also obtain a list of requirements and design changes that act as mitigations for those risks. The main purpose of testing in medical devices is to ensure those mitigations are effective. Therefore, we then decide the set of test cases (manual and/or automated) to verify mitigations that must be executed for each official release.

20.2.1.1   A Common Case for a Medical Device Target Test Scope

For projects PHOENIX and MINIWEB, our target from the beginning was to ensure 100 percent coverage of features that act as risk mitigations. For instance, in project MINIWEB, the features related to validation and calculation of the parameters were the most risky and critical ones. Of course, we also wanted to make sure the application was performing as expected for non–risk-related functional areas. Additionally, in both projects, new features would be verified using test cases that were rerun in following versions together with the rest of the test suite as regression. In project PHOENIX, the test suite (manual and automatic tests) grew bigger and more complex with crossed-referenced functionalities as the application grew.

Automated test scripts would be used to integrate all automatable tests into a test suite that would run them one after the other as the starting point of the qualification test. The qualification test, executed on a version just released to test, provides feedback on whether or not the test shall continue or the version shall be returned to development for lack of basic quality. As a secondary use, the automated test would also yield a set of prepared databases to be reused as scenarios for the subsequent qualification and manual tests. This additional use of the automated tool should not be underestimated, as we see later.

20.2.1.2   Great Expectations

By the time STA was becoming established, project DOITYOURSELF had been in development for 5 years. An approach similar to that taken with project PHOENIX, although harsher, was devised. According to the test plan, all test cases would be run for each release, irrespective of their relation to patient risks. Furthermore, stakeholders established complete test automation as a goal. With the exception of a few test cases, the whole test suite should be run automated.

Despite stakeholders thinking that total automation would be a good choice to ease testing and reduce time in test cycles, from our previous experience in STA, we knew this was an unrealistic scenario. Although we put forward some arguments to illustrate this, the goal was unfortunately not ruled out.

Lesson

It is not a good idea to try to automate all tests, but this can be a difficult point for managers and stakeholders to accept.

20.2.2 Test Flow

20.2.2.1 When to Automate: The Early Bird May Catch the Worm, but the Second Mouse Gets the Cheese

When a test project is being planned, at some point it seems reasonable to consider if and when to start STA activities. But it is not easy to know where this point is located in time. If the automation is started too early, the application could vary greatly, which would notably increase the cost of automated test maintenance. If started too late, automated tests would be executed too infrequently to justify the expenditure on automation. If not automated, regression test cycles might delay releases and time-to-market. Whatever the decision, it would have consequences on the success of the test activities and the whole project.

Good Point

Choosing the right time to automate is important; costs and potential benefits need to be balanced.

20.2.2.2 Early Automations: What to Automate and What Not to Automate

Both project PHOENIX and project MINIWEB adopted a common approach. A qualification test was planned to be executed in manual mode before major releases. All defined test cases were planned to be executed in manual mode, at least the first time, to avoid automatic executions being blocked by bugs and also to minimize maintenance.

STA tasks were planned to take place from the very beginning. They were included on the V&V plan and on the schedule in parallel with the project code implementation tasks. Because of our STA experience, we had a clear idea about what we wanted to use automation for:

- To run a limited set of maintainable automated test cases because of reduced testing resources and strict time constraints.
- To perform regression testing, saving time in manual executions over specific stable features (the critical ones or the ones that required the same verification with several combinations of data, or dull and repetitive actions).
- To provide test preconditions (it does not matter if the scripts are generated by recording actions and then some parameterization is done; don't be ashamed of this seemingly poor code—sometimes it is more than enough).

Tip
Use the right level of automation to do what is needed; know what is sufficient, and don't overengineer the automation.

And we wanted to avoid using automation for:

- Hardware-related features or features whose requirements looked unstable in the medium term.
- All new functionality, thinking erroneously that it would find many defects. STA's real value for us is to demonstrate that no new bugs have been introduced on stable functionality.
- Building a complex framework for STA when the number of features was either too low or unstable, especially when combined with limited automation resources.

Good Point
Knowing when *not* to use automation is just as important as knowing when to use it.

20.2.2.3 *Adapting to Reality*

An STA project may have to change its initial goal. For example, the goal for project DOITYOURSELF was to automate almost everything. To make things worse, we had to develop our own automation tool, which would end up causing a number of unforeseen problems (see project DOITYOURSELF section). Thus, the goal of the STA project had to be redefined at some point. Eventually, priorities were changed to meet more realistic objectives. Instead of automating functional tests, we addressed other testing needs that would give valuable payback: creating a smoke test, creating test cases to identify areas of poor performance, and creating test cases to catch memory leaks in our medical instrument. This new test approach was accepted, and STA efforts were redirected to smoke, performance, and stress tests.

Beyond these tests, our focus moved recently onto easing manual testing tasks. Our attention has gone to stable functionality, very time-consuming test cases, and valuable payback. As an example, we planned a set of test cases to assist language testing.

Now we will look at the individual projects, starting with HAMLET.

20.3 **Project HAMLET**

Two circumstances of project HAMLET are worth mentioning to show its main problem. First, the turnover rate in the project team was extremely high during recent years. A complete renewal of both development and quality teams occurred in a short period. Second, and most important, the ratio of developer to tester plus automator could be as high as four to one for some periods. That basically meant that test engineers would always be overassigned (and behind on schedule).

Two years ago, a new test team took over the responsibility for checking project quality and replaced the previous test engineers. An automated test suite existed, but there was no time available to maintain it by bringing it up to date according to the changes in the application. A year and a half later, a request came from management to estimate the cost to establish and execute an action plan to reestablish test automation for the qualification test.

Lesson

If the automation testware is not maintained, it will soon become unusable.

Because previous STA activities in that project were successful, the idea was to try to resurrect the existing automated test suite. However, a great deal of knowledge and work done in that STA was probably lost for good. The estimation of efforts for STA had to be realistic and justified, so it implied that STA for project HAMLET had to face a rude reality. There were three main concerns, among other considerations, that stood in the way of reusing the previous STA framework and scripts:

- *Completely redesigned GUI:* The existing automated test was dependent on the UI, so we could foresee that it would be hard work to update the existing automated test scripts, considering the new Ajax-based GUI.
- *Lack of tool knowledge:* Assigned resources had acquired solid knowledge of the application mechanics but did not have a good background in using the previous automation tool (SilkTest).
- *Adaptation costs in a tight schedule:* Assigned tasks left little time to obtain a good understanding of the existing STA framework and scripts. Either other tasks were delayed or STA was overly time consuming.

After evaluating all factors, it was concluded that a complete refactoring of test scripts was preferable over recovering old ones.

STA cost was calculated using an inhouse method. As a qualitative summary in round numbers, only 20 percent of the verification steps would be easy to automate, and 10 percent would be very hard to automate (and probably not worth automating at all). The main 70 percent could be automated if a good framework comprising enough auxiliary STA functions could be created.

After presenting our numbers to stakeholders, it was decided that STA activities would not be carried out. The cost of STA was too high, and no human resources would be assigned to this task. We discuss this decision in the conclusion.

20.4   Project PHOENIX

20.4.1   The Tools

Test automation was implemented in project PHOENIX using TestComplete from AutomatedQA. However, synching the execution of scripted actions in the software with the response of the actual instrument, sometimes subject to human interaction (loading materials, operating doors), was very complex.

The development team provided a simulated instrument to assist with some testing tasks that responded satisfactorily to test automation needs. Nevertheless, many functionalities remained tightly tied to the need for proper hardware and were discarded from the list of automation candidates because it was not cost-efficient.

20.4.2   Maintenance and Migration Issues

The test plan was started by one software test engineer for the first stage of the project. STA started when roughly 40 percent of the planned functionality set was under development. At that moment, STA maintenance did not look like a problem, because the GUI was expected to be reasonably stable and independent between different areas. However, not everything went as planned.

The original software test engineer left the company, and the test project was taken over by the current test team. STA was at that point fairly modularized, and for the next few releases, maintenance was at an acceptable cost. However, we knew that maintenance would become sludgy sooner or later because the script design was much too coupled to record and playback scripting. STA maintenance cost would increase with new functionality, and GUI changes and would soon mean that maintenance costs of the STA would no longer be acceptable.

20.4.2.1   Maintenance Critical Point. Call or Fold?

After some test cycles, development scope was nearly 70 percent of all planned functional areas. With each functionality increase, more automated test cases were affected and needed to be updated or redesigned. However, the cost of updating was high, and the cost of redesigning was higher (at least in the short term). Therefore, automated test coverage was getting behind. Newer releases required more and more automated script changes. As foreseen, the existing approach was not sustainable without an eventual complete rework of all automated test cases. A reconsideration of STA strategy, given the project situation, was mandatory.

Luckily, because of some delays related to hardware, we had some unscheduled time available. We could devote it to improving the automation and reducing its maintenance cost. The alternative was to abandon the automated test in favor of a manual test. We suggested that it was not the right time to put that much effort into improving STA because the application was not stable enough. However, we did not like the thought of getting rid of all automated scripts; they could still give some value to our test. We therefore chose an intermediate course: We would "prune" the scripts.

20.4.2.2   How to Proceed with Limited Automated Test Maintenance

First, we stopped adding new functionality to automated scripts. Meanwhile, we identified all scripts that participated in the qualification test and focused all maintenance efforts into those. All pieces of dead script code were discarded, and other scripts outside the qualification test were left abandoned until the tide might change. This situation extended for longer than 2 years.

> **Good Point**
>
> With limited time and resources, concentrate on those aspects of automation that will provide the most immediate benefit; come back to other aspects later.

When the application was finally considered stable enough, it was the time to resume regular STA activities. During this time, a proposal was accepted to gradually modularize all scripts still in use so they no longer would look and work like patched capture/replay scripts. Automated generation of scenario databases would also be improved. Although full maintenance of the script used to take 4 to 5 days of work per version, after this rework, we were in the position to improve this overhead down to 2 days.

20.4.2.3 Techniques

Originally, test scripting was based on capture/replay to obtain use cases and then have those scripts slightly modified to allow for simple modularization in a structured programming paradigm with some parameterization. Among other worries, having a clear and readable script was a critical issue for potential auditors or reviewers (refer to Table 20.2). We had to define an efficient STA framework that would enhance script maintainability and readability without dramatically increasing the cost.

We opted for a keyword-driven approach; the various functions and subroutines would mimic the tester's actions and verifications just as in the manual test cases. This technique improved the script stability and highlighted its equivalence to the manual counterpart for any potential reader without knowledge of the scripting language. There was another desirable side effect: As more tests were automated, new sets of functions were grown, and it was easier to reuse them to automate other tests.

20.5 Project DOITYOURSELF

20.5.1 The Tools

Automatability was not taken into account by the time software development of the medical device was initiated. That fact meant a difficulty when dealing with the automation of testing. Our first problem was to find an STA tool that could interact with our UI, which had no standard controls at all. We were unable to find any commercial one, so we would have to build a custom STA tool. The most critical issue in designing the tool was the interaction with a list of custom buttons, text fields, checkboxes, dialog boxes, and so on.

> **Lesson**
>
> Test automation is significantly more difficult when the software under test is not built with automation in mind.

Eventually, interaction with the UI was achieved by using the FEST Swing Java library, which simulates user interaction with the UI by means of an Abstract Window Toolkit (AWT) `Robot` class. This AWT `Robot` can generate native events (move the mouse, press keys). It had to be implemented for each single customized control. Because the number of controls was so large, the effort required to fully develop the tool was not acceptable to stakeholders; the tool would be only partially developed.

20.5.2   Maintenance and Tool Validation Issues

Maintenance was one of the key points in this project because we had to deal with both the STA tool and automated test cases.

Additionally, because of regulatory constraints (refer to Table 20.2), we had to validate all tools used in our process. Results and evidence of testing are unreliable if the tools used to get them are unreliable. If defects are found when validating the tool, they must be fixed; then the tool must be validated again. It was time consuming for the automation tool in the beginning because of defects and missing functionality in the tool. These problems had to be solved so we could move on, causing unexpected delays in our schedule.

20.5.3   Techniques

Automated test cases were very UI dependent. Changes in the label of UI objects or the control types could increase the maintenance cost dramatically. Besides automating only stable functionality, we went by the following guidelines to minimize maintenance costs:

■ Keep the definition of UI objects (label and type of control) in a unique file referred to by all test cases. Whatever the UI change, we only had to update the unique file.

- Promote code reusability by means of creating functions that could be reused in any automated test case.
- Create automated test cases compatible with all the configurations (stand-alone, client/server) and languages supported.

Tip

Use a translation table for things that may change so the automation can use a standard, constant term.

20.5.4 Unexpected Problems and Applied Solutions

An interesting feature for the customer (but probably not for the automation engineer) is that the hardware runs some maintenance routines when the internal values and the state of the instrument meet some complex rules. This feature simplifies required manual maintenance to operate it. In addition, the instrument is very hardware dependent. All these unexpected routines made it more difficult to control the flow of the automated test cases. However, after becoming more familiar with the instrument, we could identify when these routines were launched. This provided us with a better understanding of how to implement our test cases to cope with the hardware maintenance routines.

The inhouse automation tool allowed us to interact with the UI, but it was not straightforward to use it. During the validation of the STA tool, we realized that creating automated test cases was not as easy as expected. The main issue was to work through all those customized controls. We could identify buttons, text fields, checkboxes, and so on, in the screen with ease, but we could not identify their corresponding customized instances due to poor class/type wording (e.g., Textfield1, Textfield2, Textfield3). Because the automation tool was using customized controls, it was painful every time we had to find an object in the UI (which was constantly). So, how could we know the type of customized control of every single object in the UI?

To solve the identification problem, we created a framework that hid all the complexity and made the creation of test cases easier. At this point, our goal was to use standard-like controls instead of customized ones. The framework basically wrapped a set of customized controls under a standard-like control class (e.g., the standard control `Button` wrapped all the customized controls that actually were buttons). The use of this framework eased the process of creating automated test cases and enhanced the maintenance of the automation project.

20.6   Project MINIWEB

20.6.1   Tools

For the STA task of this project, we chose SilkTest from Segue (Borland). This tool had been used in the company for years, and the knowledge and experience of the assigned engineer was the determinant point for the choice.

20.6.2   Maintenance

STA was planned in order to avoid big efforts in maintenance. This goal was achieved by automating a limited number of features and only after manual verification to assure the functionality was stable enough to be automated. Nevertheless, we were not free from maintenance each time a new field or user profile was added to the application.

20.6.3   Techniques

Qualification testing was automated partially and executed many times, helping us to determine sooner whether the version was robust enough. STA grew up alongside the releases and during UI building. Access to the version under development was granted to testers to start recording or developing scripts in some cases, while at other times we waited for the features to be stable enough.

Mainly, we automated three kinds of cases:

- Cases that helped us to configure the application and fill the database with the entities that other test cases need as test preconditions.
- Functional test cases that verified the creation, editing, and deletion of basic entities, including boundary values and all possible combinations of the tables whose number of columns and rows are user configurable.
- Functional tests that covered long, repetitive, and dull actions on critical areas. We focused on actions split into several steps that implied manual insertion of a large amount of data and ended with calculations (means, linear regressions, acceptance range criteria, etc.).

20.6.4   Unexpected Problems and Applied Solutions

On web-based projects, added factors that contribute to the multiplicity of scenarios, such as web browser compatibility, incur an extra effort. Historically, and because of our limited range of potential end users, we restricted the support to just one web browser (the most used: Internet Explorer [IE]). However, we were later asked to support three or four of the most used web browsers.

After a hard negotiation, we agreed with the customer that the application would be fully verified with one browser (IE), and just a qualification test would be executed with a second one (Firefox). That was reflected in the test plan, as were the automation tasks.

In STA we faced the problem of developing automated scripts able to be executed for both browsers. The first attempt was very time consuming. The STA tool did not provide the same level of support for each browser, and its behavior was inconsistent depending on the browser in some cases. Finally, we achieved automation code that could verify exactly the same for both browsers in sequential mode for a limited number of test cases; the rest of the verification of the second browser was done manually.

There were also problems with the tool interacting with the application (not recognizing objects and controls). This forced us to find workarounds, and solving the situation required extra code in the scripts, for instance, to get values inside the cells of some tables.

20.7   Test Execution

Having looked at each of the four projects individually, now we discuss some common issues.

Moving onto the execution and eventual collection of results, each project faced different challenges and problems and provided varied solutions. The rate of success was varied. In this and the next section, we look at test execution and reporting for the different projects.

In project DOITYOURSELF, despite STA tool problems, we realized that our revised objectives were fulfilled. The smoke test was pretty ambitious, so it was divided into three phases. Before we finished the first phase, this test was demonstrated to run pretty well, and some defects were found either while writing the test or when running it for a specific build. It was also used when major mechanical changes, analytical changes, or code refactoring were done. It became another useful test before any of the previous major changes were committed. Stress testing lowered the chances of getting customer complaints by unexpectedly finding defects related to database size. Those defects are typically found by our customers who use very big databases, which are also created by the stress test.

One feature of the application under test in project MINIWEB was the computation of a statistical mean of a table of values and then the evaluation of whether or not the result was inside a range. STA allowed the ability to verify most possible combinations of different table dimensions (size was user configurable) to compare results with expected values and to capture images to have test evidence for almost every build.

Surprisingly, STA was revealed as a big help in finding defects: Using very specific values—randomly generated in an Excel sheet—it allowed us to cover all boundary values on calculations, finding a "mysterious" defect related to the rounding of decimals that was causing erroneous results.

> **Good Point**
>
> Automated tests can find defects that would not have been found with manual testing, often because more tests can be run. Random data or sequence is useful in automated tests.

Probably, if this test case had been designed to be executed manually, a unique set of values would have been used to cover the boundary values, thus reducing dramatically the chance of finding the defect. After several executions of automated test cases with randomly generated inputs, the probability of obtaining the winning combination increased.

20.8 Result Reporting

As described earlier, reports and logs that result from STA are also subject to analysis and audits. In addition, the clinical relevance of a possible defect could turn an otherwise meaningless issue into a showstopper, so failure analysis time was critical when a test failed. Despite what most automated test tool vendors will tell you, in our opinion, default result reports and logs generated by most tools are, at best, difficult to comprehend for any test engineer who did not personally write the scripts. Additional time must be devoted to clearly log the actions and verifications of automated tests.

Good Point

Design automated tests to make it easier to understand and analyze the test results. A simple pass or fail is often not enough.

This issue was addressed in project PHOENIX by preparing a set of functions that would log different types of messages (information, pass/fail steps, screenshots, warnings) with a consistent format (color, font, priority). Then calls to these logging commands were included within the action and verification functions to automatically and consistently log relevant messages, mimicking a manual test results report. However, sometimes this generated excessively large logs that made it difficult to retrieve the relevant information. To clean these logs of redundant and/or irrelevant information, we defined different levels of verification and tracing.

An example of this can be seen in a function we called `CreateUser`, as shown in Figure 20.2. Function `CreateUser` can be called in three different modes. Mode 1 (leftmost) reports an extensive verification, including handlers for particular cases. Mode 2 (center) runs just part of the code, focusing the verification of the final result and providing a reduced report. Mode 3 (rightmost) does not log anything but returns 1, meaning that 1 new user has been created; an external counter takes care of verifying and logging the success of the total of all `CreateUser` calls. Actions and verifications for a test case may require a detailed log, but reporting the creation of a database can spare some details.

In a first test in which we were testing the functionality of the `CreateUser` dialogue, we wanted to log every interaction with this dialogue: default values, all the input data, the particular cases we were enforcing and how we were handling them, and so on. When using this same function in a second test to create a particular scenario with just a couple of specific users, we did not want to log all this information; we just wanted to verify that `UserA` and `UserB` had been created with the correct values. But if in a third test we tackled a wider scenario in which we needed, for example, 1,000 users, but their particular details were not relevant, it would be unnecessary to log each user creation. In this case, we were concerned with only an external variable that counted the successful returns of every `CreateUser` call and a single log entry reporting if all 1,000 users were correctly created. Thus, this same function could be invoked with different modes that provided various levels of detail, as shown in Figure 20.3.

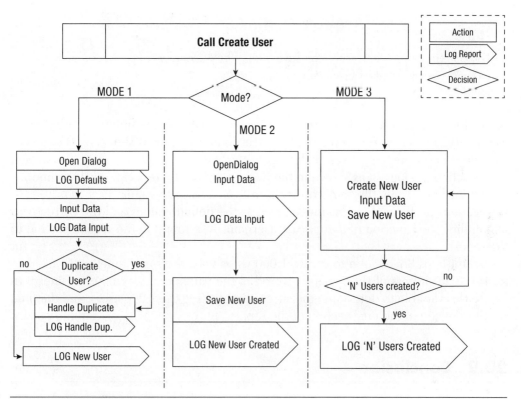

FIGURE 20.2 Function CreateUser showing the three alternative reporting modes

	SCRIPT	REPORT
1	Call CreateUser("UserA", "PwdA", Mode2)	• Data Input: (UserA, PwdA) – OK
2	Call CreateUser("UserA", "PwdA", Mode1)	• UserA created - OK
3	nUsers = 0	• Create Dialog default values:
4	For i = 1 to 1000	(<empty>, <empty>) – OK
5	User = "User" & i	• Data Input: (UserA, PwdA) – OK
6	Pwd = "Pwd" & i	• **Warning: "UserA" already exists.**
7	nUsers = nUsers + CreateUser(User, Pwd, Mode3)	• New available UserName suggestions:
8	Next	User_A, UserAA, UserB – OK
9	If nUsers = 1000 Then	• New UserName selected: UserB
10	LogPass ("1000 new users have been created.")	• UserB created – OK
11	Else	
12	LogFail ("Only " & nUsers & " have been created.")	• 1000 Users have been successfully created.
13	End If	

FIGURE 20.3 A sample script and report

> **Tip**
> Tiered reporting of test results can save a lot of failure analysis time. Report only what is needed for the objective of the test.

In Figure 20.3, on the left is the sample script that calls the function described in Figure 20.2 in its different modes. The corresponding report is shown on the right.

Script line 1 creates `UserA` with `CreateUser` in `Mode2`. Verifications performed in this action are logged as shown in the first section of the report (above the line).

Script line 2 calls the same function in `Mode1` with the same user ID. Logs of verifications performed in this mode, such as the default values and the correctness in handling the situation of a duplicate username, are found in the second section of the report.

Script lines 3 to 8 loop to create 1,000 users with the same function invoked in `Mode3`. The success of these calls is stored in the variable `nUsers`. Script lines 9 to 13 use this variable to determine the success in creating the 1,000 users, and the final result is logged in the final section of the report.

20.9 Conclusion

20.9.1 Looking Back at the Projects

Keeping STA in project PHOENIX was a daring decision, but in the end it paid off. The downside to getting rid of some scripts when pruning the code may have resulted in a feeling of wasted effort in writing and maintaining those tests. Although that was the price to be paid at that moment, over time it proved worth doing. At the same time, if the existing STA framework had to be built from scratch, it is rather improbable that the cost would have been acceptable to stakeholders. That is what happened to project HAMLET.

Failure to "revive" STA for project HAMLET was mainly caused by the interruption of STA activities due to an unfortunate combination of circumstances. As a consequence of the interruption, STA scripts became useless, and the associated knowledge was not transferred to new testers. Because knowledge was lost, even though there were scripts and data from previous activities, all work needed to be done from scratch.

A keyword-driven test approach did not provide a clear return on investment (ROI) for project PHOENIX during the first steps of the process. After the first efforts, focused on reducing costs, when STA started to produce results, this ROI became clearer. However, the real ROI is that a solid basis for automation was created. Nowadays, it allows us to diligently and successfully automate and maintain new tests for critical sections of our application. Furthermore, they are completed with clear and comprehensive evidence of all the verifications performed.

It is interesting to note that the generation of readable logs, as well as providing consistency within the reports, also provided functions bound only to the STA tool. These and other functions (file handling, object attributes verification, etc.) have been gathered in function libraries suited to automated tests for other applications, thus creating a base framework to introduce automated testing in other projects.

> **Tip**
>
> With very little extra effort, the results of good modular scripting practices can be shared with numerous other projects—potentially yielding even greater ROI for the organization as a whole.

Another lesson learned in projects PHOENIX and DOITYOURSELF was that scripting is much like programming regarding flawed design. Inherited design flaws are likely to give you trouble until you get rid of them. Scripts based on capture/replay are unlikely to ever be rid of the problems of capture/replay until the code is extensively modified.

Regarding the DOITYOURSELF project, it is worth mentioning that creating an inhouse automation tool is not necessarily a bad solution. But the way it is evaluated, planned, and executed can end up being a problem. The backbone of this challenge was having a better understanding of the code that controls the device. Delays in the startup of the automation project came from a lack of evaluation and planning and poor support from the development team. STA work was made arduous and disappointing because of the overall situation. Still, a tool was created and used and reported pretty good results.

After all the initial problems in project DOITYOURSELF, we consider that the contribution of STA was eventually positive. We believe the key points supporting this are as follows:

- Redefining the goal of the project to meet more realistic objectives with valuable payback, specifically, focusing on other testing needs that were missing (like smoke, performance, and stress tests) and also on functional test cases that could save a great deal of manual testing.

- Automating only stable functionality that required minimal maintenance.
- Creating compatible test cases for all the different configurations and different languages, which also benefited maintenance.

All these points allowed executing the automated test cases, build after build, without the need to update them. Saving time in maintenance tasks favored the creation of new automated test cases.

Good Point

With minimal maintenance of the testware, test automators can concentrate on automating more tests.

Solutions applied for the MINIWEB project led us to consider STA as one more task among others on the project schedule without incurring a delay or a bottleneck. Success of STA for this project was attributable to different characteristics compared with the other projects commented on in this chapter:

- Working in a project with little functionality, where all critical functions were well delimited (identified in the risk analysis).
- Taking advantage of the test automation experience accumulated over time, making it simple and useful.
- Not needing to spend time building a complex suite of functions and scripts.
- Having a tightly controlled product design.
- Having effective collaboration among the project manager, development team, and quality engineers.

Our expectations were not too ambitious because our intention was to automate just the identified test cases. Test cases were executed approximately 15 times. Therefore, automated testing in this project was useful and time saving.

20.9.2   What Would We Do Differently?

A critical aspect in the final success of STA is an accurate approach to goals definition. In large projects such as PHOENIX or DOITYOURSELF, the best results were obtained when STA was implemented through a series of small and attainable objectives. Once the objectives were met, new objectives could be pursued. Great expectations become treacherous in the STA world. It is advisable to make a realistic decision in spite of original expectations. Asking for professional advice is a must.

Good Point

Set small and achievable objectives, not "great expectations."

When planning for STA, the first step should be to ensure that everyone is ready to accept this type of testing. Share this information with the whole project team, including development, to determine the feasibility of the project and assess the possibility of assistance from developers. The MINIWEB project took good advantage of development collaboration, whereas the DOITYOURSELF project had more trouble because of the lack of it.

On a more technical level, the advantage of creating your own automation tool is having full control of it. But it is also true that it demands a large effort. It is highly recommended to complete the automation tool as early as possible and to create a prototype to make realistic effort estimations. As described before, in the case of medical devices, revalidating the STA tool can delay the whole test process.

For many reasons, STA maintenance can become a really choking situation leading you to be tempted to abandon automation completely. Still, there are ways to dodge elegantly and save some spoils. Those spoils can be reused to ease manual testing (with test data automatically generated) and maybe reestablish STA efforts when a more peaceful project phase is reached.

Still, a limit should be established; otherwise, resources get depleted, adding ever-more coal to a fire that is never extinguished. A milestone or a clear target must be set beforehand, and when it is reached, STA should take care exclusively of maintenance of existing features. At the same time, when new features are to be tested, STA convenience should be considered as usual.

In spite of all the problems in the process for project PHOENIX, STA generally fulfilled planned objectives and helped to keep testers motivated.

In project DOITYOURSELF, the automation project helped us exercise our devices in scenarios (in many cases, more customer-related scenarios) that would be tougher to perform manually; automated test cases can also be run more often and overnight. All of that contributed positively to increasing the quality of the medical device.

In project MINIWEB, STA helped with regression testing, allowing us to execute more test cases more often and leaving the test team to focus on the new functionality. It also allowed an early detection (even daily) of failures affecting basic functions that were introduced in the code during repair phases.

The most remarkable point is that the automation project contributed positively in increasing the quality of the medical device and confidence in the final product. After all, this is what our job is all about.

20.9.3 Plans for the Future

STA coverage for project PHOENIX is currently being increased because the cost of maintenance is the lowest ever. However, due to limited resources, the increase is produced step by step in a very smooth way.

In a similar way, project DOITYOURSELF is adding new critical functionality to STA, and the automated smoke test is being updated to cover this functionality. The stress test is also being updated to fulfill new testing needs.

On the other hand, development on project MINIWEB has stopped, awaiting new requirements or changes. Automated scripts will definitely be used for the next version.

Finally, after recently discarding STA, it seems unlikely to be applied in project HAMLET in the near future.

The test team has grown an STA development team that will provide advice and assistance for other test team members to achieve successful and better STA for their projects. First actions have been focused on generating utility frameworks (such as the one to provide clear reports) and other automation artifacts that are reusable by all projects.

CHAPTER 21

AUTOMATION THROUGH THE BACK DOOR (BY SUPPORTING MANUAL TESTING)

Seretta Gamba

Seretta Gamba tells of the difficulties she and her team experienced in trying to progress automation, even though it had a good technical foundation. She shows how they addressed the real needs of the testers and provided support where testers needed it most, which was in manual testing. The really interesting twist is how they were able at the same time to harvest things that would progress the automation—win-win situations. Their approach is described in detail, showing how they implemented levels of abstraction, separating tests from application detail such as the GUI, and they include an example of a user interface (UI) to the tests. They developed what they call command-driven testing, which is based on a form of keyword-driven testing and worked well for them. This case study takes place in the insurance industry in Germany. See Table 21.1.

21.1 Background for the Case Study

To improve the rate of test automation in our organization, we modified our test automation framework to also support manual testing. The idea was to obtain the information necessary to automate more of our product domain even though neither

Table 21.1   Case Study Characteristics

Classification	This Case Study
Application domain	Insurance
Application size	500,000 LOC tested with the automation
Location	Germany
Lifecycle	Iterative
Number on the project	27
Number of testers	5
Number of automators	2
Time span	12 months
Dates	2009
Tool type(s)	Commercial and inhouse
Pilot study undertaken	Yes
ROI measured	No (project done in my spare time)
Successful?	Yes
Still breathing?	Yes

testers nor developers had time to support the test automation team. We reached this objective by offering testers a number of extra comforts, such as integration to often-used tools and support for test case documentation.

The firm I work for, Steria Mummert ISS GmbH, develops and sells client/server or web service–based software for insurance companies. Our products range from standard applications that deliver yearly releases to highly customizable solutions that can be adapted to the requirements of any customer. Our success is founded on the quality of our products, and we realized early on that we could keep up or better our quality standards only through test automation.

I was charged with introducing and maintaining test automation. In my long IT career, I had been mainly a developer (the whole process, from interviewing the customer to writing the specs and the code, to testing and deployment both with small and big teams). Being new to test automation, I had the opportunity to study the known approaches with no preconceived opinion and so finally developed a framework (ISS Test Station) that is based on a form of keyword-driven testing that we called command-driven testing.

21.2   Our Technical Solution

21.2.1   Command-Driven Testing

Command-driven testing uses keywords that are simple commands (like SELECT, Button) that don't contain any application know-how. The interpreter scripts are thus the same for all our products, no matter what functional requirements are implemented or which development environment is to be used. We extracted the test and application know-how from the proprietary tool scripts. This again means that if we want to migrate to a different tool, we only need to rewrite the interpreter script for the basic commands; our test scripts don't have to be touched. Furthermore, remembering the advantages coming from the separation of navigation instructions and data (as in data-driven testing), we split the data files into a navigation part (DRIVER-File) in which all data is substituted with placeholders (DATA-Codes such as <FirstName>) and a data part (DATA-File such as a specific first name) in which the placeholders point to the real data. In this way, we need only one DRIVER-File for any number of DATA-Files. The DRIVER-File and the appropriate DATA-File together build what we call a *command script*. Figure 21.1 shows how the command scripts are interpreted and executed by the script-runner.

> **Good Point**
>
> Build in independence from specific tools for long-lasting automation.

The instruction INPUT, FirstName, <FirstName> in the DRIVER-File goes to the associated DATA-File and finds the DATA-Code "John" in the place referred to by <FirstName>. If there was nothing in the DATA-File after <FirstName>, then the DRIVER-File would not enter a first name but would leave it blank. If there was no DATA-Code (e.g., if <FirstName> wasn't there), then the corresponding line in the DRIVER-File would not be executed.

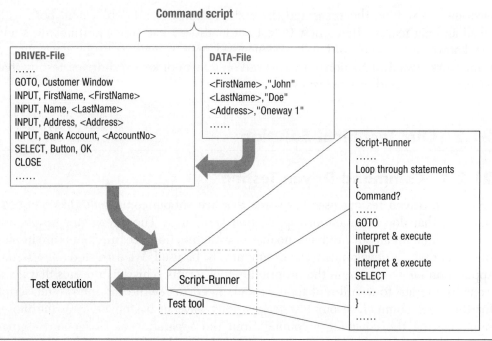

FIGURE 21.1 How command-driven testing works

The script-runner reads sequentially the commands in the DRIVER-File. DATA-Codes are substituted with the data from the DATA-File. If there is no data for a particular DATA-Code, then the statement is not executed. Every command is translated to the respective command in the script language of the currently used test tool and executed.

> **Tip**
>
> Allow flexibility such as skipping a data field if no data is available. This gives the testers control over the test using only data.

In the beginning, testers gradually learn to use the command scripts and may sometimes capture a script or map a GUI object using the tool. Other than that, only the developers of the framework do any tool scripting. As the testers gain experience, they use tool recording only for new or complex windows. Because our command scripts are quite elementary, they start "programming" directly using DRIVER-Files and DATA-Files. An advantage of this is that they don't necessarily have to wait for the software to be ready before they can start automating.

To summarize, with command-driven testing:

- Testers don't necessarily need to learn tool scripting.
- The separation in navigation and data sections makes the command scripts flexible and reusable.
- DRIVER-Files can be easily ported to different applications.
- DRIVER-Files need not be changed on migrating to another tool.
- The test tool is needed only to prepare the templates and to run the tests (so you don't need that many licenses).

21.2.2 ISS Test Station

To facilitate development of the command scripts, we created a specially designed framework (ISS Test Station). It consists of two parts, a client (ITS-Client) that supports development, execution, and logging of automated tests and an engine (ITS-Engine) that interprets and executes the command scripts in the chosen capture/replay tool.

21.2.2.1 ITS-Client

One of the basic functions of the client is to automatically translate scripts generated with the capture functionality of the deployed capture/replay tool into our command scripts. It generates a DRIVER-File and a template for the DATA-File (DATA_TEMPLATE) in which the recorded values can later serve as models for all kinds of test cases. The original capture/replay scripts are recorded window-wise by touching (recording) every element so that the derived command scripts are as generalized as possible. Mostly, the testers only have to copy the template, throw away what they don't need, adjust the data contents, and they're finished. The fact that the interpreter script (the engine) doesn't execute commands for which it doesn't find corresponding data enables the testers to effectively control the navigation of the test just by giving more or less data.

Additionally, the client offers all kinds of functionalities to create and maintain the automation test suites and control and log test execution. These are described in Section 21.5.1 and shown in Table 21.2.

21.2.2.2 ITS-Engine

The engine is nothing more than an interpreter script in the script language of the test tool. It reads the commands and translates them back into the script language of the tool in order to execute them. We have written a specific engine for every tool that we deploy, including TestPartner, TestComplete, and TestExecute.

If the script languages are not too different, for instance, different basic dialects, then it takes about 2 to 3 weeks to implement an engine for a new test tool. It takes longer when some needed functionalities are not supported and have to be developed from scratch. For instance, in SilkTest, which we implemented for a presentation, there was almost no support for string processing, so we had to write that functionality ourselves. Also, when implementing a new engine, we usually start doing the most used commands and add the less frequently used just as they are needed. In this way, we can change pretty quickly even if we are not properly "finished."

21.3 Implementing Test Automation with ISS Test Station

21.3.1 The Automation Process

21.3.1.1 Prerequisites

You cannot start if you don't know the application and the test cases that are to be automated. This is especially important for test automation. A tester can usually imagine what should be tested and what kind of results to expect, even if the test case specifications are poor, but a tool is really "stupid." You have to plan everything, the expected and the unexpected. After all, test automation is programming, so if you don't have good specs, you'll not be able to produce anything of value.

Second, you need a working engine that can interpret all the commands you are going to need for your test cases. New commands must be introduced to the framework engine only in the special case that some new element has been added to the application's GUI. In our experience, this happens quite rarely.

Finally, you must have registered all the GUI elements that will be used in test execution in the proprietary mapping of the deployed capture/replay tools. In this way, you normalize the names of the GUI controls, and by keeping the names identical in all test-tool environments, you effectively keep the scripts independent from the particular test tool. In our case, because we often have similar elements in different windows (think of an OK button), we build the normalized names in the form `Windowname_Elementname`. If known, we use the same names as are used internally by the developers; otherwise the names on the labels.

Good Point

Use standard names for objects throughout the automation to keep independent of specific tools.

21.3.1.2 *Preparing the Test Suites*

Figure 21.2 shows our automation process. The test automation team prepares the templates, as shown in steps 1 and 2; in step 3, a tester develops the actual test cases using the templates.

The first step in the automation process consists of recording the test case with the capture functionality of the tool. This generates a script in the tool's proprietary script language.

In the second step, we translate the generated script to command-scripts with the appropriate functionality in the ITS-Client. These first two steps are generally executed by the test automation team that also assembles these "pilot" test cases to create a template test suite. Generally, a number of test cases have the same "structure," meaning that they navigate between the same windows and perform on them the same actions with different data. In the template suite, there is only one occurrence for any particular "test case structure."

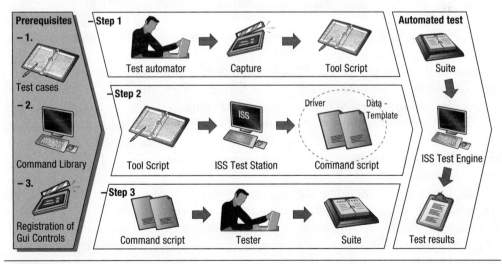

FIGURE 21.2   Our automation process

The third step consists of developing the planned test cases from the templates and building the structured test suites, which can be later executed as automated tests. To implement a test case, the tester makes a copy of the appropriate template test case and has only to tweak the data accordingly. This last step is generally executed by the testers who wrote the test cases to be automated in the first place.

Sometimes, an experienced tester with technical skills can slip into the automator role, but an automator cannot substitute for the tester.

21.3.1.3 *Test Execution*

The test suite can now be executed. Every element in the test suite can be individually prioritized (high, medium, low, irrelevant). On starting execution, we must specify the priority of the tests to be run. For instance, if we specify *medium*, then only the test elements with high or medium priority are executed. In this way, the same test suite can be executed not only for regression testing but also for smoke tests or for retest. This extra priority enables testers to execute only the selected test case or group of test cases for retest. We can also input the number of the defect item, and only the test case related to it will be executed.

> **Good Point**
>
> Devise a way for testers to select which tests to run. With more selection criteria, the automation is more flexible in practice.

During test execution, all performed steps are logged. If one step cannot be executed (e.g., because the expected window has not been displayed), then the framework sets it as not passed. Finally, after all steps have been executed, the contents of specific tables in the database (the data that we want to check) are extracted to text files, using special SQL statements, and compared with files whose contents have been extracted in the same way but checked in advance to form our expected results. If the files are identical, then the test is classified as passed. Of course, we are careful not to compare variable data—dates, indices, and so forth—that does not interest us.

We try to avoid checking directly on the GUI, because in the long run this requires much more maintenance (our developers are very creative!). To ease the reviewing of the test results, these are color-coded (green for passed tests and red otherwise) so that the testers only need to examine those that didn't generate the expected results.

Before I started with the manual testing thing, we had (for this product) about 150 test cases—actually, test scenarios (that roam between lots of windows and do a lot of inputs and checking). We stayed with these 150 test cases for 2 or 3 years. Now (2011) we have more than 300. Of the new test cases, about half were implemented from manual tests.

An automator needs about a day per test case. Without the "manual" test support, it would be more like 1.5 or 2 days. How much effort have we saved? Not as much as we would like. Because we don't have enough personnel, we have implemented test automation only for the application kernel—the regression tests for the customer variants are still in the planning stage. Even so, when we changed our current development environment, we would have needed at least 20 days of manual testing. With the automated tests, it was possible to reduce this effort to a couple of days!

21.4   Implementing Test Automation

With such a sophisticated framework, the ratio of automated to manual tests at Steria Mummert ISS might be expected to steadily grow. That has not been so.

> **Lesson**
>
> Even good toolsets do not guarantee long-term automation success.

We did develop a whole set of automated test suites for most of our software products. Our most important product (portfolio management for insurance) has been a huge success, and we have been having trouble getting new personnel at the same speed as we get new customers! This is wonderful news, of course, but it has been devastating for test automation: The more the application has grown, the fewer automated tests have been developed! The reason is that because we are a small company (about 50 employees), anyone with just some domain knowledge has been sent to the field, so no one is left on the automation team who really knows the extended application or the new test cases.

> **Lesson**
>
> Success for the company may have a negative impact on the automation effort. Management support is needed.

To keep the test automation machine running, the test automation team needs a thorough knowledge of the application to be tested and must have a good working idea of the planned test cases. In this case, our framework can create an appropriate test suite for every kind of test case template from which the testers can autonomously develop the automated test cases. The test automation team depends completely on the product teams for support. But this gives us a classic catch-22 situation: Because of the workload in regression testing, nobody has time to support the automation team, so the automation team cannot automate those same regression tests that would effectively reduce the regression test load!

To overcome this stalemate, we decided to extend our automation framework to also support manual testing. We hoped that if the testers executed their tests within the framework, they would provide, as a beneficial side effect, the necessary information to the test automation team.

> **Good Point**
>
> The purpose of automation is to support testers; find out what tasks could be better supported and provide what they need now.

We figured that we could get the testers to use the framework for manual testing only if we offered them something that they had been missing all along, maybe without even knowing it, so we had to find out how to best support them.

21.4.1   Original Procedure

The original procedure for manual regression testing was to use spreadsheets as test templates. These sheets contain the specifications for all test cases to a particular application area. Every line details a test case and is divided into two parts. In the first part (see Figure 21.3), the test case is specified. In this area, the tester finds all the relevant information to identify, prepare, execute, and check the test cases. They are written in a very terse way; testers are expected to know what they are supposed to do.

In the next area (see Figure 21.4), the tester logs how the test case was executed and whether or not it passed. He or she can add extra information, such as the probable cause for a defect and the number of the defect item that was created or a reference to some attachment.

To execute the tests, a tester makes a copy of the template spreadsheet and enters the new results, as well as eventual corrections, improvements, or new test

Test case specification										
Business process No.	Test case No.	Test area	Business case	Priority	Short description	Test instructions	Prerequisites	Expected results	Export files	Ref. No.
BP001	001	Testarea1	Business case 1	High	Test case a	1.do a 2. do b 3. do c 4. do d	Prerequisite 1 Prerequisite 2	1. Result 1 2. Result 2		
BP001	002	Testarea1	Business case 1	High	Test case b	1. do x 2. do y 3. do z	Prerequisite 1 Prerequisite 3	1. Result 3		
BP001	003	Testarea1	Business case 1	High	Test case c	1. do f 2. do g 3. do h 4. do i 5. do j 6. do k	Prerequisite 4 Prerequisite 5	1. Result 4		
BP001	004	Testarea1	Business case 1	High	Test case d	1. do s	Prerequisite 1	1. Result 5		

FIGURE 21.3   Original test specification in a spreadsheet

Test execution					
Test state	Possible cause	Performed by / on	Description	Defect-Item No.	Attachements
OK		Tester A mm.dd.yyyy			
Defect		Tester A mm.dd.yyyy	1. did s 2. system error xyz	1234	
OK		Tester A mm.dd.yyyy			
To do					

FIGURE 21.4   Test execution report for manual testing (also in the spreadsheet)

cases. Metrics to show how many test cases have been executed, how many were successful, and so on, are easily calculated with the spreadsheet functions. If defects are found, the tester creates a defect item in the development control system so that the defect can be fixed. Our development workflow is driven by development items (stories, tasks, change requests [CRs], or, as here, bug fixes). The project lead decides if and who implements the bug fix, and the selected developer is notified by email. When the developer is finished, he or she sets the item status to ready for retest, and the tester gets an email that the bug has been fixed, and he or she can do the retesting.

21.4.2 Weaknesses

To induce the testers to use the framework, we needed to know what would improve the test process, so we interviewed them more or less directly. With some testers, I could say that I wanted this information in order to do more automation. With others, if I just said the word "automation," they would send me away, and they also hadn't time just to chat, so I had to be careful how I approached them. These are some of the issues that were most often mentioned:

1. Corrections or improvements to a test template are easily lost if more than one tester works simultaneously on the same template. In this case, the changes to all versions must be consolidated. This step is often deferred to a later time (meaning never!). This problem gains steadily in importance as the number of testers grows; the cause is that the same file is used for test case specification and for logging. (If the tester works alone, then the new template can be created by simply erasing all execution information from the modified spreadsheet. But if more than one person works with the same template and both make changes, then someone has to merge the changes—not a nice job!)

Lesson

Configuration management is an important issue in test automation.

2. Reporting the defects to the development control system implies interrupting the test flow: Logging into the system is not the problem (it is done only once at the beginning), but for every defect, the tester must create a defect item, register the item number in the test sheet, report what was done, and write the defect description.
3. Many testers told me that when they find a defect, they have to repeat the test in order to be able to report exactly what they have done.

Good Point

Automation involves more than just executing tests—defect logging, debugging, and status reporting also need support.

4. On the other hand, insufficient details in the defect item makes extra work for the developer, who must locate the test description in the particular test sheet, find out who did the test, further investigate the defect, and so on.

5. There is no way to automatically create a statistic of the executed test cases versus the defects found, versus their fixing status, because the test cases are listed only in the test sheet and the defect status is maintained only in the development control system. This information has to be merged manually. Again, this wasn't a problem as long as the tester was also the test manager, the project lead, and the developer who fixed the bug!

6. To work with our data files, a text editor must be started. Also, there is also no easy way for the testers to directly examine what is happening in the database (unless the tester is also a developer).

7. New employees need a lot of support at the beginning, because the scant descriptions in the test templates require a profound knowledge of the application.

21.5   Supporting Manual Testing

We considered these issues from the point of view of test automation: Which features would be needed in order to offer the same functionalities as the testers were used to? Which new features had to be implemented to convince the testers to switch to the framework? And most important, which features would bring us forward with test automation? Also, which features could we use that were already available in our framework? We didn't want to start from scratch but just to add the functionalities that were necessary to improve the manual process.

21.5.1   Available Features

Table 21.2 overviews the features already available in the framework.

21.5.2   Features Not Currently Available in Our Framework

The next step was to discuss which features, not available in the current version of the framework, would be needed to support manual testing. To begin with, we agreed on the list shown in Table 21.3.

Table 21.2   Features Already Available in Our Framework

Manual Testing Issue	Framework Solution	Importance
Maintain test cases	Test maintenance features: Add, update, copy, and remove objects on every level of the test suite or suite list hierarchy Completely integrated configuration management	Critical: This feature must offer the same comfort as in the current process but in a different format
Overview of the available test cases	Test suites group the test cases in a hierarchical structure that is displayed in tree form; related test cases can be displayed by expanding the tree nodes A suite list groups a number of related test suites	Critical: The new process must offer at least the same comforts as the old one; no tester would do without
Logging of test results	Logging information is automatically recorded in separate logging files	High: Resolves weakness 1 by separating update functionalities from the logging functionalities
Result reports or overviews	Result reports, overviews, and cross-reference lists can be displayed (or printed) with different contents and different granularities: Command script Test case Test suite Suite list	Critical: By offering statistics that include both the completion status of test execution and the defect tracking data, we offered an important incentive to use the framework (solution to weakness 5)
Prioritization of the test cases	Priority feature: Test cases can be easily prioritized to specify which are to be executed in a particular test session; this feature allows us to use the same test suites for regression and smoke tests	High: Prioritization was a feature that they valued and would certainly not want to miss
Defect reporting to development control process	Integration with development control process: New defect items can be created directly out of the result reports; all known data is automatically transferred, so testers in most cases have nothing else to do	High: Ability to report defects to the development control system with the push of a button resolved weakness 2

Table 21.3 Features Needed in Our Framework to Support Manual Testing

Manual Testing Issue	Solution	Importance
Support for manual test execution	Test cases that should be executed (selected by priority) must be displayed sequentially Testers must be able to see simultaneously both the test specifications and the application under test (paperless execution) Testers can perform any of the following actions: ■ Perform the test case and set the test status ■ Move to the next planned test case ■ Skip the test case ■ Interrupt the test session ■ Continue the test session ■ Finish the test session ■ Change the current test case specifications ■ Create a new test case ■ Eliminate the test case ■ Create a defect item ■ Start test recording ■ Interrupt the recording ■ Restart the recording ■ Stop recording	Critical: If testers don't get this kind of support, there is no way they will ever switch over Note that the recording of the test was both by the test execution tool and a video clip (see point about what is given to developers)
Import test template sheets to framework suites	Original test cases must be imported from the current spreadsheets (CSV files) to the test suites in the framework format Import functionality should be driven by an external table to support the different formats of the test template sheets; the table pairs the original columns with the target fields in the framework suite	Critical: Testers must be able to continue to use their current test cases, although in the new suite format This step is also crucial to test automation, because it generates nothing less than the structure for the future automated test suites

Continues

Table 21.3   Features Needed in Our Framework to Support Manual Testing (Continued)

Manual Testing Issue	Solution	Importance
Detail test execution for developers	Capture facility must be integrated into the framework; it must be possible to generate not only a script for later automation but also some kind of recording (screenshot or film) that a developer can view without needing the expensive capture/replay tool license Tester can decide if and when to capture the test and for how long; starting and stopping must be performed directly from the framework without having to call external tools The produced recording is attached to the defect tracking item automatically The script produced is made available to the test automation team for further processing	High: Testers currently do without, but this feature could be a great incentive to switch over to the framework This feature is also crucial for test automation: Both the recorded screenshots (or film) and the captured script illustrate exactly the test execution that we want to automate; these can be attached to a defect item for the developer This feature resolves weaknesses 3 and 4.
Support the creation of input data or compare files	Integrate SQL scripts that extract data from the database to build initial conditions or compare values for test cases	High: Would enable testers to save the inserted data without breaking the flow of test execution (solution to weakness 6) Essential for test automation, because in this way the testers would not only disclose the test case specifications but also deliver the necessary data to create the test preconditions, the expected results, or both

21.6 The New Manual Test Process

21.6.1 Migration to the Framework

The spreadsheets were transformed into framework suites, which were then structured into business processes, business cases, and test cases. Identifiers, names, descriptions, preconditions, and expected results were either imported or filled with the appropriate default values. It took us 2 hours to adjust the import definition tables, 10 seconds each to import the Excel tables, and 1 hour to adjust each of the new test suites. This task was done only once because the test suites were thereafter maintained directly in the framework.

> **Tip**
>
> When you migrate to a new form of test documentation, make sure it is at least as easy to maintain the tests in the new format—don't go back.

21.6.2 Manual Testing with the Framework

The new process looked like this.

21.6.2.1 *Test Case Development and Maintenance*

Test case development or maintenance is one of the oldest features in the framework and offers all the standard functionalities. The GUI is different (see Figure 21.5), but there wasn't a real change in the process.

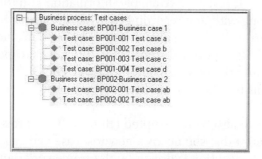

FIGURE 21.5   Structure of a business process test suite

21.6.2.2 *Test Execution*

Test execution is now supported in many ways, and so the process has become more complex:

1. The tester selects, by specifying the priority, which test cases should be executed.
2. The tester then starts execution for the current test suite.
3. A small window (shown in Figure 21.6) with the first (next) test case to be executed pops up. Preconditions, description, and expected results are shown side by side. The current large monitors enable the simultaneous display of the test specifications and of the application under test.
4. The tester checks if the preconditions are met and, if not, sets them up.
5. The tester can export the precondition settings to external files by clicking a previously configured button (e.g., button ①). The names of such files refer to the particular test case ID for easy later reference.
6. By pressing the Record button ▶, the tester can start the recording functionality.
7. The tester performs the manual test.
8. The tester can export the current state of the application ②. These files can then be used as input for subsequent test cases. And, as a useful side effect (from the automation point of view), they constitute the expected results that will be needed to check the actual results when the test is run next time (if the test has passed).
9. If the test case is completed without defects, the tester checks that it's OK ■ and goes on to the next test (Button ▷). The process continues from step 3.
10. If the test case discovers a defect, then the tester can classify it ■ and, by pressing the *Report* button, create a defect item in the development process system to have it resolved. Available information is automatically attached to the item, along with any recording, so that the tester has to step in only in exceptional cases (to fill in fields that can't be filled in automatically and aren't usually needed). Afterward, the tester can select to perform the next test (Button ▷), and the process continues from step 3.
11. The tester finishes the test, and the test results are displayed automatically.

Of course, the tests can also be interrupted (Button ◣) and restarted at a later time, or the tester may realize that she needs a new test case and can just insert it (Button ◻). To conclude, test execution is driven by the framework, but the tester is free to decide what to do next and how to do it.

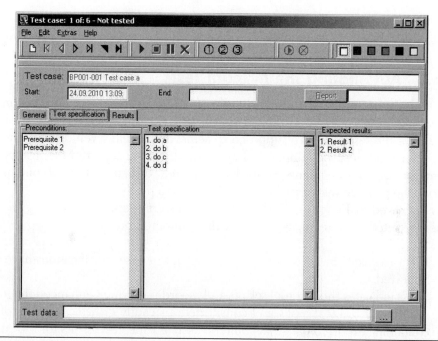

FIGURE 21.6   The current test case being executed

Good Point

Design the automation so that the testers are in charge of what happens in testing.

21.6.2.3 Defect Tracking

When a defect item is created, an email is sent to the project lead so that he or she can assign the task to a developer. After solving the problem, the developer sets the defect item state to "ready for retest," and the tester gets notified to check whether the defect has really been removed. The framework supports retest by allowing the tester to just enter the number of the defect item, and the test case connected with it will be automatically displayed (or it could be run if the test is automated).

21.6.2.4 Statistics

The framework provides both the project lead and the test manager with an over-view of the number of tests still to be executed and the number executed, passed, and failed. It also automatically connects the defect-solving tasks to the original test cases to show the actual state of the bug fixes.

21.6.3   Automating the Manual Tests

After the testers started working with the framework, creating more automated tests became much more rewarding. Also, because the automation team now knows exactly what the test cases are supposed to achieve, they can even develop the final test suites and not just the templates. In this way, the team can offer the testers extra support because they only have to check that the new test suite actually contains and performs the planned test cases before it is moved to production.

As displayed in Figure 21.7, the "friendly" testers are now generating material for the test automation team, as shown by the numbered boxes:

- Box 1 (top left) indicates that all the known test case specifications have been imported.
- Box 2 indicates the test tool scripts and recordings, which enhanced the understanding of the test cases and constituted a steadily growing number of files containing exported data that could be used as expected results for the current test or as a start condition for the next test.
- Box 3 shows the test suite structures, imported from the spreadsheets in which the test cases were specified in some detail. Only half of the suite icon is covered by the box to show that the imported structures represent only part of the necessary contents to implement automation.

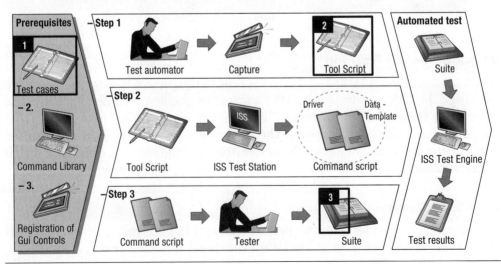

FIGURE 21.7   Where the manual testers are helping automation (without realizing it)

21.6.3.1 *Development*

In our framework, the execution steps are called test procedures—a test procedure defines which command script (DRIVER and DATA) has to be performed. We try to modularize these steps as much as possible so that a typical test case will be executed with 5 to 10 test procedures. A test case is automated by inserting all the test procedures necessary to perform it in the appropriate test case structure in the suite. The test team had to create from scratch only test procedures that performed some action that hadn't been automated yet. For example, test procedures have already been implemented for the existing automated tests to generate the initial test conditions or to check the results against the expected results. In most other cases, as illustrated previously, the work consisted of copying the appropriate DATA-TEMPLATE script and adapting the data accordingly.

The input from manual testing reduced the effort to automate a test case to the following steps:

- Call the framework functionality to transform the captured tool scripts into command-driven scripts.
- Because the recording engine of our tool didn't insert the mapped names of the GUI objects in the generated scripts, the automation team had to rework them by replacing the generated names with the correct ones.
- Create the new test procedures by extracting the necessary statements from the converted command-driven scripts.
- Insert the test procedures to perform the test cases in the test suite structures.
  - Add test procedures to set the preconditions.
  - Add test procedures to execute the test cases.
  - Add test procedures to compare the results with the expected results.
  - Add test procedures to reset the application or react to special events.
- Test the test suite. We usually check the automated test cases one by one, so that when we copy and paste, we don't use unchecked contents.

Good Point

Don't forget to test the automated tests; they are software, too!

When all the test cases have been included, the test suite is checked by the testers, and they can release it into production: Automatic testing can begin.

21.7 Conclusion

After some time to allow the testers to get acquainted with the new process, we started to get the first results. Here is a summary of our experiences:

21.7.1 Starting Phase

- The import facility, test-sheet ➜ test suite, was well accepted from the beginning.
- The testers had a hard time getting used to the new formats. They were used to the list format of the spreadsheets, whereas the suites in our framework have a hierarchical tree structure.
- Some testers had problems adapting to a paperless world.
- The recording feature was also welcomed and not only by the testers—developers were really sold on it, too, because they could immediately see what the tester had been doing to generate a defect: no more vague descriptions.
- In the beginning, the testers were recording either too much or too little. For example, too much would be recording every one of n tests that just differ by one or two entries, too little would be when only part of a test case was recorded so that it was impossible to guess what the tester had done to get to that point in the application. With time, though, they got a good feeling for when it was appropriate to record and when it wasn't.
- Another problem was that, especially at the beginning, testers would start recording and forget to shut off. This would generate *big* files and was practically useless for documentation because the developers didn't care to spool a film for half an hour to get to the test case they were working on. We solved this problem by automatically shutting off recording when a new test case was started.
- At first, the testers didn't realize that when they exported data from the database, they could also reuse it for manual testing. This feature took some time to be fully accepted.
- The filming of the test execution proved to be a great additional help for the automation team because it showed exactly what the tester had done.

Tip

Look for ways to automate small things that can make a big difference.

21.7.2 Status in 2010

- Testers have realized that they can actually help the test automation team with no extra work and have become much more cooperative.
- Testers from other product families, where we actually never had problems with getting support for test automation, also started to use the framework for manual testing.
- We have implemented a feature that supports the execution of partially automated tests. In this way, a tester can automate the tedious test preparation chores but can choose to execute the actual tests manually. For the test automation team, it means being able to deliver some automation already very early in the development process.

The "real" automation runs only on a specific production machine with a specific test database and test configuration. Testers in the field are usually operating in customer-specific conditions that aren't supported yet. What is being used a lot is the partial automation (see third point in the list).

21.7.3 Next Steps

We are using just the simplest of metrics: We only record how many test cases there are, how many were performed, how many passed or failed, and how many have been retested. As more and more testers start using the framework, we expect to be able to introduce more sophisticated metrics.

Another issue will be the integration of the framework with test planning and management tools.

21.8 References

Buwalda, Hans, Dennis Janssen, and Iris Pinkster. (2002). *Integrated Test Design and Automation Using the TestFrame Method*. Boston: Addison-Wesley.

Dustin, Elfriede. (2002). *Effective Software Testing: 50 Specific Ways to Improve Your Testing*. Boston: Addison Wesley.

Dustin, Elfriede, Jeff Rashka, and John Paul. (1999). *Automated Software Testing*. Boston: Addison-Wesley.

Fewster, Mark, and Dorothy Graham. (1999). *Software Test Automation*. Harlow, UK: Addison-Wesley.

Gamba, Seretta. (2005). "Command-Driven Testing, A Step beyond Key-Driven Testing." EuroSTAR 2005 TE7.

Koomen, Tim, Leo van der Alst, Bart Broekman, and Michiel Vroon. (2006). *TMap Next for Result-Driven Testing*. 's-Hertogenbosch, Netherlands: UTN Publishers.

CHAPTER 22

TEST AUTOMATION AS AN APPROACH TO ADDING VALUE TO PORTABILITY TESTING

Wim Demey

Wim Demey describes how he developed an inhouse tool to work with commercial and open source tools to enable parallel testing of different configurations. Testing the installation of packages that are developed with a common core but customized for different customers is important because failures in installation may have serious impacts not just on the system but on market perception as well. But testing the ports of the different packages on a large variety of configurations (operating systems, browsers, databases) can be a time-consuming and resource-hungry process, so it is a good candidate for automation. Wim used virtualization to run portability tests on many configurations at once through a custom-built tool that launches the portability tests in the virtual environments. The chapter offers many good lessons, including the importance of automating the activities surrounding test execution, for those considering a similar task. This story comes from Belgium and involves financial client software. See Table 22.1.

Of all kinds of test types, portability testing is not the one most commonly performed. However, if you have to support multiple configurations, you can't bypass portability testing.

Table 22.1 Case Study Characteristics

Classification	This Case Study
Application domain	Financial client software
Application size	
Location	Belgium
Lifecycle	Traditional based on V model
Number on the project	
Number of testers	5
Number of automators	2
Time span	4 months
Dates	2008
Tool type(s)	Commercial, open source
Pilot study undertaken	Yes
ROI measured	No
Successful?	Yes
Still breathing?	Yes

In most cases, portability testing is just a subset of the functional tests you redo on the supported configurations. But what about the installation of packages? Have you thought about the impact of installation errors on the perception and trust of end users of your software? This is definitely a hidden area where portability testing could add value. Furthermore, if you want to test all possible combinations, you need a lot of human resources and infrastructure. Therefore, in our case, we jumped on the test automation train and elaborated the possibilities of using virtual images in combination with test automation.

22.1 Background for the Case Study

Some years ago, I was working as test manager in a company that was developing a software package in the same way as I describe here for the fictitious company "Soccer Is My Passion."

Soccer Is My Passion develops web-based software to plan the calendar and manage the standings of national football leagues all over the world. Some core modules (such as team management and calendar planning) are developed centrally in the company.

In each region (Asia, Africa, Europe, etc.), another team is responsible for adapting the core modules to the needs of each interested association (e.g., number of teams, playoffs, regulations, how to calculate points for win, loss, or draw).

Finally, they build an installation package (a .msi or .exe file) and ship it to the interested association.

Here is a simplified example of the lifecycle of a package:

- Core development
- Customization
- Shipping package

The software must support a combination of operating systems (e.g., Linux, Windows XP, Windows Vista, and Windows 7), browser versions (Internet Explorer 7 and 8, Firefox), and database versions (Oracle 9, 10 and SQL2005, SQL2008).

The testing activities were split up between functional testing and portability testing. I was managing the offshore test team, which was responsible for doing manual portability testing of software packages (.msi files).

This was the last quality gate before the package was shipped to the customers and had been added to the quality process following complaints about failing installations.

Based on a checklist, my test team went step by step through the installation wizard and focused especially on syntactic items (e.g., display of correct version numbers, spelling errors). This consumed a lot of time, and the tests were very repetitive. On average, one test round took 2 person-days.

This last quality gate consisted of a maximum of three test rounds for each package. Because my team was working in India, the tests were performed before the European development teams came into the office in the morning, so there wasn't much delay or idle time for my offshore team between each test round.

22.2   Portability Testing: Love or Hate It

In the manual portability testing, we have different configuration parameters to take into account:

- *Operating systems:* four types
- *Browser versions:* three types
- *Database versions:* four types

Testing all possible combinations leads to many configurations for each test case: $4 \times 3 \times 4 = 48$ if all combinations are tested.

Even if you can reduce these numbers by applying systematic techniques such as orthogonal arrays or pairwise testing, in more complex situations, it can still mean a lot of testing. In our team, we listed all the combinations for each package and went through them with the requestor who indicated the most critical/important ones to be tested.

The manual testing lasted days even with several people performing the tests. For some packages, two people were needed over the three test rounds, giving a total of 6 person-days. It is understandable that the huge effort can become a reason for skipping or lowering the priority of portability testing.

> **Good Point**
>
> Good candidates for automation are tests that are repetitive and boring to do manually.

Portability testing can be considered as a duplication of regression testing and hence repetitive and not challenging (enough) for testers. Testers risk losing their focus when they are running portability tests time after time.

Portability testing was situated at the end of our software development lifecycle (the V model) and consequently was often the first candidate in scope to drop when a project and particularly testing were under time pressure.

22.3   Combination of Both Worlds as a Solution

Within the company, an automation framework was available, which was a library of functions that used Hewlett-Packard's QuickTest Professional. Together with my colleague, who was managing another offshore test team, we looked at how we could introduce the existing test automation framework into our portability testing.

The problem of having all required configurations was solved by using images based on virtual hard disk (VHD), a virtualization solution from Microsoft. Using this approach saved us some time per package (e.g., 20% of total test effort per test round). The only problem was that the automated tests had to be run in sequential mode because we had only one dedicated workstation for running automated scripts.

Knowing this context, I was looking for a solution that combined both test automation and virtualization to expand the added value of portability testing. I was especially interested in solutions that would allow us to run the portability testing in parallel.

I developed my own solution, shown in Figure 22.1, which I called LA-PORTA (Launch Automated Portability testing).

The key concept in this solution is a package that represents a certain version of an application that you want to test on one or more configurations (test run). It doesn't matter if the package is a custom development or third-party software.

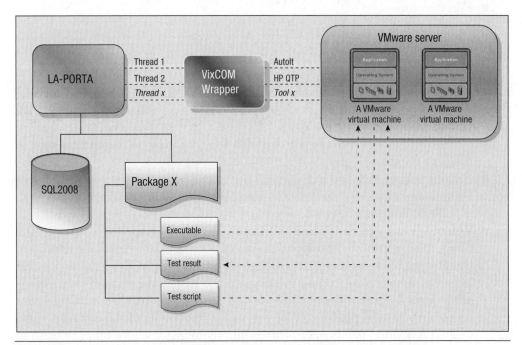

FIGURE 22.1 Overview of LA-PORTA (Launch Automated Portability testing)

The package is physically represented by an executable. For each package, an automated test script is developed.

The test run contains all information about the virtual configuration (operating system, database, and so on), which can be managed within the tool. If necessary, you can even add the installation mode (install, remove, repair) as a parameter.

Once a test run is defined, it is added to the test set where you can select which test run(s) will be executed.

Finally, the execution of the test set—each test run in a separate thread—is launched using the predefined virtual configurations. When a thread has finished the execution, the test results are gathered and sent back.

From an architectural point of view, my solution consists of the following five components, which are explained next:

- Custom .NET application (LA-PORTA)
- Virtualization product (in this case, VMware)
- VixCOM Wrapper (API to enable automated interaction between custom application and virtualization product)
- Test automation tool (e.g., AutoIt and QuickTest Professional)
- File structure

22.3.1 LA-PORTA

LA-PORTA is an application developed in .NET, and it has four main functionalities:

- *Configuration* allows you to use dropdown lists to manage parameters such as available databases, operating systems, and other values.
- Besides parameters, you can manage the virtual images representing the configurations on which you test and the packages (such as Windows XP with SQL2005, Windows XP with Oracle9).
- Through a *test run*, you can link the package to a certain virtual image. You can define the pre- and postconditions as well. These are especially important if you want to reuse a certain configuration and keep it as clean as possible (e.g., by removing all copied folders and the installed package). My experience showed me that if you continue with testing the installation of packages on an already used platform, it could impact the results of the test, especially when information needs to be written into the registry where other or existing entries could impact the behavior of the installation and/or package.

- In *test set* (submenu of test run), you select the test run(s) you want to execute. During the test execution, a log is updated in real time and can be saved.

Good Point

Having a clean starting point for a test is particularly important when testing installation—and the cleanup should be automated, too.

Figure 22.2 shows the Virtualization Selection screen where you can select the virtual image you need and check the current status (for example, Powered_Off).

Figure 22.3 shows the Compose Test Run screen where you link the package to a certain virtual configuration.

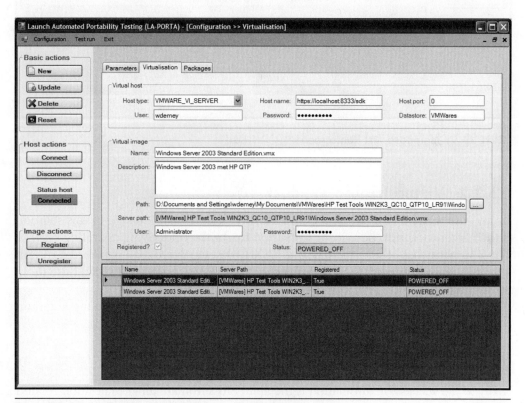

FIGURE 22.2 LA-PORTA Virtualization selection screen

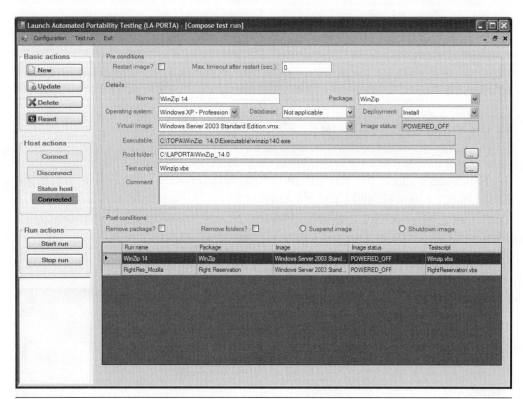

FIGURE 22.3   Compose Test Run screen

22.3.2 Virtualization Product

In my case, I used VMware Server, which is free. One disadvantage of this solution is the bigger footprint, because it installs on top of the underlying operating system. The VM family has other products, like ESX/ESXi, which are hypervisors and rely on a built-in operating system to perform core virtualization tasks. But I didn't use them for my tests.

The VMware server hosts several VMware images, each representing a certain configuration.

22.3.3 VixCOM

A key to the success of automation is the ability to automate all virtualization-related tasks (e.g., start/stop server, create snapshots, log in/log off, suspend/resume image).

The great advantage of using VMware is the availability of a well-documented Vix API (written in C#), and it is easy to use and practical both for script writers and for application programmers.

To make it still easier, I chose the VixCOM wrapper (www.codeplex.com), which wraps the original API into a library and hence could be used in .NET.

> **Good Point**
>
> Good automation is more than execution of tests; it also includes the automation of other activities (e.g., setup, suspend/resume).

The main benefit of this wrapper is the synchronous implementation of all functions, which hides the need to use callback functions and/or polling/blocking mechanisms. Otherwise, technically you need to "listen" regularly to determine if the launched actions are still running or are already finished. If they are finished, you still need to capture the feedback or result, which leads to a lot of complex programming.

The big challenge I ran up against was getting my test runs executed in parallel. Finally, I have solved this by putting each run into a separate thread.

22.3.4   Test Automation Tool

During my investigation, I was wondering which tools could be used to automate a portability test in a virtualized test environment. In addition to the commercial ones (of which I have used QuickTest Professional), I found an interesting open source tool called AutoIt.

This freeware Basic-like tool is designed for automating Windows GUI and general scripting. It is possible to automate keystrokes and mouse movements.

Initially, the goal was to automate the PC rollout of packages, such as the ones I used in LA-PORTA.

Besides being simple and easy to learn, AutoIt has some important benefits:

- The tool contains a freeware script editor with built-in function libraries (e.g., open and write to a text file).
- The generated script can be compiled into standalone executables (no need for agents to launch AutoIt scripts).
- Just like the commercial tools, it has a spy function that allows it to get the necessary information about object properties.

By using this tool, I was able to run—in an automated way—the .msi installation wizard step by step while I did some checks on titles in windows and so forth.

However, the commercial tool was better for handling complex installation wizards or applications.

22.3.5 File Structure

A folder structure, such as that shown in Figure 22.4, increases the reusability of the solution and makes it independent of the test tool you use for the automated portability test.

Each package has a separate folder in which you find the same recurrent folders:

- *Executable:* Contains the package/application that is the object of the portability testing. Usually, this is a file with an extension .msi or .exe. Optionally, the executable can be an input for the test script.
- *Test_result:* At the end of a test run, the result files (no matter what type they are, e.g., just a text file or test tool result files), are copied back to the host. This folder also contains an execution log of LA-PORTA.
- *Test_script:* The driver script is just a simple Visual Basic script, which calls a specific test tool script. This mechanism guarantees that it doesn't matter which test tool you use as long as you can launch the script through a VBS file.

Good Point

Structure your tests to be where you want them, and automate copying files to where the tools need them to be. Separate the test results from the definitions of the tests.

FIGURE 22.4   LA-PORTA directory structure

AutoIt is the tool in which you can write simple scripts to automate tasks or applications. In Listing 22.1, the commands are compiled by AutoIt to an executable that can then be called. The compiled script contains all the statements to install WinZip.

Listing 22.1   Shell Script to Launch the AutoIT Script

```
Option Explicit
Dim wshShell
Set wshShell = WScript.CreateObject("WScript.Shell")
wshShell.Run "C:\LAPORTA/WinZip_14.0\Test_script\Install_WinZip14.exe"
```

22.4   Conclusion

Although portability testing is not often performed, it is definitely a valuable type of test. Not only does it check if your package works properly on different configurations, it also checks the installation process itself. In our case, this prevented a lot of frustration for end users.

Portability testing can be used in a broader context to build a bridge toward infrastructure people to support them with testing of the installation process itself.

Using test automation and virtualized test configurations really helped us overcome the bottleneck created by our need for having all the required configurations and the time to test all combinations.

Take into account that the benefits of automated portability testing will only become true if you can run your tests in parallel. The LA-PORTA solution has shown that you don't always need expensive commercial tools to realize this kind of automation.

22.5   Acknowledgment

An earlier version of this chapter was published in *Testing Experience* magazine (www.testingexperience.com).

CHAPTER 23

AUTOMATED TESTING IN AN INSURANCE COMPANY: FEELING OUR WAY

Ursula Friede

Ursula Friede describes the experience of "feeling their way" to better automation. She and her team did not plan the steps they ended up taking, but it would have been a good plan if they had. They began by just experimenting with a tool but soon realized its limitations, so they decided to focus on the most pressing problems by changing their automation. In each of four phases, they successfully addressed an existing problem but then encountered new problems. They calculated an impressive saving per release after they had implemented their improvements. Ursula was based in Germany at the time and was automating tests in the insurance sector. See Table 23.1.

23.1 Background for the Case Study

I started my working life at the "doing front." I worked 10 years in the claims department of an insurance company. Not always fun, but at least you learn the frontend system very well. But what is behind the frontend? Out of curiosity and in parallel

Table 23.1   Case Study Characteristics

Classification	This Case Study
Application domain	Insurance
Application size	Inhouse software, based on client/server technology
Location	Germany
Lifecycle	Traditional (V model)
Number on the project	30
Number of testers	10
Number of automators	2
Time span	Vague (approx. 6 months)
Dates	2005–2006
Tool type(s)	Commercial (Quality Works, QTP)
Pilot study undertaken	No
ROI measured	No, but quantified savings: €120,000 per release
Successful?	Yes
Still breathing?	Yes

with my job, I started studying information technology (Was I bored? Nothing on TV? No boyfriend?) and got more and more involved in the technical side of this insurance company.

I started software testing 7 years ago in Germany, the land of efficiency. At this time, most of the test scripts were manual and only a few attempts to automate tests had been made.

Imagine some testers who have Quality Works installed on their machines and yet are fed up with manual testing. They know little about automated testing but are keen to try things out and and very nosy, of course.

Therefore, just random steps had been captured and replayed, such as the step Make a Payment. This script worked for one policy number only, and the payment was running with the same figures repeatedly because nothing had been parameterized.

Nobody knew what scripts were on anyone else's PC, and the script was just used for saving some seconds here and there. But we weren't able to reuse the scripts long term.

How efficient is this? Not so efficient—thus my automation test experience started from scratch.

23.2   The Application

The frontend software design is built into the process of claims management. All processes related to claims management are embedded in inhouse software that is based on client/server technologies. It is installed on about 25,000 machines as a fat client system. The client contains all business logic and presentation layers, and all of the data storage is centrally held on a mainframe host system. For purposes of analyzing, reporting, and balance accounting, all data is loaded from the operational system into a data analysis system at regular intervals.

The operational system is installed on 25,000 machines and nine different platforms. There are 850,000 database updates and 5,000 new claims on average per day. Because of the nature of this system, we had a big manual regression pack. This pack contained around 3,000 test cases.

Under normal circumstances, we weren't able to execute the whole manual regression pack within a test cycle of 4 weeks. Usually, approximately 50 percent had been completed by the end of the cycle. We tried to reduce the risk by eliminating test cases with low importance.

To complete the whole regression pack, it would have taken 10 testers 20 working days.

Luckily, only a few defects were introduced into production because of the lack of regression testing. Unfortunately, these were mainly medium to severe defects, and they had an impact on production and the business as usual (BAU).

The existing scripts mentioned earlier were only captured and replayed, but after 1 or 2 weeks, they were no longer usable. This was largely due to a lack of parameterization. For example, 1 to 2 weeks after a Future Payment test was captured, the future payment date becomes invalid. It is only possible to make a payment for 1 week in advance.

To edit the automated test to change the *cause of loss* (insurance term) required a bit of an effort. Furthermore, the fix could sometimes cause other fields to become mandatory, something that the script wasn't able to cope with at all. Hence, rerecording was frequently required.

> **Good Point**
>
> Automating tests done as a background task rarely works well; it needs full-time attention, particularly when starting out.

Everyone was aware that this wasn't the optimal way and couldn't even be called automated testing. In the team, existing automated testing skills were very little to none, except for one colleague who had recently come on board. His previous experience offered a different solution for automated testing. He came up with the idea to automate the regression pack with more structure and more efficiency.

The tool we had installed (Quality Works) was a good tool, but we didn't know how to use it properly. My colleague and I rolled up our sleeves and were ready to start.

This task wasn't set up as a project. Back in those days, people weren't aware of the importance of automated testing. We had our plan to automate the regression pack approved from our team lead. Only the two of us worked on this task. The automation of the regression pack developed alongside the "normal" project work. Because of this, it was not properly organized and it was more a learning-by-continuous-development process. The timescales were, of course, "as soon as possible."

> **Good Point**
>
> Having a good testing tool is one thing; knowing how to use it effectively is another.

23.3 Objectives

Our planned objectives for automation were as follows:

- Automated tests should be reusable and repeatable.
- It should be easy to amend all scripts at the same time (e.g., payment page changes because of release).
- All test cases of the regression pack should be covered.
- Automation should be easy to use for nonautomated-test people.

- It should provide effective passed/failed checks and error handling after a run.
- Automated tests should be run out of hours (OOH).

23.4 The Work

The following phases weren't planned, as mentioned, but these were our phases of improvement during the development process.

23.4.1 Phase 1

We realized early on that it was not worth the hassle of checking which of the existing scripts could be reused. So we made an executive decision to send all scripts straightaway to the filing cabinet: the recycle bin!

Wow! This felt good. But . . . what do we do now?

We needed a plan. We identified all the areas that had to be covered by automated tests and prioritized them. Then we scripted all these areas with the code of the latest software release.

Because we wanted to improve on our capture/replay concept, we identified which variables needed to be parameterized. We clicked through the frontend system and identified all fields that were either an edit box or a combo box. From the edit box fields, we identified which ones were time dependent (e.g., date) and which ones we wanted to change (e.g., claims number, bank account number, claims amount). From the combo box fields, we took a note of all entries so that each combination of existing scenarios was covered.

> **Tip**
>
> A good way to make a start on reusable automated scripts is to identify inputs that will change (and need maintenance), inputs that you want to vary (to cover more options), and things that are most likely to change.

Furthermore, we identified the most used procedures within the claims management system and created functions for them. In case of a code change, we only had to change these individual functions, not all of the scripts, manually.

This was an improvement over the situation we had before. We were now able to run tests multiple times and could create different scenarios because of the parameterization. But we soon realized that this solution was still high maintenance. Each script needed to be changed if new variables for parameters were required.

23.4.2   Phase 2

First, we wanted to solve the complexity of changing parameters. It took too long to open every script to parameterize a new variable. The idea was born to store all parameters in a central database.

> **Good Point**
>
> Continually review maintenance effort to identify where new approaches are needed to keep maintenance costs low.

We created a database connection. All parameters were stored in a database, and the scripts were connected to the database. This made it much easier to make amendments.

At this stage, we thought that our test automation framework was finished. But later, in real-life testing on a new project, we had to admit that, especially after a test run, the amount of time investigating the failed cases was still too high. We had to open every failed script to check which step had failed and which error message came up.

> **Good Point**
>
> Failure analysis cost is often overlooked in automation but can be significant unless it is addressed early on.

23.4.3   Phase 3

We extended the database with a field for error messages. Every time an unexpected error message appeared (client, host, or operating system), the script would write the text of the error message back to the database. After a run, it was now easy to analyze why some of the scripts failed. We were also able to see at a glance if all error messages were the same (e.g., if the environment wasn't available for a while). This saved a lot of time.

Another improvement made, but still a long way to go to perfection.

This error handling only worked for errors that didn't cause the frontend system to shut down. If the frontend system shut down, any remaining test cases weren't able to run. This made manual monitoring of the automated test cases necessary, and in case of an error message that would shut down the frontend system, a manual restart of the frontend system and a new start of the automated test cases were required.

From our point of view, there were still too many manual resources required. Even though we were able to run the scripts much faster than a tester could run them manually, one person was still needed to monitor the automated tests run. This couldn't be right; there must be a better solution.

Good Point

Test automation is never finished. There will always be further improvements that can be made; you need to decide when it is appropriate to do so and when it isn't.

23.4.4 Phase 4

By enhancing the automated framework, the frontend system restarted itself in the case where errors caused the frontend system to shut down. We implemented a simple if/then/else statement that checked if the window of the frontend system was active or not. If it was not active, the script restarted the frontend system before continuing with the remaining test cases. In the end, we were able to run the whole regression pack out of hours without anyone monitoring.

This doesn't include a restart of a computer after a power down. However, these were exceptional circumstances we weren't able to cover, but fortunately, they didn't happen very often.

23.5 Lessons

Here are the things that we should have known earlier.

23.5.1 Screen Resolution

Typical beginner mistake: We just assumed all people were working with the same screen resolution. This, of course, was not the case. Automated test cases passed because we had on our screen the screen resolution we assumed everyone else in the world had. But the real user was not able to navigate to some pages because a different screen resolution caused graphical items to be drawn off screen and therefore become invisible to the user.

It was funny that the Submit button was missing on a specific screen resolution. Well, not really funny for the user world—this was definitely a lesson learned. After seven years, I can still hear my manager's echo.

23.5.2 Less Is Sometimes More

Be wise with the decision as to which and how many tests should be automated. If you test everything and all possible combinations, you might overdo it, and the maintenance of the test pack becomes too high.

It is important to have good coverage, no doubt, but keep it simple and on the spot.

We realized later that we had too many test cases and too many combinations. The test cases were not very different from other regression tests and were of little value. It was not a problem at that time, but if you add more test cases over the years, you might lose the overall overview.

23.6 Conclusion

Here I summarize our greatest success and provide a word of advice.

23.6.1 Greatest Success

My greatest success was in this context where we designed an automation test pack that saved 200 person-days per test cycle. Because we were providing this automation alongside the normal project work, it took us about 6 months to finish the automation test pack. Nevertheless, we were running scripts already in between our test automation development phases.

This provided a cost benefit of €120,000 per release to the organization. On average, there are four releases per year. Previously, every manual test cycle lasted 4 weeks (20 working days) and involved 10 manual testers. Now only one tester, who is trained in test automation, is required to start the scripts and check the results. This tester was trained within our company. One part of the training was the test tool itself, the other part was how to use the test tool and maintain the scripts. Running the scripts takes approximately half a workday altogether. If the tests reveal lots of defects, more work is required. The other manual testers are able to concentrate more on specific manual tests for the new release and on doing other project work. We are able to improve the quality of testing on each release.

> **Good Point**
>
> Calculate what automation has saved in terms of manual effort, but don't forget to tell people about it, too!

As mentioned before, the task was not set up as a proper project, so we didn't track the costs of creating the automated test pack. At that point, it didn't create problems for us. It was just out of curiosity that we calculated the benefit. But this information was held within the team and never ended up as a proper business case or ROI calculation. If this information had been published outside the team, the work of the test team would have been more valued by the company.

23.6.2 Don't Get Carried Away

Looking back I can now say that the more specialized an automated test person becomes, the more it is required to get a person with business knowledge on board. When I started to automate scripts, I was a manual tester with lots of business knowledge. But now, I have hardly anything to do with it. There is a risk that I automate a test but completely miss the meaning of the original test: what it was supposed to test or show. This is particularly the situation if the manual test is an older one and I'm not aware of any business changes that happened in the meantime (e.g., a new maximum payout for hiring a car).

> **Good Point**
>
> Testing and automating are different skills; both are needed for best results from automation. Business knowledge is needed to devise good tests.

Therefore, when a manual test is automated, the manual test has to be 100 percent accurate, or if a new test is created, it needs to be reviewed by people with business knowledge, to make sure the new automated test is fit for purpose.

CHAPTER 24

ADVENTURES WITH TEST MONKEYS

John Fodeh

John Fodeh tells of his experiences with automated random test execution, also known as "monkey testing," for medical devices used for diagnosis and in therapeutic procedures. John describes the limitations of automated regression testing and why few bugs are found that way. Using test monkeys enabled him to find many bugs in the devices that otherwise would not have been found before release. Inputs are selected from a list at random, and all crashes are investigated. Test monkeys can be implemented with commercial execution tools or inhouse tools. This approach borders on model-based testing and also is close to exploratory test automation. John's team was able to calculate the reliability of the devices over time, which helped in the release decision. Many other interesting metrics are described in this chapter as well. An honest assessment of the limitations of the technique makes this a well-balanced description of an interesting use of tool support in testing. This story takes place in Denmark. See Table 24.1.

24.1 Background for the Case Study

This chapter describes how automatic random test execution tools, commonly known as test monkeys, were used for testing medical devices. The test monkeys were applied to enhance the existing testing capabilities, detect defects, and evaluate the reliability of the system under test (SUT).

The chapter presents the general concept, the pros and cons, as well as examples taken from projects involving medical devices and applications. The experiences

Table 24.1   Case Study Characteristics

Classification	This Case Study
Application domain	Medical applications/devices.
Application size	Approximately 800 to 1,200 KLOC
Location	Denmark
Lifecycle	Traditional (V model), incremental
Number on the project	30
Number of testers	6
Number of automators	2
Time span	6 years
Dates	2000–2005
Tool type(s)	Commercial and inhouse
Pilot study undertaken	Yes
ROI measured	No
Successful?	Yes
Still breathing?	Yes

shared in this chapter are based on several projects involving embedded and Windows-based systems.

This case study is concerned with applying automated random test execution tools in a company that develops medical devices. These devices are used for diagnostic purposes and in therapeutic procedures. Software development in this highly regulated domain is subject to various verification and validation activities throughout the development lifecycle. The company had already introduced automation tools and established a few automated regression test suites covering some of the functional aspects of the system.

Obviously, it is critical that a medical application or device is able to perform its required function and to sustain its operation for long periods of use. However, it is also of great significance that the SUT can function correctly in the presence of invalid inputs or stressful conditions and that it is able to recover "gracefully" in case of failure (i.e., the system can detect failure, recover data, and reestablish the specified level of performance). Some of the challenges that the company was facing were related to testing the nonfunctional quality attributes such as reliability, robustness, and recoverability. At the same time, the company had decided on a process-improvement initiative, looking at ways to achieve better testing in general and to increase the effectiveness and efficiency of the existing test automation in particular.

24.2 Limitations of Automated Regression Testing

Typical test automation approaches concentrate on high-level regression tests using a test execution tool. Automating regression tests was also the starting point at this company.

After successful implementation of regression test automation, the company wanted to investigate how to achieve further benefits from automation. Analyzing the existing automation strategy revealed that this approach had its flaws and limitations and, despite many advantages, was still missing serious defects in the software. Some of these shortcomings were related to the scope and quality of the automated tests, such as lacking tests to replicate long and compound usage period, stress situations, and combinations of negative input. Other shortcomings seemed to be closely related to the characteristics of regression test automation, as discussed here.

Good Point

Regression automation, although useful, has drawbacks and limitations.

24.2.1 Automated Regression Tests Are Static

Each time a test is run, the same actions are executed in the same order. Of course, repeating previously executed tests is the very nature of regression testing. Nevertheless, this means that, when executed, the tests traverse the same path in the software. Unless the software underneath is changed, the probability of finding new defects is unquestionably low. Repeating the test would not yield additional code coverage either.

24.2.2   Automated Regression Tests Are Simple

Because the tests have to be reused and maintained, most automated tests consist of short and simple sequences of commands. The tests use a limited range of input and combinations that are mostly positive tests.

As is well known, negative testing is effective in finding defects. Many defects reside in the error-handling routines of the software (or the lack of them) and are often revealed when using illegal input and actions or combinations of these. Because of limited negative input, many tests (manual as well as automated) failed to detect critical defects in the software.

24.2.3   Reinitialization of Automated Tests

Automated tests are characterized by frequent *initialization* procedures; after the short command sequence is executed, the application under test is typically reset to a known *base* state. A *cleanup* is then performed to restore databases, delete created files, and so on. This use pattern varies significantly from the way real users use the SUT. Users rarely initialize and clean up after completing a certain command sequence. Instead, they perform many different and long sequences creating extensive and composite use patterns.

24.2.4   Synchronized with Application

The playback of the automated tests is synchronized with the application under test. This feature, which is incorporated in most test execution tools, means that the tool will halt the playback and wait for a certain "visual cue" (the appearance of a specific window, button, etc.) before resuming the test. This feature is useful when running regression tests, but it also prohibits some testing—while waiting for a synchronization point, no testing is being done!

24.2.5   Vulnerable to Changes

Software typically undergoes many changes during its lifecycle. To keep up with changes in the software and the requirements, the corresponding tests need to be maintained.

This is also the case for automated tests: If automation is not structured properly, changes in the SUT (even minor GUI adjustments) may affect the automated tests, in worst cases making large parts of the tests obsolete. For this reason, special attention must be given to building solid automation architecture supporting automated tests' maintainability and reducing their vulnerability.

Besides improving the existing automation architecture, the company was seeking an automation approach to cope with volatile applications in which rapid changes were made and where the GUI might not be finalized until late in the development process.

24.3   Test Monkeys

To resolve the limitations and improve the existing strategy, we decided to investigate complementary automation approaches. The objective was to think out-of-the-box and expand automation into new areas, helping us detect defects early and ultimately helping the company improve the software reliability, robustness, and recoverability.

> **Good Point**
>
> To really use the power of automation, go beyond regression test automation.

This emerged into the idea of automatic random test execution, also known as monkey testing. Monkey testing refers to the process of randomly exercising the SUT. A *test monkey* is an automated tool for random testing. Unlike automated regression tests, test monkeys explore the system in a new way each time the test is run. The idea was the result of a few brainstorming workshops inspired by methods typically used in hardware testing, such as highly accelerated life testing (HALT) and endurance and reliability testing.

24.3.1   Characteristics

The primary function of the test monkey is to transfer input to the application under test, register the performed actions, and monitor the system response (see Figure 24.1).

The input to the application under test is specified in an action list script (a plain text file that can be created and edited in any text editor). When executing a script, the commands are read randomly by the test monkey, interpreted, and advanced to the interface of the application under test.

The test monkey monitors the response from the application under test and detects if the application crashes or hangs. If the application becomes nonresponsive, the test monkey restarts the application and resumes the test.

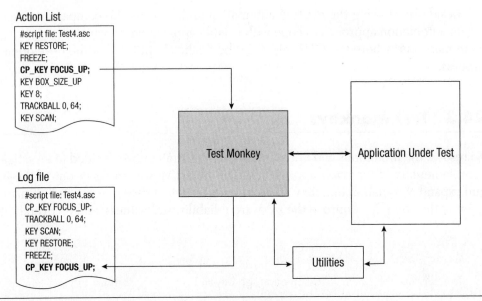

FIGURE 24.1   Schematic diagram of a basic test monkey

24.3.2 Basic Features

The test monkey was designed with the following basic features. This feature set emerged after a brainstorming session and was followed by a short pilot (1 week) to validate the concept and the technical feasibility.

- *Select randomly from the input range:* This is the main idea of the random test. Ideally, the input range would cover all possible inputs for the application under test.
- *Enter input to the application under test:* The test monkey should enter the input through the normal interface as used by the real user (e.g., the application GUI).
- *Detect "life signs" of the application under test:* This is a very important feature, as the test monkey should sense if the application under test is nonresponsive.
- *Log all executed commands:* Because it is important later on to be able to reproduce any defects found, a test monkey should have a robust logging facility, which can preserve the log in case of serious application breakdowns. The log should even survive a blue screen of death. To reproduce a defect, the test monkey should be able to play back the log. The test monkey was programmed

to capture a screen shot of the application under test when a defect was found and extract "postmortem" dump and resource utilization information (e.g., used memory) from the kernel.

- *Restart and initialize the application:* When the application under test breaks down, the test monkey should be able to restart and initialize the application so the test can be resumed.

24.4 Implementing Test Monkeys

The first test monkey was developed in Turbo Pascal and used to test an embedded system (medical device). It was implemented as a standalone tool communicating with the SUT through the device's serial interface (RS-232), the same interface and protocol that was used by the user input device (keyboard and pointing device). The design, implementation, and testing of the first test monkey took about 2 months of effort involving one developer and a tester.

The next generation of the medical device involved a Windows-based application. Initially, the company believed that the new Windows-based platform together with the new development tools and methodology would make the test monkey redundant. However, I had an experience that made me challenge this assumption.

One day, I was working from home testing the new application. It happened that I left my PC unattended for a couple of minutes to get a cup of coffee. When I came back, my (at the time) 3-year-old daughter was sitting in front of the PC clicking the mouse and banging on the keyboard. What was interesting was that she apparently was able to bring the application into an invalid state, where two dialogues of the same type were on top of each other (a situation that was not supposed to happen). Closing the dialog crashed the application!

Later, I discovered that this was related to the hotkeys (keyboard shortcuts) used in the application. Apparently, it was possible, by repetitively hitting the hotkeys, to generate a race condition, ultimately crashing the application. The defect proved to exist in other parts of the application.

I thought it was interesting that in a matter of 2 minutes, my daughter was able to reveal a defect that had slipped many weeks of testing by a professional testing team. This was a good reminder that the concept of test monkeys was also applicable in the new environment (and gives me a good story to tell).

Lesson

Good ideas for testing can come from unexpected places.

The company therefore decided to develop a test monkey running in this platform. This test monkey was implemented using Rational Robot, a commercial test execution tool (the same that was used in the company for the automated regression tests). The implementation and testing effort was 4 months and involved one developer and a tester.

Developing a test monkey, with the basic features described previously, proved to be uncomplicated. We discovered that the main challenge of monkey testing was to determine the level of application knowledge the test monkey should possess. "Primitive" monkeys would only recognize a few states in the application, such as the state where the application is idle (waiting for user input) or when the application is running in a certain mode. Test monkeys with wide application knowledge are programmed to handle multiple states (ideally all). The most suitable approach that we found for handling wide application knowledge proved to be using a finite state machine, modeling the states of the application under test, and building in the oracles (i.e., verifying the expected end state for each action, also known as model-based testing).

Test monkeys with limited application knowledge proved cheap to develop and maintain but overlooked many defects in the application. On the other hand, test monkeys with wide application knowledge can be effective at finding defects but are costly to develop and maintain.

Estimating the cost and benefit, the company decided to go for a basic primitive test monkey, limiting the application knowledge to very generic global events (e.g., at any time pressing the Abort button should cancel any ongoing operation and bring the user back to the start screen). The test monkey would only verify these generic events but would otherwise be ignorant of the application functionality.

Although it was tricky to decide how much application knowledge a test monkey should have, we learned that it was indisputable that the test monkey should have good environment awareness. The test monkey should constantly monitor the application and operating system. It should be able to recognize error messages and keep an eye on system resources (such as memory and CPU usage). This feature is needed for detecting life signs as well as for restarting and initializing the application under test.

24.5 Using Test Monkeys

Putting the test monkeys to use showed immediate benefits. Test monkeys do not require a full, stable UI. Tests can be limited to the areas that are ready and can be applied as soon as the first versions of the application under test are built.

Furthermore, test monkeys can be used whenever the test systems are not used for other purposes, and they are ideal for overnight and weekend tests. They can operate in parallel on multiple systems and run unattended for many hours or days until a predefined limit is reached (e.g., the application has completed 80,000 operations) or until the test is interrupted manually. As a result, the tool was adopted by developers and testers and used throughout the entire development process.

> **Lesson**
>
> A tool that is easy to use and provides good benefits will be used by people who can appreciate its value.

Developers used the test monkeys to get valuable feedback on the state of the application under test. The test monkeys were used as a part of the "daily build of smoke" to verify the reliability of the latest software build. If the reliability suddenly dropped, the developer would investigate the latest changes implemented in the software and make the necessary corrections before building an official (labeled) version of the application.

As the release date approached, the test monkeys provided vital information about the release candidates' readiness for release.

Testers used test monkeys to check conformance to an entry criterion (e.g., for the system test phase). If the application under test failed to pass a certain minimum number of random operations, the software was rejected and returned to the developers (for more details, see the next section).

Logs of previously found crashes were used as a part of the automated test suite to ensure that these defects did not reemerge (the notorious "Haven't I seen this bug before?" phenomenon).

When new functionality was implemented in the application under test, it was possible to direct the test monkey to a specific area of interest. This was accomplished using the following methods:

- Adding multiple entries of a particular command in the action list script, thus increasing the probability of executing this command during testing.
- Excluding specific commands from the action list script (such as commands that exit the area of interest).
- Running combinations of sequential and random tests. A sequence of commands will bring the test monkey into the area of interest and subsequently start the random test.

Test monkeys proved to excel at constructing complex combinations and sequences (especially those that were not considered during design), stress conditions, and finding defects that only emerged after a long period of use, such as memory and resource leaks and overflow problems.

24.5.1 Metrics

As mentioned earlier, the test monkeys delivered vital information about the reliability of the application under test. A useful metric was the mean number of random operations between failures. This metric is equivalent to the widely used mean time between failures (MTBF) metric (e.g., used for hardware reliability testing). This metric is calculated by counting the total number of system breakdowns encountered and the number of random operations performed. The following formula is used:

$$\frac{\sum random\ operations}{\sum failures + 1}$$

Plotting this measure as a function of the build number gives a graphical presentation of the reliability trend. Figure 24.2 shows an example. The trend visualizes the progress in the system reliability throughout development and up to release.

The chart contains two limits: The lower limit is the entry criterion for system testing, and the higher limit is the release criterion. If the software failed to comply with the entry criterion, the reliability of the software was clearly not good enough for system testing and the software was rejected.

Tip

Automate the testing of the entry criteria for system testing so people don't waste time on an application not yet ready for testing.

Using the upper limit, it was straightforward to confirm if the system reliability was adequate for release. These limits were established on the basis of experience in the company using the test monkeys in the context of the projects.

Another useful metric was the number of new defects found during 24 hours of random testing. Unlike the reliability metric in which all system breakdowns are counted, this metric takes into account only the number of new defects found during 24 hours of random testing (it is necessary to determine if the defect found by the test monkey is new or already known).

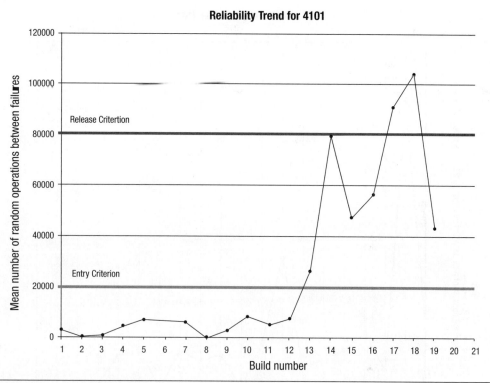

FIGURE 24.2   Reliability trend. In this example, the trend shows a significant drop in reliability for build 19, which proved to be the result of an uninitialized variable.

The following formula is used:

$$\frac{\sum new\ defects\ found}{\sum test\ hours} \times 24$$

Plotted as a function of the build number, this metric shows the effectiveness of the test monkey throughout the development process. Figure 24.3 shows an example. In the beginning, the application under test was error prone, and the test monkey didn't require a lot of time to find new defects.

Because only new defects are taken into account, this graph tends to go down as it becomes harder to find new defects. Ultimately, the trend approaches zero as the test monkey fails to find any new defects.

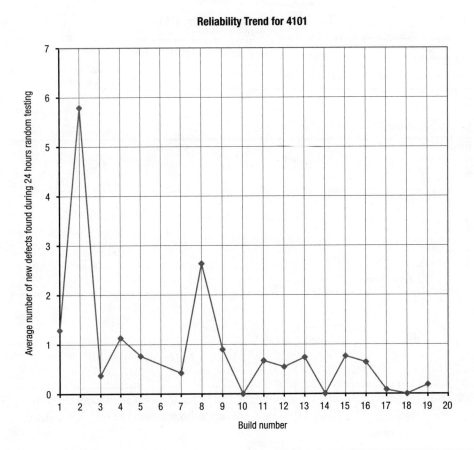

FIGURE 24.3   Test monkey effectiveness

It is worth mentioning that like any other metric, a solid statistical basis is important. If the metrics are based on only a little data (such as a few hours of random testing on a single test system), they can be misleading. Having a number of test monkeys running many hours on multiple systems helps establish confidence in the reliability of the metrics.

24.6   Benefits and Limitations

Using the test monkeys revealed that it was possible to compensate for many of the limitations and gaps in the existing regression test automation. The main benefits gained were as follows:

- *Early testing:* Test monkeys do not require an established GUI or a highly stable application under test and can therefore be applied early in the applications lifecycle.
- *Valuable feedback:* Test monkeys are used as a reliability indicator providing vital information to both developers and testers.
- *Cost-effective automation:* Test monkeys are cheap to implement and do not require considerable maintenance effort. Test monkeys can be put to use overnight and during weekends to find severe system breakdowns (nasty surprises we don't want our customers to find).
- *Long and complex test runs:* Test monkeys can run for a long period of time covering wide areas of the application under test. Test monkeys do not need to synchronize with the application under test nor initialize the application to a known start state as in traditional test automation. The long test runs create compound situations that are very useful for detecting defects that only surface after a long execution time. Moreover, test monkeys excel in negative and stress testing, creating combinations and sequences that were not considered during design.

Tip

Defects can be found by running long sequences of automated tests that would not be found otherwise.

It is important to emphasize that the company did not rely on test monkeys as the only form of testing. Test monkeys were used as a supplement to, not a replacement for, the existing automated and manual testing.

Test monkeys have a number of limitations. They do not emulate real use situations and will, depending on the level of application knowledge, miss obvious defects (test monkeys are only looking for life signs of the application under test; they will not detect a missing function, a corrupted screen image, or a wrong font type).

24.7 Conclusion

Test monkeys were successfully applied to test medical applications (both embedded devices and Windows-based), and it was possible to cover some of the gaps in the existing automated regression tests. When test monkeys were implemented early in the development process, it was possible to do more testing in the available time and find severe defects.

To implement test monkeys cost effectively, the degree of application knowledge must be carefully considered. At a minimum, the test monkey should be able to detect if the application under test has stopped responding.

Test monkeys provide an effective testing tool and the means to establish a practical reliability metric. However, test monkeys have some obvious limitations and should therefore be considered an enhancement to the test strategy, not a substitution for manual testing activities or automated regression testing.

24.8   Additional Reading

Fewster, Mark, and Dorothy Graham. (1999). *Software Test Automation*. Harlow, UK: Addison-Wesley.

Kan, Stephen H. (1998). *Metrics and Models in Software Quality Engineering*. Boston: Addison-Wesley.

Kaner, Cem, Jack Falk, and Hung Quoc Nguyen. (1993). *Testing Computer Software*. London: International Thomsen Computer Press.

Li, Kanglin, and Mengqi Wu. (2004). *Effective Software Test Automation: Developing an Automated Software Testing Tool*. New York: Wiley.

Musa, John. (1998). *Software Reliability Engineering*. New York: McGraw-Hill.

Nyman, Noel. (2000). "Using Monkey Test Tools." *Software Testing and Quality Engineering*, 2(1): 18–23.

Patton, John. (2005). *Software Testing*. Indianapolis, IN: Sams. Note that this book has a chapter on automated testing and test tools that addresses test monkeys.

Robinson, Harry. (2000). "Intelligent Test Automation." *Software Testing and Quality Engineering*, 2(5): 24–33.

Utting, Mark, and Bruno Legeard. (2007). *Practical Model-Based Testing: A Tools Approach*. Amsterdam: Morgan Kaufmann.

CHAPTER 25

SYSTEM-OF-SYSTEMS TEST AUTOMATION AT NATS

Mike Baxter
Nick Flynn
Christopher Wills
Michael Smith

Mike Baxter, Nick Flynn, Christopher Wills, and Michael Smith describe the automation of testing for NATS (formerly called National Air Traffic Services Ltd.). Among its other responsibilities, NATS provides air traffic control services for the airspace over the eastern North Atlantic Ocean. Testing a safety-critical system where lives are at stake requires a careful approach, and the requirements included special technical factors, human factors, and commercial considerations. The tool used was able to test the software without affecting it, and it was also useful in some unexpected ways, such as in training. The authors provide a helpful checklist for deciding which tests to automate and describe lessons learned, both general and technical. This case study is from the United Kingdom and involves commercial, open source, and inhouse tools. See Table 25.1.

25.1 Background for the Case Study

This chapter tells the story of a UI test tool and how it was used to support software maintenance and development in a system-of-systems (SoS) air traffic control (ATC)

Table 25.1 Case Study Characteristics

Classification	This Case Study
Application domain	Air traffic control
Application size	>1.2 million LOC
Location	Prestwick, United Kingdom
Lifecycle	Traditional
Number on the project	15–20
Number of testers	5–7
Number of automators	0–2
Time span	Variable, cycles typically lasting 3–12 months
Dates	Project entered its operational phase November 2006. Use of system-of-systems test execution automation commenced during the summer of 2009.
Tool type(s)	Commercial, open source, and inhouse
Pilot Study undertaken	Yes
ROI measured	No
Successful?	Yes
Still Breathing?	Yes

environment known as the Shanwick Automated Air Traffic System (SAATS). SAATS is the flight data-processing system used to support operations in the Prestwick Air Traffic Control Centre, which is responsible for the area Shanwick, the eastern half of the North Atlantic Ocean, as shown in Figure 25.1. (The other areas shown are Oceanic Transition Areas.)

25.1.1 System-of-Systems Operational Context

SAATS was originally developed in close collaboration with NAV CANADA, the Canadian Air Traffic Control organization, and is a system-of-systems comprising

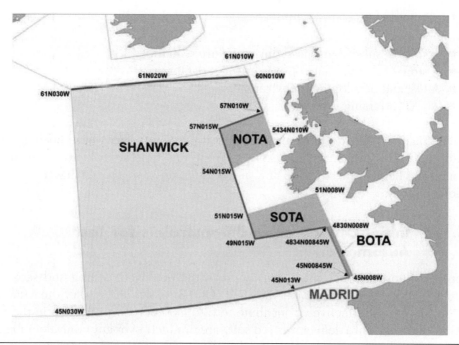

FIGURE 25.1   Map showing location of Shanwick area

DEC, Hewlett-Packard Alpha Workstations, and PC hardware, hosting a mix of OpenVMS and Windows XP operating systems, interconnected by a fiber distributed data interface (FDDI) and Ethernet LAN.

SAATS supports air traffic management through the provision of:

- Controller and assistant real-time data of all aircraft flying in the area.
- Conflict detection and resolution assistance using internationally agreed separation standards (both lateral, longitudinal and altitudes at which aircraft can fly in a given direction).
- Interfaces to adjacent area control centers for flight-coordination purposes.
- Interfaces to relevant centers for high-frequency (HF) air-ground communication and receipt of position reports from aircraft.
- Data link interfaces to aircraft to support clearance delivery (authorization to enter airspace), position reporting, and controller-pilot data link communications (CPDLC) applications.

In addition, this asset provides:

- A suite of subsystems used during failure scenarios.
- A store of the current copy of the flight database.
- A test and development environment.
- An ATC training simulator.

The many complex graphical and command-line interfaces have been assessed and optimized by human factors experts. These real-time systems are permanently manned and help ensure the safe flow of the thousand or so aircraft that traverse this region each day.

25.1.2   Initial Objectives and Constraints for Test Automation

A process improvement initiative to improve the quality of testing and save time evaluated various commercial off-the-shelf (COTS) tools. The goal of the test automation was to cost-effectively contribute toward a 30 percent reduction in the time and effort necessary to deliver assured software products over any equivalent manual process. Our objectives and anticipated benefits for the tool were as follows:

- It should be a well-established product.
- It needs to be platform independent.
- It should be straightforward to use by domain experts who are not software-development specialists.
- It should reduce mundane activity by freeing testers from repetitive tasks liable to be susceptible to human error.
- It should make shorter test cycles possible and have the potential for increased test coverage.
- Improvements in overall consistency might lead to higher-quality deliverables.
- We should have efficiency gains resulting from the integration of logging, report generation, and audit trail capabilities.
- If we can combine test automation tools with KVM-over-IP technology, then base-loading and failure-mode testing could be scripted. (KVM is keyboard video mouse inputs.)
- Potential safety/performance issues would be alleviated if the architectural approach means that no test tool application software need reside on the system under test (SUT).

Our evaluation found that eggPlant appeared to be closest to our requirements.

Good Point

Define your objectives and constraints for a tool, taking into account technical, commercial, and human factors.

25.2   Test Execution Tool Integration

eggPlant interacts with SUTs by means of virtual network computing (VNC) technology, and Figure 25.2 shows the two approaches we adopted to achieve the required connectivity.

It would have been cheaper to install a VNC server on each system, but some systems are locked down by a third party, preventing a VNC server from being installed on them without infringing support contracts. The solution is to connect a KVM and drive it remotely, as depicted by approach 2.

The first and most common integration approach (approach 1) involved hosting VNC directly on the SUT. The second approach (approach 2) needed the use of an

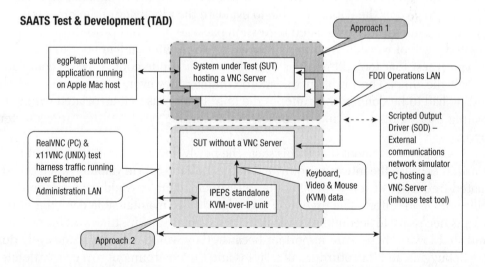

FIGURE 25.2   SAATS test and development (TAD) environment

IP Engine per Server (IPEPS) KVM-over-IP unit giving the benefit of having no testware resident on the SUT but at the expense of a slower response time for that interface.

By including a connection to the inhouse-developed scripted output driver (SOD), it also became possible to functionally interact with and monitor the whole environment from a single instance of the eggPlant application. The SOD simulates the external environment by generating reports that represent aircraft data and communication exchanges with adjacent air traffic service providers.

25.3   Pilot Project for the Tool

Our next step was straightforward: Find out if the tool would give us the benefits we wanted. A representative cross-section of manual test cases was identified for the pilot project, and an extra software engineer was tasked to automate as many of these tests as possible during the target time allocated. This was important because the lab facilities were always heavily used, and it would be necessary to fit systems training and automated script development around other operationally related requests for the lab facilities.

Because we already knew from past experience what human and time resources were required to execute our test procedures manually, all we had to do was keep track of the total effort and the time used when running the automated equivalents. This would give us the data to be able to evaluate the efficiency of the process.

After 3 months, an automated regression package of 12 test procedures had been created, each of which would take between a few minutes and an hour to complete. A typical test that took 20 minutes to do in manual mode could now be completed in half the time. The problem was more complex, however, because much of the testing had to be done in real time, so the only saving was that associated with automating user inputs, checking responses, and recording results at the various system peripherals.

It's important to note that at this stage the newly developed suites were not modularized because the intent was only to demonstrate long-term viability based on estimated frequency of reuse. Making the suites maintainable would have required significantly more effort. The exception was a handful of maintainable common library scripts necessary to accomplish basic activities such as startup, time synchronization, and shutdown. These were important because they would get used extensively during debugging and for returning all systems and the environment to a clearly defined base state between reruns.

> **Good Point**
>
> "Quick wins" may be in peripheral activities such as setup and shutdown tasks
> rather than in automating the tests.

25.4   In-Service Model

Our use of eggPlant at Prestwick does not follow a standard pattern. For example, the only scripts in constant use tend to be those supporting ATC training. In this environment, they enable operational staff to start up their simulator (a replica of the operational system) and load the required training scenario without having to call on the services of other specialists.

eggPlant-based automation is also used when there is a program constraint, resulting in the need to increase TAD use and accelerate the regression test cycle. In this circumstance, additional resource is contracted in to update the test suites. Typically, testing of new software packages can take anywhere from a few days to several months before our safety standards are met.

The reason for this limited implementation is the concern that too much reliance on automation for SoS regression may result in the gradual decline of detailed system knowledge within the test team. This is more of an issue than you might think. For example, regular refresher courses for our engineers are essential precisely because our systems are so complex and reliable. Otherwise, the potential inexperience and associated risk of an extended service interruption could result in aircraft being grounded due to flow restrictions being imposed and National Air Traffic Services (NATS) becoming the main news item of the day!

25.5   Implementation

We had concerns such as the following about trying an automated testing regime when manual testing worked reasonably well:

- Scope creep, which could cause excessive script maintenance.
- Unrealistic expectations.
- The pesticide paradox: Not all defects would be discovered.

To overcome scope creep, it was decided early on that the project must work to a clear and fixed set of requirements and that the system design being tested must be relatively mature. The unrealistic expectations would also be addressed by a good requirement set. The pesticide paradox is partly mitigated if the test scripts are rotated, modified, and enhanced so that new defects can be discovered.

An incremental approach to the introduction of automation was proposed whereby opportunities were assessed and tracked on a case-by-case basis. To achieve this objective, to capture quantitative metrics, and to create a baseline, it was further planned that a small proportion of potentially automated tasks were checked against their manual equivalents so that the time and resources consumed could be tracked in support of future decision making.

The checklist shown in Table 25.2 was used as a guide to determining whether a task was a viable candidate for automation.

> **Tip**
>
> Devise a checklist to assess the suitability of tests for automation, and automate the most suitable tests first.

Automated test suites were designed to be exact replicas of the manual test procedures. For consistency, automated suites retain the same naming convention as the manual test procedures. Automated suites were always archived as a complete set in a folder named after the software build they were used to test.

> **Tip**
>
> Avoid the potential for the inadvertent introduction of diverging baselines by adopting common naming conventions.

NAV CANADA taught us the importance of maintaining a common image library of human–machine interface (HMI) components (indexed by subsystem) that all test suites refer to. The benefit is that it significantly reduces the maintenance overhead, because when a UI changes, updates only have to be made in one place.

Table 25.2 Automation Checklist

	Assessment Criteria	Note
1.	Is the test likely to be repeated many times?	
2.	Does executing the task require the support of more than one individual?	Some tests cannot be accomplished by one person, whereas following the implementation of automation, this might become possible.
3.	How much time could be saved?	
4.	Is the task on the critical path?	Even if a test suite is not regularly reused, the future time saving during a critical project phase might justify the implementation cost (e.g., early or unattended overnight completion of core regression).
5.	Are the requirements the task is verifying low risk, stable, or unlikely to be impacted by significant change?	This might necessitate a disproportionate level of product maintenance, thereby negating benefit.
6.	Is the task common to other projects or likely to be of value as part of a collaborative effort?	We might be able to share benefit and associated development cost (e.g., common test harness).
7.	Is the task particularly susceptible to human error?	
8.	Is the task time consuming? Does it contain significant idle periods of inactivity between test steps?	
9.	Is the task mundane/highly repetitive?	
10.	Does the task require specialist knowledge, and is the skill to execute it likely to be in demand by others?	Minimizing reliance on domain experts could simplify test planning and improve TAD facility use. In the absence of significant errors, executing a test script automatically is usually much easier and quicker to accomplish than running it manually.

25.6 Typical Script Template

Listing 25.1 and Listing 25.2 show examples of standard test scripts used. The first box contains the code to run test procedure ATC_FDM_001 comprising three test cases: TC01, TC02, and TC03.

Listing 25.1   Code to Run Three Test Cases

```
(** ATC FDM 001 ALL
@author(s) Mike Baxter
@baseState S241710
@buildTarget S237114 (ENSURE)
@dependencies
@platform Eggplant v4.2
@duration 17 minutes 36 seconds
@revisionHistory  Ver   Date      Tag     Reason
@revisionHistory -----------------------------------------------------
@revisonHistory  0.1    20/10/09  MB      Initial Release for Review
Notes
- Each test case follows consecutively (i.e. no intermediate stop/
restarts)
- Begin State: SAATS stopped
- End State: SAATS stopped
**)
runWithNewResults ATC_FDM_001_TC01
runWithNewResults ATC_FDM_001_TC02
runWithNewResults ATC_FDM_001_TC03
//****************SCRIPT END******************
```

Listing 25.2 contains the script used to run only one of the test cases, ATC_FDM_001_TC01. This test case can be run on its own or as part of the procedure of three from the previous script.

Listing 25.2   Script to Run One Test Case

```
(** ATC FDM 001 TC01
@author(s) Mike Baxter
@baseState S241710
@buildTarget S237114 (ENSURE)
```

```
@dependencies StartSAATS, getVMS_Time, LoginSAATS_With_CPE &
  LoginSAATS_Without_CPE
@platform Eggplant v4.2
@duration 7 minutes 44 seconds
@revisionHistory  Ver   Date       Tag    Reason
@revisionHistory  ------------------------------------------------------
@revisonHistory   0.1   09/10/09   MB     Initial Release for Review
@revisonHistory   0.2   18/03/10   MB     Added support for use of
  universal variables
Notes
- Each test case follows consecutively (i.e. no intermediate
  stop/restarts)
- Begin State: SAATS stopped
- End State: SAATS running (TC02 follows on directly from TC01)
**)


//****************TEST HARNESS START******************
//Time & Date supplied as defined within the manual test script
set SystemTime to "09:00:00"
set SystemDate to "17/3/2005"

set CPE_Included to False

//Eggplant default value is 0.7 seconds
set ScriptSpeed to 0.7 - delay (seconds) between test steps
setoption RemoteWorkInterval, Scriptspeed

//Eggplant default minimum image search time is 1.8 seconds
setoption ImageSearchTime, 1.8

//Lower pane of Run Window shows next step before it's executed
setoption ScriptTracing, on

//Highlights step being executed and keeps it centered within the top
//pane of the Run Window
setoption ScriptAnimation, on

//Permitted values: on, off, minimal & silent
setoption Scriptlogging, on
//****************TEST HARNESS END******************
```

```
//*****************TEST CASE 1_1 START*****************
log "Step 1"

connect "ssitad0" & TADNumber & "Planner2"
wait 3

click "bt_SWS_QAB_A_Flight_Plan"

if not imagefound("t_SWS_Flight_plan_-_New") then
          logerror "Could not match Step 1 image - Flight Plan - New"
end if
//*****************TEST CASE 1_1 END*****************

//*****************TEST CASE 1_2 START*****************
//NEXT STEP GOES HERE...
//*****************SCRIPT END*****************
```

Although basic eggPlant scripts can be created relatively quickly using the tool's interactive development capabilities, producing more complex test suites that are maintainable requires knowledge of software development best practices. Furthermore, as with most COTS products in this category, gaining a quick return on investment is unlikely, due to the initial setup costs and time necessary to create the supporting framework.

25.7 Lessons Learned

The following lessons were learned from the introduction of eggPlant at Prestwick to support regression testing of SAATS.

25.7.1 General Lessons

These are some lessons we learned along the way that are general to test automation rather than specific to our situation.

- It's useful to develop a tailored user guide and other necessary documentation during the project evaluation stage. This will cut down the time for implementation because preparing the documents in advance can help in the planning process. Also, it means the documents will be in hand during implementation and development, so they can be edited, which makes for better quality documents by the end of the project.

- Where practicable, scripts should be constructed in such a way as to make them self-documenting to avoid unnecessary duplication. TestPlant provides a free utility called eggDoc, which automatically documents and indexes your test cases and procedures in HTML format.
- For ease of maintenance, it is useful to ensure scripts are developed according to a style guide or template. They should also be developed in a way that makes them independent of TAD (e.g., using a configuration file, mapping common resources to their unique IP addresses).
- Automated script development and debugging can potentially consume considerable TAD time and ideally requires dedicated resources for optimum productivity.
- Before they are baselined, automated scripts should be run in slow time and witnessed by the customer (ATC/engineering) to ensure they are representative. Just like requirements, all automated scripts should be assigned an owner/custodian. This individual should be the person accountable for script maintenance.
- An automated script should incorporate a reference in its header to any equivalent manual script together with other potential dependencies.
- Where more than a small number of testers/developers will be involved in using a tool, it is useful to give early consideration to how the integrity of testware products will be maintained and archived (e.g., adopting a robust software configuration management check-in/check-out process).
- It is worth documenting COTS tool success criteria in parallel with your requirements and, where necessary, having a simple process in place to track productivity metrics during any proof-of-concept.
- If the tool is to be hosted on standard company-branded desktops, it is worth considering the reoccurring costs associated with having your IT provider wrap/package subsequent product updates and fixes. In NATS, we say the software has been wrapped when it has passed a series of tests designed to ensure it will not interfere with our existing suite of applications.
- SoS testing using platform-independent test execution tools has many other benefits that are not always obvious. For example, a relative novice could potentially learn the basics of using a system simply by observing it effectively test itself. This is possible because the script execution speed can be varied and even paused and then restarted again by the tool if required. This attribute is also useful, along with the functions of script animation and script tracing that allow you to visually follow script execution when debugging, so we recommend implementation of these in a programmatically switchable fashion.

> **Good Point**
>
> Look for different ways to use the automation, such as by slowing down the tests to form a tutorial for training purposes of how the system works.

25.7.2   Technical Lessons

During the production of automated scripts, the availability and adoption of a Text Image Generator (TIG) has the potential to improve productivity and maintainability. A TIG in this context is a software utility that helps to generate text dynamically for image-matching purposes based on a generic/reusable predefined style description.

During the development of scripts, it is important to remember to immediately close any open VNC connections as soon as they are not needed. Failing to do so can have a severe impact on execution performance because of the cumulative reduction in available LAN bandwidth.

Also learned during the project were the following:

- A common VNC problem was leaving CAPS lock on.
- The performance of VNC can be reduced by textured backgrounds commonly found on today's desktops. It is important when defining the base state for SoS testing to make sure solid background colors are preselected.
- When developing scripts interactively or debugging, a large screen area will help improve productivity because otherwise the user must keep switching or resizing windows.

> **Lesson**
>
> Technical problems will arise that will need to be solved. Although they may not be difficult, they still take time.

25.8   Conclusion

The adoption of tools such as eggPlant in NATS will probably continue to grow because ATC systems have a long life expectancy, so the payback period is substantial.

Another potential benefit associated with the use of VNC is that it may eventually result in the adoption of remote testing. Remote testing would allow testing to be done from other sites so problems can be diagnosed by a centralized expert team.

Other future developments include the following:

- Extending the use of parameterized scripts with data- and keyword-driven test techniques to increase test coverage combinations of environments and system commands.
- Extending use of the TIG to improve productivity.
- Extending use of the eggDoc utility to automatically generate more of the supporting documentation.

The use of the automated test tool eggPlant has been a success based on time savings. However, greater efficiency gains could have been achieved through the use of a dedicated test team rather than using pooled resources, because knowledge of how to maintain and develop new scripts inevitably reduces over time.

CHAPTER 26

AUTOMATING AUTOMOTIVE ELECTRONICS TESTING

Ross Timmerman
Joseph Stewart

Ross Timmerman and Joseph Stewart tell about the inhouse testing tools they developed over the years to test automotive electronics systems at Johnson Controls. In 2000, no commercial tools were available for this niche area, so the Johnson Controls team chose to develop their own tools, which was done initially by the test team and later by an offshore team. Both benefits and problems arise from writing your own tools, but the team dramatically increased the number of tests they were able to run. They also discovered ways to automate things they initially thought had to be done manually. In their second initiative, they built on the success of the earlier tools but provided more functionality, using off-the-shelf hardware modules with their own software to get the best results. This case study covers 5 years and is based in the United States. See Table 26.1.

26.1 Background for the Case Study

Johnson Controls is a global, diversified technology and industrial leader, serving customers in more than 150 countries. The company's 142,000 employees create quality products, services, and solutions to optimize energy and operational efficiencies of buildings; lead-acid automotive batteries and advanced batteries for hybrid and

Table 26.1 Case Study Characteristics

Classification	This Case Study
Application domain	Embedded software for automotive systems
Application size	4 K to 512 MB
Location	United States
Lifecycle	Phased waterfall
Number on the project	8 test engineers who did the automation
Number of testers	8 test engineers
Number of automators	8
Time span	5 years
Dates	2004–2009
Tool type(s)	Combination of commercial off-the-shelf hardware and inhouse software
Pilot study undertaken	No
ROI measured	No, but number of automated tests and test hours were counted
Successful?	Yes
Still breathing?	Yes

electric vehicles; and interior systems for automobiles. Johnson Controls' commitment to sustainability dates back to the company's roots in 1885, with the invention of the first electric room thermostat.

Johnson Controls Automotive Experience is a global leader in automotive seating, overhead systems, door and instrument panels, and interior electronics. The company supports all major automakers in the differentiation of their vehicles through products, technologies, and advanced manufacturing capabilities. Through its 200 plants worldwide, Johnson Controls supplies automakers with products ranging from single components to complete interiors. In total, the company's technology ends up in more than 30 million cars per year.

This case study comes from the electronics department at the Johnson Controls Holland, Michigan, technical center (part of the Automotive Experience business). It outlines the circumstances that led to the creation of the software test engineering functional group and the subsequent efficiency and performance gains made through test automation.

The electronics department designs embedded electronic modules for the automotive market throughout the world. The electronics modules are grouped into three categories: driver information products, connectivity products, and specialty products. Driver information products are items such as instrument clusters and information displays in the cabin of the vehicle. Connectivity products are modules that allow voice control of phones and other devices via a Bluetooth link. Specialty products are modules such as HomeLink, a device that allows drivers to communicate wirelessly to operate garage door openers, gate systems, home lighting, electronic compasses, and trip computers.

The memory size of the products ranges from 4 KB of ROM on the low end to 512 MB of Flash on the high end. The size, in lines of code (LOC), ranges from a few hundred LOC on the low end to approximately 500,000 LOC on the high end.

In 2000, all software testing was done by the individual software engineers writing the code. Later in the year, a small group was formed to independently test the software because the complexity and code size of the products was beginning to increase. At the time, there was no automation of tests, no defined process, and no systems in place to manage the testing.

In 2003, a software functional group under a single senior-level manager was formed.

Lesson

Improvements are often kicked off by an issue or need.

This group:

- Established software requirements engineering as a role.
- Deployed the RequisitePro requirements management tool.
- Developed a software quality management system using the Software Engineering Institute's Capability Maturity Model Integration (CMMI) framework.
- Created an independent software test engineering team responsible for testing the product according to requirements traced to test cases.

The creation of the software test engineering team led to significant improvement in the ability to deliver high-quality products to our customers.

26.2   Objectives for Automation Project

Although the Software Test Engineering group yielded positive results early on, it was quickly becoming evident that the method of testing products had to change. Projects were becoming more complex in scope, and manual tests could not support the increase in the number of tests required without a significant increase in workforce. Increasing the workforce was not an option, so the solution was automation. Introducing automation to test software would solve two increasing problems at the same time. It would allow for the same workforce to create and test more complex projects, and it would remove the human variable from the loop so tests could be performed in a more repeatable way.

26.3   Brief History of the Automation Project

26.3.1   Our First Tools

The first tools used to automate the tests in the software test engineering group were based on the type of communication that the product used to communicate with the vehicle. There were test tools for both controller area network (CAN) communication and J1850 (single wire, automotive specific) communication. These tools were created inhouse by the software test engineers. The tools that were needed were determined by necessity, and the necessity to send messages on a vehicle bus (communication network) was by far the greatest need. Prior to the creation of automated software test tools, the test engineer worked from Microsoft Word documents that specified messages to be sent using a manual tool that required each byte in the message to be entered manually, and then sent by a button press.

> **Good Point**
>
> If you develop your own tools, you can make them do what you want.

The CAN and J1850 test tools were similar in functionality. Each could send single and periodic messages and could check for expected messages sent from the product under test within a specified time limit. The initial goal of automation was to use the existing bus tools to automate testing the product's specified bus communication requirements. This was accomplished by writing software that would read text files with specific commands. Software testing was now testing whole features at a time using a script instead of message-by-message testing.

Now that there was a tool that could send communication messages to the product, the engineers thought about how this new capability could be used to test other aspects of the software. The software test engineering group realized they needed test hooks in the product software to determine the position of a stepper motor, or the status of an LED. To expand the amount that could be tested by these tools, further development of the tools was necessary. The software test team began to have a voice in the development of diagnostic requirements. To increase the range of automatable test cases, the test team also began creating diagnostics for the development team to embed in the product.

Good Point

Give the testers a say in the choice and design of embedded diagnostics within the software to aid test verification.

26.3.2 Limitations of the First Tool and Creation of the Next-Generation Tool

The shortcoming of this first generation of test tools was always that we would never be able to fully automate all of our tests because the testing was limited to bus communications only. Any input that was not a CAN or J1850 signal bus still had to be tested manually to verify proper voltage levels, timing, and so on. This was true with the exception of the voltage of the power supply. Late in the use of the CAN automated tester, the ability to change the voltage of a programmable power supply was added. All other inputs, such as buttons pushed by the user, resistance ladders for multiple position switches, open circuit, and short circuit tests, had to be done manually.

Tip

Look for things done manually that could be automated even if not everything can be.

In the 2005–2006 timeframe, the next-generation test automation tool was under development. The approach for creation of this tool was different than for the CAN and J1850 tools; this time it focused on non-bus inputs.

The expected functionality of the new tool was defined in a requirements document similar to that used for the product being tested. The development of the software to control our next-generation tool was contracted to an offshore development center. Contracting this work to the offshore development center kept the cost down, but visibility of the day-to-day progress required a lot of time in meetings. On-site support from the offshore development center was needed, which drove the cost higher, but eventually the tool came together for less cost than if the work had been done inhouse.

> **Good Point**
>
> Tool development at an offshore development center has advantages, but there may be hidden costs in terms of time needed in support.

The new test hardware was to be commercial off-the-shelf (COTS) modules that would be integrated into the whole test system. These modules include, but are not limited to, programmable power supplies, digital multimeters (DMMs), resistance cards, switch modules, and data acquisition cards. All these cards would be controlled by the tool software being developed by the offshore development center. The job of the software test engineers would remain what it was intended for them to be. Instead of creating the software test tools, as was done with the CAN and J1850 automated software tools, the creation of the test tool was done by the offshore development center. The software test engineers at Johnson Controls returned to writing test cases and testing products. The only difference was that the tool being used had changed. The next-generation tool would be known as GenBlue 2 (GB2).

GB2 addressed the limitations of the previous test tools discussed earlier. The test team now had the ability to change voltages, read DMMs, set resistances, and set open/short circuits all with the automated tool. This is where the test group is today, but the evolution is not going to stop here. In the past couple of years, Johnson Controls has started to create products that involve visual displays. This always requires visual verification of graphics, menu structures, and so on. The test group plans to develop automated visual inspection in the near future to address these new challenges.

26.4   Results of the Automation Project

With a staff of eight full-time software test engineers, the number of tests executed increased significantly from the beginning of the project in 2003 to the maturity of the project in 2006.

In 2007, using the new software test tool, it was not fully understood what test steps needed to be counted in the results page. The reason for a large number of tests counted that year was that with GB2, the report that was originally created counted all steps as either a pass or fail, even steps that were just to set up conditions for the intended verification. We needed the report to count only the steps involving a test that checked an output of the software. That error was fixed shortly into 2008. This is the reason for the big jump in 2007, then the decrease in 2008, and it explains why there is not much of an increase between 2008 and 2009: Some of this discrepancy made it into the 2008 numbers.

> **Good Point**
>
> Don't be afraid to change what you base your metrics on, but explain the apparent anomalies that result.

Figure 26.1 shows the number of tests executed by the automated test equipment, which ramped up significantly beginning in 2003. Figure 26.2 shows the number of hours of testing done by the test automation over the years 2004 to 2009.

26.5   Conclusion

Looking back on the progression of software testing in this organization, it is clear that the capabilities of the team at the beginning of this study would not support the complexity of the products produced and the level of testing supported today. The new test tool was born out of necessity as it became clear the old test tools had serious limitations. Despite having these new capabilities, the challenge for the software test team is still the ability to test increasingly complex products as accurately and quickly as possible. The difference now is that the test system created has the flexibility to evolve. Through off-the-shelf components and a dedicated team to update the automation software, the software test engineer is left to think like a test engineer and create the test cases.

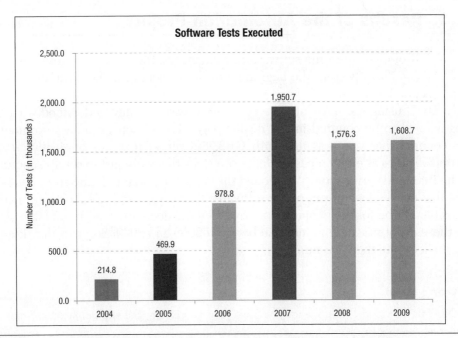

FIGURE 26.1   Software tests executed by the tools from 2004 through 2009

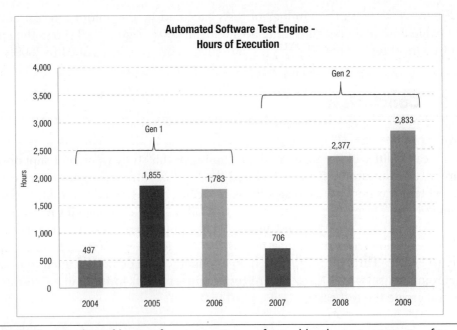

FIGURE 26.2   Number of hours of test execution performed by the test automation from 2004 to 2009

BHAGs, Change, and Test Transformation

Ed Allen
Brian Newman

Ed Allen and Brian Newman tell of their experience in automating the testing for a customer relationship management system. The problems they encountered ranged from technical issues such as environments, testware architecture/framework, and "script creep" to people issues, including management support, working with developers, and when to ignore a consultant. After several false starts, they were challenged by some "Big Hairy Audacious Goals" (BHAGs) and were given support to meet them. They achieved good benefits in the end and provide some intriguing metrics about the number of defects found by different ways of testing (automated, manual scripted, exploratory testing, and bug fixes). This story is based in the United States with a team of 28, including 25 from quality assurance and 3 from development. See Table 27.1.

27.1 Background for the Case Study

The authors of this chapter work at RightNow Technologies, a publicly traded company based in Bozeman, Montana, with offices worldwide. At the current writing, RightNow employs approximately 1,000 people. We develop a software product called RightNow CX, a customer relationship management (CRM) solution primarily

Table 27.1   Case Study Characteristics

Classification	This Case Study
Application domain	Desktop, web-based, mobile devices, social channels: voice, chat, email
Application size	5,000 KLOC tested with the automation
Location	United States
Lifecycle	Traditional
Number on the project	QA = 25; Development = 3
Number of testers from QA	20 (18 of whom were also automators)
Number of automators from QA	5 dedicated to automation
Time span	1 year
Dates	2009
Tool type(s)	Commercial/inhouse
Pilot study undertaken	No
ROI measured	No, but benefits measured: 58% regression test acceleration, from 12 weeks to 5
Successful?	Yes
Still breathing?	Yes

found in large contact centers. The software resides on the customer service agent desktop along with voice integration, social communities, and marketing and sales automation. Another key component of RightNow CX is a highly customizable web framework that allows our customers to interact with their customers via a web portal typically found in the support pages of a company's website. Our software is delivered using a SaaS, or software as a service, model in which we host the software in our private cloud. The scope of this automation project was to automate only the agent desktop, marketing, sales, and the web experience tests.

This automation project was conducted during the entire year of 2009 and was concerned only with automating the in-scope UI tests using the commercial UI automation tool TestPartner.

We look at how the first attempt at creating an automation framework failed and how we rebuilt the framework using a dramatically different approach. We also look at our plans for the future.

Of course, there is much more to the success of test automation than the choice of tools or the framework design. Other major factors that contributed to the success of our automation project were buy-in from executive management, finding the "why" for the developers, and empowering the quality assurance (QA) team to succeed.

In this chapter, we walk through each of these items and give you some insight into what we did to ultimately succeed in our test automation effort.

27.2 Buy-In

27.2.1 The Executives

At the beginning of 2009, our executive management adopted the automation of QA regression tests as one of the top three corporate initiatives for the year. Several factors played into this decision, the key among them being quality issues reported by customers and the cost of supporting, diagnosing, recoding, retesting, and issuing patches outside the normal release cycle.

As executives questioned why these issues were occurring and what could be done to correct them, one answer was that QA spent most of our time during each release cycle—a corporate mandate is that we release a new version of our product every quarter, and we absolutely do not miss release dates—executing the same set of regression tests every quarter. In other words, we had no time to approach the software testing differently even though the software was changing every quarter. We were running right into Beizer's pesticide paradox: "Every method you use to prevent or find bugs leaves a residue of subtler bugs against which those methods are ineffectual."[1]

We also had a mandate to run the regression tests each release. One possible solution to this problem of how to approach testing differently while continuing to run the same tests in the same timeframe would have been to add people to the QA team, but budget constraints made this impossible. However, in the short term there

---

1. Boris Beizer, *Software Testing Techniques*, 2nd ed. (New York: Van Nostrand Reinhold, 1990).

was an opportunity to invest significant funds in this project. With that, we were given a year to engage in a project to highly automate the regression testing, thus freeing up existing testers for other types of high-value-added testing outside our traditional regression test realm, such as exploratory testing, performance testing, and load testing.

As we explained this to the executive team, they saw the vision of what we wanted to do and threw their backing fully behind it.

Good Point

A problem can often be a catalyst for change, provided that the change is seen to address the problem.

27.2.2   The Developer "Why"

With the backing at the highest level within the company, we next moved to get development support for our efforts. At the beginning of this project, we required 10 weeks to execute the full suite of manual regression tests and an additional 2 weeks to execute and maintain the automated regression tests, for a total of 12 weeks for regression testing. Given this, we talked to the developers about how we could automate regression testing so we could reduce our manual regression time from 10 weeks to 5 weeks and run a full automated regression test every 24 hours. More frequent testing of their code meant we could give more frequent feedback on any issues in the core of the product. We also explained how we would then be able to perform additional testing and provide even more helpful feedback.

Good Point

Find a way to give the developers something they want if you want them to write code in a way that helps you.

Development bought in and even provided several developers who were dedicated to our effort for nearly the full duration of our project. Having this help was huge. With the developers on board, they were able to quickly make code changes to improve the testability of their code, which in our case meant having easily recognizable objects. Beyond this assistance, they also became champions of our efforts throughout development, working with other developers to ensure testable code.

27.2.3 Empowering QA

27.2.3.1 BHAGs

We already had some automation in place before this project. The role of test automation was assigned to a team under a different manager from the manual test team. This created some tension between the teams because priorities as well as opinions on what should be automated and when often differed. Those who owned the tests felt they had little say in how or when the tests were automated, and those who owned the automation felt they had no say in what tests should be created or how they should be written. Little differences of interpretation became major sore spots. Also, the automation was created in a vacuum with each automator working independently without a managed framework in place. This often resulted in fragile scripts that required a long lead time for maintenance during each release.

As mentioned in our discussions of development, the QA team was challenged with some specific goals that came to be called Big Hairy Audacious Goals (BHAGs). These goals stated that within the 1-year timeframe of this project, we would, via automation, reduce the amount of time for the manual regression run from 10 weeks to 5 weeks and, even with this increase in automation, run the automated regression in less than 24 hours.

These goals generated a lot of excitement and provided tremendous motivation for the team. They also gave the team something specific and measurable to work toward. We could now track and show progress toward reaching the goals.

> **Good Point**
>
> A clear measurable goal is the best starting point for automation.

27.2.3.2 Realigning Roles

One of the first things we realized was that even with the backing of the executive team and of development, we couldn't accomplish this project with the current small team of automators. So we entirely did away with the distinction between a tester and an automator. Everyone was now a tester who used automation as one tool for accomplishing their testing. We did maintain a smaller group of dedicated automation developers. To make this merger of roles successful required training. We conducted the training via a lot of "on-the-ground" mentoring as well as formal in-class training. The formal training was conducted by a consultant brought in from the vendor of the tool we were using for the automation. This consultant also stayed with us for several months beyond the training for continual assistance and mentoring. Additionally, we hired an outsourcing firm to conduct the manual regression testing while our testers worked almost exclusively on this project.

Though there was resistance from a couple of testers who had no interest in writing code, there were several positive outcomes of the realignment of roles. The key one was that we now had the people power to make this project work. But even more exciting was that it raised the technical skills across QA. This had the unintended but incredibly positive consequence of making better testers—testers who were subject matter experts previously were also now knowledgeable in writing code; they understood coding principles. This allowed for better communication with developers, better bug reports, and more thorough analysis of issues found during testing.

We allowed those testers who resisted to continue working as they were. Over time, their resistance lessened, and they eventually came to accept the change. Of course, it was only possible to take this laissez-faire approach because the resistance was limited to a small minority.

27.2.3.3 *Test Automation Leadership Team*

Early in the project, we established a Test Automation Leadership Team composed of the QA managers, the vice president over QA, a project manager, the tool vendor consultant, the developers on loan to QA for this project, and several testers. Each person on this team had equal voice in the team, and there was no hierarchy in meetings. The team was established as a temporary team whose mission was to establish milestones, monitor progress, coordinate work, make course corrections, and resolve technical issues. This team also ensured information flowed both up and down within the QA organization.

27.2.3.4 *Constant Improvement*

The QA team met at least every other week to discuss what was working and what was not specifically as it pertained to the automation project. This meeting was also used for continual training and as a kind of show-and-tell to highlight good scripts and to talk about what was new. This proved to be an effective measure, because everyone had a say in the process and many good ideas were implemented that may not have been identified otherwise. This also gave everyone on the team a sense of ownership of the project.

Good Point

Keep looking for ways to improve the automation, and solicit ideas from everyone. Keep the communication flowing!

27.3   The Story of Building the Automation Framework

27.3.1   Creating Test Points

It may be helpful to back up a bit from the framework and explain how we create tests. Each company or testing organization seems to have a slightly different definition of what constitutes a test, or a test case, or a test point: stories, business cases, scenarios, use cases, to name a few. As Lloyd Roden illustrated in his *Weakest Link Lightning Keynote* at STAR WEST 2010, four testers, when asked how many test cases they had completed in the past hour, gave four very different results ranging from 0 to 300. This dramatic difference in responses was attributed to the differences in definitions of a test case.

In our organization, we refer to one specific test and its single expected result as a test point. These test points were created from a top-down approach, where first we divided our entire application suite into modules. We then subdivided the modules into their different editors and page sets; pulled out common areas for many-to-one testability; and separated smart client, thin client, end-user pages, utilities, APIs, and so forth, until we had a list of components that represented logical compartments of our product suite.

> **Good Point**
>
> Structure your tests for ease of automation and ease of maintenance.

From there, we decomposed each component into subcomponents and kept going until we had every area broken down into groups of the simplest objects to test in the application. We then created individual test points that performed various combinations of positive and, where applicable, negative actions against those objects. We now had a solid foundation for our manual regression testing.

Two major payoffs resulted from this approach:

- When new features were introduced into the product, it was easy to find where test points should be added, because the test point tree (comparable to your directory structure on your computer) was the roadmap to the feature's test point location.
- The test points were already logically grouped, making strategizing for creating test scenarios (written instructions for automating a group of test points) much simpler.

27.3.2 The Beginning

During the years leading up to this project, we used several commercial automation tools, and we learned three key lessons:

- *Record and playback did not work:* The scripts created using this approach inevitably required a high degree of maintenance and constant rework.
- *Separating the QA team into testers and automators was often fraught with difficulty:* The tests written by the testers would not suit the purposes of those doing the automating, and vice versa; there was often conflict between what a tester believed should be automated and what an automator believed should be automated. Also, once a test was automated, who owned that test—the tester or the automator?
- *Even after you have automated a test, the work is not done:* There is maintenance involved in ensuring the script continues to run, in verifying script failures, and in updating the script for new versions of the software.

27.3.3 The Consultant

With the QA team motivated, the budget secured, the goals set, the process defined, and the training complete, we were ready to really get moving on this project.

Note that, prior to this project, we didn't have the concept of an automation framework. Each script was essentially created as its own standalone entity. There was very little modularization within the scripts and none among the scripts. The scripts were kept on the scripter's local computer and run when needed. We knew we wanted and needed some kind of highly modularized, centralized, and lower-maintenance framework that would really drive success. But we really weren't sure what this would look like. Enter the consultant.

As previously mentioned, we had brought in a consultant for this project. Knowing we wanted to create a robust and sustainable framework through which we could add automation scripts, the consultant came up with a framework that essentially relied on record and playback. The idea was to use record and playback to identify each of the objects under test and then create a repository of object maps we could call from each script. Based on our previous experiences with record and playback, we were not at all convinced this would work. Needless to say, we were disappointed.

27.3.4 Redoing the Framework

We basically ignored the consultant from that point on. We rethought everything and asked the question, *If we were to start completely from scratch, how would we do this?* That is when the project really took off.

> **Tip**
> If a consultant gives you bad advice, ignore him!

The first thing we did was move up a layer of abstraction with our automation. Rather than looking at the individual tests and starting to script at that level or finding ways to make the existing scripts "work better," we moved up to the component level. By component I mean individual editors or widgets on a screen (e.g., the calendar widget could be a common component throughout the application). At that level of abstraction, we gained a new perspective. The proposal was made that we should be able to write modules to identify, attach to, and perform basic operations against each component of the software. The individual scripts could then call those modules. Though there was a tremendous amount of work involved in this approach, the idea sounded much better than the consultant's proposal, so we dug in and made it happen.

27.4   Description of our Automation Framework

27.4.1   Modules in Our Framework

Each editor, dialog, common object, and so on, receives its own module. Functions are created within each module to interact with each object in that module. Listing 27.1 shows an example of a module for the `IncidentEditor` where we set the value of some field in that editor (both the value and the field are variables passed to the module).

Listing 27.1   Example Module for the IncidentEditor

```
' Sub: SetField
'
'     Sets the specified field to the provided value
'
' Parameters:
'
'     eField - The field to set
'     sValue - The value to assign to the field
'
Public Sub SetField(ByVal eField As IncidentEditorField, ByVal sValue As
```

```
String, Optional ByVal bAttachToUnderLyingObject As Boolean = True)

    Select Case eField:
        Case ieIncContact:   'The Contact Field is a look up field
                             'so it requires special steps to set
                             'it
                  .
                  .
                  .
        case Else:
              ClientScriptUtils.SetField
                    GetFieldAttachName(eField), sValue,
                    GetFieldType(eField),
                    GetFieldFriendlyName(eField)
    End Select

End Sub
```

The script would then call the `SetField` module and pass in the desired string value, as shown in Listing 27.2.

Listing 27.2   Example Module for the IncidentEditor

```
'Incident

'Open a new Incident
IncidentUtils.CreateNewIncident
IncidentEditor.WaitForReady

'Fill in required fields for Incident
IncidentEditor.SetField ieIncSubject, "Add Org/Contact Incident"

IncidentEditor.ValidateFieldValue ieIncSubject, "Add Org/Contact
Incident"
```

Using this approach, we can quickly write scripts for any field on any editor or dialog to cover a variety of checks, such as boundary conditions, special characters, alpha versus numeric, whether or not a field is required, and so on.

One of the big obstacles we ran into was trying to reduce and eliminate timing issues within our automation tool. Such issues caused a large number of scripts to fail unnecessarily due to timing problems not with the application under test but with the automation tool itself. To overcome this, we created a module referenced in the previous script called `WaitForReady`.

> **Lesson**
>
> Timing and synchronization problems can occur with the testing tools as well as with the application you are testing.

Creating a subroutine to wait for controls is one of the biggest things that improved script reliability because it reduces or eliminates timing issues with the automation tool. To ensure we are not masking bugs in the product, we conduct separate tests specifically looking for timing errors.

This modularized approach dramatically reduced our maintenance overhead from previous approaches we had taken to automation. With this approach, we have one centralized place to make necessary changes. Because changes are at the module or function level, the scripts never need to know there is a change and can run without interruption.

27.4.2 Considerations for Modules

27.4.2.1 Module Conventions

Module and function naming conventions are used that map to the product modules, editors, dialogs, utilities, and so forth, making it easy for testers to write because they just need to know the name of the editor or dialog they are working in and the applicable modules are made available. For example, Figure 27.1 shows where, after you type IncidentEditor, you get a list of the available modules that can be used in that editor.

> **Tip**
>
> A good user interface to the automation both helps and restricts the tester by showing what keywords are available.

27.4.2.2 New Modules

Each time a new dialog, component, or other element is introduced to the product through our new features process, a new module is created. The automation

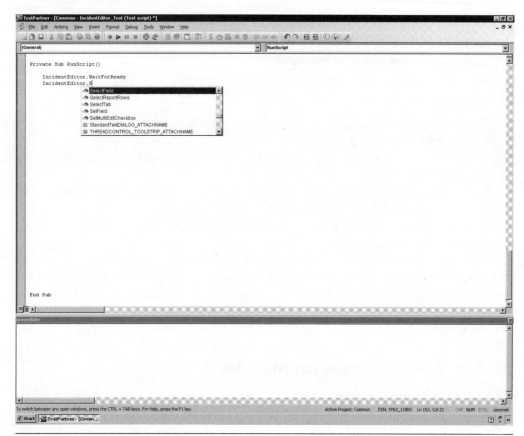

FIGURE 27.1   Incident editor example

developer builds the module, its functions, and all of the interacting attributes by
identifying every object in the new feature that it can be interacted with and every
way the objects can be manipulated. Once the automation developer feels the
module is complete, it is checked into the framework and made available to the
scripting team.

27.4.2.3   Issues with Modules

When using a module, if a scripter finds a missing or improperly working function, an
incident is created and assigned to the appropriate person. This incident-submission

process uses the same product we already use to submit defects to our product development team, which is also the same product we sell—we use our own product to create, track, assign, escalate, and perform analytics on the defects written against our own product (i.e., we eat our own dog food).

27.4.3 Script Execution

With over 1,300 scripts that use nine different starting data sets, and with the scripts being able to change configuration settings on the test site, resetting the site after each script run is vital. For a brief moment in planning, we considered returning configuration settings back to their original state and deleting any data that was changed after each script run, but that would quickly turn into a problem the first time a script failed to run all the way through, leaving the site in an unknown state and the next script starting from where the previous script died. To avoid this state, we moved the cleanup to the beginning of each script so that each script cleans up whatever mess is left behind by the script before it.

27.4.4 Failure Capturing Method

When a check fails in a script, the script itself and the results of the checks are printed out to a Word document. At the point of failure, a screenshot is captured and placed in the document to show where the failure occurred. This makes troubleshooting much easier and helps minimize the cost of failure analysis.

> **Good Point**
>
> Give enough information (automatically) to make it easy and quick to find out what went wrong when an automated test fails. This will minimize failure analysis time.

27.5 The Test Environment

Developing a sound automation framework was one of the keys to our success, but this framework didn't succeed without a sound test platform. What really clinched the success of our automation project was the creation of a test environment that was automated, robust, predictable, and synchronized with the automation framework.

> **Good Point**
>
> Don't neglect the test environment, and automate as much as possible in its setup.

In our development process, a new product build is compiled every evening that includes all of the new or updated code that was checked in that day. Each night, an automated process is kicked off that automatically compiles and builds the latest code base. From this, test sites are then automatically created for both the automation run that evening and for the manual testing the next day. Once the sites are ready for the automated run, the automated regression begins running the automation test scripts.

27.5.1   Multiple LANs

In the beginning, we had a single LAN where all of these sites resided. Today we have separate LANs for test automation, manual testing, and load testing, and another for the developers, all of which reside in our cloud. This prevents events such as load testing from impacting the productivity of the testing team, and the automation runs are not impacted by any environment issues that can be introduced by an unfortunate database query, or the sudden creation of several sites, or clones of massive sites.

27.5.2   Virtual Machines

As mentioned, our prior automation approach was to run scripts on local machines as needed. We drastically rethought that approach and now use 50 virtual machines (VMs) to run the scripts. This is accomplished overnight while everyone is sleeping. We began by using QADirector, a commercial tool that allowed us to schedule scripts, assign them to a pool of machines, and automatically farm them out as a VM became available. In this way, we can run the scripts overnight without intervention and verify failures in the morning. Since starting this project, we have built our own tool to replace QADirector.

We have realized many benefits from this approach, including the following:

- A pool of VMs is easier to maintain and control. We can quickly and easily make needed changes to all machines at once. We also can specifically control the environment to introduce or leave out variables as we deem necessary.
- We can quickly introduce more machines to the virtual environment as the number of scripts increases.

27.6 Metrics

27.6.1 Benefits of Automation

Although we haven't measured ROI by comparing to automation costs, we have measured the efficiency gain through automation.

27.6.1.1 Previous to This Project

The manual regression tests took 10 weeks, or 50 days, to run; the previous automation took 2 weeks, or 10 days, for a total of 12 weeks, or 60 days.

27.6.1.2 After This Project

The manual regression tests took 5 weeks, or 25 days, to run; the automation takes less than 1 day and is run concurrently and repeatedly with manual testing for a total of 25 days. The efficiency gained is calculated as

$$(60 - 25) \div 60 = 58\% \text{ regression test acceleration.}$$

This clearly met our BHAG of reducing manual regression testing from 10 weeks to 5 weeks and to run the automated regression in less than 24 hours. There were two key reasons we were able to reduce the amount of time it takes to run our manual regression tests:

1. Using the new automation framework meant scripts could be created in less time, so more tests could be automated. We took full advantage of that efficiency. Concurrently with this project, additional tests were being automated, resulting in a dramatic decrease in the amount of time required to run the remaining manual regression tests. For example, at the beginning of this project, we had approximately 400 automation scripts. By the end of this project, there were over 800, thus cutting our manual regression runtime by nearly half.
2. Because the scripts are now run overnight, those testers who formerly were devoted only to running, troubleshooting, and maintaining scripts are now free to run manual tests. This further reduces the time required to complete a full manual regression run.

27.6.1.3 *Daily Regression Run*

What really makes us smile is that what took 12 weeks of testing for 20-plus testers now takes 5 weeks, and we have turned the automated regression into an overnight operation. This means that we can now run full automated regression every night on each day's new build as we near the end of the release cycle. Whereas before, we would go into production with test points that were manually tested 10, 20, or even 30 builds ago, we now can execute our entire automated test suite on the build that will go into production.

27.6.2 Effect on Customer-Found Defects

We have been told it is a fool's game to measure quality. But one way we fools attempt to do this is to simply count the number of customer-submitted defects. Is the number going up or down? If down, then maybe we have an indication that product quality is improving. Of course, there are any number of caveats to measuring this, but we believe it can be one useful metric. Overall, what we are finding is a significant drop in customer-submitted defects in the releases after this project completed even with more features and more customers. This is shown in Figure 27.2.

Another way to look at this is to compare the number of defects found by customers with the number found by testing. This is shown in Figure 27.3. One thing to note is that over time this will decrease as more customers adopt the newer releases and as they have more time on those releases, but the bottom line is that we are seeing a definite trend toward increased efficiency.

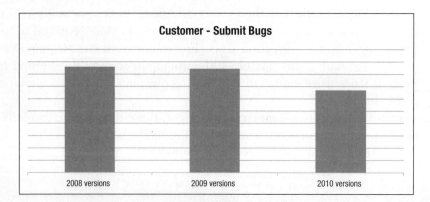

FIGURE 27.2   Number of customer-submitted bugs

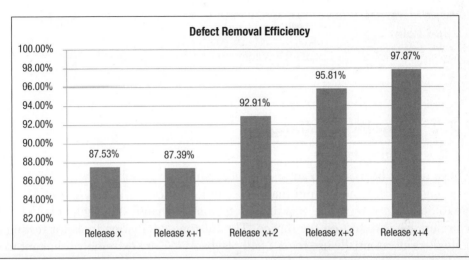

FIGURE 27.3 Defect detection percentage (DDP) (also known as defect removal efficiency)

27.7 Conclusion

27.7.1 Lessons Learned

We have found that one of the easiest mistakes to make when writing a scenario for an automation script is to fall prey to what I call "script creep."

Script creep begins when you find yourself armed with easy-to-use modules and functions and begin thinking, "While I'm validating the configuration settings of this functionality, why don't I just go to the user interface and validate the object by manipulating it with data; and while I'm inputting data, why not do a little analytics testing by running a few reports and knocking those tests out, too?" This becomes a nightmare to troubleshoot, especially if something at the beginning of the script is the cause of the failure at the end of the script.

The lesson we learned was to keep the scripts small. Focus on one area of your product at a time. Strategize your major areas of testing first. Then write your test scenarios based on your currently existing manual test points. Using the scenario, automate a small group of test points that are tightly related, keeping the script short. The great thing about this method is you have lots of little celebrations along the way as you knock out test after test.

The most important thing about keeping scripts small is that they are easy to maintain, keeping maintenance costs low and automation success high.

Good Point

Beware of script creep. Keep each automation module simple and focused.

27.7.2 Ongoing Challenges

27.7.2.1 Mobile Devices

We have not yet been able to automate successfully on a mobile device. We considered using emulators and found that they had limitations as a testing tool. We continue to find bugs using the actual devices that aren't manifest using an emulator. So our preference is to test on the device. The existing automation tools for testing on mobile devices essentially use record and playback. We are extremely reluctant to go with this approach even for mobile testing.

27.7.2.2 Automated versus Manual Testing

We continue to push the approach that our scripted tests should largely (though not entirely) be automated and our manual testing should largely (though not entirely) be exploratory. However, we find that some testers are reluctant to let go of their scripted tests and allow the machines to run them. The more we use exploratory test approaches, the more comfortable these testers become with that approach, but it takes patience. Also, although we are finding that where exploratory tests work very well in most areas of the product, it may be wiser to continue with a more scripted approach in another area.

One example where a more scripted approach fits well is our set of tests for calculating user sessions. Our company invoices customers based on their number of end-user sessions. Needless to say, some very precise requirements are in place to calculate a session and to ensure we get our invoicing correct. We have to ensure these requirements are met with each release and that our software correctly counts (or doesn't count) a user session. This is not as straightforward as it might seem. In this case, it is very important we follow the scripts. Of course, even within this tightly scripted feature there is flexibility beyond the requirements where exploratory testing can work well, particularly as we ask questions not directly answered by the requirements.

Exploratory testing has worked especially well for us with new features. In many cases, we may not have a strong set of requirements and minimal design documentation (or any at all, for that matter). Exploratory testing has proven to be very useful in that context where we have a lot of questions to ask of the software under test. We also have found good success employing exploratory testing when testing across features to understand how one feature interacts with another, seemingly unrelated, feature.

27.7.3 What's Next

The really cool thing is that we can actually ask, What's next? For so many years, we were stuck in a rut and couldn't see a way out. Now we really feel transformed as a team and can tackle that next project. Here are some of the things we are currently working on:

- Inhouse development and investigation into open source tools to replace our commercial UI automation tool for which MicroFocus is ending support in the next year.
- Automated defect logging, including video capture and automated server-side logging/tracing of errors.
- Gathering more metrics on what bugs the automation scripts are finding and why scripts are failing.
- Automated exploratory testing, an approach introduced to one of the authors while he attended the CAST conference in 2010. We have been thinking of ways this could be useful for us. One idea—still very much in its infancy—is to create automated scripts that randomly or semirandomly "discover" two or more objects in an editor and then use combinatorial testing to explore the interactions between those objects.
- Manual testing—the whole point of this automation project was to increase the time we had available for additional approaches to manual testing. Our new mantra is, "The scripted tests are largely automated and the manual testing is largely exploratory." Table 27.2 shows how bugs have been found over our last three releases. Note the significant percentage of defects found via exploratory test versus other approaches.

Table 27.2 Percentage of Bugs Found by Different Approaches

Automation Defects	Manual Scripted Defects	Exploratory Test Defects	Fix Verification Defects
9.3%	24.0%	58.2%	8.4%

Note that the automation defects are found via running the automated regression suite repeatedly during the period of the release and are not all found during a single run. The manual defects are all found during the 5-week (25-day) period of manual regression testing. The exploratory defects are found in the new time gained by this project (5 weeks saved from the previous manual regression test effort). The fix verification defects are found at any point throughout the release while we verify fixes concurrently with the regression and exploratory testing. We also track defect severity and have so far found the percentages are roughly the same, with the automation and manual script defects being 2 to 3 percentage points higher and exploratory defects being 3 to 4 percentage points lower for high/medium severity defects.

Perhaps we are on to something good here. It is exciting!

CHAPTER 28

EXPLORATORY TEST AUTOMATION: AN EXAMPLE AHEAD OF ITS TIME

Harry Robinson
Ann Gustafson Robinson

Harry Robinson and Ann Gustafson Robinson describe Harry's experiences in doing what seems on the surface like an oxymoron. How can testing be both exploratory and automated? There are a number of requirements to make it possible, but when it can be done, it provides a way to explore test input spaces that are far too large to be tested in any other way. This chapter takes us step by step through Harry's journey of implementing what has now become known as model-based testing. The effort was far more successful than anyone thought possible at the time, which had an unexpected side effect on Harry's career! Although this story takes place rather a long time ago, the techniques described are now "coming into their own" because better tool support makes them applicable to more systems in a wider context. (Note: Although this chapter has two authors, it is told from Harry's viewpoint for easier reading.) This story comes from the United States. See Table 28.1.

28.1 Background for the Case Study

After completing my electrical engineering degree, I spent about 10 years working for AT&T Bell Laboratories. In the mid-1990s, Bell Labs was the research and development arm of the AT&T phone system and was the preeminent site worldwide for the development and testing of communications software.

Table 28.1   Case Study Characteristics

Classification	This Case Study
Application domain	Problem reporting for telephone systems
Application size	1,100 function points
Location	United States
Lifecycle	Waterfall
Number on the project	30 on Actiview, 4 on Trouble Manager project (developer, tester, specification writer, and project manager)
Number of testers	1
Number of automators	1
Time span	1.5 years
Dates	Mid-1990s
Tool type(s)	Inhouse
Pilot study undertaken	No
ROI measured	No
Successful?	Yes
Still breathing?	No

I started at Bell Labs as a developer and later specialized in supporting the X.25 communications protocol that was the basis for many data networks in the Bell system. While testing fixes to an X.25 implementation, I became interested in verification problems and moved into a testing role. In Bell Labs at the time, there was no strong distinction between developer and tester, so migrations between the disciplines were common.

I had no formal training in software testing, so I spent several months reading books and papers on the subject. Given my background in engineering, I was surprised that much of the writing about software testing treated it as a clerical activity concerned with step-by-step instructions rather than an engineering problem about how to find software defects effectively.

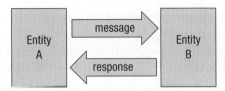

FIGURE 28.1   One system communicating with another

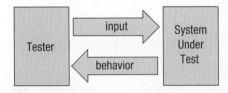

FIGURE 28.2   One system testing another

I also realized that software testing had underlying similarities to the communications systems I had been working with for several years:

- In a communications system, entity A sends a message to entity B; entity B reacts by altering its internal state and/or sending a response back to entity A, as shown in Figure 28.1.
- In software testing, a human tester sends an input to the system under test (SUT); the SUT reacts by altering its internal state and/or exhibiting a behavior that can be evaluated by the tester, as shown in Figure 28.2.

My background in communications and my readings in software testing convinced me that it would be possible to write a test program that could interact with the SUT the way a human tester did, providing inputs and evaluating the system's responses. In early 1994, I was assigned to test the Trouble Manager module of a project called Actiview. Actiview was a version 1 product staffed by a small, high-caliber, fast-moving team. It seemed like a great opportunity to try out ideas for improving testing.

28.2   What's a Trouble Manager?

Trouble management tools coordinate repair workflow within an organization. For instance, bug databases are a type of trouble manager, tracking the progress of a defect from the moment it is opened to the time it is finally resolved. In the case of

Actiview, the Trouble Manager coordinated the diagnosis and repair of malfunctioning equipment in the phone network.

When customers have a problem with their phone line, they contact the repair service bureau to report the issue. The workflow of a typical phone service repair goes as follows:

1. Create a trouble ticket to track the problem.
2. Run automatic electrical tests on the phone line.
3. Diagnose the problem.
4. Fix the problem.
5. Notify the customer that the problem is fixed.
6. Close out the ticket.

In the early days of the telephone system, a trouble ticket was a physical piece of paper that was passed around the repair bureau and updated as work on the ticket progressed. Once computers became widely available, tickets were stored as entries in a central database, and workers updated the ticket information by running transactions such as `CreateTicket` and `AnalyzeTicket` against the database engine.

To execute a transaction, a technician in the repair bureau filled out a standard form about the problem and sent the form to the Trouble Manager as a tab-separated list of fields and field values describing the problem. For instance, if customer Elisha Gray reported a problem with his phone line (206-555-1234), the `CreateTicket` transaction buffer would contain the following list of tab-separated field names and values:

```
TransactionName<TAB>CreateTicket
TelephoneNumber<TAB>206-555-1234
CustomerName<TAB>Elisha Gray
```

(Note that, for sake of clarity, this example is a very small subset of the 58 fields in `CreateTicket`.)

Some fields, such as `TelephoneNumber`, are required for the `CreateTicket` transaction to succeed. Other fields, such as `CustomerName`, are optional—nice to have, but not necessary.

It turns out to be useful to construct a table of the fields and whether they are required (see Table 28.2).

If the `CreateTicket` transaction contains all required fields, the transaction succeeds. Trouble Manager saves the data to the database, assigns a unique `TicketID`, and begins tracking the ticket. If, however, a required field is missing from the `CreateTicket` buffer, Trouble Manager fails the transaction and returns a response indicating which field is at fault.

Table 28.2 Required Fields for `CreateTicket`

Field Name	Is Field Required?
TelephoneNumber	Yes
CustomerName	No

28.3 Testing a Trouble Manager Transaction

Testing the individual transactions was simple in theory. A UNIX utility called ud (for utility driver) took an ASCII file as input, submitted the file to the Trouble Manager, and returned the Trouble Manager's response.

28.3.1 Testing That a `CreateTicket` Transaction Succeeds When All Required Fields Are Present

A tester sends a valid `CreateTicket` buffer to Trouble Manager:

```
TransactionName<TAB>CreateTicket
TelephoneNumber<TAB>206-555-1234
CustomerName<TAB>Elisha Gray
```

Because all required fields are present, Trouble Manager returns a `Transaction Succeeded` message and assigns a `TicketID`:

```
TransactionName<TAB>CreateTicket
TransactionResult<TAB>Transaction Succeeded
TicketID<TAB>19203
```

28.3.2 Testing That a `CreateTicket` Transaction Fails When a Required Field Is Missing

A tester sends Trouble Manager a `CreateTicket` buffer where a required field is missing (or commented out by a prepended #):

```
TransactionName<TAB>CreateTicket
#TelephoneNumber
CustomerName<TAB>Elisha Gray
```

Since the required field `TelephoneNumber` is missing, Trouble Manager returns a `Transaction Failed` message specifying the problem:

```
TransactionName<TAB>CreateTicket
TransactionResult<TAB>Transaction Failed
Error<TAB>Missing Required Field: TelephoneNumber
```

There were a dozen required fields in the `CreateTicket` transaction, so constructing test buffers by hand worked well enough to test basic Trouble Manager functions, but handcrafted tests did not scale well to testing the wider range of behavior, such as multiple missing fields. The number of tests needed would quickly overwhelm a tester's ability to construct test buffers by hand.

The traditional automated test approach involved a lot of work and didn't solve the essential problem of how to find lots of defects in the product. My inner engineer rebelled against that inefficiency. I looked into how I could generate and evaluate transactions programmatically.

Good Point

Always be on the lookout for ways to make testing more efficient.

28.4 Constructing Test Cases Programmatically

I designed a simple way to construct a transaction buffer and populate it with known errors. The basic idea was as follows:

1. For each field in a transaction:
   a.   Decide if the field is to be present or missing.
   b.   If present, write the field name and value to the buffer.
   c.   If missing, comment out the field name in the buffer.
   d.   If the missing field is required, log that fact to a temporary file.
2. Submit the constructed transaction buffer to Trouble Manager.
3. Use the temporary file contents to determine if the transaction is expected to succeed or fail.

As an example, suppose we want to construct a `CreateTicket` buffer where the telephone number is missing and the customer name is present.

The test program would do the following:

1. Write `#TelephoneNumber` to the buffer file.
2. `TelephoneNumber` is a required field, so write "Missing Required Field: TelephoneNumber" to the temporary file.
3. Write `CustomerName<TAB>Elisha Gray` to the buffer file.

The completed transaction buffer looks like this:

```
TransactionName<TAB>CreateTicket
#TelephoneNumber
CustomerName<TAB>Elisha Gray
```

The temporary file indicates that the transaction buffer contains an error and should fail with the message:

```
Missing Required Field: TelephoneNumber
```

So the expected response from Trouble Manager is

```
TransactionName<TAB>CreateTicket
TransactionResult<TAB>Transaction Failed
Error<TAB> Missing Required Field: TelephoneNumber
```

28.5   New Ways to Think about Automated Tests

Constructing input buffers in this way made the test automation very flexible:

- The error messages saved in the temporary file provided a handy test oracle for predicting the transaction's success or failure. Test automation was not shackled to comparisons with previous test results and could move beyond simple regression testing.
- Trouble ticket information in the database could be checked against the contents of the successful transaction buffer. Even when a value could not be

predicted, as with timestamps assigned by Trouble Manager, it was possible to check that the timestamp value was reasonably close to the time the transaction had run.

- Test automation became an active tool for exploring Trouble Manager's behaviors. For instance, when Trouble Manager appeared to have difficulty processing long strings, I modified the buffer constructor to generate mostly long string values. When character encoding caused problems, I inserted random control characters into the field values.

- Test design became an active concern. For instance, what was a good way to test for multiple errors in a single buffer? Randomly inserting errors seemed haphazard. But exhaustive testing was out of the question; there were literally trillions of ways to combine errors in the 58 fields of the `CreateTicket` transaction alone. Fortunately, I ran across two early pairwise combination tools called OATS (Orthogonal Array Testing Strategy) and CATS (Constrained Array Test System) that reduced the number of needed tests from a trillion to a paltry 243.

- The ease and flexibility of generating tests made it possible to run dynamic test automation almost as soon as the developer's hands left the keyboard. This fact had a far-ranging impact on how the developer and I worked together on the project.

> **Good Point**
>
> A partial oracle (where you can know something about the result of a test but not every detail), if it can be automated, can enable far more tests to be run and checked automatically.

But test generation also prompted many new questions that didn't have easy answers:

- Because field values were generated on the fly, each transaction buffer could be different from any that went before it. That meant that this test automation could find previously undiscovered bugs and that there was therefore a benefit to letting this test automation run on its own, even around the clock. What would be the criteria for stopping a test run?

- Many fields had values that needed to meet a given constraint. For instance, the value for the `TelephoneNumber` field had to be 10 digits in NNN-NNN-NNNN format; any other format would cause the transaction to fail. Once I was able to generate field values, what types of values would be most likely to find bugs? Would I find bugs in the `TelephoneNumber` field using random strings, such as `lkljlkjkjs`, or would it be better to use invalid strings that were almost valid phone numbers such as `206-555-123Z`?

- Finally, how should I count these generated test cases? Test case counts were an important metric in Bell Labs, but the number of generated tests would be proportional to the time and resources available to run them. That could easily amount to millions of tests, but were all these tests really worth counting? This question would haunt the later stages of the project.

28.6 Testing the Trouble Manager Workflow

The real power in a Trouble Manager is not at the individual transaction level but in how a dozen different transactions combine to produce a workflow. After a trouble ticket is created in the system, it needs to be guided along a path toward eventual repair. The repair center staff updates the ticket with additional information as they analyze, diagnose, and ultimately fix the problem.

Trouble Manager uses transactions, such as `CreateTicket` and `AnalyzeTicket`, to move a ticket through the workflow, and it uses a variable called `TicketState` to identify where the ticket is in the process.

In Trouble Manager, a typical workflow (annotated here with transaction names and `TicketState` values) was as follows:

1. `CreateTicket`: Records the trouble information. (The ticket is now in the *Created* state.)
2. `AnalyzeTicket`: Appends test results to the ticket. (The ticket is now in the *Analyzed* state.)
3. `DiagnoseTicket`: Appends a diagnosis and recommended repair(s). (The ticket is now in the *Diagnosed* state.)
4. `RepairTicket`: Records the repairs performed. (The ticket is now in the *Repaired* state.)
5. `CloseTicket`: Notifies customer and closes out the ticket. (The ticket is now in the *Closed* state.)

It is helpful to visualize the workflow as a map of states through which the trouble ticket moves. Maps like the one shown in Figure 28.3 were often found on the whiteboards of engineers throughout the team.

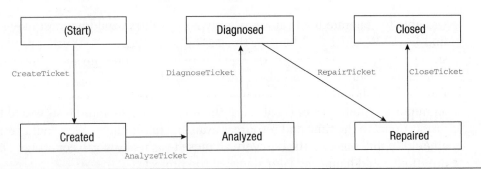

FIGURE 28.3   Basic trouble ticket workflow

Not all trouble tickets follow this five-step plan. A ticket's path can vary depending on the circumstances:

- If the ticket is in the Analyzed state, a staffer can rerun the `AnalyzeTicket` transaction to append additional test results to the ticket.
- If the ticket is in the Diagnosed state, and the customer called to say the problem went away, a staffer can run the `CloseTicket` transaction to send the ticket to the Closed state.
- If the ticket is in the Repaired state, but the customer's problem persists, a staffer can run `AnalyzeTicket` to return the ticket to the Analyzed state.

Incorporating these new actions gives us three more lines in our diagram, as shown in Figure 28.4. And, importantly, we now have two loops in the paths a ticket can take. One is a three-step loop {DiagnoseTicket-RepairTicket-AnalyzeTicket}; the other is a self-loop {AnalyzeTicket} at the Analyzed state.

However, note that our original sequence is still present as a path through the new map, as shown in Figure 28.5.

In fact, every ticket's processing can be viewed as a path through the map, and I found the path concept to be a productive way to think about the workflow testing. Because my test program could construct transaction buffers automatically, I could create a path through the workflow simply by listing the desired transactions in order and letting the program construct the transactions.

The first test path would be the original five-step sequence just presented:

1. `CreateTicket`
2. `AnalyzeTicket`

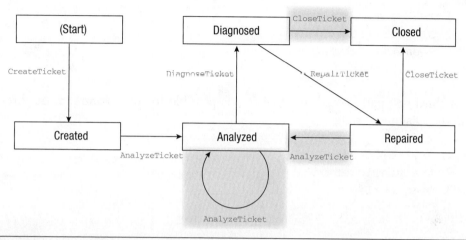

FIGURE 28.4 Improved trouble ticket workflow

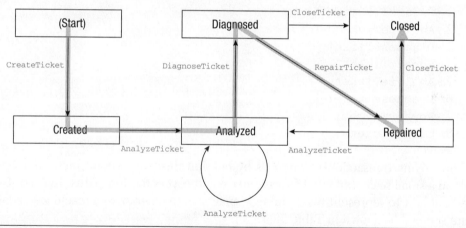

FIGURE 28.5 Original path through trouble ticket workflow

3. DiagnoseTicket
4. RepairTicket
5. CloseTicket

The second test path could introduce the AnalyzeTicket self-loop:

1. CreateTicket
2. AnalyzeTicket

3. `AnalyzeTicket`
4. `DiagnoseTicket`
5. `RepairTicket`
6. `CloseTicket`

A third test path would test that it was possible to run `CloseTicket` directly from the Diagnosed state:

1. `CreateTicket`
2. `AnalyzeTicket`
3. `DiagnoseTicket`
4. `CloseTicket`

A fourth path would explore the three-step `DiagnoseTicket-RepairTicket-AnalyzeTicket` loop:

1. `CreateTicket`
2. `AnalyzeTicket`
3. `DiagnoseTicket`
4. `RepairTicket`
5. `AnalyzeTicket`
6. `DiagnoseTicket`
7. `RepairTicket`
8. `CloseTicket`

Specifying transactions sequences by hand in this way is convenient and works well on a small scale, but it is labor-intensive and covers too few paths. Instead, I figured out how to represent the Trouble Manager state diagram as a machine-readable finite state table, shown in Table 28.3.

Once the workflow is represented as a state table, many algorithms can generate test paths through the workflow. For instance, a random walk algorithm will select an action from a state, execute the action to reach a new state, and begin the process again. Here is a possible random walk showing the action taken:

1. `CreateTicket`
2. `AnalyzeTicket`
3. `AnalyzeTicket`
4. `DiagnoseTicket`
5. `RepairTicket`

6. `AnalyzeTicket`
7. `AnalyzeTicket`
8. `DiagnoseTicket`
9. `CloseTicket`

Each type of path generation has its strengths and its drawbacks. Random walks, for instance, generate interesting test sequences but they have difficulty ensuring good overall coverage. A slightly more sophisticated random walk overcomes this weakness by using probabilities to steer the test generation toward areas that need to be tested.

At the other end of the sophistication scale, an algorithm called the Postman traversal provides a minimal length path that hits all the actions in the workflow. Normally, the effort to write a Postman program would outweigh the benefit derived, but Bell Labs had an internal tool (called POSTMAN, no less!) that implemented the algorithm, so I was able to run the tool on my own state table easily.

Good Point

Check within your organization for useful tools that you can use.

Table 28.3   Finite State Table for Trouble Ticket Workflow

Starting State	Action	Ending State
(Start)	`CreateTicket`	Created
Created	`AnalyzeTicket`	Analyzed
Analyzed	`AnalyzeTicket`	Analyzed
Analyzed	`DiagnoseTicket`	Diagnosed
Diagnosed	`RepairTicket`	Repaired
Diagnosed	`CloseTicket`	Closed
Repaired	`CloseTicket`	Closed
Repaired	`AnalyzeTicket`	Analyzed

In the case of the Trouble Manager diagram shown in Figure 28.4, the Postman algorithm covers the workflow in two sequences for a total of 13 steps:

1. `CreateTicket`
2. `AnalyzeTicket`
3. `AnalyzeTicket`
4. `DiagnoseTicket`
5. `RepairTicket`
6. `AnalyzeTicket`
7. `DiagnoseTicket`
8. `CloseTicket`

and

1. `CreateTicket`
2. `AnalyzeTicket`
3. `DiagnoseTicket`
4. `RepairTicket`
5. `CloseTicket`

Being able to generate test sequences automatically found many bugs and provided excellent feature coverage, but I was still dogged by the earlier questions:

- What kinds of sequences would be best at finding bugs?
- How would I know when I had covered enough sequences?
- How should I count test cases?

28.7   Test Generation in Action

As the Actiview specifications firmed up, the development and test teams began to write their respective code. It was standard procedure at the time for developers and testers to work completely independently of each other until the official system test period several months away. The notion was that this separation kept testers from being influenced by how the code was written, but what usually happened was that many bugs that could have been fixed if caught early were deeply entrenched in the product by the time official testing started.

Because I was eager to try out my rudimentary test generation scheme, I approached Bill Stafford, the developer for the Trouble Manager module, to see if

I could get early releases of his code to experiment against. Many developers are reluctant to share newly written code, but I was fortunate that Bill was comfortable with the idea and felt it might be a good way to find bugs early.

Good Point

Cooperation can benefit both testers and developers.

Traditional test automation can be fragile and difficult to change, so it is a common rule of thumb that automation should not be introduced until the codebase has stabilized. However, since I was not crafting the tests individually, the automation was relatively unaffected by feature changes. When a feature changed, I modified the test generation program to accommodate the change and had my automation running again within minutes.

The early use of automated tests was so successful that I began running generated tests against the modules as soon as they were coded. In fact, it was usually cost-effective for Bill to code a feature, run a few sanity tests, and then load the freshly built feature to a machine where my test program would begin generating and executing tests.

Because the testing of the feature was much simpler than the coding, it was usually the case that the tests could be ready as soon as the code was. This early intervention of testing enabled us to detect problems with the transactions very early, and because bugs were stopped early, we did not encounter problems later in the development cycle with bugs that had been missed.

After working together for a few weeks, Bill and I fell into a regular mode of operation. We worked feature by feature so that the code and tests were ready at the same time. Often we ran tests against the code all night and reviewed the results the next morning. These test results identified discrepancies between the expected and actual behaviors but did not assume that a behavior was a bug in the code. It could just as easily be a bug in the testing. A few minutes of inspection usually made it clear which of us needed to fix his code.

The question of whether to file bugs (i.e., write up a bug report) for code defects found at this time popped up occasionally. Because the development code being tested was fresh and had not been thoroughly tested yet, the fixes were simple, and it was often easier to just fix the problem than to write up a bug report on it. Also, Bell Labs often used bug counts as a way to rate developers—a developer with too many bugs filed against his code might have a difficult time at performance review. On the other hand, if I, as the tester, never filed any bugs, my management would question how I was spending my time. I never did find a satisfactory solution to the bug-filing question. I trusted that we were doing the right thing to deliver high-quality software, and I kept my management informed in the hope they would agree with me.

> **Lesson**
>
> Early model-based automation was effective as a testing strategy, although it defied the usual practice of using bug counts to evaluate the performance of testers and developers.

An important advantage of the test sequence generation work was that the tests did not require human oversight. We were able to run hundreds of sequences overnight and on the weekends. Once we discovered that the three other VAX computers in the test lab were idle most of the time, we arranged to have our sequences run on those machines as well. In this way, we picked up hundreds of hours of extra test time over the course of the project.

> **Tip**
>
> Make use of idle machines for unattended testing when appropriate.

28.8 Home Stretch

As the Trouble Manager project entered its final stages, my test generation approach continued to function well. My simple state machines were creaking under the complexity of Trouble Manager's later phases, but they held up. Generated tests were running on multiple VAXes around the building, and last-minute feature changes were accommodated easily.

Because of scheduling issues and the addition of several last-minute features, the final system test period was collapsed from 6 weeks down to 1 week. We were testing around the clock anyway, so this schedule change was a formality that actually had little effect on our testing.

> **Lesson**
>
> If the testing has been thorough throughout the development, reducing the time for testing at the end of the project may be a realistic option.

The main question we had to answer was what subset of the possible tests to run as a certification test during the final week. We finally settled on roughly 10,000 transactions that gave us good coverage of all the functionality. Bill made the final change to the system on December 26, 1994, in preparation for a January 1 delivery.

After running some targeted regression tests to make sure the latest change had not broken anything in its immediate vicinity, I kicked off the first round of the 10,000 tests I would run that week. Two of my kids were home with strep throat and the third was in the hospital getting his tonsils removed, so I worked from home for most of the week. As the week ended, I was pleased to see that the 10,000 tests ran cleanly without encountering a single bug.

But if the lack of bugs was a blessing, it was also a curse. Management became suspicious of a system test period in which no bugs were found. To tell the truth, I was a little uncomfortable about it myself. But I knew the software was solid. I went around to all the stakeholders in the system engineering, development, and test teams to confirm that they felt Trouble Manager was ready to ship. They all did. We shipped on January 1, 1995.

28.9   Post-Release

My performance review was held shortly after the release of Trouble Manager. My manager, who had no background in software development or testing, didn't know how to judge my work on the project. It turned out that this manager's only metrics for judging testers were the number of automated tests written and the number of bugs found.

Depending on how you counted test cases, my automated test case count was either a few dozen or a few million. I had actually filed few bugs during the development period, and zero bugs during official system test. Not surprisingly, given that strange combination of metrics, my January 1995 performance review was not stellar.

> **Lesson**
>
> Simply doing great work may not be recognized by managers who don't understand what you have been doing.

As the New Jersey winter melted into spring, I found that the absence of bugs detected during system test had started some people wondering if Trouble Manager was really as complex and difficult to test as we had claimed. Because Bell Labs at that time had an internal group that calculated software complexity, the group was brought in to offer their opinion.

In March, the assessment group concluded that Trouble Manager was complex enough that we should expect to see 12 high-severity bugs, 24 moderate-severity, bugs, and around 60 low-severity bugs in the first 6 months after release. I pointed out that Trouble Manager had already been in the field for 3 months with no reported bugs. Shouldn't we have seen a few bug reports by that point?

In fact, Trouble Manager ran in the field for 8 months before someone filed the first bug against it (a low-severity bug against a sorting routine). We were unable to reproduce the bug on our own systems but accepted the bug anyway.

In midsummer, I got word that the complexity assessment team had nominated me for an award based on the quality of the Trouble Manager deliverable. A few months later, an AT&T vice president gave me the 1995 AT&T Award for Outstanding Achievement in Quality. By that point, however, the effects of my January performance review had affected my ability to move within the company. Shortly thereafter, I left New Jersey for opportunities on the West Coast, but that's another story.

28.10 Conclusion

Test generation brought many advantages. Because my programs constantly tested new areas of Trouble Manager and automatically evaluated the results, I was able to run tests all hours of the day and night on idle hardware. I therefore found more bugs and found them earlier than would have been possible otherwise. I was even able to prevent many bugs by uncovering issues in the specification while creating my test generation program.

Test generation also brought difficulties. The paradigm change away from static scripted automation threw our metrics into a tailspin. Counting test cases or bugs became irrelevant. Eventually, we found better metrics such as code and model coverage, but justifying this approach to management was a struggle.

In the years since the Trouble Manager project, I have worked in several high-profile software organizations. Somewhere along the way, test generation methods became part of the mainstream. I now spend much of my time teaching test engineers how to apply similar techniques in their own work.

28.11 Acknowledgments

It is a pleasure to acknowledge Bill Stafford and Mary Ann Parker of the Actiview team for their extraordinary hard work and their support for this new way of approaching software testing. Our paths haven't crossed for a long time, but my gratitude to them and high regard for their work hasn't dimmed.

TEST AUTOMATION ANECDOTES

An anecdote is a short account of an incident (especially a biographical one). Numerous people told us short stories (anecdotes) of their experiences, and because they merit retelling but don't constitute full chapters, we collected them in this chapter. The stories vary in length from half a page to five pages. They are all independent, so they can be read in any order.

29.1 Three Grains of Rice

Randy Rice, United States
Consultant, speaker, and author

As a consultant, I see a number of different situations. The following describes three short experiences I have had with a couple of clients.

29.1.1 Testware Reviews

I was a consultant once on a project where we were trying to bring best practices in test automation into a large organization that had only tinkered with test automation. The company's environment spanned web-based, client/server, and mainframe applications. About 15 test designers and 15 test automators were brought in to work on this effort. The test tools in use when we first arrived were old versions not even being supported by the vendor because of their age. Only a small portion of the applications were automated to any degree. The automation that was in place consisted of large test scripts that were very difficult to maintain.

The project was initiated as one of several aggressive projects to technically reengineer the entire IT operation. The chief information officer (CIO) who was the original champion of these projects was a believer in test automation. Her successor inherited the projects but did not share the same commitment and enthusiasm for many of them. There was also a 6-month vacancy while the new CIO was being recruited, so things had just coasted along. When the new sheriff came to town, people started trying to figure out who would survive.

Supervising this effort were three senior test automation consultants who really knew their stuff and had a very specific approach to be followed. We had six test automation gurus on the managing consultant side, and we had regular communication based on metrics and goals. In fact, we developed a very nice dashboard that integrated directly with the tools. At any time on any project, people could see the progress being made. We gave demonstrations of how the automation was being created (this went over management's heads) and also the results of automation, so we had plenty of knowledge and communication.

To their credit, the contracting company trained all the incoming test design and automation consultants out of their own pocket. Although these were experienced consultants, the contractor wanted to set a level baseline of knowledge for how the work would be done on this project.

After about 3 weeks, it became apparent that some of the test automators were going their own way and deviating from the defined approach. This was a big problem because a keyword approach was being used, and certain keywords had to work consistently among applications. There were too many people who wanted to do things their way instead of the way that had been designed.

To correct the issue, the senior consultants required all test designers and consultants to attend daily technical reviews of testware. Technical reviews are not just for application software code or requirements. To get 30 people (more or less) from diverse backgrounds on the same approach is not a trivial achievement! Before long, this became a peer review type of effort, with critiques coming from peers instead of the senior consultants. It had turned into a forum for collaboration and learning.

Good Point

Reviews of automation testware are beneficial not just from a technical standpoint but also from an idea-sharing and brainstorming standpoint.

Some of the test consultants resisted the technical reviews and didn't last on the project. They were the same test automators who refused to follow the designed approach.

After a few weeks, it was no longer necessary to maintain the frequent reviews, and the test automation effort went a lot more smoothly.

Unfortunately, test management and senior technical management (at the CIO level) in this organization never saw the value of test automation. Therefore, much of the fine work done by this team was scrapped when senior management pulled all support for this effort. They terminated the contracts of everyone who knew anything about the automation and ended up "achieving" a negative return on invest-ment (ROI)—millions of dollars were spent with very little to show for it. I see little future for automation at this company now, in spite of the great work that was done.

> **Lesson**
>
> Technical success is no guarantee of lasting automation; management support through good communication is needed.

This was a huge and very visible project. But the test manager was like many test managers and had been thrust into the role with no training in testing. The client staff were thin in numbers, skills, and motivation.

My bottom line assessment is that the organization simply was not ready for such an aggressive project. Then, when the sponsoring CIO left, there was no one to champion the project. Also, the software wasn't engineered in a way that was easily automated; it was old and very fragile. The expectations for ROI were very high and it would have been better to take smaller steps first.

29.1.2 Missing Maintenance

There was a move in the late 1990s to go from fractional stock prices to decimal prices. For decades, stock prices had been shown as "$10 1/2" instead of "$10.50." There were many benefits to the decimal representation, such as ease of computa-tion, standardization worldwide, and so forth. This was a major conversion effort that was almost as significant for the company as the Y2K maintenance effort.

Because the conversion effort was so massive and time was so short, manage-ment decided not to update the test automation during the project. This decision later proved to be significant.

By the time the decimalization project was complete, work was well underway for the Y2K conversion effort. We wanted to update the test automation for both efforts—decimalization and Y2K—at the same time. However, the schedule won again, and by the time the Y2K effort was complete, the test automation was deemed to be so out of date, it would be easier to start all over in a new, more modern tool. This was indeed the case. One of the problems was the platform, the DEC VAX. There was only one tool on the market for that platform. An emulator-based PC tool could have been used, but then there would be issues of character-based testing.

At the time, keyword-driven or even data-driven approaches were not widely known, and the automators and test managers encountered for themselves the difficulties of maintaining the automation code with hardcoded values. The first decision not to keep up with maintenance of the automated testware proved to be the death of the entire test automation effort for that application. This was a highly complex financial application, taking about 3 years to create the original test automation. There were new projects being developed on client/server platforms. Starting again from square one might have been a good idea, but the company hadn't yet realized the ROI from the first effort. Basically, the manual test approach just seemed too compelling.

Lesson

Once you abandon the maintenance of the automation, it is likely to die. For a better chance of success, choose an automation approach that will require the least maintenance.

29.1.3   A Wildly Successful Proof-of-Concept

I was hired by a large Wall Street company to assess the quality of its software testing process and make recommendations regarding a workable test automation approach. This company was not new to the idea of test automation. In fact, it already had three major test automation tools in place and was looking for another test automation solution. There was no integration between the various test automation tools, and they were applied in functional silos.

One particular system at this company was being manually regression tested every day! This one very unfortunate lady performed the same tests every day for about 8 hours a day.

As we were considering which tools might be the best fit for this system, I suggested that we contact the various candidate vendors and see if any were willing to send a technical consultant and perform a proof-of-concept using the the vendor's tool and my client's system.

My client thought this was an excellent idea, so we contacted the vendors and found one that was willing to send in a consultant at a reduced daily rate. We felt it was worth the risk to pay for the proof-of-concept. It would have taken us weeks to try to get an unfamiliar tool working, and we didn't want to pay for a tool without knowing it would work.

It seemed to me a good test project for the proof-of-concept was the 8-hour daily manual regression test, so we asked the vendor's test automation consultant to tackle that application.

After 3 days, the regression tests were completely automated! We were hoping just to get an idea that the tool would work in the environment. What we got instead was our first success! We probably broke even on ROI after 1 month.

> **Tip**
>
> Tool vendors can be a great help to get you started "on the right foot."

My client was thrilled, I looked good for suggesting the idea, and the vendor made a big sale. However, the person happiest with the outcome was the lady who had previously performed the manual regression tests for 8 hours a day. Now, she started an automated test and 15 minutes later, the test was done. Her time was now free for designing better tests and performing more creative tests.

29.2 Understanding Has to Grow

Molly Mahai, United States
Test manager

When we started looking at automation, I read everything I could get my hands on. I knew I couldn't automate everything. I knew automation would not replace people, and I knew it would require investment. I read *Software Test Automation* (Fewster and Graham, Addison-Wesley, 1999) at a recommendation, and I learned about the steps to take.

The funny thing is that even knowing all that, I felt I could not accomplish the first steps to set up an architectural framework. I know that sounds simple, but what does an architecture look like? How do we want to capture our tests? How will we set it up so that we can reuse scripts? All these questions kept preventing us from making progress. So, in my usual fashion, I made a decision and picked an architecture. I had no idea if it would work or not, but we needed to get moving with something. This freed us up to learn, and learn we did. We created a regression suite that addressed a handful of our applications, and it looked like we were moving in the right direction, but we ran into problems. There were too many scripts, and the initial grouping (directory structure) was not sufficient for our use.

This time, though, I knew a lot more and figured out that our architecture was lacking. We had too many projects, the library was cumbersome, and so on. So, I redesigned the architecture and created staging areas, including a sandbox area for development scripts, a place for scripts in use, and a place for scripts that were part of the production suite. We also enforced the naming conventions that we had put in place. These simple changes fixed a good many of our organizational problems.

The key is that we knew about this potential pitfall, and we knew how important it was to have an architecture that worked for us, but we couldn't design that architecture until we knew more of what we wanted to accomplish. For us, this was not a pitfall that we could avoid: We had to learn our way through it. The great thing was that I was intently aware of this potential problem (from reading the book), and I kept my eye on it. We redesigned the architecture as soon as we realized it wasn't working for us, and the impact on our automation effort was negligible.

I relate this to trying to explain to teenagers that they will view things differently when they are older. They cannot grasp it through hearing from someone else; they must learn it for themselves.

> **Lesson**
>
> Experiencing the problem is often the best (or only) way to see a better solution.

29.3   First Day Automated Testing

Jonathon Lee Wright, United Kingdom
Consultant and speaker

In the past decade, I have dealt with a number of ways of creating testware frameworks and found advantages and disadvantages in each of the following approaches:

- Modularity driven
- Keyword driven
- Data driven

In 2009, I was tasked with automating the testing of a new package for the New Zealand Lotteries Commission. The requirements phase had only just been completed, and the scheduled testing was looking very tight—less than a month (the schedule was imposed on us by marketing, who had already overcommitted their advertising!).

With just 2 months until the release would be delivered, this was an opportunity to adapt the testware frameworks I had used before, combining them with the latest technologies to develop what I refer to as a hybrid (keyword-/data-driven) automation framework.

Not only would this meet all the requirements set by the business, but more important, it would allow us to start the development of the testware framework immediately.

29.3.1   Initial Investment

The inherent problem with the hybrid approach is the large initial investment in time and effort to design the testware framework. Consequently, it was important that the development of this framework be treated as a legitimate project in its own right with its own planning, design, development, and testing phases together with the necessary resources. Table 29.1 shows our estimates for the effort required to create 100 test scenarios.

In essence, the hybrid approach would take roughly twice as long as the previous automation approach, which in turn would take twice as long to automate than the preparation for manual testing.

29.3.2   What Is to Be Automated?

Given the limited time available and the increased initial effort required, it was critical that we identified the optimum test coverage. To avoid developing unnecessary test components, we used the MoSCoW method:

- What *must* be automated?
- What *should* be automated?
- What *could* be automated?
- What *won't* be automated?

Table 29.1   Simple Calculations for Initial Testware Preparation Effort

Approach	Effort
Manual	2 weeks
Existing framework	1 month
Hybrid framework	2 months

This method allowed us to focus our efforts on those test components that were necessary and would give the greatest value by assessing the associated business risk, reusability, usage, complexity, and feasibility of each test component.

The test components were regarded as individual jigsaw pieces, but we kept in mind what was needed to complete the entire puzzle.

Business process modeling (BPM) was used within the centralized test management tool (Quality Centre) to represent the individual puzzle pieces (test components); mapping the pieces revealed the workflow through the system.

Figure 29.1 shows how one BPM may only include 5 puzzle pieces but enable more than 20 different paths through the system under test (SUT), with each path having a different business risk and impact assessment.

This made it easier to decide which automation modules to develop first by starting small and automating only the most critical business processes—keeping it as simple as possible while recognizing that the test coverage could be increased as the framework matured over time.

The decomposition of the workflows into a high-level model visualizes and enables an agile approach to the framework development. The development's build order and resource focus becomes obvious.

Each path through the system represents an agile feature, which may be in or out of scope depending on time and resources. Another benefit of this approach is that the model becomes an artifact that may be shared between the test framework and target application developers.

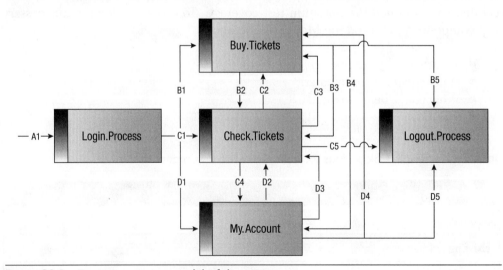

FIGURE 29.1   Business process model of the SUT.

> **Good Point**
>
> Start by automating the most valuable tests, but plan for later growth.

29.3.3   First Day Automated Testing

The key to first day automated testing is to create a dynamic object repository based on a combination of fuzzy logic and descriptive programming supporting the design and development of test scenarios before the actual delivery of the SUT.

Traditionally, because of the dependency on building the object repository, test automation is carried out at the end of the software development lifecycle once the SUT is delivered. However, because we had only a single month in which to execute testing but a full 2 months before the SUT was delivered, it seemed logical to develop the testware framework beforehand while the application was still in development.

> **Good Point**
>
> Automation can (and should) start before the software being tested is delivered, so the automated tests are ready to run on the first day the software is released. But this requires good planning and good testware architecture.

29.3.3.1   Business-Level Keywords

To allow the creation of test scenarios ahead of the SUT delivery, a high-level keyword approach was used to represent:

- Specific BPM and business process testing (BPT) modules
- Specific/collections of user stories
- Assigned work items
- Queries against the test asset database

Using high-level business-level keywords, such as `Login.Process`, allows complexity hiding and reusable encapsulation. `Login.Process` contains a number of low-level keywords, such as `Enter Username Text` and `Press Login Button`.

The collection of application keywords represents natural domain-specific languages that translate into a number of lower-level actions performed before and after the core event. This included checking that the pretest and posttest conditions were met and the actions and reactions, including any popup/error recovery, were processed correctly.

Good Point

The more automation code is reused, the more worthwhile it is to build in recovery from unexpected errors or events and the more robust the scripts are.

Using this approach meant we had a foundation upon which to design and develop reliable, domain-specific, and reusable test scenarios before the release of the SUT.

Writing the test scenarios (manual or automated) as business-level keywords combined with natural language made it accessible to application domain experts, business analysts, and developers. The test language was self-validating and human readable, which removed the requirements to educate the end user in the tool. The verbs and nouns in the domain-specific language were written in natural language using context-sensitive validation. This improved the utilization of resources by encouraging joint collaboration between multifunctional teams while supporting behavior-driven development (BDD).

The Scrum team was made up of a number of multidiscipline team members (business analysts, testers, and developers) sharing the various roles of the test design phase without any previous automation experience. This allowed teams to collaborate and share test assets such as BPM/BPT modules, user stories, and work items. They could also run queries against previously created test scenarios and reuse shared test cases and steps.

The flexibility of having the test scenarios stored in a database also allowed for full/partial fallback support for legacy manual testing because the test data could be easily extracted into a traditional test scenario format. It was easy to read because of the use of natural language combined with valid test data that could be easily used in manual test execution.

Good Point

Automated tests should be accessible and readable by all and should enable the tests to be run manually if necessary.

In summary, this approach of managing centralized test assets to generate sanitized test scenarios validated against business rules provided ready-to-use tests and data in the correct format. This was evidenced by the ability to generate tests featuring over 10,000 ticket number combination states covering all possible combinations of ticket types and amounts (this excluded specialized test runs such as boundary and negative tests, which were run separately) before the SUT had even been written.

29.3.4   Problems and Solutions

We found problems stemming from procedures not being followed consistently. For example, changes to the functionality of reusable test components' jigsaw pieces were not being checked in correctly. This was caused by not having an enforceable gated check-in procedure and consequently resulted in limited reusability of some of the test components. The problem was solved by enforcing the check-in procedures in the Configuration Management tool.

> **Lesson**
>
> Automation development requires the same discipline as software development.

It became apparent when the testware framework entered the execution phase and was distributed across a pool of remote test clients generated by a virtual machine (VM) dispenser that there was limited direct visibility into the test execution status.

While it was relatively easy to identify primary core modules failing on startup, more subtle changes to reusable test components were much harder to spot. The requirement for a test asset loader to validate the current SUT build against the test asset database before execution could have prevented this.

Without the ability to monitor runtime failure, especially controlled failure (i.e., scenario recovery), a significant amount of execution time was wasted. For example, a discrete change to a test component could cause a false-positive error, which in turn caused the testware framework to repeatedly retry the current test scenario before attempting to continue through the remaining test cases. What was needed here was a suitable real-time dashboard that could provide notifications regarding the SUT health as well as progress of test client execution.

We solved this problem by devising a way to flag the overall status of a test set— In Progress, Ready, Repair, or Blocked—to keep the tester informed. This would affect the current test run and associated test client VM's state where, for example, a Blocked status did not allow the test run to be continued until the necessary pretest conditions were met (e.g., the Lotto product draw had been successfully processed).

> **Tip**
>
> Keep track of things that affect the test execution to avoid wasting time running tests that will fail for reasons you are not interested in. There is a danger, however, that tests that are turned off will never be turned back on.

29.3.5 Results of Our First Day Automation Approach

This approach worked extremely well, and we realized a good return on investment (ROI) for the additional effort in developing the framework.

Once the release was delivered, the execution was run constantly, day and night. This was made possible by having dedicated resources available during the day to deal with basic debugging of failed scripts and execution. Developers based in another time zone were also available in the evening to maintain the framework and provide additional support for improved test coverage.

Overall, this approach was found to work well in this case study by demonstrating its innate advantages, reflected in what I like to call the approach: Hybrid Keyword Data-Driven Automation Framework.

- *Hybrid:* Utilizing the best technologies and resources to do the job.
- *Keyword:* Creating simple and robust test scenarios written in business-level keywords combined with natural language.
- *Data:* Effective use of dynamic business data to provide an input source.
- *Driven:* Reusable component modules and libraries to provide reliable processing of generic actions, objects, and events.
- *Automation:* That is collaborative, distributed, and scalable.
- *Framework:* Independent of application, technology, or environment under test.

The best aspects of these proven approaches demonstrate how they have evolved over the past decade; this echoes some of the progress toward leaner and more agile business methodologies. They are in a constant state of evolution—just as the underpinning technologies evolve over time.

A significant benefit was that the framework had the ability to support multiple browsers, platforms, and technology stacks under a unified engine with the capability to deal with generic object classes as well as application-specific classes.

29.4 Attempting to Get Automation Started

Tessa Benzie, New Zealand
Test engineer

My company was keen to get into test automation. We had a couple of days of consultancy (with one of the authors of this book) to explore what we wanted and the best ways of achieving our goal. We discussed good objectives for automation and created an outline plan. We realized the need for a champion who would be the internal enthusiast for the automation. The champion needed to be someone with development skills.

We hired someone who was thought to be a suitable candidate to be the champion for our initiative. However, before he could get started on the automation, he needed to do some training in databases, as this was also a required area of expertise, and we needed him to be up to speed with the latest developments there.

After the training, he was asked to help some people sort out some problems with their database, again "before you start on the automation." After these people, there were some other groups needing help with databases. When do you think he finally started automation? As you may have guessed already, he never did! Of course, it can be very hard for a new person to say no, but the consequences should be pointed out.

A few months after that, a new test manager came in who was keen to get the automation started at the company. He did some great work in pushing for automation, and we chose and acquired a test tool that looked suitable. There were a couple of other contractors (the test manager was also a contractor) who were coming to grips with the initial use of the tool and began to see how it could be beneficial.

So we had a good start, we thought, to our automation initiative.

Shortly after this, there was a reorganization, and the contractors and test manager were let go. A new quality assurance manager was brought in, but test automation was not on her list of priorities. Some people were trying to use some of the automated tests, but there was no support for this activity. However, there were many, many tests that needed to be done urgently, including lots of regression tests. Now we had "football teams" of manual testers, including many contractors.

Lesson

Organizational support is needed to get a significant automation initiative started; be sure you choose a champion who will stay on task and be the driving force behind your initiative. Beware of knowledge walking out the door with your contractors—it's far better to involve permanent staff.

29.5 Struggling with (against) Management

Kai Sann, Austria
Engineer and test manager

I have had some "interesting" managers over the years who had some challenging effects on the way we did test automation.

29.5.1 The "It Must Be Good, I've Already Advertised It" Manager

We started software test automation in 2002. The management's intention was to reduce time for the system test. Furthermore, the management used automation as a marketing strategy before the automation was developed.

At this time, there was no calculation for return on investment (ROI). The approach was this: Software test automation must pay because manual testing is no longer needed. The goal was to automate 100 percent of all test cases.

I had a hard time explaining that software test automation is just one of many methods to achieve better software and that it is not free—or even cheap.

29.5.2 The "Testers Aren't Programmers" Manager

We started very classically and believed the promises of the vendors. They told us, "You only need to capture and replay," but we found this was not true. In our experience, this leads to shelfware, not success—it does not pay off.

After some trial and mostly error, we started to write automation code. At this point, we were far away from developing automated test cases. We needed some lessons in writing code. We were lucky to have very good mentors on our development team who taught us to write libraries and functions so we didn't have to code the same tasks repeatedly.

I had a discussion with my boss about what programming is. He explained to me that he consciously hadn't hired testers with an informatics degree because he didn't want to have more developers in his department. You can imagine his surprise when I told him that our automation code included libraries and functions.

He told his superiors that the testers do "advanced scripting" rather than coding because he was afraid that the testers would otherwise be forced to write production code!

Good Point

Beware of political issues and fears.

29.5.3 The "Automate Bugs" Manager

An idea provided by one manager was to automate bugs we received from our customer care center. We suffer the consequences to this day. How did this work? Our developers had to fix our customers' bugs. We were told to read this bug and automate this exact user action. This is where the consequences come in: Not knowing any better, we hardcoded the user data into our automation. After 2 years, we were one major release behind the development. We didn't know anything about data-driven tests at that time.

We were automating bugs for versions that were not in the field anymore. Most of these test cases still exist because we haven't had time to replace them.

Lesson

Holding the title of manager doesn't necessarily mean a person knows best (or anything) about test automation! You may need to educate your manager.

29.5.4 The "Impress the Customers (the Wrong Way)" Manager

My boss had the habit of installing the untested beta versions for presentations of the software in front of customers. He would install unstable versions and then call our developers from the airport at 5:30 a.m. and order immediate fixes to be sent to him by email.

Our programmers hated this so much that we introduced an automated smoke test. This test checks if we have a new build; then it installs the beta, and finally it checks the basic functions of our product. Our boss was told to only install smoke-tested beta versions.

Today we don't have this boss issue anymore, but we continue the automated smoke tests for our nightly builds because they provide us with a good guess about the state of our software. Here we really save money because smoke tests must be done anyway and we can provide our development with a lot of issues concerning the integration of new modules at an early stage. We expand this test every few months. The coolest thing is that we are informed about the latest test results by email.

So in spite of some challenging managers, we are now doing well with our automation!

> **Good Point**
>
> Sometimes an approach adopted for one reason turns out to be good for other reasons.

29.6   Exploratory Test Automation: Database Record Locking

Douglas Hoffman, United States
Consultant and speaker

Pre–World Wide Web (late 1980s), I was the quality assurance (QA) manager, test lead, and test architect for the second-largest relational database management system (RDBMS) software company at the time. Before landing the job, I got my bachelor's degree in computer science, started out as a systems engineer, and had worked my way up into hands-on engineering services management (QA, tech support, sales support, and tech writing).

The company had about 300 employees, mostly in San Mateo, California. The relational database engine had evolved over more than 10 years and had a well-established, fairly stable codebase. At the time, the code had to be ported across 180 hardware/software platforms (most were variations of UNIX). The QA team was small (initially with a ratio of about 1:20 with developers, growing to ~1:5 over 18 months) and nearly completely focused on testing. Most new testers were recruited from other companies' development organizations.

To support the large number of versions, the product was developed using internal switches to enable or disable different code functions. Therefore, most of the porting was done by selecting the proper combinations of switches. This meant that once features or bug fixes had been incorporated into the base code, the various ports would pour into QA.

Because the test team was small, we spent almost all our time running tests on the various platforms. Little time was available for design and implementation of tests for new features. A thorough test run for a new release on a platform could take 2 weeks, and the dozen testers could receive 150 versions in a few weeks. The management and technical challenges dealing with this situation are other case studies in themselves. This case study focuses on one particular exploratory automated test we created.

Unlike regression tests that do the same thing every time they are run, exploratory automated tests are automated tests that don't have predetermined results built in; they create new conditions and inputs each time they're run. Exploratory test automation is capable of finding bugs that were never specifically conceived of in advance. These are typically long-sequence tests and involve huge numbers of iterations because they are only limited by available computer resources.

> **Tip**
>
> When the input space of an application is huge, exploratory automated tests can find defects that are difficult to find manually.

29.6.1 The Case Study

Bug being sought: Errors in database record locking (failure to lock or release a lock on a record, table, or database).

When I took over the QA organization, the existing test cases were simple applications written in the various frontend languages, mostly our proprietary SQL. Most existing tests were applications and data sets collected from customers or scripts that verified bug fixes. Automation was achieved using a simple shell script that walked through the directories containing the tests and sequentially launched them. Most of the testers' efforts were in analyzing the results and tweaking the tests to conform with nuances on the various platforms.

One area of concern that wasn't well tested using our regression tests was record locking. A few intermittent bugs that locked up the programs or clobbered data had been found in the field. The locking mechanism was complex because of the distributed nature of the database. For example:

- Parts of the database might be replicated and the "master" copy moved around as requests were made.
- Different parts of the database needed to communicate about actions before they could be completed.

- Requests could occur simultaneously.
- Common data could be updated by multiple users.
- One user's request for exclusive access (e.g., to update part of a record) could cause some other users' requests to wait.
- User requests for nonexclusive access might proceed under some circumstances.
- Non-overlapping parts of interlocking records might be updated by different users.
- Timeouts could occur, causing locks and/or requests to be cancelled.

Most multiuser database systems at the time were hardwired and LAN based, so Internet and cloud issues weren't part of the picture. (This was before widespread Internet use, browsers, or the World Wide Web.) Frontend programs were built out of compiled or interpreted programs written in proprietary languages. The use of LANs meant that interrupt events came directly through hardware drivers and were not processed by higher-level system services.

Prior to the test automation project, the straightforward locking sequences were tested using manual scripts on two terminals. For example,

1. One user would open a record for nonexclusive update (which should lock the record from being modified but allow reading of the record by other users).
2. A second user would open and attempt to modify the record (thus successfully opening but then encountering a record lock).
3. Another test would have the first user opening for nonexclusive read (which should not lock the record and should allow reading and modifying of the record by other users).
4. The second user would read and update the record (which should work).

The regression tests confirmed the basic functioning of the lock/unlock mechanisms. Only a subset of condition pairs could be manually tested this way because of the amount of time it took, and complex sequences of interactions were out of the question. Figure 29.2 shows an example of the interaction of two users attempting to access the same record.

In relational databases, updating a record can write data in many tables and cause updates to multiple indexes. Different users running different programs may reference some common data fields along with unique data. The data records are contained in multiple files (called tables), and programs reference some subset of the fields of data across the database. Intermittent, seemingly unreproducible problems could occur when the requests overlapped at precisely the wrong times. For example,

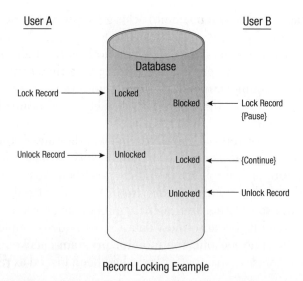

Record Locking Example

FIGURE 29.2   Record locking example

the second read request might come in while the first was in the process of updating the database record. There might be tiny windows of time during which a lock might be missed or a partially updated record returned. These kinds of combinations are extremely difficult to encounter and nearly impossible to reproduce manually. We decided that the best way to look for errors was to generate lots of database activities from multiple users at the same time.

Good Point

Good candidates for automation are tests that are difficult to run manually and those that are too complex for manual testing.

The challenge was to create multithreaded tests that could find timing-related problems of this type. The goal was to produce tests that would generate lots of conditions and could detect the bugs and provide enough failure information to the developers so they could isolate the cause and have some chance at fixing the bugs.

Automated tests: We created a single program that accessed a database using various randomly selected access methods and locking options. The test verified and logged each action. We then ran multiple instances of the program at the same time (each being its own thread or on its own machine). This generated huge numbers of combinations and sequences of database activities. The logs provided enough information to recreate the (apparent) sequence of database actions from all the threads. If no problems were detected, we discarded the logs because they could get quite large. While the tests were running, a monitoring program observed the database and log files to ensure that none of the threads reported an error or became hung.

Oracle: Watching for error returns and observing whether any of the threads terminated or took excessively long. The test program did very trivial verification of its own activities. By the nature of multiple users updating overlapping data all the time, data changes might be made by any user at any time. We couldn't reliably confirm what was expected because some other user activity might change some data by the time the test program reread it. Because most database activities completed in fractions of seconds, if there was no lockout, the monitor program checked for multisecond delays on nonlocked transactions or after locks had been logged as released.

> **Good Point**
>
> A test oracle, especially for automated exploratory testing, may just be looking for system failures rather than functional correctness. Use an oracle that is appropriate to the testing you are doing.

Method summary:

1. Created a program that independently, randomly accessed records for update, read, insert, and delete. Different types of record locking were randomly included with the requests. Each program logged its activity for diagnostic purposes and checked for reasonable responses to its requests.
2. Ran multiple instances of the program at the same time so they potentially accessed the same data and could interfere with one another. Access should have been denied if records were locked by other processes and allowed if none of the other threads was locking the referenced record.
3. Created and ran another program to monitor the log file and the database engine to detect problem indications and shut down if a problem occurred.

Because the threads were running doing random activities, different combinations and sequences of activities were generated at a high rate of speed. The programs might have detected errors, or the threads might hang or abnormally terminate, indicating the presence of bugs. Each instance of the test generated large numbers of combinations of events and different timing sequences. The number of actions was limited by the amount of time we allocated for the lock testing. We sometimes ran the test for a few minutes, but at other times it could run an hour or longer. Each thread might only do hundreds of database actions per second because of the time it took for waiting, error checking, and logging. We ran from three to a dozen threads using multiple networked systems, so a minute of testing might generate 100,000 to 300,000 possible locking conditions.

Results: We caught and were able to fix a number of interesting combinations, timing-related bugs, and one design problem. For example, a bug might come up when:

- User A opens a record for update.
- User B waits for the record to be unlocked to do its own update.
- User C waits for the record to be unlocked to do its own update.
- User A modifies the data but releases the lock without committing the change.
- User B modifies the data but releases the lock without committing the change.
- User C updates the data, commits it, and releases the lock.
- User C's data was not written into the database.

I was surprised because a few of the timing- and sequence-related bugs were not related to the record locking itself. If the commits occurred at the same time (within a tiny time window), the database could become corrupted by simultaneous writes of different records by multiple users in a single table. Although the records were not locked because the users were referencing different rows, the data could become switched.

We couldn't be certain that we caught all the bugs because of the nature of these kinds of timing- and sequence-related problems. Although millions of combinations were tried and checked, there were myriad possibilities for errors that we couldn't detect or didn't check for. Trillions of combinations wouldn't amount to a measurable percentage of the total number of possibilities. But, to the best of my knowledge, there were no reported field problems of that nature for at least a year after we created these tests. (I moved on and no longer had access to such information.)

Good Point

The benefits of exploratory automated tests may be significant even if you can't know what you didn't test.

We didn't leave reproducibility to chance, although even running the same series of inputs doesn't always reproduce a problem. The at-random tests used pseudorandom numbers; that is, we recorded seed values to be able to restart the same random sequences. This approach substantially improves reproducibility. We generated a new seed first when we wanted to do a new random walk, and we reused the seed to rerun a test.

> **Tip**
>
> Even random tests should be reproducible in order to confirm bugs and bug fixes. Use the same starting point (the "seed") to reproduce the same random test.

The archiving system is critical for tracing back to find the likely cause and also as the test oracle. Much of the data being recorded can be checked for consistency and obvious outliers to detect when likely bugs are encountered. I tend to log the things developers tell me might be important to them as the test progresses and then "dump the world" when a bug is suspected.

We used some functional test suites that were available for SQL, including from the National Bureau of Standards (which later became the National Institute of Standards and Technology), but they only checked basic functionality. We used them to some degree, but they were not random, asynchronous, or multithreaded. TPC-B wasn't created until several years later.

Recognizing the root cause of reported bugs required serious investigation because the failures we were seeking generally required multiple simultaneous (or a specific sequence of) events. Many of the factors we looked at were environmental. We were primarily looking for fundamental violations of the locking rules (deadlocks and data corruption), so recognizing those failures was straightforward. Identifying the cause was more difficult and frustrating. It sometimes took a lot of investigation, and once in a while, we gave up looking for the cause. This was frustrating because we knew there was a bug, but we couldn't do anything about it other than look for other symptoms. Most of the time, though, the developers were able to identify the probable cause by looking for the possible ways the failure could have happened.

> **Good Point**
>
> Unreproducible failures are worth reporting because sometimes developers can trace the cause in the code if they know that something is wrong.

29.7   Lessons Learned from Test Automation in an Embedded Hardware–Software Computer Environment

Jon Hagar, United States
Engineer, trainer, and consultant

Embedded systems comprise specialized hardware, software, and operations. They come with all of the problems of normal software, but they also include some unique aspects:

- Specialized hardware that the software "controls" with long and concurrent development cycles.
- Hardware problems that are "fixed" in the software late in the project.
- Limited user interfaces and minimal human intervention.
- Small amounts of dense, complex functions often in the control theory domain (e.g., calculating trajectories, flight dynamics, vehicle body characteristics, and orbital targets).
- (A big one) Very tight real-time performance issues (often in millisecond or microsecond ranges).

Products that make up embedded software systems now span the automotive, control, avionics, medical, telecom, electronics, and almost every other product domain one can think of. I have been involved in space avionics (guidance, navigation, and control software), but many of the approaches and lessons learned are applicable to other embedded software systems. In this section, we use examples drawn from a hypothetical but historically based space flight software embedded system.

The goal of verification, validation, and testing (VV&T) is to show that embedded software is ready for use and the risk of failure due to software can be considered acceptable by the stakeholders.

Development programs can be small—for example, 30,000 source lines of code (with staffs of 10 to 60 people)—yet these programs are time and computationally complex and are critical to the successful control of the hardware system.

29.7.1   VV&T Process and Tools

We typically have four levels of testing and tools that support each level. The lowest level is probably the most different for embedded systems because it is nearest to the hardware. It uses a host/target configuration and cross-compiled code (including automation code). Cross-compiling is where source code is compiled on one computer, not into the binary (executable) of that (host) computer but rather into binary executable code that will run on a different computer (the "target") that is too limited to be able to run a compiler on. Our testing at this level aims to check against standards and code coverage as well as requirements and design and is automated by the developer.

We call this "implementation structural verification testing" (some places call this unit testing). This testing is conducted with a digital simulation of the computer and/ or a single-board target hardware-based computer.

The implementation test tools were customized in the beginning, but other off-the-shelf tools were added later. Examples include LDRA TBrun, Cantata, and AdaTEST. The project used both test-driven development and code-then-test implementation approaches. The comparison and review of results, which include very complex calculations, is done using test oracle information generated from commercial tools such as MATLAB, BridgePoint, and Mathmatica.

The middle level, which we call design-based simulation tools, uses tools that are based on software architecture structures and design information, which have been integrated across module boundaries. These tools allow the assessment of software for particular aspects individually. In some projects, model-based development tools, BridgePoint, and MATLAB were used, and this enabled the integration efforts to go better than in past systems, because the models enforced rules and checks that prevented many integration defects from happening in the first place.

> **Tip**
>
> Using models can help to prevent and eliminate defects that otherwise would be found in testing (or not found), but nothing guarantees that you find 100 percent of them.

The next level is requirements-based simulation (scientific simulation tools). These simulations (driven by models) are done in both a holistic way and based on individual functions. For example, a simulation may model the entire boost profile of a system with full vehicle dynamics simulation, and another simulation may model the specifics of how the attitude thrust vector control works.

This allows system evaluation from a microscopic level to a macroscopic level. The results from one level can be used as automated oracles to other levels of VV&T test supporting "compare" activities.

This approach of using simulation/models to drive and analyze test results comes with a risk. There is the chance that an error can be contained in the model or tool that replicates and "offsets" an error in the actual product (a self-fulfilling model result). This is a classic problem with model-based test oracles. To help with this risk, the project used the levels of testing (multiple compares), a variety of tools, different VV&T techniques, and expert skilled human reviewers who were aware of this risk. These methods, when used in combination with testing, were found to detect errors if they exist (one major objective) and resulted in software that worked.

Finally, at a system level, VV&T of the software uses actual hardware in the loop and operations. An extensive, real-time, continuous digital simulation modeling and feedback system of computers is used to test the software in a realistic environment with the same interfaces, inputs, and outputs as in the actual system. The system under test runs in actual real time; thus there is no speed-up or slow-down of time due to the test harness. Additionally, with hardware in the loop and realistic simulations, complete use scenarios involving the hardware and software could be played out with both for typical usage scenarios (daily use) and unusual situations such as high load, boundary cases, and invalid inputs.

29.7.2 Lessons Learned

This section summarizes some general observations that the projects had during the initial setup and use of automated VV&T tools:

- *Training:* It is important to allow both time and money for training on tools and testing.
- *Planning:* Tools must be planned for and developed like any software effort. Automated VV&T tools are not "plug and play." To be successful, plan for development, establish a schedule and budget, integrate with existing processes, plan the test environment, and also test the test tools. Test tools must be "engineered" like any development effort.
- *Have an advocate:* Test tools need a champion in order for them to become incorporated into common use. The champion is someone who knows the tools and advocates their use. Success comes from getting staff to think "outside the automated tool box." The new tools must "integrate" with the existing staff, which means education, mentoring, and some customization. Advocates work these issues.
- *Usability of a tool must be reasonable for the users:* While people will need training on tools, and tools by nature have complexities, a tool that is too hard to use or is constantly in revision by vendors leads to frustration by users that, in the extreme, will lead to shelfware. Ensure that the user interface is part of the selection evaluation before purchasing any tool.

Good Point

Usability of the tools is important—even for "techies."

- *Expect some failures and learn from them:* Our project explored several tools that were abandoned after an initial period of time. While failure is not good, it is really only total failure when one does not learn from the mistake. Also, management must avoid blaming engineers for the failure of an idea because doing so stifles future ideas.

Good Point

If you learn from your mistakes, you have not totally failed. Any failure or mistake becomes a source of information to share.

- *Know your process:* Automated test tools must fit within your process. If you lack process, just having tools will probably result in failure. Expect some changes in your process when you get a new tool, but a tool that is outside of your process will likely become shelfware.
- *Embedded systems have special problems in test automation:* Despite progress, automated test tools do not totally solve all embedded VV&T problems. For example, our projects found issues in dealing with cross-compiling, timing, initialization, data value representation, and requirements engineering. These can be overcome, but that means vendors have more functions to add and projects will take more money and time. Plan for the unexpected.
- *Tools evolve:* Plan on test tool integration cycles with increments.
- *Configuration management (CM):* Even with VV&T tools, projects need to manage and control all aspects of the configuration, including the test tools as well as the test data.

29.7.3 Summary of Results

Although I am not permitted to reveal specific data, when compared to custom-developed tools and manual testing, establishing an automated commercial-based VV&T environment took about 50 percent fewer people. The projects tend to take these savings to create more and/or better automated tests. While adding to test automation, the projects maintained and improved functionality and quality. Further, maintenance-regression costs decreased because vendors provided upgrades for a low annual fee (relative to staff costs for purely customized tools). Commercial tools have a disadvantage of lacking total project process customization, but this has proven to be a minor issue as long as the major aspects of the process were supported by the tools.

Additionally, the projects reduced test staff work hours by between 40 and 75 percent (based on past VV&T cycles). We found that our test designers were more productive. We created the same number of tests and executed them in less time and found more defects earlier and faster. We had fewer "break-it, fix-it" cycles of regression testing, which meant that less effort was needed to achieve the same level of quality in the testing and the same defect detection rates.

In an embedded software VV&T environment, automated test tools can be good if you consider them as tools and not "magic bullets." People make tools work, and people do the hard parts of VV&T engineering that tools cannot do. Tools can automate the parts humans do not like or are not good at. Embedded projects continue to evolve VV&T automation. VV&T automation tools take effort, increments, and iterations. Tools aid people—but are not a replacement for them.

Good Point

The best use of tools is to support people.

29.8   The Contagious Clock

Jeffrey S. Miller, United States
Developer

Sometimes a good testing idea is contagious. Once it meets one need in your system, other uses may emerge that were quite unexpected when you began.

29.8.1   The Original Clock

I had just been hired at Google as a developer on a project during its preparation for public release. The system under development embedded a timestamp when recording certain events. Depending on how long it had been since the events were recorded, the system needed to present, interpret, or process the events in different ways.

The project had a strong mandate for developers to demonstrate the features they created via automated unit and system tests. As my first development task, I took on the job of designing and coding an application clock to make developer testing of time-based behavior simpler. In production, the application clock follows the system clock, but for testing, it wraps a test clock that can be manipulated to simulate the passing of minutes, hours, or days.

29.8.2   Increasing Usefulness

At first, the application clock was used for automated testing of portions of code encapsulating the core logic for time-dependent features. However, the system under development could be driven as a whole via a scripting language that could simulate one or more users interacting with the system to accomplish a set of tasks. Script-driven system tests were the common property of developers, feature owners, and a team of testing specialists. The testing team used script-driven system tests alongside manual verification to exercise the system in detail before each version was released to production. Soon I helped add commands to the scripting language to control the clock, allowing nonprogrammers to set up scenarios that included the passage of time.

29.8.3   Compelling Push

The original application clock was limited by design so that the clock could never be manipulated in the production system and thereby create troublesome inconsistencies. However, the testing team needed to exercise the system and its features interactively in a staging environment similar to the production setup. However, for testing time-based behavior, sometimes they set up a scenario before a weekend and returned after the weekend to verify the correct behavior. Other times the testing team changed the system clock so that the application would pick up the changed time and demonstrate the desired behavior. Both of these techniques were laborious and error prone, with the system clock manipulation frequently causing side effects that would ruin the test.

At the request of a primary tester and another developer familiar with the application clock, I revisited the application clock design. By this time, the system supported a mechanism for enabling and disabling features in production without having to redeploy a new system binary. This mechanism allowed me to guard the application clock from being manipulated on the actual production servers while allowing the testing team to control time interactively on their own simulated production servers.

29.8.4   Lessons Learned

The main thread of this story follows a version of a software developer's adage: "Wrap external dependencies." While the runtime library is normally considered internal, the clock it provides is a service outside the system. When the passage of time is important in system logic, wrapping the clock is a beneficial move.

The unexpected bonus was that adapting to successively larger scopes (isolated code, scripted captive system, interactive deployed system) provided benefit to more and different groups of people and for different types of tests. Although the larger scopes required modestly more architectural plumbing, in each case the wrapped clock fit into configuration systems that had been built to bring other benefits to the system. With hindsight, it would have been better to build them earlier had we known more of the operational and testing uses for the application clock.

I've now moved on to other work within the company, but I can see the application clock has been maintained and adapted to fit the system's new configuration mechanisms. I'm glad it continues to prove useful.

> **Lesson**
>
> Look for wider application for any useful utilities that help to automate some aspect of testing.

29.9   Flexibility of the Automation System

Mike Bartley, United Kingdom
Lecturer and consultant

We developed our test automation system ourselves and devised ways to adapt our automated testing to be more efficient in ways that we have not seen elsewhere.

Because we had already developed an inhouse software version control and build system, it was fairly easy to integrate our automation tool with our build system. This made our testing more efficient because we could selectively test only those modules that had changed, as shown by our source code dependency tree. If nothing that a particular test depended on had changed, that test would not be executed. This dramatically reduced the build and cycle time and thus allowed us to put in place continuous integration of builds and tests. We did keep an option that forced all tests to rebuild and run if we wanted to run a full regression test.

We made it easy to remove tests from the test suite when a test needed updating because of changes in the software it was testing. Although we were then cutting down on the test coverage because the test(s) were not run, it meant that the maintenance of those tests didn't have to be done immediately, thereby stopping the rest of the test suite from running.

We extended this to a way of "banning" specific tests for various reasons:

- The software has changed, but the tests have not yet been updated.
- A test is known to be giving a false failure (i.e., it fails but it should pass).
- A test is not restoring test machines to a known good state.

This idea proved to be a major benefit to our efficiency.

> **Tip**
>
> Being able to selectively choose tests to run or not to run can make the automation quicker and more efficient. Make it clear which tests are active and which are not.

29.10   A Tale of Too Many Tools (and Not Enough Cross-Department Support)

Adrian Smith, United Kingdom
QA lead

I have been involved in five automation projects over 5 years, with varying degrees of success.

29.10.1   Project 1: Simulation Using a DSTL

The first project was written in Python and batch scripts, running functional and performance tests on 85 to 145 PCs, simulating more than 20,000 machines. It was not originally an automation project, but I made it so. What started as a simple control program ended up growing into a fully flexible domain-specific test language (DSTL), as it would now be called, that enabled the tester to write test steps in a simple though unstructured keyword/parameter language. Expand the tests, alter them, chain them, and add new elements to the language as needed. The potential 9-month project was still being used 6 years later, It has ended up having a much better ROI than expected as its scope has increased over time. Thousands of man hours were saved and vastly more test runs were performed than a could have been run manually and with fewer execution errors.

About halfway through the automation project, my manager wanted me to do some manual testing for a different project because it was way behind. I knew this would be the end of the automation, so I managed to convince him that it would be better for me to stay with this (ad hoc) project—and this contributed to its success.

> **Lesson**
>
> Have the courage to argue your position with your manager.

29.10.2   Project 2: Testing a GUI Using TestComplete

The second automation project was to automate system-level applications. A tool was bought to experiment with: TestComplete 3. I had high hopes for another success using a DSTL for the testers, but this would take a long lead time to build. We then came across problems of automating GUI interfaces written in an automation-unfriendly way. I naively asked development to assist by modifying their code to help with the automation but was flatly refused. I had no support from management for this, so I had to go it alone. I probably should have stopped there and then.

> **Lesson**
>
> Without the cooperation of developers, test automation will be more difficult than it needs to be.

But I didn't. I persevered with the DSTL framework, though with little abstraction because I wanted to have something working sooner for management. At the time the first beta was just about ready, a new director of testing was appointed. The good news was that he thought automation was a good thing. The bad news was that he decided we needed to get "the right tool" with a single solution of manual test creation, results gathering, and reporting. I had to suspend my work with TestComplete and was given a 2-month task to evaluate a number of GUI automation tools. The final three were Rational Robot, Quality Centre QTP, and guess what: TestComplete. After the evaluation, I thought TestComplete was the most flexible and wanted to continue with it. The company thought differently, so this framework was never completed.

29.10.3   Project 3: Rational Robot

A 3-month proof-of-concept was then initiated for Rational Robot. If I had got further in the previous project, I could have at least reused the tests written. It was decided to do something similar with this tool, framework, abstraction, and tests being a thin layer on top. After 8 months, another automator and I had abstracted the tests and had a GUI object action library that could be generated automatically. Many hundreds of lines of code were automatically generated to do simple GUI actions as click a button or check a textbox. All that was changing was which control in which window to use. We had a good feeling about this framework because it was simple, and we were just starting to settle on a project to automate when, at this point, management decided to do a proof-of-concept for QuickTest Professional (QTP).

29.10.4   Project 4: Final Python Project and QTP Proof-of-Concept

Management were now getting involved and wanted to see some ROI that could be quantified to justify the purchase of this tool. We set to work on a single-use framework in Python, eventually automating 15 end-to-end smoke tests using GUI libraries. I had made a Python frontend so that testers could create and maintain tests without needing a lot of technical knowledge. The number of bugs that it found was too low to justify extending this automation to other areas. However, we were beginning to get occasional cooperation from developers. There were a couple of interfaces that could be called directly from Python to C written specifically for us to enable the tests to function.

We had one problem that we lost many days trying to figure out: The tool would crash but didn't report any error. It turned out to be a bug in the tool itself.

Good Point

Don't forget that the tool itself is also software and may have bugs.

For the proof-of-concept project for QTP, we had trouble trying to work with QTP in the way we wanted to, and a lot of time was wasted coming to grips with it. Eventually, we found a workaround to allow us to put many methods in one QTP file. At the end of this proof-of-concept, I would still have opted for one of the *other* tools.

Management chose QTP, and we had a real project to do with deadlines and end dates, so many of our ideals were curtailed, sidelined, or dropped. We again ran into problems with GUI objects and no help from developers.

29.10.5   Project 5: QTP2

With a new release of QTP, we tried to integrate our framework and Python code so that test results would be received centrally while still allowing us to launch tests including rebooting machines. This was using VMware virtualization and CruiseControl. We added extensively to application libraries, which were QTP libraries that did lots of specific tasks in a GUI, passing in a number of parameters. We also wanted to bring the test creation tool up to date so that the testers could use the automation easily. The thought behind this was that the easier it was to write a test, the quicker it would be to add tests, while the application libraries could be maintained by the automators.

However, management didn't want "extraneous time" spent on this perceived nonproductive activity!

Lesson

Managers sometimes think they know best even when they don't. As an automation champion, dare to say "Mission Impossible" when necessary.

The way we automators wanted it was that testers would not have to learn much programming, but because there would be no tool to help with creating tests, then testers would have to learn programming and know much more about the internal workings of the automation system. This is not a bad thing, but with a lot of pressure on the test department, it seemed (and was proven to be true) that testers rarely had time to dedicate to automation programming before being taken off again by another project. In a lot of cases, they never made it to do any automation because of deadline changes. At this time, automation still was not at the forefront of management thinking, but it was definitely starting to get their notice.

Progress was being made, libraries were expanding, and the tests were nearing completion, having overcome many of the problems of GUI fragility.

Now a problem that we automators had "forgotten about" came back. For the first time in a couple of years, the GUI interfaces began to be amended or over-hauled on a much more frequent but ad hoc basis (to us automators). We were not informed of changes as they happened, so our tests started failing, and it took a long time to find out why. After 2½ months of battling this upset (hundreds of changes to GUIs rendered even the smoke tests useless), I called a halt.

> **Lesson**
>
> Changes to the user interface can derail the automation if it cannot cope with such changes.

29.10.6   The End of the Story

Of the five automation projects I was involved in, only the first one achieved success. It was non-GUI and an isolated project. The others failed because of what seemed to be management decisions and lack of cross-department cooperation, but perhaps better communication would have helped.

Management had a bit of a shock and a rethink about automation after all the previous high-profile problems. Automation is now a deliverable for *developers*— one of the key problems before was that there was no incentive for developers or development managers to support or even cooperate with automators, as they had their own targets. Direct GUI automation has been abandoned, and automation is now at API level.

The final irony is that developers now have to maintain the APIs and automation code; if only they had agreed to maintain object libraries or had added a few lines to object maps earlier, there would have been less work for them now.

29.11   A Success with a Surprising End

George Wilkinson, United Kingdom
Test manager, trainer, and consultant

This anecdote describes some of my experiences on a large test automation proj-ect undertaken in 2007 and 2008. This project was to automate the core processes of the system validation tests of the National Health Service (NHS) Care Records System (CRS) application as rolled out within England by a large health IT Systems Integration company. This was being undertaken as part of the wider National Programme for IT (NPfit). The study covers 8 months of continuous progress, though with a surprising end.

An automation team was formed from a number of locations, including the North of England, the Midlands, and the West Country. Rather than looking for an exact skills match, we wanted people experienced in the CRS application who were enthusiastic about getting involved in automation. Because the team was geographically distributed, we decided to meet most weeks in a geographically central location for 2 days.

Good Point

Team-building is important for automation teams, too, especially when they are geographically dispersed.

29.11.1 Our Chosen Tool

TestStream was a commercial validation suite from Vedant Health, a United States company specializing in test health-care automation targeted at laboratory information systems (LIS) and health informatics systems (HIS). Our representative from Vedant traveled from the United States to start the project going and to run the training in the product set and the TestStream methodology.

Good Point

Take advantage of learning from others when the opportunity arises.

One of the useful features of TestStream was called Scenario Builder. It provided a way to construct automated patient journeys, which are made up of a number of predefined actions. The analyst simply pulls together these actions to create a longer test. There are over 600 actions for our CRS application system, and they include elements such as Register a Patient, Add Allergy, Schedule Surgery, and Check in a Patient. The Scenario Builder allows the sequence of events to be defined and viewed as a true patient journey.

No scripts, scripting, or further script development was required by either my team or Vedant Health, because the Scenario Builder's actions provided the components or scenarios required. The only requirements were a solid familiarity with the application under test and a thorough understanding of the test case (normally a patient journey).

We built a comprehensive library of automated scripts and devised standards and procedures about how they were to be stored and maintained. We developed a customized comparison and data collection tool, which we called CAT (collection analysis tool).

29.11.2 The Tool Infrastructure and an Interesting Issue as a Result

The product was installed and accessible by the user via a secured network to servers running virtual machines (VMs), as shown in Figure 29.3. Access to the VMs and thus to the test environments was provided to both the automation team running tests and company IT support staff.

Vedant's access for support could be from anywhere in the world because some of the highly experienced Vedant support staff moved around the world assisting other clients. This required remote access to our infrastructure, but we soon discovered that it didn't work. The system was so secure (in order to prevent fraudulent access into any test environment that may hold live patient data) that it prevented the remote access facility from working.

> **Good Point**
>
> Don't forget to test your support facility, especially if you have stringent security requirements.

We resolved the issue by allowing both companies independent access to another test system that was clean of any patient data. This solution was foolproof from a security perspective but provided only limited support, which was to be mitigated by the test system holding the same application version that the majority of systems were holding in the field. Although the solution was not perfect, because the deployments were not always running the same system version, it was a step in the right direction—and one on which we could make progress.

Looking back, we realized that no feasibility study had been conducted on support, which could have prevented the remote access issue from arising.

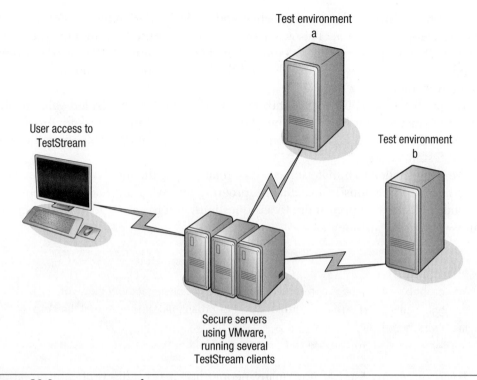

FIGURE 29.3   TestStream infrastructure

29.11.3 Going toward Rollout

Over the next 3 to 4 months, the team grew from 6 to 10, with an additional four part-time support members. We produced a catalog of the automation tests that were available to the deployment projects to build their own scenarios. As we progressed with the pilot, we identified data and configuration requirements that were localized to the individual projects as they moved away from a standard. This meant that our current generic approach needed to be tailored for the deployment-specific test environment. What we had done was created a process but lost some sight of our individual customer's requirements.

Lesson

Don't invest too much effort in designing your automation without testing it out in a real situation.

We ran a sample of the data collection and clinical ordering features of the CRS for a particular deployment. This was a great success because we found many defects that were thereby prevented from entering the live environment. We found between 10 and 100 defects on well-built and established test environments and thousands on other environments.

We published a report to the stakeholders showing how we added value to the current manual test approach. We found that we could automate tests for around 70 percent of the installed CRS functionality and save approximately 30 percent of our current testing effort.

We now decided to initiate some public relations for the tool. We scheduled several educational sessions to explain the program and what we had been doing, to give stakeholders the opportunity to ask questions, and to gather feedback from the teams working on customer sites.

Lesson

You probably need to do more public relations and communication than you thought. Make pilots or demonstrations part of project milestones so that they are more visible.

I was quite surprised at how many people had a very different interpretation than we did of the product set and its intentions and of software test automation itself. Most people's experience with automation test tools is that they require constant scripting or maintenance to work. Fortunately, these sessions helped to convince people that our automation was an improvement on that.

We also dispelled some illusions and misperceptions about automation and set more realistic expectations. The public relations meeting also raised the team's confidence and gave them some well-deserved recognition.

The automation team were elated by the results from the pilot project and the fact we were now in the rollout stage. Their confidence was really growing; after all, they had made it work. TestStream was out there and making a real difference! We were positioning ourselves well, and the future, at last, after a good deal of effort, was looking more positive.

29.11.4 The Unexpected Happens

In late May 2008, after discussing our success so far and the rollout plans, the overall project was cancelled because of a breakdown in the contract with the systems integration company. Therefore, our automation project was also cancelled. I gathered my team together for the last team meeting and officially announced the cancellation. They had worked extremely hard, but the automation project was over; all those many late evenings, weekends, sheer determination, and extra miles traveling to make this work were now history. What a heartbreaking end to what should have been a great success.

Good Point

Sometimes in spite of a great effort, things don't go the way we expect because of factors entirely out of our control. Take what you can from the experience to use next time.

29.12 Cooperation Can Overcome Resource Limitations

Michael Albrecht, Sweden
Test manager, consultant, and speaker

I was in a test team that was testing technical aspects of banking system processing without access to a GUI. For this project, we needed not just domain knowledge but more technical skills than we had. Rather than take the traditional project approach and try to hire someone, we got everyone together, both testers and developers, and developed the skills we needed between us, although we did need to bring some testers with coding skills into the team.

We had no money for tools, so we just started to use the same open source tools that the developers were using. The difference in the way we used them was that we needed to do some coding to create scenarios for our tests rather than just exercising each one individually. We also needed to verify our expected results and double-check with the database directly.

We didn't spend any money on tools, but we did spend a lot of time (we also built our own performance-testing tool). Sometimes it is easier to explain (or hide) these costs: The purchase of a tool would appear to be a large single cost, but time being spent over months or years doesn't appear to be as significant even if it is the same or even more money!

We found that close cooperation with the customer and working as a team enabled us to succeed in our automation. Being forced to use the same tools was a blessing in disguise in the end.

P.S. from Lisa Crispin: In one project (a good while ago), I knew I needed to get help from the developers to progress the automation, so I decided to use the same programming language for the tests that the developers were using. I bought myself a book and started writing scripts. When I needed help, the programmers were happy to help me because they knew the language.

> **Lesson**
>
> Cooperation between testers and developers is good for automation, and so is extending the tools you already use. And sometimes deviousness works!

29.13   An Automation Process for Large-Scale Success

Michael Snyman, South Africa

Test manager

I work for a large bank in South Africa, employing 25,000 staff. We adopted test automation from 2006 to 2008 with a clear aim of reducing costs and increasing productivity.

It was Edward Deming who said, "If you can't describe what you are doing as a process, you don't know what you are doing." In our case, this was true; any success in the area of automation was due to individual skill and a large amount of luck. The challenge was in taking what the successful individuals did and describing this practice in the form of a process.

29.13.1   Where We Started

Our shelves were littered with numerous tool acquisitions and implementations with varying degrees of success. Each of these individual attempts had been focused on very limited and sometimes selfish objectives. The habit of looking only at accomplishing immediate project goals had significantly affected the ability of the organization to optimally use its selected tools. Such a one-sided view of automation had a considerable negative effect on operational activities such as regression testing and on justifying the investment made. Compounding the problem was the loss of valuable information in the form of test cases, test scenarios, and test data.

> **Lesson**
>
> Focusing on too low a level in the organization does not optimize automation as a whole.

Automation was involved too late in the process. How often is automation viewed as the savior of the behind-schedule project? When automation does not deliver on these unrealistic expectations, it becomes yet another automation failure. In reality, it is very different; my experience points to automation requiring multiple cycles and project releases for it to become fully effective and provide an acceptable ROI.

We weren't capitalizing on what we could have learned. For example, a failure experienced in production is an example of a test missed and one that should be included in the test cases for the next release. Test automation should provide an interface for both manual testers and incident management systems with the aim of capturing lessons learned during any phase in the project lifecycle.

The seeming lack of success in test automation initiatives and the large upfront investment required deters projects from planning and implementing test automation. The reluctance to learn from unsuccessful implementations and the habit of blaming the tool for failure in automation projects has resulted in a stigma linked to specific tools and automation in general.

Past attempts to justify automation focused on quality as the key attribute to be considered and measured. The difficulty in dealing with quality is that it is extremely complex. We clearly needed a way of providing a cost–benefit calculation for test automation using an attribute other than quality.

> **Good Point**
>
> Appropriate objectives are critical. Automation does not improve the quality of the tests or the software being tested.

In the absence of a detailed automation framework and process, a large dependency was placed on the skill and ability of individual team members.

29.13.2 The Key to Our Eventual Success: An Automation Process

In 2006, a formal project was launched with dedicated resources, a champion for automation, a good technical framework, clear goals, and a detailed plan. In this anecdote, I describe one aspect that was critical to our success in achieving automation on a large scale.

It was clear, based on past experience, that a standard approach for automation should be defined and documented in the form of a test automation process. However, this process could not exist in isolation but had to be integrated into the newly defined manual test process and should be compatible with the organizational software development lifecycle (SDLC). For example, in the requirement for a defined automation process, the framework required high-level activities described as *specification analysis, script creation, scenario documentation, validation,* and *data sourcing* that needed to be satisfied by a detailed process. The full process is shown in Figure 29.4.

> **Tip**
>
> The more people who are involved in automation, the better the documentation about it needs to be.

From the documented automation framework, we were able to extract the key process activities required to perform and support most automated testing activities. Here follows a brief description of the objective of each step.

- *Analysis and design:* Understand the client's requirements, and establish if it is possible to satisfy each requirement with current technology at our disposal.
- *Scripting and configuration:* Implement the client's requirements via an automated solution. This might include recoding, coding, and building special utilities.
- *Parameter definition:* Assess scripts against system user–defined scenarios with the aim of identifying elements to be parameterized.
- *Parameter management:* Manage large amounts of data in customized spreadsheets.
- *Scenario collection:* Populate spreadsheets with scenarios provided by stakeholders of the system.
- *Validation:* Check the spreadsheets and parameters, incorporating pass and fail criteria in the spreadsheets and allowing the automated script to validate results of executed tests.

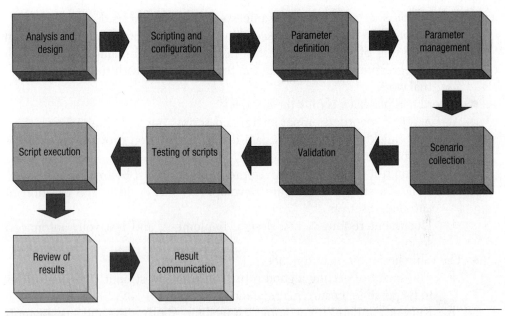

FIGURE 29.4 Automation process

- *Testing of scripts:* Ensure that the scripts run as expected, and remove any bugs in the scripts.
- *Script execution:* Run the scripts with the scenarios and parameters defined.
- *Review of results:* Internally review the results of script execution, what tests passed and failed, any common problems such as an unavailable environment, and so on.
- *Result communication:* Summarize the results sent to managers, developers, stakeholders, and others.

29.13.3 What We Learned

These are the main lessons we learned on our journey through test automation:

- Having a tool is not an automation strategy.
    a. The tool is nothing more than an enabler of a well-thought-out set of automation activities.
    b. We believe that if you approach automation correctly, you should be able to switch between tools with little or no impact.

- Automation does not test in the same way as manual testers do.
  a. Automation will never replace manual testers. We view automation as an extension of the manual tester, taking care of mundane activities such as regression testing, leaving the tester to get on with the more intellectual work.
- Record and playback is only the start.
  a. A set of recorded, unparameterized scripts has very limited reuse and ages quickly. The focus on data-driven automation provides us with the flexibility and reuse required.
- Automation test scripts are software programs and must be treated as such.
  a. Follow a standard software development life cycle in the creation of automated scripts.
  b. Document requirements; design, implement, and test your automated scripts.
- The value lies in the maintenance.
  a. The secret of getting a good return on your investment is reuse; for this to be possible, ensure maintenance is simple.
  b. Keyword or data-driven approach facilitates both reuse and easy maintenance.

29.13.4 Return on Investment

Our automation process enabled us to achieve consistency of automation practices across the bank. We showed a benefit of $8,600,000 after 3 years. This benefit calculation method was reviewed by our finance team at the highest level, and the benefits were confirmed by the individual system owner for whom the testing was done.

The total amount invested in the testing project, of which automation was a subproject, was in the area of $4,200,000. The amount spent on automation was less than 20 percent of this total budget, including the acquisition of functional testing tools, consulting, and the creation and execution of automated test scripts.

The benefit calculation was primarily based on the saving achieved in human resource costs. For example, one of our main systems used in the sales process took, on average, 4 weeks with 20 human resources to regression test. With automation, we reduced that process to 5 days and two resources: a reduction from 2,800 manhours to 70 man-hours. This translated to a financial savings of about $120,500 per regression cycle. If you take into account that, on average, we run two full regression cycles per release and have multiple system releases per year, and that we are involved in various other systems, the savings soon start adding up.

We have a spreadsheet that uses parameters as the basis for all calculations. It allows us to compare the manual execution time per parameter to the automated time. We refer to parameters as the inputs required by the system under test (e.g., if we are testing a transfer from one account to another, parameters might be "from account," "to account," and "amount"). So, if we say that conservatively we invested $850,000 in automation and had benefit of $8,600,000, then the ROI for automation (ROI = (Gain − Cost)/Cost) was over 900 percent.

From a project testing perspective, the organization viewed the return on the total investment in testing, which was still over 100 percent. (Usually, if ROI is 10 percent or more, it is considered an excellent investment!)

It is also interesting to note that the automation part was the only initiative within the project testing that could be measured accurately, and as such, it provided justification for the entire project.

Good Point

Keep good records of the costs and benefits of automation (and testing) to make sure the highest levels in the organization realize what a good investment they have made in automating testing.

29.14   Test Automation Isn't Always What It Seems

Julian Harty, United Kingdom
Tester at large

I strongly believe testing can and should use automation appropriately, and conversely, we should be careful not to waste time and resources on automating garbage (e.g., ineffective, misguided, or useless tests). Also, we should beware of being beguiled by shiny automation for its own sake, and over the years, I've sadly met many people who believe, without foundation, that because they have automated tests, these tests are appropriate or sufficient. One of my self-assigned responsibilities as a test engineer is to challenge these flawed tests and retire as many as practical.

Good Point

Just because a test is automated doesn't make it a good test.

This anecdote includes several experience reports of test automation, both good and bad. Generally, I was directly involved in them, but sometimes the analysis was done by other team members. They are taken from companies I've worked with and for over the last 11 years. Project teams ranged from about 10 to 150 technical staff and typically ran for several years.

In every case, test automation was core to the project.

29.14.1 Just Catching Exceptions Does Not Make It a Good Test

A large global application included several APIs that allowed both internal and external groups to integrate with it. Java was the primary programming language. Over the years, before I was involved, hundreds of automated tests had been written for the respective APIs. For one API, the tests were written as a separate application, started from the command line, and in the other, the open source JUnit framework was used. Each set of tests ran slowly, and several days were required to update the tests after each release from the application's development team.

Our team of test engineers was asked to assume responsibility for both sets of tests. Each engineer was assigned to one set of tests. We spent several days learning how to simply run each set of tests (the process was cumbersome, poorly documented, and simply unreliable). We then started reading through the source code. What we found horrified us: There was an incredible amount of poorly written, duplicated code (implying little or no software design or structure), and worst of all, the only thing each test did to determine success or failure was catch runtime exceptions (e.g., out of memory, network timeout). When an exception was caught, the test reported a failure.

> **Good Point**
>
> Just because automated tests can be run doesn't make it good automation. You need to know the details of what the test does in order to assess whether or not it is a good test.

API tests should provide known inputs and confirm the results received are as expected without undesirable side effects or problems. For example, if we have an API for a calculator program, a typical method may be

```
result = divide(numerator, denominator);
```

A good test should check that the calculated result is within the error range for the sum (for real numbers, the answer may be approximated, truncated, or rounded, etc.). It should also check for what happens when invalid inputs (e.g., trying to divide by zero) are provided. For example, what should the result be, and should an exception be thrown? (And if so, which exception, and what should the exception contain?)

After spending several more weeks working on the test automation code, we ended up deleting all the tests in one case and effectively rewriting the tests for the other API. In both cases, we decided to focus on enhancing the lower-level unit tests written by the developers of the respective APIs rather than propagating or sustaining inadequate tests written by testing "specialists."

> **Good Point**
>
> Don't be afraid to throw away bad automation code and poor automated tests.

29.14.2   Sometimes the Failing Test Is the Test Worth Trusting

We decided to restructure our web browser–based tests because the existing tests had various problems and limitations, including high maintenance and poor reliability. The initial restructuring went well, and we also migrated from Selenium RC to WebDriver, which had a more compact and powerful API designed to make tests easier and faster to write. At this stage, the tests ran on a single machine, typically shared with the web application under test when run by the automated build process.

The tests took a long time to run (tens of minutes), which was much longer than our goal (of having them run within a few minutes). Thankfully, we had existing infrastructure to run the tests in parallel across banks of machines. The tests needed to connect to the appropriate test server, which was compiled and started by the build process, so the test engineer made what seemed to be the appropriate modifications to the automated tests to take advantage of the distributed testing infrastructure. Perplexingly, however, one of the tests failed every time he ran the tests using the distributed infrastructure.

Over the next few days, he dug into his code, the configuration scripts, and so on, but was unable to get the now embarrassingly obdurate test to pass. Finally, he discovered that a network configuration issue prevented any of the tests from reaching the newly built server; however, *only one of the tests detected this!* At this point, he was able to fix the network configuration issue and finally get the failing test to pass.

> **Good Point**
>
> Just because the tests pass, it doesn't mean that all is well. Tests need to be
> tested, too.

Several valuable lessons were learned:

- The other existing tests had effectively been worthless because they didn't fail when they could not reach the server at all.
- Even expert engineers can be fooled for days when test results don't conform to expectations.
- The failing test was actually the friend of the project because it exposed the problems with the rest of the—very flawed—tests.

One concept worth embracing is to consider how easily the current test could be fooled, or misled, into providing an erroneous result. For example, would an automated test for an email service detect missing menu options? Then consider how to strengthen the test so that it will not be fooled by this problem. While this concept can be applied iteratively to a given test, I suggest you limit yourself to addressing potentially significant problems; otherwise, your test code may take too long to write, maintain, and run.

29.14.3 Sometimes, Micro-Automation Delivers the Jackpot

In this story, 10 lines of Perl cracked open a critical nationwide system.

I learned many years ago that I'm not a brilliant typist. On one project, my poor typing helped expose a potential security issue when I accidentally mistyped some commands for a file transfer protocol in a telnet application, which led to a potential problem. Although I wanted to explore the potential flaw more scientifically, I continued to mistype commands in different ways and found that my mistakes were now hampering my ability to explore the application effectively. At the time, I lacked UNIX or Perl skills, so although writing an automated script to enter the commands seemed sensible, I was unsure whether it was worth spending the time to learn how to write a suitable script.

Salvation came in the form of a gnarly system administrator who knew both UNIX and Perl inside-out. Furthermore, the system architect had unilaterally decreed there were no security flaws in his file transfer protocol, and the system administrator saw a great opportunity to potentially prove the architect wrong, so he immediately offered to write a simple command-line script in Perl that would start telnet and issue various preliminary commands (those I'd been mistyping). The work took him less than 30 minutes.

Good Point

Don't hesitate to ask for help; it can save a lot of time (and hassle).

Once I had this basic script, I was able to experiment with the script through interactive typing, once the script had completed the initial steps, or by adding additional file transfer commands to custom versions of the script. With this script, we eventually proved that there were serious issues in the implementation of the file transfer protocol that resulted in buffer overflows in the underlying program, which we could then exploit to compromise the security of the system. I also identified several design flaws in the software update mechanism and proved that these flaws allowed an attacker to effectively disable the entire nationwide system. Not bad for a few hours work (and a few days to get permission to reproduce the problems in various environments, including the live production system).

TOOLS

Table A.1 contains the tools referred to in this book and the chapter(s) where each is mentioned. Tools are classified into commercial tools (Comm) and open source tools (Open). Because this table is intended to help you find more information about tools, it does not include inhouse tools. Such tools are mentioned only in the chapter in which they are described but are not available to the general public. A brief description of the type of tool is included in the table.

We included a web address for each of the tools listed here. There is a similarity here to the expression "All models are wrong, but some models are useful" (George Box). This list is guaranteed to be wrong (by the time the book is printed) but was correct at the time of the last checking (November 2011). As well as being a historical snapshot of the tools at this time, we hope that this list, although wrong, will be useful as a starting point to finding these tools.

Table A.1   Tools Referred to in This Book

Tool name	Type	Description
A-Tool	Comm	Test execution and performance test tool
ACTS (formerly FireEye)	Open	Combinatorial testing tool
AdaTEST	Comm	Unit test tool
Ant	Open	Java-based build tool
Apache Web Server	Open	Web server
Araxis Merge	Comm	File compare
ATRT	Comm	Automated test and retest (automated testing framework and solution)
ATS4 AppModel	Open	Modeling tool for GUI flow and test
AutoIt	Open	Shell scripting tool
Automator QA (replaced by Rational Testing Suite)	Comm	Record and playback assisted automation tools
BIRT	Comm	Business and intelligence reporting tool, part of Eclipse
BridgePoint	Comm	Model-based tool for embedded systems
CA-VERIFY	Comm	Mainframe test execution tool
Cacti	Open	Monitoring/graphing tool
Canoo WebTest	Open	Web application test tool
Cantata	Comm	Unit test tool
CATS (Constrained Array Test System)	Inhouse now Comm	CATS generates pairwise test combinations and allows for system constraints such as invalid pairings
CruiseControl	Open	Wrapper for automating builds

Web site	Chapter
www.symbio.com/products/a tool/	14
http://csrc.nist.gov/groups/SNS/acts/index.html	7
www.ipl.com	29
http://Ant.apache.org	1
http://httpd.apache.org	11
www.araxis.com/merge/index.html	21
http://idtus.com/autotestretest	7
http://ats4appmodel.sourceforge.net	14
www.autoitscript.com/autoit3/	22
www.ibm.com/software/rational/	10
http://eclipse.org/birt/phoenix/	7
www.mentor.com/products/sm/model_development/bridgepoint/	29
www.ca.com/us/products/detail/ca-verify-for-cics.aspx	5
www.cacti.net	19
http://Webtest.canoo.com	1
www.ipl.com	29
www.testcover.com	28
http://cruisecontrol.sourceforge.net	1, 29

Continues

Table A.1 Tools Referred to in This Book (Continued)

Tool name	Type	Description
CVS (Concurrent Versions System)	Open	Source code configuration management
Diff Doc	Comm	File compare
eCATT	for SAP customers	Extended Computer-Aided Test Tool, SAP's own automation test tool
Eclipse	Open	Java integrated development environment
Eclipse plug-ins	Open	Plug-ins for Eclipse
Eclipse Rich Client Platform	Open	A software development and deployment environment
eggPlant	Comm	Image-based remote access user interface test execution tool
EMMA	Open	Java coverage tool
FASTBoX Framework	Comm	Test execution framework
FEST Swing Java Libraries	Open	Java libraries that support test automation; used to create the software test automation tool
FireEye, now called ACTS	Open	Combinatorial testing tool
Fit	Open	Framework for acceptance tests
FitNesse	Open	Framework for acceptance tests
Hiperstation	Comm	Mainframe testing tool
Hudson	Open	Continuous integration server, continuous build tool
IDATG, now TEMPPO Designer	Comm	Model-based test design and test case generation

Web site	Chapter
www.nongnu.org/cvs	1
www.softinterface.com/MD/Document-Comparison-Software.htm	21
www.sdn.sap.com/irj/sdn/ecatt	15
www.eclipse.org	7, 12
www.eclipse.org/pde/	7
www.eclipse.org/home/categories/rcp.php	7
www.testplant.com	7, 17, 25
http://emma.sourceforge.net/	2
www.ctg.com/europe/we-know/testing/test-automation	16
http://fest.easytesting.org	20
http://csrc.nist.gov/groups/SNS/acts/index.html	7
http://fit.c2.com/	19
http://fitnesse.org	1
www.compuware.com/mainframe-solutions/hiperstation-automated-mainframe-testing.html	12
http://hudson-ci.org	1, 7, 18
http://at.atos.net/temppo	9

Continues

Table A.1 Tools Referred to in This Book (Continued)

Tool name	Type	Description
IP Engine Per Server (IPEPS)	Comm	Standalone KVM-over-IP device for attaching to system under test
JET (Java Engine for Testing) and JAG (JET Agent)	Inhouse, then Open	Test execution tool and framework
JMeter	Open	Load testing tool
JUnit	Open	Java framework for unit tests, unit test framework, and test execution tool
LabVIEW	Comm	A graphical programming environment used to develop measurement, test, and control systems
LDRA TBrun	Comm	See TBrun
Liberation (formerly ATAA)	Comm	Test automation framework
Lotus 123	Comm	Spreadsheet application
Mathematica	Comm	Computation application
MATLAB	Comm	High-level computing language and interactive environment for data analysis, etc.
Microsoft Visual Studio	Comm	Interactive development environment (IDE) used for test automation and debugging. Integrates with Visual Studio Team Foundation Server.
Model 204	Comm	Database management system
Model Designer	Open	A test modeling tool, part of the TEMA toolset
Nagios	Open and Comm	Monitoring, visualization, reporting tool

Web site	Chapter
www.adder.com/uk	25
http://kenai.com/projects/jet	2
http://jakarta.apache.org/jmeter/	19
www.junit.org	1, 18, 29
www.ni.com/LabVIEW	13
www.simplytesting.com	5
www.ibm.com/software/lotus/	10
www.wolfram.com/mathematica/	29
www.mathworks.com/products/matlab/	7, 29
www.microsoft.com/visualstudio/	3
www.rocketsoftware.com/m204	12
http://tema.cs.tut.fi	14
www.nagios.org	19

Continues

Table A.1   Tools Referred to in This Book (Continued)

Tool name	Type	Description
Net-SNMP	Open	Simple Network Management Protocol tool suite
NMAP	Open	Security scanner
Nunit	Open	Automated unit testing tool
OATS (Orthogonal Array Testing Strategy) Now called rdExpert	Home, then Comm	OATS uses mathematical techniques called orthogonal arrays to generate pairwise test combinations
OpenSTA	Open	Performance testing tool
PDF Forms plug-in	Comm	Automation interface
PICT	Comm	Pairwise independent combinatorial testing
QADirector	Comm	Test management
QARun	Comm	Capture/replay
QEMM (Quarterdek Expanded Memory Manager)	Comm	Memory management tools for MS-DOS
Quality Center (QC)	Comm	Test management tool
Quality Works, See SilkTest	Comm	Test tool suite
QTP (QuickTest Pro/ Professional)	Comm	Test tool suite
Rational Robot	Comm	Test execution tool
RealVNC	Comm	Virtual network computing (VNC) GUI-sharing application
RequisitePro	Comm	Requirements management tool
Selenium	Open	Test execution tool

Web site	Chapter
www.net-snmp.org	11
http://nmap.org	11
www.nunit.org	7
www.phadkeassociates.com	28
www.opensta.org	9
www.adobe.com	16
http://msdn.microsoft.com/en-us/testing/bb980925	15
www.microfocus.com/assets/qadirector-data-sheet_tcm6-6890.pdf	27
Ex Compuware; no longer supported	21
No longer available	10
www.hp.com	23, 29
Quality Works is the previous version of SilkTest	23
www.hp.com	5, 6, 16, 22, 23, 24, 29
www-01.ibm.com/software/awdtools/tester/robot/	24, 29
www.realvnc.com	25
http://www-01.ibm.com/software/awdtools/reqpro/	26
http://seleniumhq.org	17, 29

Continues

Table A.1 Tools Referred to in This Book (Continued)

Tool name	Type	Description
Selenium RC	Open	Test tool for writing automated web application UI tests in any programming language against any HTTP website using any mainstream JavaScript-enabled browser
SendMail	Open	Email tool suite
SilkTest	Comm	GUI test automation tool
SLIM	Open	Templating engine using JSP syntax
SOAP UI	Open	Functional and load testing tool for web services
SPSS	Comm	Statistical package; tool for manipulating large data files; and comparing expected and actual results
Subversion (aka SVN)	Open	Source code configuration management
SuperSMITH Visual	Comm	Scientific plotting software to make Crow-AMSAA reliability growth plots
T-Plan Robot	Comm/Open (reduced scope)	Uses VNC technology to run tests remotely
TEMPPO	Comm	Test management tool
TBrun	Comm	Unit testing tool
TEMA	Open	A toolset for model-based testing
TestComplete	Comm	Test execution
TestExecute	Comm	Test execution
TestPartner	Comm	GUI test automation tool
Teststream	Comm	Validation suite for health-care automation

Web site	Chapter
http://seleniumhq.org/projects/remote-control/	29
www.sendmail.org	11
www.microfocus.com/products/SilkTest/index.asp	9, 20
http://java-source.net/open-source/web-testing-tools/slim	1
www.soapui.org	19
www-01.ibm.com/software/analytics/spss/	10
http://subversion.apache.org	1, 7
www.weibullnews.com	13
www.t-plan.com/robot/	7
http://at.atos.net/temppo	9
www.ldra.com/tbrun.asp	29
http://tema.cs.tut.fi	14
http://smartbear.com/products/qa-tools/automated-testing/	20, 21, 29
http://smartbear.com/products/qa-tools/automated-testing/testexecute/	21
www.microfocus.com/products/TestPartner/index.asp	9, 21, 27
www.vedanthealth.com	29

Continues

Table A.1 Tools Referred to in This Book (Continued)

Tool name	Type	Description
Text Image Generator (TIG)	Comm	Generates text images from text descriptions for use with eggPlant's embedded image-recognition engine
"The Automator" (not its real name)	Comm	Test execution
TwinText	Comm	Documentation generation
Visual Source Safe	Comm	Configuration management tool
Visual Test (formerly MS-Test)	Comm	GUI test execution tool
VixCOM	Open	API to enable automated interaction between custom application and virtualization product
VMware	Comm	Virtualization product
VNCRobot	Open	Uses VNC technology to run tests remotely
Watir	Open	GUI test driver
WDK (Windows Driver Kit)	Inhouse and Open	A software development kit for Microsoft Windows device drivers
WebDriver	Open	Test execution tool, test automation framework for web browsers. (WebDriver and Selenium have been merged into a single framework.)
WebLOAD Open Source	Open	Load testing tool (commercial version also available)
Windows PowerShell	Comm	Task automation framework
WinRunner	Comm	GUI test automation tool. (WinRunner is no longer supported.)
x11vnc	Open	VNC server for real X displays

Web site	Chapter
www.testplant.com/products/eggplant/	25
A fictitious tool	4
www.ptlogica.com/TwinText/	16
http://msdn.microsoft.com/en-us/vstudio/default.aspx	4
www.ibm.com/	5
http://vixcomwrapper.codeplex.com/	22
www.vmware.com	22, 29
http://vncrobot.en.softonic.com/	7
http://watir.com/	1, 19
www.microsoft.com/whdc/devtools/wdk/default.mspx	8
http://code.google.com/p/selenium/	17, 29
www.webload.org/	19
http://msdn.microsoft.com/en-us/library/dd835506(v=VS.85).aspx	3
www.hp.com	5, 9
www.karlrunge.com/x11vnc/	25

ABOUT THE CASE STUDY AUTHORS

This section contains biographical information for the authors of the major case studies presented in Chapters 1 through 28.

Chapter 1: Lisa Crispin

Lisa Crispin is the coauthor, with Janet Gregory, of *Agile Testing: A Practical Guide for Testers and Agile Teams* (Addison-Wesley, 2009), coauthor, with Tip House, of *Extreme Testing* (Addison-Wesley, 2002), and a contributor to *Beautiful Testing* (O'Reilly, 2009). She has worked as a tester on agile teams since 2000 and enjoys sharing her experiences via writing, presenting, teaching, and participating in agile testing communities around the world. Lisa was named one of the 13 Women of Influence in testing by *Software Test & Performance Magazine* in 2010. For more about Lisa's work, visit www.lisacrispin.com; @lisacrispin on Twitter; gplus.to/lisacrispin on Google+.

Chapter 2: Henri van de Scheur

Henri van de Scheur has worked for more than 20 years in the IT industry and more than 10 years in testing and general quality assurance. In 2007, he established the interest group Software Testing within the Norwegian Society for the middle of Norway and has been chairman since then. In addition, he is the chairman for the yearly conference Free Test (see http://free-test.org), covering the use of open source tools.

The experiences described in his case study were from a previous job. Since 2009, he has been working as quality assurance lead at Verdande Technology AS in Trondheim, Norway.

Chapter 3: Ken Johnston and Felix Deschamps

Ken Johnston is currently (2011) the principal test manager for the Bing shopping, travel, and entertainment domains. Since joining Microsoft in 1998, Johnston has filled many other roles, including test lead on Site Server and Microsoft Commercial Internet System; test manager on Bing infrastructure, data modeling, and visualization; and live site engineer, Hosted Exchange (an early attempt at cloud Exchange), knowledge worker services, Net Docs, Microsoft billing and subscription platform services, and group manager of Office 2010 Internet platform and operations team. For two and a half years (2004–2006), he served as the director of test excellence for Microsoft. Ken is a regular presenter at software testing conferences in the United States and Europe and is coauthor of the book *How We Test Software at Microsoft* (Microsoft, 2009), www.hwtsam.com.

Felix Deschamps joined Microsoft in 2005 as a software development engineer in test (SDET) on the Exchange Server team shipping Exchange Server 2007 and 2010. For several years, Felix worked as a senior SDET on the Exchange cloud service now shipped as part of Office 365. In this role, he was instrumental in helping develop the team's live site test automation infrastructure. Prior to joining Microsoft, Felix was a software developer at Decision Software.

Chapter 4: Bo Roop

Bo Roop is currently (2011) employed as a senior software quality assurance engineer at the world's largest designer and manufacturer of color measurement systems. He is responsible for testing their retail paint matching systems, which are created using an agile-based software development methodology. Bo helps gather and refine user requirements, prototypes user interfaces, and ultimately performs the software testing of the final product.

This offers a unique opportunity for a tester to perform in the same arena as the software developers. Testers in this organization are held with the same esteem as developers; and while

their responsibilities are quite different, the common goals cannot be achieved without total group effort.

Testing is a passion of Bo's, and he is involved with local software groups as well as a few online forums. He's an advocate for software that meets the customer's needs and expectations and can frequently be heard trying to redirect teams toward a more customer-centric point of view.

Bo is also an avid motorcyclist, enjoys snowboarding and skateboarding, and has recently taken up disc golf. He learned to cook and sew from his mother and still takes pleasure in both. Most of all, he enjoys spending time with his family.

Chapter 5: John Kent

John Kent has been working in the software industry for over 25 years and has specialized in test automation and test management for the last 20. He designed and built the Liberation automated testing framework and is CEO of Simply Testing Ltd. He is coauthor of the *Official Netscape JavaScript Book* (Ventana, 1996). He was a key contributor to the development of the T-Plan test management tool and more recently has been developing an Entity Model for Testing. John often writes for software testing magazines, including his "View From Kent" column for *Professional Tester Magazine*. He regularly presents to international audiences on software testing subjects. John has a MSc in computing and lives in West Sussex with his wife and two children.

Chapter 6: Ane Clausen

Ane Clausen lives in Copenhagen, Denmark. She has an MSc in computer science from the University of Copenhagen. She has worked with IT systems for insurance and pension companies for over 20 years, the past 10 years as a test manager and team lead. She has been automating testing since 2005. She has also been a project manager, analyst, developer, method specialist, and teacher in the technical university of Denmark, and she presents at conferences. Since 2010, she has been working as a test manager and team lead on an outsourcing project to India that also included test automation.

Chapter 7: Elfriede Dustin

Elfriede Dustin enjoys researching new ideas and discovering new approaches to the automated software testing challenge. Software development is still an art, and that makes automated software testing a special challenge. Elfriede has a BS in computer science and over 20 years of IT experience, implementing effective testing strategies on both government and commercial programs.

Elfriede is author and coauthor of a number of books, including *Automated Software Testing* (Addison-Wesley, 1999), *Effective Software Testing* (Addison-Wesley, 2002), *Quality Web Systems* (Addison-Wesley, 2002), *Testing SAP 3/R* (Wiley, 2007), *The Art of Software Security Testing* (Addison-Wesley, 2002), and her latest, *Implementing Automated Software Testing* (Addison-Wesley, 2009). She is a frequent speaker at international conferences and a frequent contributor to magazines and various online publications.

Chapter 8: Alan Page

Alan Page began his career as a tester in 1993 and joined Microsoft in 1995. He is a principal SDET on the Xbox platform team where he splits his time between coaching testers across the division and helping to improve the skeletal tracking system of Kinect. Alan also leads Microsoft's test architect group and other internal quality- and testing-focused communities.

Before coming to Microsoft, Alan worked at a small software company, developing and testing multimedia applications for Windows 3.1. His first job at Microsoft was testing networking functionality on Windows 95. Since then, he's worked on Internet Explorer (versions 2 and 3), Windows 98, Windows . . . ahem . . . Millennium, several versions of Windows CE, and the most recent version of Microsoft Lync.

Alan is also a frequent speaker at industry testing conferences and has published several articles on testing and quality in testing and software engineering magazines. Alan writes about testing on his blog (http://angryweasel.com/blog), was the lead author of *How We Test Software at Microsoft* (Microsoft Press, 2008), and recently contributed a chapter to *Beautiful Testing* (O'Reilly Press, 2009).

Chapter 9: Stefan Mohacsi and Armin Beer

At the time of the project, both authors worked for Siemens, Beer as an external contributor to Public and Healthcare Solutions, and Mohacsi as head of the Support Center Test.

Stefan Mohacsi (right) studied computer science at the Technical University of Vienna. In 1997, he joined Siemens and became project manager of the research project IDATG (Integrating Design and Automated Test Case Generation). Over the years, the first simple prototype developed into a powerful tool. Its most notable application has been as a core part of the test automation framework of the European Space Agency (ESA). Today, Stefan is senior consultant for model-based testing at Atos. In addition, he is a member of the Austrian Testing Board and has held numerous lectures at international test conferences. Stefan's email address is stefan.mohacsi@atos.net.

Armin Beer (left) has been working in the area of test management and test automation for about 20 years. He is currently an independent consultant for the test management group at the social insurance institution BVA (Versicherungsanstalt öffentlicher Bediensteter). He is also participating in the research project SoftNet of the Technical University of Graz and lecturing at the University of Applied Sciences in Vienna and the Technical University of Graz. Armin's email address is beer@arminbeer.at.

Chapter 10: Simon Mills

Simon Mills has more than 30 years of experience in the field of software quality, having transferred into the world of system testing from a business role. Simon has been involved in testing software in both business and technical or scientific environments from major investment and insurance systems to laser control, cryogenic control, and superconducting applications. He is the founder of Ingenuity System Testing Services, the preeminent testing authority in the field of electronically traded insurance in the United Kingdom. Simon is widely published internationally in conference proceedings, papers, and contributions to books and has presented as an invited speaker in the United States, at EuroStar, and at the World Congress for Software Quality.

When he isn't buried in running his testing practice or trying out new testing methods, he can be found driving his Bentley, flying his European Eagle Owl, maintaining his medieval house, or repairing and restoring clock mechanisms—all of which are equally as temperamental as any computer system.

Chapter 11: Jason Weden

Jason Weden has been testing software, building software test infrastructures, and developing software for over 13 years. He currently works as a senior quality assurance engineer. As a member of a Scrum sprint team, his recent testing endeavors have focused on story-based automated tests of cloud-computing services. His experience in test automation spans various programming languages such as Groovy, Java, and C#. His recent interests involve the application of functional programming techniques to his software test automation architectures, especially using the Scala programming language. His profile can be found at www.linkedin.com/in/jasonweden.

Chapter 12: Damon Yerg (A Pseudonym)

In June 1958, Damon was born the youngest of three in the tropical North Queensland town of Townsville. In the months leading up to his birth, Qantas began flying to London for the first time, Nikita Khrushchev became Premier of the Soviet Union, and Castro attacked (or began liberating, depending on your perspective) Havana. Soon after Damon's birth, Charles became Prince of Wales, and NASA, Madonna, and Michael Jackson were born. Australia's population didn't quite top 10 million that year.

Damon grew up on a fruit farm near Stanthorpe, the coldest town in Queensland (sometimes it even snows!).

He started working for "the Agency" in 1993. Beginning in customer service, he moved on to system support, team leader, and business analyst. He managed automation services and has now moved on to new challenges.

Damon is happily married with two adult children and lives quietly in his West Ipswich (a small historical city about 45 km west of Brisbane) home with his beautiful island girl (lovely partner Celia), his aged and venerable father, their ADHD-afflicted Blue Cattle dog, and their just plain weird cat called Mong. From there he pursues such pastimes as brewing beer, bushwalking, gardening, and writing. As Damon says, "It's a good life."

Chapter 13: Bryan Bakker

Bryan Bakker received his master's degree in computer science in 1998 and has worked as software engineer on different technical systems. Since 2002, Bryan has specialized in testing of embedded software in multidisciplinary environments; in these environments, the software interfaces with other disciplines like mechanics, electronics, and optics. He has worked on, for example, medical products, professional security systems, semi-industry products, and electron microscopy systems.

Bryan currently (2011) focuses as a test architect on test automation, integration testing, reliability testing, and design for testability. Bryan is also a tutor of several different test-related courses, including ISTQB training.

Chapter 14: Antti Jääskeläinen, Tommi Takala, and Mika Katara

Antti Jääskeläinen is a teaching associate at Tampere University of Technology, Department of Software Systems, where he has completed his doctoral thesis on model-based testing. He has been involved in model-based testing research for several years and has published a number of related papers.

Tommi Takala is a researcher and a postgraduate student at Tampere University of Technology, Department of Software Systems.

Mika Katara is an associate professor at Tampere University of Technology, Department of Software Systems, where he is in charge of software testing research and education. He earned his doctorate from the same institution in 2001. He has published more than 40 papers on model-driven development and testing and has supervised and cosupervised more than 30 testing-related MSc theses. Katara is also the main organizer of the TUT software testing days, a biennial industry seminar that typically draws 200 testing professionals from across Finland.

Chapter 15: Christoph Mecke, Armin Gienger, and Melanie Reinwarth

Dr. Christoph Mecke joined SAP in 1997 and has always worked in the area of quality management for several SAP products. At the moment, he is a test architect, driving new concepts especially in the area of test automation.

Dr. Armin Gienger joined SAP in 1998. Most of the time, he has worked as a test automation expert in various application areas within SAP.

Melanie Reinwarth joined SAP in June 2001. Starting in 2009, she took over product management tasks in the area of test management focusing on the eCATT test tool.

Chapter 16: Björn Boisschot

Björn Boisschot is a consultant with 8 years of experience in test tools, the last 5 years of which he has served as a test tools consultant for CTG Belgium. He is a coach and certified trainer in different quality tools suites. He has worked in numerous projects in various industries such as telecommunications, government, industry, health care, and utilities. His specialty is test automation, and he has implemented frameworks for a number of the top 10 Belgian companies.

Björn is a strong believer in test automation and is the founder and prime developer of CTG's test automation framework FASTBoX.

Chapter 17: Michael Williamson

Michael Williamson worked at Google as a software engineer in test on Webmaster Tools for about a year and a half. Before Google, he worked as a software developer for various other companies, most notably a startup developing network security systems and a research laboratory working on next-generation routers. Google was his first opportunity to dive into the testing world.

Chapter 18: Lars Wahlberg

Lars Wahlberg has been working with testing of marketplace systems for about 10 years in roles such as test engineer, test manager/leader, and test strategist. Before that, during the 1990s, he worked with testing of flight-control systems for military aircrafts and has a MSc degree in aerospace. He also teaches ISTQB test foundation courses in Stockholm with Hans Schaefer.

Chapter 19: Jonathan Kohl

Jonathan Kohl is an internationally recognized consultant and technical leader. Based in Calgary, Alberta, Canada, he is the founder and principal software consultant of Kohl Concepts, Inc. In addition to assisting teams with testing, Jonathan helps companies define and implement their ideas into products, coaches practitioners as they develop software on teams, and works with leaders helping them define and implement their strategic vision. He is also a popular author and speaker. As a thought leader in exploratory testing, mobile application testing, developing policy and strategy, and helping teams adjust to methodology changes, Jonathan doesn't just write and talk about developing software, he actively helps teams deliver the best products they can.

Chapter 20: The Systelab Team: Albert Farré Benet, Christian Ekiza Lujua, Helena Soldevila Grau, Manel Moreno Jáimez, Fernando Monferrer Pérez, and Celestina Bianco

Albert Farré Benet is working currently (2011) as a project manager on a software project for an in vitro diagnose (IVD) instrument. He has spent many years working as test leader and software quality engineer and has published software test automation results in *Testing Experience* magazine and presented at Software Quality Systems conferences.

Christian Ekiza Lujua is a software test engineer with several years of experience in software quality. He has worked since 2007 as test leader and test automation engineer for an IVD instrument software at Systelab Technologies SA. In 2011, he was employed as Sw QA analyst at QAD, Inc.

Helena Soldevila Grau is currently responsible for automation testing for a project at a customer location after many years working as software test engineer for IVD-related applications.

Manel Moreno Jáimez is Systelab's test manager, after 10 years in the company working in different internal projects. He also works as a consultant for external companies. Apart from functional testing, he has experience in software test automation, performance testing, usability, web testing, risk management, and requirements management.

Fernando Monferrer Pérez is a software quality engineer with more than five years of experience testing patient clinical information management systems, many of them including software test automation.

Celestina Bianco is director of software quality at Systelab. She has been working in health care software for 23 years, both in development and quality. She regularly presents papers at international conferences and has been part of the working group or review committee for international standards in software quality.

Chapter 21: Seretta Gamba

Seretta Gamba started programming for her physics thesis back in 1972 and found this kind of work so satisfying that she never started a scientific career. Instead she worked as an IT-specialist first in her home country, Italy, and since then, more than 30 years in Germany. She has experience in very different branches of IT, such as furniture warehousing, semiconductor manufacturing, automotive process controlling, and insurance. Currently (2011) she works full time as developer, test manager, and automation lead at Steria Mummert ISS.

She has developed command-driven testing and the framework ISSTestStation.

Seretta Gamba was a speaker at EuroSTAR in 2005 and 2009.

Chapter 22: Wim Demey

Wim Demey is a senior test consultant who started his career in 1997 and has extended his knowledge and expertise over the years by working in several areas (pharmaceuticals, utilities, telecommunications, nonprofit, social security) and roles (test manager, test tools specialist, coach, presales).

Driven by an eagerness to learn new things, Wim is always looking forward to where he can cross the borders of traditional testing with a special interest for technical topics (infrastructure testing, test tools). This allows him not only to get a good helicopter view on a project but also to be able to discuss with customers and project teams the low-level details of testing.

His motto is "Make IT happen," which means doing your daily job in a pragmatic, constructive, and collaborative way and not being afraid of the real hands-on stuff. That's the way to deliver the added value that customers expect from a consultant.

Chapter 23: Ursula Friede

Ursula Friede was born in Germany and started working as a claims manager in an insurance company after school. For over 10 years, she concentrated mainly on the business side. She studied for the Bachelor Professional (CCI) of Insurance in parallel with her job to gain a better business understanding.

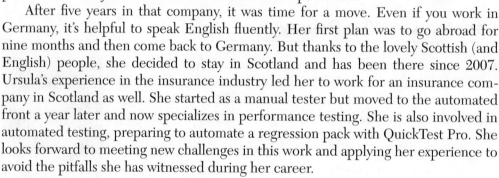

Ursula got involved in a project in which the whole IT system was changed. She trained all users with the new system and became a supervisor. At this point, she became increasingly interested in IT.

She then applied for a job as an inhouse consultant in another insurance company. Her advantage was her business knowledge, and the plan was to share her knowledge with the IT people in the team. This worked reciprocally: They shared their IT knowledge with her. Ursula then studied IT in parallel with her job and became more and more specialized.

After five years in that company, it was time for a move. Even if you work in Germany, it's helpful to speak English fluently. Her first plan was to go abroad for nine months and then come back to Germany. But thanks to the lovely Scottish (and English) people, she decided to stay in Scotland and has been there since 2007. Ursula's experience in the insurance industry led her to work for an insurance company in Scotland as well. She started as a manual tester but moved to the automated front a year later and now specializes in performance testing. She is also involved in automated testing, preparing to automate a regression pack with QuickTest Pro. She looks forward to meeting new challenges in this work and applying her experience to avoid the pitfalls she has witnessed during her career.

Chapter 24: John Fodeh

John Fodeh is a consultant. He has many years of experience in software testing, quality management, and process improvement. He has been involved in almost all major aspects of test automation, from design and implementation to test and maintenance. John is an active member of a Danish special-interest group in software testing and is a frequent speaker at testing conferences. He holds an MSc from the Technical University of Denmark and is a certified software tester. He was Programme Chair for the EuroSTAR conference in 2010.

Chapter 25: Mike Baxter, Nick Flynn, Christopher Wills, and Michael Smith

Mike Baxter started his career in 1980 as a Royal Navy technician, specializing in the support of signal intelligence systems. Returning to full-time education in 1991, he studied communication engineering at the University of Plymouth before gaining employment in a government-sponsored applied research program investigating satellite and data link technologies. He joined NATS in 1998 and over the years has contributed in a number of different departments, including research, safety, systems development, and more recently, verification and validation.

Nick Flynn began his career working for financial institutions in London. After setting up and running a tourism business, he went back to university and gained his masters degree in software engineering. Nick has worked on a variety of high-profile engineering projects across the globe. He currently works for NATS, where he specializes in developing soft skills for system engineers and presents regularly on this topic. Nick is on the UK Advisory Board for INCOSE and represents the United Kingdom at JTC1/SC7 for Systems and Software Engineering Standards within ISO/IEC.

Christopher Wills joined the army in 1974 at age 16 and trained and worked as a telecommunications technician before leaving to go to university for a degree in electrical and electronic engineering. Then he served as an officer in the Royal Navy, mostly involved in technical training of weapons and marine engineers and, for a spell, with the Royal Marines as a training specialist. Christopher has since qualified as a teacher and taught A-level physics and mathematics and postgraduate management studies. He earned an MBA and an MA in creative and critical writing and currently works for NATS as a technical author.

Michael Smith has held a variety of air traffic control and engineering roles within the Royal Air Force and the United Kingdom's air traffic control provider (NATS). He is currently the chief engineer in NATS, responsible for engineering standards and processes at all the UK air traffic control centers. Mike also represents the United Kingdom at JTC1/SC7 for Systems and Software Engineering Standards within ISO/IEC. Mike has lectured and presented internationally on a range of engineering topics and is also an experienced business coach and acts as mentor to a number of senior engineers within industry.

Chapter 26: Ross Timmerman and Joseph Stewart

Ross Timmerman has been with Johnson Controls since 1996 and is currently the North American manager of the engineering process (EPG). He is a 1988 graduate of Calvin College, Grand Rapids, Michigan, where he obtained a BSE in electrical engineering. Ross enjoys giving presentations on process improvement and innovative technology and was a speaker at the 2009 National Software Engineering Institute SEPG Conference, the 2009 Great Lakes Software Excellence Conference, and most recently the Grand Valley State University Pew Campus IEEE chapter, where he spoke about battery management systems in hybrid electric vehicles.

Joseph Stewart was with the Johnson Controls software test engineering team for more than 6 years (2004–2010) and was a key member of the automation team. He is a graduate of the University of Michigan–Dearborn, where he obtained a BSEE degree in 2002. Since 2010, Joe has worked for General Motors as a controls integration engineer at the Milford Proving Grounds in Milford, Michigan.

Chapter 27: Ed Allen and Brian Newman

Ed Allen began his career as a professional software tester in 1997. He joined RightNow in 2004 and is currently a quality assurance manager. Before joining the dark side of management, he was instrumental in championing exploratory test approaches at RightNow. He continues to be fascinated by the cognitive challenges encountered in software testing and encourages his teams to be distracted by the "shiny objects" seen while testing. When not working to improve software quality, Ed loves to rock climb and to play, coach, and watch soccer.

Brian Newman has been with RightNow Technologies since 2000 in various leadership roles, including quality assurance, technical support, and RightNow product-upgrade projects. Prior to that, he spent 15 years testing, deploying, and operating a variety of global communication systems for L-3 Communications, Lockheed Martin, Loral, Unisys, and Sperry Univac. Testing, exploring test methodologies, and implementing automation have been ongoing areas of focus throughout Brian's more than 25 years of communications hardware and CRM/CX software experience.

Chapter 28: Harry Robinson and Ann Gustafson Robinson

Harry Robinson (left) is principal software development engineer in test for Microsoft's Bing team. He has 25 years of software development and testing experience at AT&T Bell Labs, Hewlett-Packard, Microsoft, and Google, as well as time spent in the startup trenches. While at Bell Labs, Harry created a model-based testing system that won the 1995 AT&T Award for Outstanding Achievement in the Area of Quality. At Microsoft, he pioneered the model-based test generation technology, which won the Microsoft Best Practice Award in 2001. Harry holds two patents for software test automation methods and speaks and writes frequently on software testing and automation issues.

Ann Gustafson Robinson (right) has a professional degree in architecture and has had careers as an architect, a database developer, a systems consultant, and a remodeler. She currently teaches classes in comics, moviemaking, street art, and game design. Over the past 20 years, she has spent considerable time editing and reworking articles on model-based testing.

ABOUT THE BOOK AUTHORS

Dorothy Graham

Dorothy Graham is an internationally renowned consultant, a popular speaker, and an author who has been in software testing since the 1970s.

Originally from the United States, she has spent most of her working life in the United Kingdom. She has a BA from Calvin College, Grand Rapids, Michigan, and a master's from Purdue University, West Lafayette, Indiana, both in mathematics. She was a software developer for Bell Labs for two years and a developer and team leader for police command and control systems at Ferranti before joining the National Computing Centre as a trainer, becoming an independent consultant in the 1980s.

Dorothy is coauthor with Tom Gilb of *Software Inspection* (Addison-Wesley, 1994), coauthor with Mark Fewster of *Software Test Automation* (Addison-Wesley, 1999), and coauthor with Rex Black, Isabel Evans, and Erik Van Veenendaal of *Foundations of Software Testing* (Thomson Learning, 2008). She was initiator and coauthor of *The CAST Report* (Cambridge Market Intelligence Ltd, 1993), a compilation of information about commercial testing tools in the 1990s.

Dot was program chair for the EuroSTAR conference in 1993 and 2009. She has been on the boards of a number of conferences and publications in software testing. She was a founding member of the ISEB Software Testing Board and was a member of the working party that developed the ISTQB Foundation Syllabus.

She founded Grove Consultants in 1989, which provides consultancy and training in software testing. In 2008, Dot left Grove to become "semiretired." Since then, she has spoken at many conferences around the world but also has more time for extended holidays and her main hobby of choral and madrigal singing.

She was awarded the European Excellence Award in Software Testing in 1999 and was named one of the 13 Women of Influence in testing by *Software Test & Performance* magazine in 2010.

Mark Fewster

Mark Fewster has 30 years of experience working with software, specializing in software testing for over 20 years.

Mark has a BSc (Hons) in electronic computer systems from Salford University, United Kingdom. Mark was a software developer and manager for a multiplatform graphical application at Racal-Redac where he was responsible for improvements to testing practices and the development of a software testing tool that provided dramatic and lasting savings for the company. The successful principles developed then formed the basis for *Software Test Automation*, the book that he coauthored with Dorothy Graham and was published in 1999.

After working as a consultant for Performance Software for two years, Mark joined Grove Consultants in 1993, providing consultancy and training, particularly in the application of software testing techniques and test automation. He has published papers in respected journals and is a popular speaker at national and international conferences and seminars.

Mark has contributed to the British Computer Society's Specialist Interest Group in Software Testing as committee member and program secretary. He has worked on the ISEB Software Testing Board and the UK Testing Board of ISTQB. At Eurostar 2006, Mark was awarded the Mercury BTO Innovation in Quality Award for his presentation on keyword-driven test automation. He is a member of the ISTQB Working Party, developing a syllabus for the Expert Level Test Automation Certificate.

INDEX

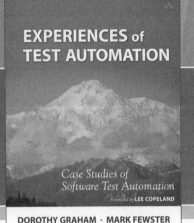

EXPERIENCES of
TEST AUTOMATION

Case Studies of
Software Test Automation

Foreword by LEE COPELAND

DOROTHY GRAHAM · MARK FEWSTER

FREE
Online Edition

Safari
Books Online

Your purchase of **Experiences of Test Automation** includes access to a free online edition for 45 days through the **Safari Books Online** subscription service. Nearly every Addison-Wesley Professional book is available online through **Safari Books Online**, along with thousands of books and videos from publishers such as Cisco Press, Exam Cram, IBM Press, O'Reilly Media, Prentice Hall, Que, Sams, and VMware Press.

Safari Books Online is a digital library providing searchable, on-demand access to thousands of technology, digital media, and professional development books and videos from leading publishers. With one monthly or yearly subscription price, you get unlimited access to learning tools and information on topics including mobile app and software development, tips and tricks on using your favorite gadgets, networking, project management, graphic design, and much more.

Activate your FREE Online Edition at
informit.com/safarifree

STEP 1: Enter the coupon code: LNBMPEH.

STEP 2: New Safari users, complete the brief registration form.
Safari subscribers, just log in.

If you have difficulty registering on Safari or accessing the online edition,
please e-mail customer-service@safaribooksonline.com